1975

May
73
Bonus

book may be kept

FOURTEEN DAYS

THE
STRUCTURE
AND
MEANING
OF
PSYCHOANALYSIS

Judge Baker Foundation Publication No. 6

WILLIAM HEALY, M.D.
AUGUSTA F. BRONNER, Ph.D.
Directors, Judge Baker Foundation, Boston
Research Associates, Institute of Human Relations, Yale University
Formerly Directors, Juvenile Psychopathic Institute, Chicago
ANNA MAE BOWERS, A.B.
Research Assistant, Judge Baker Foundation

THE
STRUCTURE
AND
MEANING
OF
PSYCHOANALYSIS

AS RELATED
TO PERSONALITY AND BEHAVIOR

New York · ALFRED · A · KNOPF · *mcmliii*

PREFACE

Our interest in this structural presentation of the theory and practical issues of psychoanalysis has grown, first, out of long-standing appreciations and confirmations of psychoanalytic values as seen in application to the problems of personality and human conduct, especially as we have had to meet them in the lives of young people. As part of our program of work, we, though with some conservatism, have had the desire ever to make these values increasingly clear to ourselves and to our staff and students.

Then, in attempting a thorough-going review of the literature for the purpose of showing psychoanalysis as one of the scientific approaches to understanding of personality in a projected manual of methods of personality study, we found ourselves involved in a veritable maze of material. It became evident that a distinct service could be rendered to others interested in the fields of psychology and psychiatry through an organized statement of what has been contributed to date in psychoanalysis. The work of presenting the main issues, even in outline form, has grown beyond the limits of a section of the proposed manual and in its present proportions is only suitable for a separate publication—although we trust it may be regarded as merely one of the various approaches, which properly should be utilized coordinately, in a well-rounded study of human personality.

v

While, for this presentation, we have drawn upon many sources, we have by no means attempted a complete summary of all available material. Hence, we strongly urge any student of psychoanalysis to become familiar with the original, often brilliantly expressed, writings of Freud himself, and with many of the works of his followers.

Certain advantages of our method of presentation will be plain to the reader. On the left hand pages are what, for want of a better term, may be called the orthodox theories and fact-findings of psychoanalysis—for the most part consisting of Freud's own statements. On the right hand, in smaller type on account of the mass of material, are introduced (a) contributions of exegetical value, (b) some notable accessions to the psychoanalytic structure by "Freudians," and (c) on account of their attempt constructively to modify psychoanalytic doctrine, various ideas set forth by those, who, still holding to the major concepts of Freud, offer divergencies of theory or practice.

Unavoidably, in the arrangement of the material, it has been necessary to anticipate definitions and theories when using terms. Our carefully prepared index will, however, be an aid in fuller cross-referencing than has seemed advisable in the body of the book.

We have felt also that it would be an unnecessary burdening of the text if bibliographical references were cited. In the appendix we have given the main sources utilized by us. The most comprehensive listing of psychoanalytic literature is that by Rickman, Index Psychoanalyticus, 1893–1926.

In the attempt to be unbiased expositors of the various principles, theories, and fact-findings of psychoanalysis, we have allowed ourselves very few criticisms, comments, or suggestions.

Concerning the great amount of reading and thought which obviously has been involved in this production, we would here pay tribute to the finely critical work of our co-author, Anna Mae Bowers, who for over two years has continuously been engaged with us in attempting to organize the ideas of the psychoanalytic school and, to some extent, its offshoots. We together have discovered the great intellectual challenge which serious reading in psychoanalysis brings and have, too, found not a little satisfaction in our task of attempting a fair-minded understanding and representation of the tremendous structure that psychoanalysis has built.

Boston, February, 1930　　　　　　　　　　　W. H.

A. F. B.

CONTENTS

ix

SECTION VI

BEHAVIOR—PERSONALITY FORMATION—CONDUCT

SECTION ViI

THERAPY

INTRODUCTION

INTRODUCTION

Psychoanalysis investigates the dynamics of mental life, conscious and unconscious, through studying mental content by a special technique. Psychoanalysis began as a method of treating some psychoneurotic ailments, but based on its accumulation of facts, it has gradually developed not only its own technique, but also a vastly important psychological theory which Freud has called "metapsychology," and it has evolved interpretations which have important bearings on character and personality formation.

Freud early interested himself in the relationship of the psychoanalytic theory and point of view to fields other than that of the neuroses. He turned his attention to art, wit, the psychology of primitive peoples, and other sources, from whence he drew material that threw light upon psychoanalytic concepts and which, in turn, psychoanalysis explained and illuminated. More recently there has been a steady growth of the application of psychoanalysis to problems in child psychology and to the understanding of various aspects of human behavior, for example, some forms of delinquency and criminality. Then, too, group psychology and other sociological phenomena are coming under consideration.

Thus psychoanalysis has attained the status of having, in method, become an "instrument of psychological research" into the depths of human nature; from its own interpretation of its findings it

Freud gives as one definition of psychoanalysis, "A dynamic conception which reduces mental life to an inter-play of reciprocally urging and checking forces."

Freud himself clearly states that psychoanalysis, while originally the name of a particular therapeutic method, has now also become the name of a science, the science of unconscious mental processes. Its development is shown by the gradual attempts at systematization, not only of its great body of observational data, but also of its concepts as reported recently in "metapsychology" in which there is an attempt at definition of dynamic, topographical, and economic considerations.

The fact that psychoanalysts have not carefully organized their material makes, after all, very little of a case against them. Perhaps they work all the better without such careful organization; it may be that much of their theory is worked out more advantageously without the hamperings of too closely knit formulations or, for the present, without too rigid adherence to even their own previous statements. Freud, in one place, speaks of continuing on with his own phantasies.

Though starting from an empirical standpoint and with pragmatic values emphasized, it should be clearly realized that conceptual formulations, altered from time to time, have deeply influenced the outlook, modes of thought, terminology, and even the therapeutic aims of psychoanalysis. To follow through even our sketch of the cardinal formulations of psychoanalysis will make this plain.

For general understanding of the personality there can be no minimizing the importance of psychoanalytic fundamentals, but Freud himself warns that it is unsafe to judge the normal entirely by the standards of the pathological, from the study of which psychoanalytic theory has been evolved. Other psychoanalysts have made the same point; Alexander, for example, has emphasized the need of studying for comparative purposes the normal, adequately-functioning personality.

has constructed an edifice from which it is possible to get many a new outlook on human life.

From all this it seems plain to us that, since no systematic publication of psychoanalytic theories and discoveries has appeared, the time is right for depicting the structure of psychoanalysis, so far as it has been erected. As a matter of fact, there is small chance for accurate appreciation of what psychoanalysis has contributed or is likely to bring forth without some such carefully organized portrayal. Lacking this, the off-hand opinions commonly expressed concerning psychoanalysis, not only by casual thinkers but also by those with psychological training, as well as unripe popularizations, are likely to be continued. It has been often stated that underlying emotional attitudes cause either ardent acceptance or antagonistic rejection of psychoanalysis. Be this as it may, it at least appears certain that the great amount of study, almost insurmountable for those much occupied with other matters in our busy world, but necessary in order to gain a fair view of the foundations and structural growth of psychoanalysis, militates immensely against realization of its true significances.

Even some of those engaged in practical psychoanalytic work can often hardly "see the forest for the trees," and it is for these, as well as for students younger in the subject, that an organized setting forth of the main contributions will be valuable. Indeed, it is self-evident that the utilization of interpretations, as in medical science, can only safely be carried on when founded upon thorough acquaintance with basic attitudes and formulations. And then one might dare to hope that for critical self-growth among the espe-

Other writers have stated their belief that much of psychoanalytic theory is applicable to the normal. Mitchell, after asking the question, "How far are the doctrines derived from the study of neuroses applicable to normal people?" himself answers that they are applicable in some degree to all people; peculiarities of mental functioning, found well marked in neuroses and psychoses, are only exaggerations of modes of mental functioning common to all.

"Almost every principle that has been invoked in explanation of abnormal mental processes is found to be of equal value in the interpretation of normal behavior." Repression, the unconscious (whatever its content), analytical theories of dreams and their interpretation, all belong to the normal mind.

"The light thrown by analytical doctrine upon the workings of the normal mind is one of the strongest arguments in favor of the general truth of these doctrines. Did they not contain much truth, it is hardly possible that hypotheses put forward in explanation of mental process of behavior that are admittedly abnormal should be so illuminating when applied to the workings of the normal mind and to the conduct of normal people."

Mention should be made of some disagreement with this point of view on the part of leading psychologists who, although not psychoanalysts, are friendly to psychoanalysis. Bernard Hart makes the point that the "facts (of psychoanalysis) are reached by the employment of a peculiar method . . . of such a character that the possibility of distortion cannot with certainty be excluded"; "the influences at work are, at any rate so far as our present knowledge goes, of an incalculable character." Others, too, have offered similar criticisms, among them McDougall, who, nevertheless, asserts his belief that "Freud has done more for the advancement of psychology than any student since Aristotle."

It will take time for the philosophers to have their innings with Freud, playing the game either with or against him, but already some of them have shown themselves deeply concerned with his theories and discoveries. We may give one example of how the Freudian psychology, at least as it was earlier stated, may enter into philosophical discussion.

cially well equipped psychoanalysts, the illuminati, this endeavor to assemble their own material may not prove valueless.

But not a word further should be written in this introduction without bringing to the reader's attention Freud's great insistence that psychoanalysis is not "a closed system." Far from maintaining that the final word has been said about psychoanalytic discoveries anywhere along the line of scientific advance, he and his close co-workers earnestly proclaim that psychoanalysis opens to view matters pertaining to the understanding of individual human lives and of social forces which will afford material for research during generations to come. Part of what has been produced is fundamental, Freud asserts; other parts represent mere coping-stones which may be removed without damage to the main structure. And he himself acknowledges that he does not know just which of the added portions will survive. "Only such 'true believers' as expect from science a substitute for the creed they have relinquished will take it amiss if the investigator develops his views further or even transforms them."

Psychoanalysis presents itself as a structure erected within the field of psychobiologic science. Closer observation shows with fair distinctness what the foundations of psychoanalysis are and the psychobiological bedrock upon which they rest. In some places the line of demarcation is not very clear, particularly because the psychological and biological bedrock is to some extent used in the foundations. In the attempt carefully to study psychoanalysis it becomes evident that in the interests of better understanding the foundational concepts should be clearly discerned.

E. B. Holt, whose contributions to the most technical aspects of philosophy are well known in his field, states that Freud's work is epoch-making because he has given to the science of mind a "causal category," he has given a key to the explanation of mind, the first key that ever has fitted—and that is the Freudian "wish." This "wish" is all that Freud gives under the term and also includes whatever is called impulse, tendency, desire, purpose, attitude—and we may ourselves add urges and strivings.

The "wish" is a "course of action which some mechanism of the body is set to carry out, whether it actually does so or does not." It is "any purpose or project for a course of action" even if it is merely entertained by the mind. It is "dependent on a motor attitude of the physical body, which goes over into overt action when the wish is carried into execution." It is in the interplay of compatible or antagonistic wishes "that one finds the text of the entire Freudian psychology."

Holt goes on to say that in the Freudian psychology "all emotions, as well as the feelings of pleasure and displeasure, are separable from the 'wishes'; and this precludes any thought of a merely hedonistic psychology."

Holt is not only Freudian, but also calls himself a behaviorist. For him, the "wish" is of cardinal importance and he readily turns it into the "specific response relation." For him, the "wish" is "function"; "it is that motor set of the organism which, if opposed by other motor sets, is functional attitude towards the environment, and which, if unopposed, actuates the organism to overt behavior, which is a constant function of the environment."

But when it comes to ethics, Holt, in special chapters on the implications of the Freudian theory for ethics considers the term "wish" most unfortunate. The idea of purpose, seemingly implied in the "wish," is not involved; the "wish" contemplates no end whatsoever. "The doctrine of the 'wish' shows us that life is not lived *for ends*. Life is a process; it is a game to be played on the checkerboard of facts." "Its motive power comes not from in front (from 'ends') but from behind, from the wishes which are in ourselves." We play the game rightly if, instead of suppressing wishes, we lucidly discriminate the facts. For ethics, the Socratic teaching is upheld by Freudian theories—virtue is wisdom.

Most distinctly to be recognized are the following psychobiological facts accepted as foundation stones of psychoanalysis: (a) Biological and psychological development are inseparably interrelated. (b) The essential nature of the individual consists in strivings and urges, innate or unlearned, which originally are quite independent of environment. (c) Whatever the individual is or does at any given moment is very largely predetermined by his earlier experiences and his reactions to them. (d) The earliest years of life represent the period when biological and mental experiences most profoundly influence the individual because he is then less pre-formed or conditioned. (e) Existing actively in the mental life of the individual there is a vast amount of which he is unaware. (f) The biological and consequently the psychological, constitution varies in different individuals.

SECTION ONE

CARDINAL FORMULATIONS

SECTION I

CARDINAL FORMULATIONS

In order to draft a working sketch of the structure of psycho-analysis, it is best, first, systematically to outline certain cardinal formulations. Just where one shall begin and the order in which these formulations shall be presented is not so easy to decide. The main effort must be to show the findings and theories with their organization as related to the whole structure, a picture that will not only be comprehensible but will demonstrate the significance of psychoanalytic formulations and their relationships to each other. These cardinal formulations are based on "clinical discoveries." We present a discussion of these under the following headings:

Libido
Cathexis
Polarities
Ambivalence
Divisional Constitution of Mental Life
Fundamental Principles
General Instinct Directions

LIBIDO

"That force by which the sexual instinct is represented in the mind, we call libido." To this definition there should be added another statement of Freud's, namely, that libido is "the energy . . . of those instincts which have to do with all that may be comprised under the word 'love.' "

Freud says quite explicitly that for psychoanalysis the term "sexual" has a very wide meaning. He feels justified from the scientific point of view of his researches, he says, in viewing as "sexual,"

2

On account of the reproach that so frequently is made against psycho-analysis for its "sexuality," it is essential that readers and students acquaint themselves thoroughly with what is meant by "libido" and "sexual" in psychoanalytic usage. Earlier Freud preferred to speak of *psychosexuality,* "thus laying stress on the point that the mental factor should not be overlooked or underestimated." Both he and his adherents have recognized that the main opposition to and misunderstanding of psychoanalysis lies in the extensive use of the word sexual. In defense of Freud, Jones points out that the part played by sexual impulses in the unconscious is much greater than the part they play in consciousness, and thus in many ordinary activities there may be some underlying element of sexual pleasure because of their unconscious sexual significance.

Freud fair-mindedly acknowledges that it is through psychoanalytic work with neurotics that the emphasis upon sexual has been placed, and that his "one-sidedness" has arisen through finding that in neurotic disorders "by far the most significance attaches to the sexual instincts; in fact the neuroses are the specific disorders, so to speak, of the sexual function." "Our one-sidedness is like that of the chemist who traces all compounds back to the force of chemical attraction. In doing so, he does not deny the force of gravity; he leaves that to the physicist to reckon with."

Formerly in defining libido, Freud stated that it might be regarded as "analogous to the force of hunger or will to power and other such trends among the ego tendencies," that is, he made a definite distinction between the energy (libido) derived from those instincts which had an object as their aim, or the sexual instincts, and other forms of energy derived from what he called the "ego instincts," and manifested chiefly as a self-preservative urge. Later he came to the conclusion that at least a part of the self-preservative energy is also of a libidinal nature, i. e., self-love as well as object-love must be reckoned with. Freud termed all these "love" impulses "Eros."

3

or "love," or "libido," or "Eros," not only desires for sexual union but much else. "The nucleus of what we mean by love naturally consists (and this is what is commonly called love, and what the poets sing of) in sexual love with sexual union as its aim. But we do not separate from this—what in any case has a share in the name 'love'—on the one hand, self-love, and on the other, love for parents and children, friendship, and love for humanity in general, and also devotion to concrete objects and to abstract ideas. Our justification lies in the fact that psychoanalytic research has taught us that all these tendencies are an expression of the same instinctive activities." Thus Freud recently states, as he did in 1910, that in psychoanalysis the term "sexuality" "goes lower and also higher than the popular sense of the word."

His extension of the term "sexual," Freud says, means first that sexuality is to be considered as not simply referring to the genitals and the function of propagation; it must be regarded as "a more comprehensive bodily function having pleasure as its goal, and only secondarily coming to serve the ends of reproduction." Secondly, the sexual impulses are to be considered as including not only body or organ-pleasure, but "all those merely affectionate impulses to which usage applies the extremely ambiguous word 'love.'"

In defending his use of the word sexual, Freud points out that he has employed it in the same sense as the German *"Liebe."* He not only includes but stresses the element of mental satisfaction.

Libido as conceived by Freud has certain important characteristics. (1) It varies in intensity even in the same individual; there is a certain quantitative ebb and flow, corresponding to the different periods of physiological development. (2) Libidinal urge is always present even in early childhood though differing then from normal adult manifestations. It exhibits itself in childhood as the so-called partial or component impulses. (See Infantile Sexuality.) (3) Libidinal sensitizations do not belong to the sexual organs alone but become attached in succession to various body areas, namely, the organs of nutrition, excretion, procreation (erotogenic zones), and are manifested in localized excitability which is relieved by ap-

Jung took over the term libido and applied it to a more general energetic concept underlying the dynamics of mental life, representing the urge or push of life, which no expansion of the meaning of the term sexual would ever adequately express. For Jung there is a primal libido which is necessarily utilized in the service of nutrition, of growth, of sexuality, and of all the human activities and interests.

Freud, always dualistic, even though he has widened his conception of libido to cover both the sexual and self-preservative impulses united under the term Eros, still insists that Jung's libido, a monistic conception of primal energy, cannot possibly hold true. He finds energy running in another channel, namely, in the direction of the Death or Destructive Instinct.

Mitchell has pointed out that Jung has created confusion by his unfortunate application to his own conception of an undifferentiated primal life force of a word with prior meaning.

Jung's specific criticism of Freud's sexual theory is as follows: "The sexual theory is entirely correct up to a certain point, but it is one-sided. It would therefore be just as false to repudiate it as to accept it as universally valid." He contends that even what presents itself in sexual form need not always remain sexual in its inmost nature. "For it is conceivable that one instinct may disguise itself under another." (*Two Essays on Analytical Psychology*.)

McDougall suggests the use of the term hormé for the striving principle, and points out that Jung's conception of libido, which he himself accepts, is practically identical with Bergson's *élan vital*, vital urge.

Attention should be called to the fact that Freud has never used the term libido in the sense of an all-embracing primal urge. In view of this it would seem that his critics in charging him with pan-sexualism have distinctly misunderstood his conception.

Adler who has broken away from the Freudian school regards the one great driving force as not a sexual but an Ego urge (the urge to power)—which manifests itself, however, very frequently in a sexual form.

5

propriate stimulation. The whole localization process has been accomplished by the end of the fifth year, according to Freud. (4) The distribution of libido, that is, the direction of the libidinal flow, is constantly changing. It may, for example, be directed outward or inward (object-love and narcism); it may be arrested in its forward flow (fixation); or it may flow to levels representing earlier stages of development (regression); it may become dammed up (repression); or it may be deflected into other more socially acceptable channels (sublimation).

CATHEXIS

Cathexis is the accumulation or concentration of psychic energy in a particular place or channel, libidinal or non-libidinal. According to the findings of psychoanalysis, libidinal energy, a part of psychic energy, is directed or accumulated in any or all of three channels—directed towards the self, towards objects, and towards inner mental creations or phantasies.

(a) Ego-cathexis (cathexis of the Ego)—libido directed toward the self (ego-libido; narcissism—narcism). This predominates in the early stages of development (see Developmental Stages) when the self represents the direction taken by the entire libidinal energy; the self is then the love-object. The child earliest looks upon the whole world as his and comprised within himself, and as he gradually comes to perceive other objects and his inability to command them, he compensates for the shrinking of his sovereignty by discovering satisfactions within himself, that is, by narcism. It is, in Abraham's words, "that stage in the development of the libido in which the child is himself the center of his own narrow world and in which he receives proofs of love from other persons without himself giving any return." One of the essential characteristics of narcism seems to be this demand for ego-gratification through receiving the attention and consideration of others; in the Freudian sense it is the need for receiving "love." Freud says, "The outside world is at this time, generally speaking, not cathected with any interest and is indifferent for purposes of satisfaction."

8

The concept of cathexis, which has become of fundamental importance in the exposition of psychoanalytic theory, has its analogy and origin in the fact of accumulation or charge or load of electricity in an object, familiar in physics. Extension of the analogy gives the idea of psychical tension, similar to an electrical charge, seeking active discharge and readily causing disturbance if dammed up.

Narcism (narcissism), a term derived from the classical story of Narcissus, was first used by Näcke to denote the perverse attitude of a person who treats his own body in the same way as otherwise the body of a sexual object is treated, that is to say, he experiences sex pleasure in kissing, caressing, and fondling his body until complete gratification ensues upon these activities. More recently, the term has been taken over by psychoanalysis, and narcism in the sense of interest in one's own self or body and its activities has been discovered to be a normal phase of development, not in the sense of Näcke, but with a modified meaning.

Until recently most psychoanalytic stress has been laid on "object-libido." Increasing consideration is now being given to "Ego-libido" which is conceived by some as being the more primary of the two. According to this concept all libido emanates originally from self-libido, there being a mutual reciprocity between the amount of libido remaining attached to the self and the amount finding external expression. Libido frequently oscillates between internal and external expression, depending to a large extent on circumstances. This is important for the concept of narcism. There can be a temporary or permanent withdrawal from objects and a return to the self. A certain freedom of movement of libido in both directions is considered requisite for mental health.

Another concept (L. P. Clark) is of an original allocation of libido in the total economy of the individual Ego with gradual division into two channels—one flowing towards the various erotogenic zones, to be placed ultimately at the service of the sexual aim; the other flowing towards the preservation of the personality (narcistic protection of Ego against own self-destructive impulses).

Psychoanalysts distinguish primary and secondary narcism. Primary narcism is original libidinal ego-cathexis, part of which normally persists while the rest is gradually transferred to objects. It was his study of the mental life of children and of primitive peoples that led Freud to this conception of a primary narcistic stage. Freud defines secondary narcism as that which arises when libidinal object-cathexes are withdrawn or called in away from external objects towards which libido has been flowing, and he says that it is then superimposed upon the primary form. Secondary narcism results when renounced or lost objects are recreated within the individual and are loved as a part of himself, a process known as secondary identification. Introjection, as well as identification, is thus involved in secondary narcism.

During the later developmental period there is, in normal individuals, a gradual reduction of primary narcism, except that at puberty and during early adolescence there comes a considerable new growth of ego-libido which is utilizable for the purpose of emancipation from parental dependencies and attachments. Maturity, however, demands relinquishing a certain amount of narcism.

(*b*) *Object-cathexis* (libidinal cathexis of the object, object-love, object-libido)—the directing of libido toward some object (person or thing). "The libidinal energy is directed towards, or rather in-

A clearer concept of narcism may be arrived at by differentiating it from several other terms with which it is often confused. Narcism *vs.* Autoerotism—Freud says autoerotism is "primordial, so there must be something added to autoerotism—some new operation in the mind—in order that narcism may come into being." MacCurdy defines autoerotism as "a blind protopathic stimulation and response of the body" into which no concept of personality enters; autoerotism can exist without self-consciousness. He thinks Freud does not make this clear. He goes on to point out that narcism may be expressed in autoerotic practices but can exist in phantasy alone without autoerotism.

Narcism *vs.* Egoism. (We wonder if a much better term is not Egocentrism—the latter as ordinarily and clearly contrasted with Egotism; there is obvious confusion of the terms among psychoanalytic writers.) Sadger maintains that narcism rests on an over-evaluation of the own body. Freud differentiates Egoism (Egocentrism?) from narcism as follows: "I believe narcism is the libidinous complement of Egoism." "One can be egoistic and still maintain strong interest in libido-objects" or "One can be egoistic and at the same time preponderantly narcissic, that is, have a very slight need of an object."

Narcism *vs.* Introversion. In narcism itself, no matter how great the self-feeling and self-appreciation, there is no loss of contact with reality. Havelock Ellis says that narcism involves a comparison of self with others and implies self-preference. In introversion there is a withdrawal of libido from reality satisfaction; often the phantasies typical of introversion are not narcistic. MacCurdy maintains that in these matters Freud has not been clear.

fused into, the idea of some object in the outer world." Object-love is essentially a motor striving towards the object primarily as a source of somatic satisfaction, and Freud points out that the word "love" does not really become applicable to the object-choice until the various motor impulses become synthesized into one predominant trend. At the same time a fusion takes place between the somatic and the concurrently evolving affectional elements of the libidinal energy. The well-being of the love-object becomes now a prime consideration.

The first external objects which force themselves upon the child's attention are those which meet his self-preservative needs and those which help him to maintain his narcism. These forms of object-finding lead the way to the first libidinal object-cathexes and definitely predetermine all later libidinal object-choice. Freud speaks of "conditions of love" being thus very early established and says that, in general, adult object-love always conforms to one or the other of two types, namely, anaclitic or narcistic.

Anaclitic object-choice—when the libidinal cathexis is of an object that has previously met the self-preservative needs, the term anaclitic (from the Greek, leaning up against) is used. In the early stages of object-love, the mother (or nurse) who met the child's nutritional and security-demanding impulses, becomes the first love-object. Later adult object-choice often follows this same pattern, (a) the woman who tends (mother, nurse and others); (b) the man who protects (father-substitutes, princes, soldiers, the man with money, the strong man).

Narcistic object-choice—when the love-object resembles the self in any way, (a) what the self is (person of the same sex, occupation, race, etc.); (b) what the self once was (child, youth, an "innocent" etc.); (c) what the self would like to be (ideal of self—a leader, a hero, a person specially endowed with some outstanding attribute of strength, intellect, virtue); (d) someone who was once a part of the self (child of one's own body—especially strong in the case of women).

12

The concept of narcism has led to a clearer understanding of why psychoanalysis has failed as a therapeutic measure in the case of certain mental disorders. The narcism may be so exaggerated and persistent that no object-love is possible, and the regular transference technique (see Therapy) is of no avail.

Abraham points out that there can be a form of negative narcism which shows itself in an exaggerated underestimation (as in the melancholiac).

Secondary narcism is really a stage in the development of the libido from autoerotism to object-love. At this stage the sexual impulses which have hitherto been engaged in various autoerotic activities unite in taking the whole body as a love-object, and only subsequently proceed from this to the choice of some other person as love-object.

Ellis, in his extensive discussion of narcism, decides that it is really the basis for all creative achievement—the making of things that are representative or worthy of the self.

Of the narcistic type of object-love Freud says that its existence had not been suspected until it was revealed by psychoanalytic investigation. "We have found, especially in persons whose libidinal development has suffered some disturbance, as in perverts and homosexuals, that in the choice of their love-object they have taken as their model not the mother but their own selves. They are plainly seeking themselves as a love-object. . . . This observation provides us with our strongest motive for regarding the hypothesis of narcism as a necessary one."

Freud thinks that the sex of the individual is usually fundamental in determining the type of object-choice. Complete object-love of the anaclitic type is, properly speaking, characteristic of the man. A man's love, he says, displays "the marked sexual overestimation which is doubtless derived from the original narcissism of the child, now transferred to the sexual object." This means that there is an impoverishment of the Ego in respect to libido "in favor of the love-object."

The "purest and truest feminine type" of object-love is narcistic. Such women, Freud says, really "love only themselves, with an intensity comparable to that of the man's love for them. Nor does their need lie in the direction of loving, but of being loved; and that man finds

The individual's first real love experience takes place in early childhood and the parent (usually of the opposite sex) becomes his first love-object. Normally, the child's libido detaches itself comparatively swiftly from the parent, but very commonly there is a clinging to some phase or aspect of his first love relationship, and all subsequent object-love bears its impress, if ever so faintly. Freud claims that he has been able to establish several types of adult object-love all of which can be traced back to the first early love experience. (See Developmental Stages and Oedipus Complex.)

(c) *Phantasy-cathexis—Introversion*—the libido in introversion is directed toward the inner world, the world of representation, instead of the world of reality. With object-love there is desire for motor discharge, a going out toward the object, but with introversion there is no desire for motor expression; satisfaction is found in imagined response, in dwelling on phantasied activities in connection with images and ideas of external objects.

The existence of phantasy-cathexis is normal; the phenomenon of introversion follows along the lines of normal activity of the pleasure principle. However, it also offers the possibility of abnormal flight from reality. The pain of reality, especially during childhood, the sensing of frustrations and incapacities, often leads to taking temporary refuge in the life of phantasy. During childhood, or later, introversion may lead to the creation of new wish-formations which normally may have relationship to quite ordinary behavior, and even to the best ambitions and the finest idealism. On the other hand, introversion may reanimate earlier repressed infantile wishes, leading to regression, shown in a striving after infantile marks of expression. (See Phantasy-formation, Fixation, Symptom-formation.)

favor with them who fulfills this condition." Freud thinks that development is responsible for the woman's narcistic object-love. The development of puberty seems to bring about an intensification of the original narcism, and this is unfavorable to the development of a true object-love. There arises a certain self-sufficiency (especially when there is a ripening into beauty) which compensates for the social restrictions upon the girl's object-choice (that is, the father). Freud goes on to say that narcistic women are of great importance for the erotic life of mankind since they exercise a great fascination for many men, their charm, like that of a child, lying in their self-sufficiency and inaccessibility. He is quite willing to admit, however, that there are countless women who love according to the masculine anaclitic type.

Even for the narcistic woman there is a way to complete object-love. "In the child to whom they give birth a part of their own body comes to them as an object other than themselves upon which they can lavish out of their narcism complete object-love." Freud thinks that "Parental love which is so touching, and at bottom so childish, is nothing but parental narcism born again, transformed though it be, into object-love. . . ." He points out in support of this how parents are always ready to ascribe to their child "all manner of perfections which sober observation would not confirm, to gloss over and forget all his short-comings. . . . Moreover, they are inclined to suspend in the child's favor the operation of all those cultural acquirements which their narcissism has been forced to respect, and to renew in his person the claims for privileges which were long ago given up by themselves. The child shall have things better than his parents. . . . He is to fulfill those dreams and wishes of his parents which they never carried out. . . ."

Freud writes, "We do not say of those objects which serve the interests of self-preservation that we love them; rather, we emphasize the fact that we need them, and perhaps add an element of a different kind in our relation to them, by words which denote a much lesser degree of love—for example, to be fond of, to like, to find agreeable."

In its early stages object-love is, as Freud points out, "compatible with abolition of any separate existence on the part of the object," and "injury or annihilation of the object is a matter of indifference." Another characteristic of the early stages of object-love is the regular co-

15

Cathexis which is non-libidinal may evidently be directed in channels which are not all yet determined. The main channel so far elucidated is that feeding the Death or Destructive Instinct (q.v.).

existence of hate—a repulsion from, rather than a striving for, the object. The attempt to increase the distance between the self and the object may take the form of aggressive destructive impulses with regard to the object, and the general attitude toward the object (love and hate) is termed ambivalent. (See Ambivalence.) Normally, as object-love develops into its mature form, ambivalence should drop out. However, various degrees of ambivalence, as well as traces of other preliminary forms of object-love are commonly found in the normal adult.

Mitchell points out that the relative quantities of ego-libido and object-libido vary in different individuals. "Some people are more narcissistic than others; but in everyone there remains a certain amount of the original narcissism of childhood, and this may become augmented to a degree that makes a normal life impossible. In infancy autoerotic acvities are the only outlet for the libido until an object in the outer world is found. Contact with the world external to the body provides the opportunity for the turning of the libido outwards, away from the self; but the need for such direction of the libido towards outer objects is probably implicit in its very nature." "For everyone there is a limit to the quantity of ego-libido that is compatible with health. Thus, from the beginning a turning of libido outwards and its attachment to real objects outside the self is a necessity for healthy life." As Freud puts it, "in the last resort we must begin to love in order that we may not fall ill, and must fall ill if, in consequence of frustration, we cannot love."

Alexander thinks there is greater persistence of primary narcism in the neurotic than in the normal. This primary narcism, having nothing to do with morality, antedating conscience, may often come into conflict with secondary narcism. The neurotic also makes relatively feeble object-cathexes—he is always ready at the slightest external difficulty to give up an object-cathexis. This weakened object-libido, Alexander explains, is due to the greater need on the part of the neurotic for narcistic libido to neutralize his self-destructive tendencies.

In the state of being in love, the lover projects his own narcism or self-idealization, and there is a tendency to idealize and thus cease to criticise in any way the love-object which is regarded, as Mitchell says, "free from imperfection and incapable of doing wrong." The lover becomes lacking in self-confidence, since he lacks the support of his own projected narcism.

POLARITIES

Polarities are certain aspects of mental life fundamentally characterized by being paired as opposites or polarities. The practical finding is that they exist in definite active antithetical relationships. Necessarily involved in the principle of opposites is the tendency of mental processes to polarize, to gather about two extremes, with the possibility of shifting positions or even of oscillation back and forth.

The polarities considered important for the dynamics of mental life in which psychoanalysis is especially interested are as follows:

a. Activity-Passivity
b. Self-Outer World (Subject—Object)
c. Pleasure-Pain
d. Life-Death
e. Love-Hate
f. Masculine-Feminine

Clearly, it is because psychoanalysis deals so much with the dynamics of instinctive life and the conflicts arising therein that it perceives as so important the cardinal principle of polarities in mental life. In an early work Freud lists the first three polarities we give as governing mental life as a whole. Other antitheses, however, are frequently referred to by psychoanalysts as being necessary for the interpretation of the directive activities of mental life, and now all six pairs of opposites listed seem to be worth considering from the point of view of psychoanalytic theory.

Polarities are somewhere defined as "the concept of certain fundamental situations which no amount of effort can alter and which the individual is experientially fated to discover." Rickman, writing of the significance of polarity in the psychical apparatus, says, "Neither can be disturbed without affecting the other."

Glueck says "Psychoanalysis throughout has shown a preference to state its contributions in terms of polarities and antitheses."

Jung speaks of the great importance of what he calls the "regulating function of the opposites"—that is, "everything tends sooner or later to go over into its opposite." This "principle of the opposites" Jung contends should be taken into account in the formulating of any sound scientific theory. Baynes, making the same contention, viz. that a fundamental psychological conception must always embrace a fundamental pair of opposites, says that Freud ignores one all important polarity— causality-goal.

Freud says of the antithesis subject-object that it "remains sovereign above all in our intellectual activity and provides research with a fundamental situation which no amount of effort can alter."

In an early writing Freud says, "The polarity pleasure-pain depends upon a feeling-series, the significance of which in determining our actions (will) is paramount and has already been emphasized," and his well known Pleasure Principle was based upon this polarity.

Of the activity-passivity polarity, Freud points out that it must not be confounded with the polarity subject-object. He says "The relation of the Ego to the outer world is passive insofar as it receives stimuli from it, active when it reacts to these. Its instincts compel it to a quite special degree of activity towards the outside world, so that . . . we might say that the Ego-subject is passive in respect to external stimuli, active in virtue of its own instincts."

Of the polarity masculine-feminine, Freud says that it has no psychological significance until the antithesis activity-passivity has coalesced with it. "The fusion of activity with masculinity and passivity with femininity confronts us indeed as a biological fact, but it is by no means so invariably complete and exclusive as we are inclined to assume."

The love-hate polarity, Freud has concluded, is allied to, or representative of, the Life-Death antithesis.

AMBIVALENCE

Ambivalence denotes contradictory emotional attitudes toward the same object either arising alternately, or existing side by side without either one interfering necessarily with or inhibiting the expression of the other.

Ambivalence is characteristic of the unconscious, of children, of neurotic behavior. In adults it points to poor integration of personality. Conflicts may or may not arise between or concerning ambivalent emotional attitudes.

The most obvious example of ambivalence is found in the love-hate relationship. Freud has attempted logically to explain this upon the psychoanalytic theory of the origin of the two feelings. Primary is hate which is based upon the Ego or self-preservative instinct, thus, at that period not derived from sexual life but from the struggle of the Ego for self-maintenance. Freud makes the point, too, that the earliest showing of love appears connected with what would seem to be impulses of hate, the desire evidently being to incorporate the love object, equivalent to devouring or annihilating it. Later, hate may exist alongside of love, since hate may represent some expression of impulses active through the Ego instincts, or what appears to be hate is really regression to the early sadistic stage of love-object relationship mentioned above. Clearest and simplest to understand is the conflict between the two forces, one deriving from the Ego, the other from libidinal demands, because then the ambivalence does not arise from the cleavage of any one instinct.

The originator of the term ambivalence was Bleuler who gave under a definition of the conception the fact that the same thing can have a positive and negative feeling-tone, and that it can be thought of in positive and negative terms, or striving towards it can have equally contradictory qualities.

Freud tends to confine his discussion of ambivalence to the love-hate situation which is characteristic of the love-life. He states that (a) some ambivalence may have its origin in the original universal constitutional bisexuality; (b) the love-hate ambivalence may be due to identifications complicating object-love, identifications ambivalent from the first, or (c) according to his recent Life-Death instinct theories, it may represent a state of incomplete fusion of these so-called primary instincts.

Students of child psychology by the psychoanalytic method note many evidences of ambivalent attitudes on the part of young children. Freud and other workers find illustrations in such overt phenomena as when a child at one moment says to its parent, "I hate you," and the next minute gives evidence of affection.

We might offer the observation that very early beginnings of hate are easily to be seen in the form of aversion and repulsion in infancy during the primary narcistic stage, before there is any evidence of a love-object having been formed. Hug-Hellmuth maintains that even the first cry of the infant shows opposition to the world.

In his essay on the subject (*Die Ambivalenz Des Kindes*) Graber insists that during intrauterine existence there is only a single feeling-tone, a unity of pleasure; and that only with the experience of birth comes the first polarity, pain-pleasure. This first polarity in the affective life is the basis of the first ambivalence.

The discussion of the love-hate ambivalence brings out what seems to be an important point properly to be mentioned here. The psychoanalysts evidently feel that there is a distinction between hate, sadism (sadistic love), and aggressive impulses (the Death or Destructive instinct), though they frequently employ the terms very loosely and confusingly in the literature.

Jung's ideas about ambivalence seem to be well expressed by Hinkle, "all impulses in their natural and unredeemed state are ambivalent; therefore, besides the creative impulse there is the destructive impulse."

DIVISIONAL CONSTITUTION OF MENTAL LIFE

I

UNCONSCIOUS, PRECONSCIOUS, CONSCIOUS

One of the great foundation stones utilized for the structure of psychoanalysis is the conception that mental life consists of much more than appears in consciousness; in other words, mental processes actively function on what may be thought of, for want of a better analogy, as diverse strata or levels. Psychoanalysis terms these conscious (Cs), preconscious (Pcs), unconscious (Ucs).

Because of the great interest attaching to the subject, Freud has devoted much effort to making his formulations concerning the Ucs very clear. Both before and in his time, the concept of the Ucs has been a storm-center of argument by philosophers and psychologists. In a number of his writings he has given carefully worded logical statements for the basis of his divisions of mental life. The reasons for thorough-going acceptance of belief in a dynamic Ucs are several, according to Freud. They are mainly (a) the post-hypnotic carrying out of suggestions held in the Ucs, (b) the evidences found through discovering the latent meaning of dreams, (c) the discoverable bases for common slips or errors of speech, memory, action, (d) the fact that ideas suddenly appear in the mind from somewhere outside consciousness or even that problems are solved without awareness, (e) the small amount in consciousness at any one time in comparison to the latent content of the mind, (f) the fact that through psychoanalytic technique various mental and physical symptoms are found to have their foundations in hidden mental life, and in general, that "analytic investigation reveals some of these latent processes as having characteristics and peculiarities that seem alien to us, or

22

"The division of mental life into what is conscious and what is unconscious is the fundamental premise on which psychoanalysis is based." The Ucs does not become conscious because life situations do not call it up, or because certain repressing forces are opposed to it. The technic of psychoanalysis offers a means by which the opposing forces can be removed and the repressed made conscious. Dream analysis is the most valuable means available for penetrating into the Ucs.

Part of what is unconscious in mental life has been in consciousness; part has not. So, too, all that is repressed is unconscious, but not the whole of the Ucs is repressed. It is important to note this because the psychoanalytic knowledge of the Ucs has been derived from study of repressed material.

Jones writes of the Ucs—when one uses the term in psychoanalytic sense one denotes by it mental processes that are (1) unconscious, (2) dynamically active in the production of external manifestations, (3) of high significance to the personality, (4) endowed with certain peculiar attributes that sharply distinguish them from the type of mental functioning with which we are familiar. (*Papers on Psychoanalysis.*)

According to Jones some of the attributes of the Ucs are: The close relation to the instincts and to infantile life; their conative nature; the prominent part displayed in them by sexuality (predominantly but not exclusively sexual); ruthless absolute egocentricity; total absence of the ideas of time and of negation. "The Ucs is quite timeless and the word 'no' has no significance for it." The Ucs is entirely regulated according to the pleasure-pain principle—that is, entirely non-moral. "In the unconscious mind social, moral, ethical, altruistic, and esthetic considerations are simply ignored, as completely as though they did not exist." Energy belonging to unconscious ideas is very mobile—"can be shifted from one idea to another in a way that is quite foreign to conscious mental life."

Already in 1900 Freud makes the distinction between mental life as it exists in the Ucs and in consciousness, to which it cannot be raised except as it is associated with word perceptions. Later he expanded the idea. In order to become conscious, the content of the unconscious system needs to be reenforced by new qualities which are only possible by association with words. Other psychoanalytic writers follow him in this theory. Jones writes, "Unconscious ideas are non-verbal representations

23

even incredible, and running directly counter to the well known attributes of consciousness," (g) finally, "an incontrovertible proof" is found in "that the assumption of the Ucs helps us to construct a highly successful practical method by which we are enabled to exert a useful influence upon the course of conscious processes."

THE UNCONSCIOUS

The Unconscious is that vast quantity of mental life which either never was in consciousness, or, previously in consciousness, has been repressed. (See Dynamisms—Repression.) It is to be particularly emphasized that the elements of the unconscious system are active constituents of mental life. Indeed, in view of their findings, psychoanalysts are convinced that the somatic and emotional effects of the Ucs (even though it is termed the latent part of the mind) are far more powerful than those emanating from consciousness. The Ucs is essentially dynamic and capable of profoundly affecting conscious ideational or emotional life without the individual's being aware of this influence.

Knowledge of the Ucs is obtained only through the transformation or translation of the material of the Ucs into something conscious. "The possibility of such translation is a matter of everyday experience in psychoanalytic work." It is true that "because of of objects or acts—words being confined to conscious or preconscious processes." Rickman says, "Unconscious ideas are unconscious in the sense that they cannot by mere increase of cathexis become conscious." In order to become conscious an idea must be "coupled with a word presentation."

Freud brought up a very difficult problem when he asked the question whether there are unconscious instinctive impulses, emotions or feelings, as there are unconscious ideas. (*The Unconscious, 1915.*) He insists that instincts themselves can never find representatives even in the Ucs except through the ideas that represent the instinct. And just so it is quite beside the mark to regard emotions, feelings, affects, as unconscious; these are not in the Ucs in the sense that ideas are. Even though such terms as unconscious love, hate, etc. are used in psychoanalysis, they have inexact meanings, but still Freud acknowledges their permissibility for practical usage, because they represent situations in which intermediate stages are in the Ucs, and because these situations are dealt with and respond to ordinary psychoanalytic technique. But with much attempt at clarification, Freud still states that the present state of our knowledge precludes adequate statement concerning the difference in status of emotional and ideational elements in the Ucs.

Concerning the possible activities of the Ucs, it should be remarked in the words of Freud that "the Ucs of one human being can react upon that of another without the Cs being implicated at all." Though not very understandable in its dynamics, "the fact is incontestable." (We ourselves wonder what part physical attitudes, facial expressions, gestures, voice qualities, play in this, and we should be inclined to ask with Freud whether preconscious mental activity as an influence can be entirely ruled out.)

Jones speaks of the "infantile nature and origin of the Ucs," and he goes on to say, "The splitting of the mind into the conscious and unconscious regions takes place in the earliest part of childhood life, probably in the first year, and . . . this splitting is the result of the conflict between the uncivilized and non-moral endowments with which we are born and the inhibiting forces." These non-moral childish impulses, since they cannot obtain any direct outlet, reach out and grasp certain experiences, even of adult life, causing them to be pushed into the Ucs. Jones says, "The infantile character of the Ucs thus persists throughout the repulsion and resistance," exertion is required for the conscious to penetrate the Ucs, but it is done through the special techniques of psychoanalysis. As a matter of fact, psychoanalysis is sometimes defined as the method of making conscious what was previously unconscious. This is in the main valid, though there still remains the question of whether *all* that is unconscious could by any technic be brought into consciousness.

From the earliest days when Freud and Breuer found that hysterical symptoms are the derivatives of unconscious memories there has been a steady accretion of knowledge and an immense development of theory concerning the unconscious, but Freud's paper of 1915 on the Ucs demonstrates the great complexity that exists for solution of the psychological problems related to this division of mental life.

The main attributes of the Ucs as portrayed by Freud are given in terms of characteristics that are not true of the other mental systems. Its "instinctual impulses . . . exist independently, side by side, and are exempt from mutual contradiction." "There is in this system no negation, no dubiety, no varying degree of certainty." "Intensity of cathexis is mobile in a far greater degree in this than in the other systems. By the process of displacement one idea may surrender to another the whole volume of its cathexis." Its processes are timeless, "they are not ordered temporally, are not altered by the passage of time, in fact bear no relation to time at all." Its processes are little related to external reality; "their fate depends only upon the degree of their strength and upon their conformity to regulation by pleasure and pain." In the Ucs an idea, in contrast to ideas in consciousness, is not verbalized; "the unconscious idea is of the thing alone."

26

whole of life, giving an added signification to the old saying that the child is father to the man." Freud, however, has said that there is no complete split until the period of puberty.

According to Jones, it is the absurdity for the adult of the persistently infantile (primitively sexual, illogical, etc.) nature of his Ucs which prevents his recognition of its relationship to his conscious desires and beliefs.

The origin of the content of the Ucs is still a controversial issue. Freud and others speak of "primal phantasies" and by these he means phantasies, the fundamental similarity of which he has found so recurrently that they assume a typical form. In the beginning he was inclined to believe these phantasies to be always traceable to real experiences, but later he was inclined to explain their typical character on the basis of a phylogenetic possession. By this he means that the individual is capable through racial inheritance of reaching out "beyond his own life into the experiences of antiquity, where (whenever?) his own experience has become all too rudimentary." The unconscious phantasies (wishes, fears, etc.) "were once realities in the primeval existence of mankind and that the imaginative child is merely filling in the gaps of individual truth with prehistoric truth."

Jung's development of the concept of the Ucs diverges from that of Freud. It is composed of two levels—the personal Ucs and the collective Ucs. Jung says that the personal Ucs "contains forgotten memories, suppressed (purposely forgotten) painful ideas, apperceptions sometimes described as below the threshold (subliminal), that is, sensory perceptions that were not strong enough to reach consciousness, and finally contents that are not yet ripe for consciousness."

The great difference is the slight emphasis placed on repression by Jung. Mitchell says that for Jung: "The personal Ucs is not the result of repression following conflict but is merely a consequence of the tendency of every individual to develop one-sidedly in his mental growth. In adaptation to life one part of his potentialities is neglected in favor of the other and the neglected part tends to become unconscious."

Concerning the collective or superpersonal Ucs, Jung writes: "In every individual there are present (besides his personal memories) the great 'primordial images,' those potentialities of human representations of things as they have always been, inherited through the brain structure from one generation to the next."

In the beginning of their investigations psychoanalysts were primarily concerned with the repressed Ucs, the content of which they found to be composed mainly of childish sexual impulses and phantasies. Thus they came to speak of the Ucs as predominantly "infantile." From his studies of the dream, Freud discovered "not only that the materials of forgotten childhood experiences are accessible to the dream, but . . . also that the psychic life of children with all its peculiarities, its egoism, its incestuous love-choice, etc., continues for the purposes of the dream in the Ucs. . . . Thus it becomes more certain that the Ucs in our psychic life is the infantile."

With the extension of the concept of the Ucs, infantilism is still regarded as one of the main characteristics of this system, and the term now seems to refer not only to the content but also to the unconscious mode of functioning.

But since more attention has been paid to the archaic psychological remnants of race history which make up part of the Ucs, the primitive nature of this part of the mind is also stressed.

Jung emphasizes "the dominants" or "archetypes" of the collective Ucs which it is very important to be able to recognize. Chief among these dominants (phantasies) are divinities, saviors, magical demons, animals. These as projections upon the physician come to light during the transference, and Jung says his clinical experience has repeatedly demonstrated these unconscious phantasies.

The collective Ucs embraces the whole sphere of inherited functional complexes which Jung terms archetypes, by means of which the historical continuity of all human experience exists as special psychic tendencies or ways of functioning in individual psychology. The validity of this concept is claimed to rest on an immense variety of empirical observations and clinical experience.

The question of the inheritance of ideas is bound to be brought up, and Jung answers: "I do not by any means assert the inheritance of ideas, but only of the possibilities or germs of ideas, something markedly different." "I must own I have never yet found indisputable evidence of the inheritance of memory-images, but I do not regard it as positively excluded that besides these collective deposits, which contain nothing specifically individual, the psyche may also inherit memory acquisitions of a definite individual stamp."

In the vast amount of discussion concerning the use of the terms Ucs much appears to be largely a matter of mere terminology. (See Northbridge, *Modern Theories of the Unconscious*.) Whatever may be meant by various psychologists in their use of the words Conscious or Unconscious or Subconscious, for psychoanalysis the main fact is the dynamics of the situation. For the psychoanalyst the conception of the Ucs centers about a working principle, clinically established. The controversial attitude of some academic psychologists is based largely on their theory that consciousness must have more definite characteristics and dynamic aspects of its own than psychoanalysis grants.

The Preconscious (formerly called the foreconscious) is that part of mental life which in appropriate circumstances, either through an effort of the will or stimulated by an associated idea, can be brought up into consciousness. The Pcs is that part of mental life which without definite release of repressions has the capability of becoming conscious. Some memories are less accessible than others, this being due to associative connection with unconscious material. On the whole, the Pcs has more of the characteristics of the Cs than the Ucs.

Long preceding his notable conception of the work of the Super-ego (see later), Freud developed the idea of a censorship of thought which emanated from or functioned through the Pcs. At first this was conceived of as protecting the Cs from the intolerable material of the Ucs, but later Freud found by clinical observations that there was also censorship existing between the Pcs and Cs. Because certain ideas in the Pcs could derive some cathexis from the Ucs, there was need of a further protective agency on the other frontier, determining what thoughts shall become conscious. But all this now has to be reviewed in the light of more recent topographical formulations of the metapsychology of the Ego, Id, and Super-ego.

The more recent theory concerning the Pcs is that it consists of what was earlier verbalized material and can again be verbalized. In this it differs from the Ucs which deals with some sort of material which remains unrecognized and unverbalized.

Since the Pcs stands as in an intermediate position between the Cs and the Ucs, it is easy to see that much involved discussion might center about it. Freud himself opened up various questions concerning the exact functions of the Pcs, how much cathexis it carries, what inhibitive powers are within its province, etc. But astutely the father of psychoanalysis warned against generalizations concerning the apportionment of parts of mental activities to the different mental systems.

Inasmuch as the Coconscious of Morton Prince is that part of mental life which, though not in awareness, normally has stimulability, it is much the same as Freud's Pcs. The mental life on the fringe of consciousness or awareness to which attention is readily drawn is part of the concept of the Coconscious. But the boundary lines are not satisfactorily drawn and there is no present agreement concerning the limits of the Coconscious and the Pcs. The same must be said for the term Subconscious which is used by some writers.

The Conscious is that part of mental life, proportionately infinitesimal, of which the individual is aware at any given time. Though consciousness is a continuum during normal waking life, its content is extremely transitory, constantly changing.

From a developmental standpoint, either of the race or of an individual, consciousness represents the upper stratum of mental life. In Freud's earlier papers, he strongly draws attention to the fact that older primary mental processes were unconscious, and in the present-day adult the Ucs contains the residues of these primary methods of thought. Consciousness developed later to meet the demands of adaptation to the external real world.

Later Freud makes it plain that the total content of consciousness is not derived from perceptions of the external world; derivates of the Ucs, if distorted or removed by an adequate number of intermediate associations, have free access to consciousness.

Concerning the origin or movement of mental activity, Freud later modifies one of his earlier theories that ideas arise from the Ucs and states that mental activity either "starts from the instincts and passes through the system Ucs to conscious mentation, or, on excitation from without, it passes through the systems Cs and Pcs till it reaches the unconscious cathexes of the Ego and of its objects."

Consciousness is only one property of mental life. It is not, according to psychoanalysis, the essential part as has been generally considered. It may co-exist with other attributes of mental life, or it may be absent, as in dream life, when others parts of the mind are active.

The study of the properties of consciousness is much more within the realm of ordinary psychology than of psychoanalysis—the latter being so peculiarly a study of the unconscious strata of the mind that it has welcomed the term, *depth psychology.*

The splitting of consciousness, "dual personality," a phenomenon familiar to students of psychopathology, greatly interested Freud in the earlier days of psychoanalysis. This hysterical state, Freud thinks, does not prove at all the possible existence of a second consciousness or a "subconscious," rather this means merely the splitting of mental activities into two groups whereby a single consciousness takes up its position alternately with either the one or the other of these groups." Students may well refer not only to Freud's very early papers, but also to his contribution in 1915, *"The Unconscious."*

ID, EGO, SUPER-EGO

The great discoverer, Freud, not finding the Ucs-Pcs-Cs concepts adequate for answering many of the practical problems of mental life, has again made a great advance in psychology by working out another formulation of the constitution of mentality. This later tripartite divisional theory is not intended to supplant the earlier, but presents another point of view which he considers is even more dynamic in its basic conceptions, though it still remains topographical in its outlines of the mental structure. The overlappings are acknowledged; they are not contradictory but rather are complementary.

The more recent formulation of the mental structure of personality is conceived of in terms of three constituents not sharply differentiated, yet each having separate specific characteristics. These are the Id, the Ego, the Super-ego.

Freud's new concepts seem to have created considerable difficulty for some concerning the functions and boundaries of the Id and the Ucs —that is, as to wherein lies the fundamental difference between them. Jones, speaking in this connection, says, "It will not be quite easy to combine the two pictures thus obtained, for the classification is in some respects a crossed one." Rickman says that it cannot be made too emphatic, that the states of consciousness postulated by Freud do not correspond to his later concepts of mental structure.

Freud himself recognizes the difficulties which arise in trying to reconcile the two concepts but insists that both are needed and in speaking of the Ucs says, "Nevertheless, we must beware of ignoring this property, for in the last resort the quality of being conscious or not is the single ray of light that penetrates the obscurity of depth-psychology." (*Ego and the Id.*)

Jones says "Psychoanalysis would find it quite impossible to set forth its findings and conclusions except in terms of an unconscious mind, for its main work consists in the unraveling of unconscious processes which can be described only in mental language, and in converting them into conscious processes."

In the light of the above, Rank's assertion that the concept of the Ucs has "become superfluous, even confusing, and was in fact given up by Freud," seems completely without foundation.

There seems to be no need whatever for giving up either of the tripartite divisional schemes of mental life. Each in its essentials offers very much of value—even though it may be that some modification of details, such as Freud recognizes, may be necessary. The fact that the Id–Ego–Super-ego theory has received such an immediate and wide acceptance and application (without in the least infringing upon the validity of the conception of the Ucs) proves the immense value of this later formulation of the dynamics of mental life.

Alexander says the "division of the total personality into fairly independent parts is the fundamental scientific contribution of psychoanalysis. Our thinking has not as yet accepted sufficiently the reality of these invisible intra-psychic part personalities." He also says that Freud's later contributions "have put us in a position to comprehend the relations obtaining between the manifestations of psychic disease as well as normal psychic manifestations within the personality as a whole."

The characteristics of the Id as variously given by Freud are as follows:

It contains all phylogenetic acquisitions.

It is the source of instinctive energy for the individual.

It forms the great reservoir of libido.

The Eros and death instincts struggle within it.

It is the region, the hinterland, of the passions and instincts, also of habit tendencies.

It is unconscious.

The pleasure-principle reigns supreme in it.

Guided by the pleasure-principle it guards itself against tension and pain.

It aims at gratification of libidinal urges.

It is unmoral, illogical; it has no unity of purpose.

The repressed merges into the Id and is then part of it.

Id: Latin, translatable "it," a term used in etymological consistency with "Ego." Both these words are peculiar to the English translation—Freud uses "Ich" and "Es."

Freud has remained convinced that mental processes possess certain characteristic attributes according to the region of the mind in which they take place—and this has led to his later ideas concerning the Id, the Ego, the Super-ego, each in and of itself, or containing, an energy system.

The structure and activities of the Id are not entirely clear even to the most advanced disciples of psychoanalysis, even though the great merit of the concept is apparent. Many of the attributes formerly given to the Ucs are apparently those of the Id, yet they are not identical. Some writers, however, seem entirely to fuse the two. It is a tribute to Freud to state that he does not claim finality for his own formulations—he bespeaks further research and further interpretation. Indeed, in one of his most recent writings he states that in the endeavor to fix some of the most important theoretical ideas of psychoanalysis, he goes far beyond psychoanalysis and it remains to be seen whether the later constructions will turn out to be serviceable.

Ferenczi says the Id is "the region where habit tendencies are piled up."

The Ego is an organization of mental life derived from that more primal structure, the Id, by modifications imposed on it by the external world. It is never entirely differentiated from the Id. Its characteristics are as follows:

It is a coherent organization of mental processes.

Just as instincts play a great role in the Id, so perceptions play a great part in the Ego.

It is not sharply differentiated from the Id; its lower portion merges into the Id.

It is representative of the external world, of reality.

It represents what we call reason and sanity.

It is an entity which starts from out the perceptual system and begins by being preconscious.

In its character it is a precipitate of abandoned object-cathexes; it is formed to a great extent out of identifications, taking the place of abandoned cathexes; it contains a record of past object-choices.

Part of it is conscious; part of it is unconscious and produces powerful effects when becoming conscious.

It regulates all its own constituent processes.

From it proceed the repressions.

It has to hold in check the superior strength of the Id.

Sublimation may take place through the mediation of the Ego—in this way erotic-libido is changed into Ego-libido.

It goes to sleep but exercises censorship on dreams.

It strives to be moral.

"By virtue of its relations to the perceptual system it arranges the processes of the mind in a temporal order and tests their correspondence with reality."

It owes service to three masters and is consequently menaced by three dangers: the external world, the libido of the Id, the severity of the Super-ego.

It controls motility and the approaches to the discharge of excitations.

The Ego occupies a position between the Id and reality. Freud says, "Like the dweller in the borderland that it is, the Ego tries to mediate between the world and the Id, to make the Id comply with the world's demands and by means of muscular activity to accommodate the world to the Id's demands." "It also offers itself to the Id as a libidinal object in view of its power of adaptation to the real world, and aims at attaching the Id's libido to itself." (Thus arises Ego-libido.)

The Ego, according to Freud's ideas, is derived from auditory impressions, verbal images (as is the Super-ego).

The Ego arises, according to J. Glover, from inhibiting internal urges when they fail to give pleasure. Its work is to adapt inner urges to the reality of the outer world. It represents the imprint of external necessity on the Id.

After the Ego has repressed any material, this material is shut off from the conscious Ego and there is no way of communication between them except by the roundabout path of psychoanalytic exploration.

The Ego is evolved to regulate instinctual life in accordance with reality as it appears, says Glover. The Ego alteration takes place through introjection and is less pliable after childhood. Rank states that the intellectual functions mature late in the Ego development.

The task of the Ego, among other things, is to substitute the reality-principle for the pleasure-principle which reigns supreme in the Id.

The Ego-synthesis is cemented by narcistic libido.

In a recent work (*The Problem of Lay-Analyses*) Freud expounds for the benefit of the layman his conception of "the forces active in and between" the Ego and the Id. The statements he makes in this connection, taken into consideration with others made elsewhere, may perhaps serve to illuminate the subject to some degree. Stated briefly, the main points seem to be as follows:

The Id produces the driving power; the Ego "takes the steering wheel in hand" in order to reach the desired goal.

The Id urges demand immediate rash gratification which will end in failure; the Ego must forestall danger by mediating between the Id's reckless demands and the practical outer world.

The Ego has two different censorial duties in respect to the Id—(a) to watch the outer world and seize the most opportune moment for a harmless gratification of Id urges; (b) to induce the Id to modify or renounce its urges, or to substitute or postpone its gratifications.

The Ego as it develops should gradually learn that another way to gratify the Id urges "consists of changing conditions in the outer world in such a way as to bring about circumstances favorable to gratification." This is "the supreme achievement" of the Ego. "Sufficient discernment to perceive when it is opportune to stifle passions and when it is opportune either to face or fight the realities of the outer world is, after all, the Alpha and Omega of practical wisdom."

There is no inherent opposition between the Ego and the Id; in the normal person it should not be possible to distinguish between the two.

The childhood Ego is relatively weak and only slightly different from the Id; it is apt to become panic-stricken in the face of an Id urge, and, instead of assisting it to some form of gratification, it may shirk its duty and attempt flight, or repression of the urge.

In spite of these indicated activities of the Ego, Freud approvingly cites the opinion of Groddeck who maintains that "what we call our Ego is essentially passive; we are 'lived' by unknown and uncontrollable forces."

Wälder says that the first feat of analysis was the discovery of the Id; the second, discovery of the share of the libido in building up the Ego; The next task is to divide off empirically the sphere of action of the two systems. He says again that the fundamental problem of psychoanalysis is the ascertaining of the part which each of the two systems (Id and Ego) play in every psychical act. "The distinction sought for is not of such a kind that, say, one group of psychical phenomena is then to be regarded as originating in the Id, and another as formed out of the Ego; the aim is rather to determine and mark the share of both in every phenomenon."

Rickman says that a failure of adaptation in healthy persons is usually more connected with the Ego than the libido development. Various Ego-capacities must be considered—e. g. has the Ego the capacity to tolerate the Super-ego, to tolerate large quantities of libido, to transfer the libido to another object, etc.?

Ferenczi brings out two points with respect to the Ego, that it "not only plays a purely passive, intermediary rôle between the Id, the Super-ego, and the outer world, but occasionally it also has certain very important active influences on the end result of the psychic occurrences." Secondly, "the Ego, despite its comparative weakness, is capable of holding in control great quantities of energy of the Id," which Ferenczi says "is explainable on the ground of its high organization which the Ego has acquired apparently in its long diplomatic service as intermediary between the various psychic forces. The Ego is weak but clever, the Id strong but crude and primitive; it permits itself to be led by higher powers. So the Ego becomes watchman at whose signal the instinctive energy takes this or that direction."

If the Ego is to exert any real influence on the Id, it must have access to all parts of the Id. If, however, it deals with an Id urge by means of repression, it must pay by losing control of the urge which will attempt in all sorts of disguises to assert its independence. A neurosis is often the result of this Ego-Id conflict; and, in any case, there is bound to be some crippling of the Ego.

The recent developments of the conceptions of the Ego are of great significance for psychoanalytic therapy. The aim now is not only to uncover repressed emotional states and urges and abreact these, but also to explore the nature of the Ego. Analysis of the Ego is to discover why the repressing faculty acted as it did, why repression of this particular material occurred at all. The idea is to learn how this particular Ego is made up in certain particulars, how it viewed reality, what identification it made. E. Glover states it well: "One aim of psychoanalysis is to discover why repressions occur, i. e., why the early Ego scented danger, wove theories, arrived at conclusions; how repression was brought about, i. e., by what manipulation of the parent-child relationship the Ego got the upper hand of the urges of the Id or what was the process of changing Ego attitudes and of modification of urges."

The Super-ego is an outgrowth of and is a modification of the Ego; it has a special position in regard to the Ego and has the capacity to rule it. Its nature and activities, according to Freud, may be given in these terms:

It is to a great extent unconscious; it is independent of the conscious Ego and is largely inaccessible to it.

It is farther from consciousness than the Ego.

It is the "heir of the Oedipus Complex"—a precipitate of identifications with the parents "in some way combined together."

It is a deposit left by earliest object-cathexes of the Id.

It also represents an energetic reaction formation against those choices.

It has a great many points of contact with the phylogenetic endowment of each individual—his archaic inheritance.

It is a borrowing by the child's Ego of strength from the father to help in carrying out the repression of the Oedipus complex—a setting up within the self of the obstacle to Oedipus desires—"a most momentous loan."

Its chief function is criticism which creates in the Ego an unconscious sense of guilt.

It acts in the form of a "categorical imperative" and assumes a "compulsive character."

It is essentially the same as conscience.

It may be hyper-moral and tyrannical towards the Ego.

It is always in close touch with the Id and can act as its representative in relation to the Ego.

There is a very free communication possible between the Super-ego and unconscious instinctual trends.

It knows more than the Ego about the unconscious Id.

It is amenable to later influences but preserves throughout life the character given to it by its derivation from the parent complex.

It is a permanent expression of the influence of the parents.

The mature Ego remains subject to Super-ego domination.

Concerning the genesis of the Super-ego it is generally agreed that an already loosely organized system of primitive morality during infantile libidinal stages is welded together through erotic strivings towards the parents, through the Oedipus struggle and its repression, through the "thou shalt" and "thou shalt not" necessities of child-parent relationship. There is an extension or development of the Ego through introjection of the parent-object, a process of identification. Perhaps, also, there are first beginnings, as Ferenczi suggests, in the training, the "thou shalt not's" of sphincter training and commands to cleanliness. The first renunciations are represented in the development of the Super-ego. Inner follow outer frustrations. There is conversion of outer to inner prohibitions.

It sounds highly theoretical to say, as Glover does, that the specific structure and tendencies of the Super-ego depend on the nature of the primitive identifications with the parents and on the fate of the libidinal strivings towards the parents, but it is upon just such factual discoveries that psychoanalysis believes itself to be firmly founded. The parents are incorporated into the individual; they continue to function as instigators of repression. The early identifications and introjections leave their strong imprint.

With regard to function, psychoanalysts (with the exception of Alexander) agree that the actual active repression is performed by the Ego rather than the Super-ego, though for the most part in obedience to the demands of the latter. (It is to be noted, however, that the Ego can repress the sense of guilt provoked by the Super-ego's attack upon it.) Alexander points out that the Super-ego treats phantasies as if they were acts. Rickman describes the Super-ego as "a technique for maintaining object-relationships while at the same time affording an outlet for instinctual energies that often tend to destroy these relationships. Its function is adaptive, it is slowly acquired, integrated with other psychical functions and liable to disorders." Again, he states "the Super-ego is a part of the regulating mechanism which slowly develops in early childhood as a specially functioning part of the Ego-system, to act as an indicator, when a certain kind of internal tension increases above a certain limit."

Psychoanalytic interest in the Super-ego seems at present to center about investigations and speculations concerning such problems as the

The injunctions and prohibitions of other authorities (teachers *et al*) remain vested in the Super-ego and continue in the form of conscience to exercise the censorship of morals.

Jones who has written much about the Super-ego regards it as "one of the most important contributions that Freud has made to the science of psychoanalysis"; and says that "as to the validity and value of the conception there will be universal agreement." Though he admits that the hypothesis involves many contradictions which must yet be solved, he says "there is every reason to think that the concept of the Super-ego is a nodal point where we may expect all the obscure problems of Oedipus complex and narcism on the one hand, and hate and sadism on the other, to meet." Freud himself says "concerning the origin and function of the Super-ego a good deal remains insufficiently elucidated."

According to Jones, there are certain formulations with regard to the Super-ego which seem to be well established:

First, it is connected with the passing of the Oedipus complex, "the nuclear and essential part of its composition may be regarded as the direct imprint made on the personality by the conflicts relating to this complex."

Second, one of its clearest features is the function it exercises, which is "to criticise the Ego and to cause pain to the latter whenever it tends to accept impulses proceeding from the repressed part of the Id."

period of its origin, the specific factors involved in its genesis, and the manner of its development—sex differences, child-adult differences. The all important question for neurosis seems to be: Does the originally constituted Super-ego remain static or is it modifiable later, and if so, how?

The rôle of the actual parents in the genesis of the Super-ego seems to be in doubt. Klein says that in her analysis of children she often finds a Super-ego which is in complete contradiction to the character of the parents and evidently depends mainly on the child's own phantasy formations. In the case of a very sadistic Super-ego, however, she points out that violence on the part of the parents may reenforce its aggressive character and lead to destructive attacks on the environment. Rickman and Payne both think that parental conduct may have a traumatic effect on Super-ego formation. The child's "discovery of a parent's gross failure to fulfill his ideal may be a factor in instigating mental regression and the onset of neurosis."

Alexander says the Super-ego is to a large extent the product of education, a result of child-rearing to the extent that parental prohibitions "clothe those stirrings which will later come under the ban of repression with prohibitions containing a punitive clause. . . . In the course of time these prohibitions and commands of the educational process become transformed into internal laws, and this internalized morality as conscience, becomes, in a large measure, independent of the presence of the original prohibiting persons." However, Alexander further describes the Super-ego as a "faculty which reflects certain phylogenetic echoes of primitive man. This code which has become relegated to the unconscious is identical with the totemistic code of primitive peoples. Its chief prohibitions are directly in the male against the incest wish and against inimical stirrings against the father."

Jones claims to have discovered clinically that the Super-ego is "normally and predominantly" derived from the parent of the same sex. He suggests that the Super-ego "is derived from the thwarting parent, irrespective of whether this happens to be the primary love object or not; normally it is a secondary love object, the parent of the same sex." Thus he lays stress on hostility arising out of frustrated object-love as the essential condition of Super-ego formation.

47

Tremendous emphasis has been placed by psychoanalysis upon Freud's recent Super-ego concept which has arisen out of the attempt to investigate and understand the repressing forces. The Super-ego is evidently closely allied to "conscience," and, it would seem, is considered of great importance by psychoanalysis for understanding normal as well as abnormal development. There is, therefore, justification for giving special consideration to it.

Freud says of the Super-ego that "it stands as the representative of the most important events in the development both of the individual and of the race; indeed, by giving permanent expression to the influence of the parents it perpetuates the existence of the factors to which it owes its origin."

The concept of the Super-ego, Freud says, answers the reproach that psychoanalysis has ignored "the higher moral, spiritual side of human nature." In reply to this he says that the Super-ego "answers in every way to what is expected of the higher nature of man." He says, "Here we have that higher nature of this Ego-ideal or Super-ego, the representative of our relation to our parents. When we were little children we knew these higher natures, we admired them and feared them; and later we took them into ourselves."

Schilder says that the identifications with the parents are the most important for Super-ego formation, but he also points out that the child will see in or ascribe to the parents, and incorporate into himself, different attitudes at different stages of his development. As a result, there will co-exist many different Super-egos, some very primitive, others highly differentiated. Certain attitudes which are common to the majority of individuals in the child's environment reenforce each other through identifications, and in this way the general requirements of society become deeply engraved on the individual.

Rickman stresses a mode of Super-ego development based on the internalizing of only some of the parental prohibitions, that is, isolated reaction formations, which, he says, will lead to an unintegrated "moral character." This type of Super-ego, he thinks, is closely related to criminal tendencies. Both he and Reich also explain criminality as due to a "defective" Super-ego, or an "ineffective capacity for self-criticism." Freud claims that "a very powerful sense of guilt may be the motive rather than the result of a crime."

Rickman deals with the problem of why the child "should accept so unpleasant a thing as a criticizing person into his psychical system." He says it is "primarily love for the parents and their surrogates which makes it well-nigh impossible for the child to neglect their injunctions, and it is at bottom the force of love which causes it to renounce its sensual pleasures." The child gives up part of itself in return for continued parental approval, thus the pleasure-principle rules.

Alexander thinks of the Super-ego as a formation based on the pleasure-principle—"the introjection of painful environmental instinct inhibition in the form of an inhibitory Super-ego took place in the interest of pain avoidance."

The frequently tyrannical or sadistic nature of the Super-ego which, according to Alexander, plays so great a part in the neuroses, is explained by Klein as due to its origin in the oral or anal-sadistic stage of development. Jones points out that the formation of the Super-ego may be accompanied by regression to the anal-sadistic. Freud, on the basis of his Life-Death instinct hypothesis, suggests that a sadistic hyper-moral Super-ego may be due to instinct defusion, the Super-ego becoming "a gathering place for the death instincts." Alexander makes much of this theory.

49

There seems to be general agreement that the earliest identifications with the parents are far more significant than any later identifications; the power of the latter to modify the first imprint is in dispute. Rickman describes the formation of the Super-ego as "a continuous process which is carried on by parent substitutes, by school teachers, superiors in business relationship, civic affairs, etc." But he adds, "the setting up of the Ego-ideal is essentially a product of the parent-child relationship, whatever its later development." To what extent the Super-ego is in touch with outer reality seems a point in question in this connection. Jones points out that its relation to outer reality was closer in infancy than at the present, but says it gains its power over the Ego through the reality which it represents and concludes that "in some obscure way it combines influences from both the inner and the outer world."

The relation of the Super-ego formation to secondary narcism is assumed by all psychoanalysts, that is, libidinal satisfaction can be attained through the achievement by the Ego of Ego-ideals. Jones says "the replacement of object cathexis by identification brings about a profound change in the libidinal situation. The image thus incorporated into the Ego serves itself as an object to the libidinal impulses proceeding from the Id, so that more of them are directed toward the Ego as a whole than previously; this constitutes what Freud calls "secondary narcism." According to Rickman, the Super-ego "is a device, so to speak, for maintaining narcism," that is, the "psychical harmony and peace" which comes from fulfillment of the Ego-ideal acts as a compensation for the renouncing of primitive organ satisfaction. The child can retain his self-love and at the same time keep the affection of his parents.

Klein contends (and thinks she is in agreement with Freud) that with the passing of the Oedipus complex the Super-ego assumes "a lasting and unalterable form." Later Super-egos will, of course, arise but in more superficial strata and at bottom determined by the original Super-ego, which, she says, she is convinced from her analysis of children, is "firmly rooted in the child," and "at heart unalterable." The child's Super-ego is not essentially different from that of the adult; "the difference is only that the mature Ego of adults is better able to come to terms with their Super-ego." The only way of reaching and influencing the activities of the Super-ego is, Klein says, through analysis.

Eder, in a recent contribution, distinguishes between the neurotic and the normal Super-ego as follows: "The super-ego is more powerful and more active in the neurotic than in others, and it would seem rather that the neurotic is less able, on that account, to come to grips with reality." He speaks of the "rancour and rigidity" of the neurotic Super-ego, and again of how psychoanalysts have from their clinical experience gained the impression "that if the id impulses could have been controlled by something less inflexible, less severe, more adaptable, and yet less fantastic than the super-ego, the individual could not have been forced into the compromise of a neurotic character or of neurotic symptoms."

Another point of difficulty which has led to much speculation is the origin and nature of the Super-ego in the girl. There are various hypotheses to explain what takes the place for the girl of the castration fear in the boy. Freud suggests fear of loss of the mother's love. Horney suggests fear of vaginal injury in the event of the fulfillment of incest phantasy. (See Oedipus.) Psychoanalysts (including Freud) seem convinced that there is a qualitative difference between the male and female Super-ego. Freud says, with regard to women, "their Super-ego is never so inexorable, so impersonal, so independent of its emotional origins, as we require it to be in men." Rickman and Payne both agree on the more infantile character of the Super-ego in the woman, that is, Payne says "it is more prohibiting and less permitting, certainly as far as sexual gratifications are concerned."

There are many theories concerning the relations existing between the Id, the Ego, and Super-ego, and special interest seems to center about the ultimate fate of the latter and how it is brought about.

Regarding the origin of the Super-ego Jones says: "We thus see that the Super-ego arises as a compromise between the desire to love and the desire to be loved. On the one hand it provides an object for the libidinal impulses of the Id when the external object is no longer available, whereas on the other hand it represents the renouncing of incest which is the only condition under which the parents' approval (i. e. affection) can be retained."

Psychoanalysts seem concerned only with the unconscious Super-ego. Jones, in showing how the Super-ego affords a bridge between the older and newer psychoanalytic concepts, says the chief novelty in the Super-ego concept lies in the discovery that its most important part is unconscious. The conscious part, he says, is accepted by the conscious Ego and corresponds to conscience in ordinary parlance. Considerations of reality with knowledge of actual life have been allowed for in its formation. With regard to the unconscious part, he describes it as much more irrational, as shaped predominantly by the parents, and with attitudes and judgments remaining on an infantile level. Rickman says that though the Super-ego "is an unconscious mental function, the effects of its action may be at times conscious."

Alexander lays much emphasis on the intimate relation existing between the Id and the Super-ego which alone, he says, "is capable of explaining the possibility that a need for punishment may arise for tendencies and wishes which are not in consciousness." He speaks of "a pact," or collusion between the Super-ego and the Id and says of the neurotic conscience, that its fundamental characteristic is its "corruptibility." Reik also speaks of the Super-ego as "the secret ally of repressed tendencies."

Both Reich and Rickman discuss the Super-ego's influence on the development of the Ego. Reich says "the real Ego develops by carrying out the wishes of the Super-ego which, as a result, become part of the Ego." Rickman says "finally, by duress it urges the Ego to change its character and assume control of instinct impulses, not according to the Ego standards but to those of the outer world."

Rickman states that the Super-ego is "under the influence of social opinion," and that normally the regulating functions of the Super-ego, which in the Phallic stage are archaic and exaggerated, should in the Post-phallic stage be supplanted by the Ego; its unconscious force should be weakened and it should retain only its function as an indicator or signaler to the Ego that there is danger to the Ego from the infantile impulses.

The survival value of the Super-ego, Eder points out, lies in a certain utility which it possesses for the Ego. "The Super-ego has a ready-made reply to Id demands; it meets these demands with an inflexible or a very nearly inflexible code—religion, ethics, superstition, good manners. The Super-ego is here the delegate of the Ego, and prepared to deal with all instinctual impulses after an approved and stereotyped pattern. In the meantime the Ego can prepare itself for new eventualities. It is very convenient for the Ego to delegate its reactive immediate responses to a mechanism that is fixed and stable, one which takes no notice of the divergent circumstances, but reacts always in the same way towards like stimuli. The Super-ego is for the Ego a part of reality, fictitious but fixed."

In contrast with Freud's view, it is of interest to note Eder's statement, that in spite of the fact that the Super-ego may be regarded as the source of many cultural achievements, psychoanalysts have discovered it to be not only "the chief obstacle to mental health, but also a handicap

According to Jones, in the normal individual the Super-ego constituted in childhood should "develop freely," and if this fails to take place "fateful consequences may follow. It is well known that children are apt at a certain age to be over-moral—that is, regard slight lapses from the standards they have recently acquired as being heinous sins, with tragic significance; much of the unhappiness of childhood comes from this. If the childish attitude just indicated persists, or if it is directed against remote derivatives of the forbidden impulses, then all sorts of quite innocent acts, even those such as walking, eating, etc., may become forbidden in adult years. To consciousness this forbiddenness appears simply as incapacity, which constitutes one form of nervous disorder. An important step in the treatment of nervous troubles is often the lightening of this burden of irrational guilt."

to the progress of civilization," and that they "look forward to the disappearance of the control exercised by the Super-ego over the Id and the taking over of this control by the Ego, as the more hopeful line of progress for the individual and even for the race."

Alexander writes of the Super-ego: "Psychological experience shows that the Super-ego, this last product of identification with reality, marks the greatest source of danger for the continuance of the psychic apparatus," since it is "highly charged with the aggressions of the external world." Though Alexander goes on to speak of the Super-ego as eventually becoming absorbed into the Ego, he also says "The Super-ego is the part of the psychic apparatus which displays least solidarity with it." This, it would appear, is the case even in the normal individual, while in the neurotic the opposition between the Ego and Super-ego is very strongly marked. Alexander speaks of pathological states "in which the Super-ego is like a foreign body within the Ego," and the Ego must give way to its demands just as it does to external reality.

Alexander defines the Super-ego as "a social faculty, one that guards the individual from the satisfaction in reality of his asocial wishes and even punishes him for the satisfaction of them in phantasy."

Rank, who accepts the existence of the Freudian Super-ego, naturally considers it from the point of view of his own particular sadistic libido theory. (See Libido.) Its basis is the mother-child relationship and it is built up genetically from inhibited sadism. Rank thinks there are three Super-egos, or three different stages in Super-ego development: (1) The biological Super-ego. Very early, Rank says, there is a libidinal missing of the breast, a privation. The unsatisfied oral sadistic libido is partially abreacted (?) as rage, etc. toward the mother; the other part is dammed up in the Ego and leads to the construction of inner privations or inhibitions. (2) The moral Super-ego. This arises in the anal stage as a result of sphincter training, the next educational stage of privation. A content is now given to the "sado-masochistic mechanism, set in biological motion at the oral stage" and a moral relation to the mother is set up. (3) The social Super-ego. This comes into being at the Oedipus through the projection on to the father of the inner maternal inhibitions, followed by identification with the father and introjection of paternal prohibitions.

Sketch suggesting topographical relationship of Cs and Ucs; Id, Ego, and Super-ego.

(Elaborated from Freud's diagram in *The Ego and the Id*)

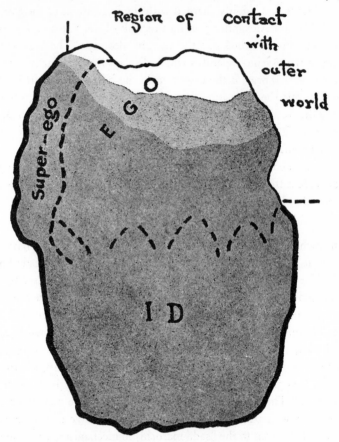

SHADED PORTIONS = THE UNCONSCIOUS—UCS
LIGHTLY SHADED PORTIONS = THE PRECONSCIOUS—PCS
UNSHADED PORTIONS = THE CONSCIOUS—CS

From the standpoint of identification Rank goes on to trace the genesis of the Super-ego as (a) love identification with the mother (mother's breast), (b) sadistic hate identification with depriving mother, with corresponding inner inhibitions, (c) projection on the father of the inner maternal inhibitions or hate identification, (d) hate identification with the father.

For Rank the real nucleus of the Super-ego is the "strict mother" (not, however, the actual mother but the mother as sadistically conceived by the child). This, he says, is ignored by Freud in his consideration of the feminine Super-ego. Rank himself, however, says that the woman's Super-ego differs from the man's, since the girl at the Oedipus retains the primary psychobiological Super-ego; the boy "builds up over the primary maternal Super-ego the paternal social Super-ego." The female Super-ego "consists much more of inhibitions than guilt feeling, whereas in the male anxiety dominates."

Rank also says that experience shows that Super-ego formations based on brother identifications are often directly contrary to and quite independent of a paternal Super-ego formation. Split personalities may be due to strong opposition between two tendencies based on different Super-ego formation.

Rank refers to a "primitive" Super-ego and a "correctly functioning" one. The primitive Super-ego will show in a constant attempt to unload itself, or reestablish the punishment from without, a part of the objective mother-relation. He says "one can understand neither the pleasure of perverse masochists nor the need for punishment of the child, the neurotic, and the criminal, unless one takes into consideration this inner unloading tendency."

FUNDAMENTAL PRINCIPLES

Several underlying "principles" of mental functioning which are fundamental to the understanding of main trends in the personality have been formulated by Freud. These principles are essential parts of the psychological theory as expounded by psychoanalysis. Briefly stated, they are as follows:

(*a*) *The Pleasure-principle*—the tendency for mental life and the development of personality to be shaped primarily according to the affective (pleasure-pain) aspects of inner and also of outer stimuli. Freud speaks of the pleasure-principle as the "sovereign tendency obeyed by the primary (i. e. unconscious) processes." He says, "These processes strive towards gaining pleasure; from any operation which might arouse unpleasantness ('pain') mental activity draws back (repression)."

In the beginning Freud defined pleasure and pain from the point of view of the quantity of excitation or tension present in the psychic life. His hypothesis was "that there is an attempt on the part of the psychic apparatus to keep the quantity of excitation present as low as possible, or at least constant," and therefore, that "all that tends to increase the quantity of excitation must be felt to be contrary to function, that is to say, painful."

The ideas set forth in the first two principles were originally expressed in *Die Traumdeutung* (1900) and were later expounded in *Formulations Regarding the two Principles in Mental Functioning* (1911).

Fechner's postulation of a psychophysical relationship of pleasure and pain to "conditions of stability and instability" influenced Freud, as he frankly admits, in formulating his pleasure-principle, which he terms "a special case of Fechner's tendency to stability."

With regard to the pleasure-principle, it is important to remember that *immediate* satisfaction is the goal. Thus the reality-principle, through its emphasis on postponement of satisfaction, comes to stand in opposition to it. In this connection, however, Freud writes, "It is . . . indubitable that the replacement of the pleasure-principle by the reality-principle can account only for a small part, and that not the most intense, of painful experiences."

The apparently conflicting statements which are to be found in Freud's writings regarding the relationship of sexuality with the pleasure-principle are perhaps largely explainable when it is remembered that he has given, not the popular connotations, but a very special and extended meaning to the term sexuality. He also makes certain very definite statements in regard to this matter. In discussing the pleasure-principle he writes, "The condition of sexual excitement is the most striking example of the pleasurable increase in tension . . . but it is certainly not the only one." And concerning the relationship of the pleasure-principle and the reality-principle to the sex impulses, he points out that the pleasure-principle maintains its sway for a long time over the sex impulses which "are not so easily educable."

Freud points out that all impulses to motor activity which are under the supremacy of the pleasure-principle are for the purpose of unburdening the mental apparatus of accretions of stimuli. Acceptance of the reality-principle involves a certain degree of restraint of motor discharge, and the mental apparatus has to develop the capacity "to support increased tension during a delay in the process of discharge."

Freud calls attention to the fact of "the tenacity with which we hold on to the sources of pleasure at our disposal" and "the difficulty with

Though he still maintains the paramount significance of the pleasure-principle for mental functioning, Freud has come to the conclusion that his earlier view of pleasure and pain—namely, "that every 'pain' coincides with a heightening, every pleasure with a lowering, of the stimulus-tension existing in the mind"— will not hold, and he now believes "that there is such a thing as pleasurable tension and 'painful' lowering of tension." He says, "pleasure and 'pain' cannot, therefore, be referred to a quantitative increase or decrease of something which we call stimulus-tension, although they clearly have a great deal to do with this factor. It seems as though they do not depend on this quantitative factor, but on some peculiarity in it which we can only describe as qualitative."

But Freud has recently again laid emphasis on the quantitative factor in psychic "pain." He now conceives of it as the state of psychic helplessness which arises when the outlets for discharge of excitation are inadequate.

which we renounce them." Phantasy-making is an example of this tenacious clinging to the pleasure-principle. It begins in the games of children and is later continued as day-dreaming.

Alexander lays much emphasis on what he feels is the essence of the development from the pleasure to the reality-principle. This consists, he says, "in the ability not merely to endure instinctual tensions at times, but even to seek out directly situations of pain or suffering in the interest of a future and assured pleasure-gain, or of the avoidance of a greater pain." He cites as examples the submitting to dental treatment in order to avoid future distress; the criminal who seeks punishment to free him from an inner sense of guilt—both the crime and the punishment "signify an unburdening for him, an economic gain in the pleasure-pain balance." Many "paradoxical self-injuring actions" may be explained on this basis.

The fact that the Ego has become so thoroughly imbued, during the period of development from the pleasure-principle to the reality-principle, with the idea that the right to instinctual gratification may be purchased through suffering accounts, Alexander thinks, for the relationship which it is bound to assume to the Super-ego. "It is . . . not surprising if the Ego applies the same methods in relation to the inner representative of the social demands, the Super-ego, as it had learnt to practice in relation to the external world. It gives in to the Super-ego where necessary, just as to external reality, and, if required, it takes suffering on itself in order that elsewhere it may thus be enabled to carry the instinctual demands through triumphantly. But upon the same principles rests the relation of the child to his educators, who behave to the child's instinctual demands in exactly the same way as impersonal reality. They inflict pain on the child if he does not obey, and reward him with pleasure prizes if he will make the needed instinctual renunciations. It is therefore only a matter of course that the behavior of the Ego to the Super-ego will conform to the same principles as are at the basis of its relations to external impersonal reality and to its educators. The behavior of the Ego to the Super-ego is, therefore, in accordance with the reality-principle."

(*b*) *The Reality-principle*—the tendency to shape mental life and personality development according to the requirements of external necessity. It is secondary to the pleasure-principle; it is, at least in its earliest development, an acquired, learned tendency, forced upon the individual by the need for adaptation to his environment. Freud contends that the reality-principle inevitably supersedes the pleasure-principle when the organism discovers that the former is "useless and indeed extremely dangerous." He says that due to the need for self-preservation, "it (the pleasure-principle) is replaced by the 'reality-principle,' which without giving up the intention of ultimately obtaining pleasure yet demands and enforces the postponement of satisfaction, the renunciation of manifold possibilities of it, and the temporary endurance of 'pain' on the long and circuitous road to pleasure."

Freud speaks of "the so-called Reality-Principle which, although striving for the same ends as the Pleasure-Principle, nevertheless considers such practical necessities as the outer world imposes." Again he writes, "Actually, the substitution of the reality-principle for the pleasure-principle denotes no dethronement of the pleasure-principle, but only a safeguarding of it. A momentary pleasure, uncertain in its results, is given up, but only in order to gain in the new way an assured pleasure coming later."

Alexander stresses the fact that the reality-principle is forced upon the Ego. "Under the pressure of a more powerful reality it has had, willy-nilly, to identify itself in part with this. . . ." However, "at bottom it may sympathize with the instinctual demands of the Id." The differentiation of the Ego from the Id is really "only for the purpose of thus securing (through identification with external reality) a more complete satisfaction of instinctual demands." Again in this connection Alexander writes, "We picture the improved pleasure-principle, the reality-principle, in this way; that the psychic apparatus only takes upon itself the precise amount of self-restriction that is necessary, just as much as is absolutely essential for the attainment of instinctual gratifications." If the Ego allies itself more with reality than is required in the interests of instinctual gratification, "it is betraying the interests of the Id. If the Ego turns its capacity for testing reality into an end in itself and does not merely apply it to the service of instinctual demand, if it looks for objective truth, it is giving up its original attachment to the instinctual life and placing itself on the side of reality."

Art brings about a peculiar reconciliation between the two principles. The artist turns from reality and allows his instinctual life full play in phantasy. He then finds a way to return to reality; with his special gifts he moulds his phantasies into a new kind of reality, and men concede them a justification as valuable reflections of actual life. "Thus by a certain path he actually becomes the hero, king, creator, favorite he desired to be, without pursuing the circuitous path of creating real alterations in the outer world. But this he can only attain because other men feel the same dissatisfaction as he with the renunciation demanded by reality, and because this dissatisfaction, resulting from the displacement of the pleasure-principle by the reality-principle, is itself a part of reality."

(*c*) *The Nirvana-principle*—the tendency of mental life to maintain "at as low a level as possible the quantities of excitation flowing into it" or to bring about a minimum of psychic tension. This relatively tensionless condition, as has been pointed out above, was Freud's original conception of pleasure. Now he states quite clearly that the pleasure- and Nirvana-principle must be regarded as quite distinct from each other.

The term Nirvana-principle was suggested by Barbara Low and accepted by Freud in the beginning as really identical with the pleasure-principle. His growing conception, however, of the death instincts, (see next section for discussion) "the aim of which is to lead our throbbing existence into the stability of an inorganic state," led him to the conclusion that the Nirvana-principle was closely related to the death instincts and distinct from the pleasure-principle. He seems inclined to regard the Nirvana-principle as preceding the pleasure-principle, since he speaks of it as having undergone "a modification in the living organism through which it became the pleasure-principle" and also of the life instinct as having "wrested a place for itself alongside the death instinct in regulating the processes of life." "In this way," he says, "we obtain a series . . . . : The Nirvana-principle expresses the tendency of the death-instinct, the pleasure-principle represents the claims of the libido, and that modification of it, the reality-principle, the influence of the outer world."

(d) *The Repetition-compulsion-principle*—the tendency in waking life, to live through again—dramatize, re-stage—in different setting some earlier emotional experience which has made a deep impression, or in dream life to re-enact it with often much the same setting. Though the pleasure-principle may be operative to some extent in such cases, Freud is convinced from his observations that there is a tendency or compulsion to revive "experiences of the past that contain no potentiality of pleasure and which could at no time have been satisfactions." He is inclined to believe that this repetition-compulsion does not only exist independently of the pleasure-principle but is also perhaps of earlier and independent origin.

Freud reached his conclusions with regard to the nature and validity of the repetition-compulsion principle on the basis of various observations. The clinical picture of war and other traumatic neuroses showed a striking peculiarity in the dream life—the patient continually dreaming of his disastrous experience. This, Freud felt, could not be explained by his wish-fulfillment theory of dreams, unless masochistic urges were the explanation. Observations also on children who frequently, Freud found, in their play re-enacted or dramatized unpleasant experiences also supported the notion that something other than the pleasure-principle was operative.

Freud found in the transference-neurosis phenomenon, his main argument for postulating the existence of a repetition-compulsion principle in psychic life, a principle more fundamental even than the pleasure-principle. Freud points out that always in the inevitably recurring transference-neurosis situation, the patient lives over again in respect to his physician one of the most deeply painful episodes of his childhood—the Oedipus situation with all its vain expectations of satisfaction and with its narcistic wounding.

Alexander calls the repetition-compulsion the "principle of inertia"— that is, the avoidance of constantly changing active psychic effort and its replacement by an automatism, and says that it "seems to be the fundamental fact underlying all mental and biological processes." He thinks that Freud gives "a profound insight into the essential unity of neurotic symptoms, transference and human destiny by his view of them as an expression of a compulsion toward the repetition of an attempt to solve an unresolved conflict, to master subsequently a real experience that had been insuperable."

Ferenczi calls attention to what might be termed the morality-principle. "The psychically healthy Ego," he writes, "must adapt itself in three directions and has to bring the three principles of pleasure, reality, and morals into harmonious relations." In this connection it is interesting to note Alexander's description of the Super-ego as "that internalized piece of reality."

GENERAL INSTINCT DIRECTIONS

In recent years Freud has engaged in some notable speculations concerning the innate trends of the fundamental urges of the human personality. He postulates two trends which, he suggests, constitute the essence of all living matter. These formulations are theoretical but are supported by biological and psychological considerations. Freud discussed them in a chapter in *"The Ego and the Id,"* entitled "The Classes of Instincts," clarifying his original speculations appearing in *"Beyond the Pleasure Principle."*

Any understanding of Freud's attempt to divide primary urges into two qualitatively different instinct classes must take into account his conception of the meaning of the word "instinct," which he has stated very clearly. He thinks the term should be reserved for primal trends only, that is, for those which cannot be resolved further. In addition, "instinct" connotes for Freud a constant psychic force attacking from within the organism, having its source in important somatic processes and needs in various organs or parts of the body. These inner psychic stimuli are always seeking to create situations which will secure for them various specific forms of motor discharge, or activity in respect to an object, thus bringing about an easing or slackening of the stimulus-tension. Complete instinct gratification (motor activity) can only be achieved through contact with the outer world. No action of flight can avail against an instinct.

The word "instinct" has been and is used by psychologists, psycho-analysts, and laymen with very diverse meanings. Just what an instinct is, and what specific instincts exist are questions to which many answers are given. Psychoanalysts as a whole use the term instinct very loosely and confusingly and apparently quite synonymously with the terms "impulses," "wishes," "urges."

In an attempt to clarify this confusing situation, we have made a dif-ferentiation that we believe is consistent with Freud's own statements. The term "instinct" is used by him in referring to the main innate trends. (In Freud's present theory there are only the two, Life and Death.) We would also regard as synonymous the term "urge." For the specific ex-perientially or clinically discovered components of these instinct-trends, we would suggest reserving the terms, impulses, wishes, desires, which, as it will be seen in later sections, psychoanalysts quite obviously mean when they use the terms "part-instinct," "instinct-component."

The undiscriminating use of the term "instinct" in psychoanalytic literature and the difficulties thus created are set forth comprehensively by Mitchell in a chapter on "The Theory of the Instincts." (*Problems of Psychopathology*.) In it he undertakes to discuss in detail Freud's con-ception of instinct, and says he has a right to formulate his own notions which are based upon his analytical experience. Though he admits Freud's neglect of comparative psychology in his endeavors to solve the instinct problem, Mitchell says in Freud's defense, "But the psycho-analytical approach is so uniquely his own prescriptive right, and leads to such a novel and suggestive point of view that psychologists of every school should welcome and treat with respect any conclusions that he may put forward."

The fact that from the beginning Freud recognized the existence of other impulses beside the libidinal led him to the perhaps rather hasty conclusion that these other impulses might be grouped as self-preservative, and for a time he was inclined to speak of the sexual and self-preservative instinct groups as qualitatively different and opposed to each other. Gradually, however, certain considerations led him to take the view that the self-preservative impulses, arising as they did out of self-love or narcism, were also fundamentally libidinal in nature and should be reckoned with as such. The earlier distinction between egoistic and sexual instincts was now converted into a contrast merely between egoistic and object cathexes, both libidinal in nature.

His new conception of what constitutes pleasure and pain, his acceptance of the Nirvana-principle, and the conviction which he reached of the existence of a repetition-compulsion, forced Freud to the conclusion that in addition to the libidinal forces at work in the human organism, there were destructive urges, related both to the self and to outer objects.

The classification of "instincts"—that is, primal unresolvable trends, "striving with each other from the very beginning"—as it now stands is still dualistic, and, Freud admits, quite hypothetical. The instincts are:

His new instinct theory, Freud thinks, perhaps throws some light on ambivalence. He says, "The question also arises whether ordinary ambivalence, which is so often unusually strong in the constitutional disposition to neurosis, should not be regarded as the product of a defusion; ambivalence, however, is such a fundamental phenomenon that it more probably represents a state of incomplete fusion."

Freud's conception of an instinct involves the consideration of its impetus, its aim, its object, and its source. The impetus is the motor element, the force of the impulse to activity inherent in every instinct disposition. The aim of an instinct is to get rid of the condition which has given rise to the stimulus. The object of an instinct is the particular means by which it can achieve its aim. The source of an instinct is for Freud a process, either physical or chemical, which is the stimulus. He says an instinct is "a mental representative of an organic force."

Mitchell points out Freud's disagreement with the biological classification of the instincts, made by many psychologists, into self-preservative, race-preservative, and herd instincts. "Freud maintains that the herd instinct is a derivative of the group of tendencies which he includes under the sexual instinct, being merely a development of the relationships which arise within the family."

(*a*) *Eros or Life Instinct.* From the physiological standpoint the life instinct represents the fundamental tendency to maintain and increase organic life; from the psychological standpoint it may be regarded as composed of (1) the uninhibited sexual or organ-gratification impulses; (2) the sublimated (aim-inhibited) impulses, derived from the original organ-satisfaction impulses; and (3) the self-preservative impulses—that is, the impulses to protect and preserve not merely the body and physical life but primarily the personality and self-ideal.

(*b*) *Death or Destruction Instinct.* From the physiological standpoint, this represents the tendency to lead organic matter back to the inorganic state, "to reestablish a state of things which was disturbed by the emergence of life." From the psychological standpoint the death instinct may be regarded as composed of (1) regressive impulses—tendencies toward the reinstatement of an earlier level of personality development; (2) self-immolating, self-injuring, self-destroying impulses; (3) aggressive impulses toward objects—through the turning outward of the instinct.

At the time of the first publication of Freud's speculations in regard to a possible two-fold classification of the instincts, it was clear that they had a purely theoretical value both for himself and most of his adherents. Rickman spoke of Freud's "tepid feeling of indulgence" towards these concepts, and seemed to feel that they had little practical value for psychoanalysis. Schilder felt compelled to disagreement as to the existence of a death instinct—he said it was "questionable." Jones said quite definitely that Freud's recent instinct conceptions "do not at present form an essential part of psychoanalytic theory."

However, from the first, Alexander found the concept of the death instinct of great practical value as throwing new light on repression, Super-ego, neurosis. References to this instinct seem to be more frequent nowadays in analytic writings, and apparently there is a more general acceptance of it for practical interpretative purposes.

With regard to the death instinct, it is important to note, as Freud himself points out, that for the Ucs the concept of death in its literal sense does not and cannot exist. It is, rather, complete passivity toward which the organism instinctively strives.

Ferenczi writes, "On account of the dazzling effect of the impressive unfolding of growth at the beginning of life, the view has tended to be that in individuals only just brought into the world the life-instincts were greatly preponderant. In general, there has been a disposition to represent the life and death-instincts as a simple complementary series in which the life maximum was placed at the beginning of life, but the zero point at the most advanced age. This does not, however, appear to be quite accurate." Ferenczi argues that the destructive instincts are just as active as the life instincts immediately upon birth, and that "the child has to be induced by means of an immense expenditure of love, tenderness, and care to forgive his parents for having brought him into the world without any intention on his part." He points out that a "slipping back into non-being" would come more easily to the child than the adult. Where the early aversion to life is extreme, it may point to "a defective capacity for adaptation."

Besides postulating the two instincts Freud has speculated upon the relationship between the life and death instincts. He believes there can be *Fusion and Defusion of Instincts*. He points out that life itself is a conflict and compromise between these two instinctual trends. Analogous to the processes of anabolism and katabolism, both instincts may be regarded as "active in every particle of living substance, although in unequal proportions." Then Freud goes on to say, that indispensable to his conception is the theory that these two classes of instincts are fused, blended, and mingled with each other, and that they also can be defused.

Though the impulses arising from these two instinct-patterns are opposed to each other, fusion, perhaps because of the economics of the pleasure-principle, occurs regularly and very extensively. The specific death or destructive impulses can be diverted away from the self and directed towards the outer world. But as it is difficult for these impulses to get entire satisfaction, they manage to discharge themselves by attaching themselves to the Eros instinct, so getting a good deal (though not all) of their satisfaction in this way. Defusion subsequently may be also a possibility, in which case there is direct emergence of the death instinct.

Since his two instincts are qualitatively different, to round out his theory and to make it work, Freud assumes a neutral, displaceable energy which is able to join forces with either the life or death instinct and "augment its total cathexis." Through this displaceable energy there may be gratification of one of such antitheses as the impulses of love and hate at the expense of the other.

Ferenczi thinks that Freud's conception of the death instinct has never up to this time been taken into consideration by biologists and psychologists, and that it is valuable as throwing light in particular on masochism. "Only through this conception are we able to understand masochism, pleasure in pain, and the destruction of the self; the purely sexual masochism, as well as those excesses against the self, which afflict one in the form of exaggerated conscience and need for punishment." Freud has called this "moral masochism."

Alexander, who defends the concept of the death instinct, points out that Freud "assigns primary significance to the impulse toward self-destruction, the death instinct, and derives outwardly directed destruction from this primary death instinct," but that some of his followers (notably Jones and Reich) believe "that self-destructive human behavior can be derived from the turning inward of the destructive instinct originally directed outwardly; i.e., masochism from sadism, and not vice versa." This view would, of course, dispense with the death instinct. The question of the existence of an endogenous death (self-destructive) instinct, Alexander thinks, can never be settled empirically. He points out that much of the self-injuring behavior of every-day life may have as its root merely the working of the reality-principle, that is, the unconscious seeking of situations of lesser pain in order to avoid future greater pain. Narcistic satisfaction may also explain the irrational seeking out of what may appear exaggeratedly painful situations. In addition, the fact that the Ego is constantly making identifications with the outer world means the internalizing of the "hostile tendencies of reality." Nevertheless, Alexander believes that an exaggerated tendency to self-injury (suicidal trends, moral masochisms, melancholia) can frequently have as its basis only a primary self-destructive instinct. "If it appears that in many cases men turn against themselves in greater degree than the pressure of reality and their love for the outer world demand, this will unequivocally testify to an endogenous self-destructive factor." Alexander speaks of the death instinct as "the disintegrative nisus of the body, active since the beginning of life." We quote a brilliant passage: "The surface tension which arrests the growth of the drop of liquid and disrupts it, the decomposition of the biological molecule into its elements during the katabolic phase of metabolism, the self-destruction of the psychic apparatus, the breaking up of states and cultures; all these

Freud admits that there is relatively little clinical evidence so far for the death instinct. Eros is more accessible to study, the death instinct he speaks of as being "elusive." It is seldom found pure; there are usually erotic components with it; for the most part it can only express itself indirectly through Eros. Again he speaks of the death instinct as being "mute" and says, "The clamor of life proceeds for the most part from Eros and from the struggle against Eros."

The death instinct can be neutralized and rendered harmless by being fused with erotic components, by being enlisted in the service of Eros. In part this instinct is directed toward the external world, mainly in the form of aggression, and in part it continues to operate within the individual organism.

are expressions of the same regressive dynamic principle, which counteracts growth and life just as the momentum of inertia opposes the formation of higher dynamic units, and which we should all so much like to forget or deny in its biological manifestation as the death-instinct."

Alexander shows how four combinations can result from the two instinct qualities (Eros and Death) and the two instinct directions (inward and outward). These are as follows:

1. "*The destruction instinct directed outward,* which we recognize in various instinct-fusions. It forms an element of the genital impulse, in which it becomes neutralized by an erotic admixture of equal rank, and is only to be seen after thorough-going analysis. When present in a relatively much stronger degree, it helps form the perversion of sadism. In its sublimated form, it contributes an important element to every *active* type of behavior (impulse to research, social activities, athletics etc.)."

2. "*Sadism directed inward,* which plays so large a part in all instinct-inhibitions, in the categorical imperative of the Super-ego—always, to be sure, with some erotic admixture. Pathologically we find it in moral masochism as well as in the masochistic perversion."

3. "*The Eros instinct directed outward.* Its most important manifestation is the object-libido or the genital impulse. It is always mixed with destructive elements."

4. "*The Eros instinct directed inward,* we know best as narcissism. Its principal task is the neutralization of the destruction-instinct remaining in the organism. The construction of an integrated system which we call the Ego is its achievement."

Alexander thinks neurosis can be viewed as the result of the excessive turning inward of the death instinct. The breaking through of the restrained impulses can be viewed as an attempt at healing in opposition to the destructive working of the death instinct when the latter no longer serves the purpose of development but instead endangers the existence of the whole system.

Primary masochism Alexander calls "an erotized remnant of the destructive instinct."

SECTION TWO

DEVELOPMENTAL STAGES

DEVELOPMENTAL STAGES

INTRODUCTORY

Psychoanalysts maintain that as a result of their observations they can establish definitely three periods in psychosexual development, namely, (I) Infancy period—from birth to about five years of age; (II) Latency period—from about five to twelve years; (III) Adolescent or Pubertal period—from about twelve to eighteen years.

The *Infancy Period* has received great stress by psychoanalysts because of Freud's discovery of "infantile sexuality." Jones says, "It is plain that we shall have radically to revise our conception of the infantile mind and especially in regard to sexuality." And again, "The sexual life of early childhood is far richer and more complex than is generally supposed. . . . It would be difficult to overestimate the importance that the mental life of early childhood possesses for the determination of the future trends of the individual."

By infantile sexuality Freud means that every child is born with an organically determined sexual excitability which during his very early years demands in varying degrees, according to the individual constitution, various specific forms of motor discharge in connection with the self or objects (persons and things). Infantile sexuality is egocentric (narcistic, and auto-erotic), primitive and asocial in its manifestations, and is most accessible to observation in the third or fourth year. The child very early senses, both consciously and unconsciously, the opposition existing between his crude desires and environmental and cultural standards. Anxieties and inner conflicts arise, and the Ego, being still relatively weak in its ability to modify urges by sublimation, may mainly attempt

Jones writes concerning infantile sexuality, "it is the most novel and important of the psychoanalytical contributions . . . it is this knowledge that furnishes the key to the understanding of adult problems. Every adult problem in the realm of sexuality, friction and difficulties in marriage, inadequacies in the conjugal relationships, the inner meaning of such social problems as the causes of prostitution or the emotions about birth-control, all jealousy, rivalry, and conflicts between the sexes, the origin of the various perverse practices and attitudes, and endless similar problems, all are capable of full explanation only in the light of our newly gained knowledge concerning the early stages in the development of this complicated instinct."

Freud writes, "The sexual instincts at first behave auto-erotically; they find their satisfaction in the child's own body and therefore do not come into the situation of frustration which enforces the installation of the reality-principle." Later they begin to find an object, but a long interruption in the latency period postpones sexual development until puberty. "These two factors—auto-erotism and latency period, bring about the result that the mental development of the sexual instincts is delayed and remains far longer under the supremacy of the pleasure-principle, from which in many people it is never able to withdraw itself at all." He goes on to point out that as a consequence of these conditions, a very close connection arises between the sexual impulses and phantasy, both in healthy and neurotic people. "The perpetuated activity of auto-erotism makes possible a long retention of the easier momentary and phantastic satisfaction in regard to the sexual object, in place of real satisfaction in regard to it, the latter requiring effort and delay."

The term "polymorphus-perverse" is used by Freud as descriptive of the child's sexual disposition. The use of this term is justified, he thinks, because of the similarity observed between adult sexual aberrations or perversions and the infantile modes of sexual gratification. Under the influence of physical or mental sexual experiences or even phantasies, the child is capable of premature arousal of some one or other of these sexual impulses and may be misled into all sorts of sexual transgressions—thus proving that he carries the potentialities for these in his constitution. The relatively slight resistance which the child offers to such "perverse" sexual activities is due to the fact that "the psychic dams defense against them by shutting the unacceptable and unpermissible wishes from consciousness and motor expression. This process, known as repression, is of the utmost importance for future personality development.

The *Latency Period* is characterized by a dropping out—though seldom complete—of the crude infantile sexual interests, and the emerging, more or less spontaneously, of new interests, activities, and attitudes, the energy for which however is believed to be still derived from the influx of sexual excitation, which Freud says, "by no means ceases at this period." As a result of the awakening within him of these new interests or transformations of libidinal energy (sublimations and reaction formations) there comes about normally a reconciliation of the child's interests with those of his environment, and social feeling develops.

As an addition to Freud's more theoretical considerations, H. Deutsch states that her experience inclines her to think that the so-called Latency Period can only be regarded as very relative in its latency.

At the *Pubertal Period* there is a recrudescence of infantile sexual impulses. This influx of the old, together with the new, flood of sex life forms what Freud terms "the double thrust of sexual development." The child is at once plunged into a struggle between the standards built up by the Ego during the Latency Period and the somatically re-inforced infantile sexual desires. The final outcome should be fresh renunciations and deflections of libidinal energy into new channels, together with a synthesis or a converging of somatic and sublimated sexual currents into one stream. However, too intensive repression is often resorted to, especially if it strongly characterized the Infancy Period.

It must be remembered that psychoanalysts do not believe that any one developmental stage is ever completely abandoned or left behind. Traces of every stage either in its primitive or in some derivative form are to be found making up the adult personality. It is believed that even the normal adult Ucs always contains some remnants of infantile libidinal cathexes. These hangings on, in

against sexual excesses such as shame, loathing, and morality—which depend on the age of the child—are not yet erected or are only in the process of formation." In this connection, Freud states clearly that "no seduction is necessary to awaken the sexual life of the child," and that such an awakening "may come on spontaneously from inner sources."

Freud says that it can be discovered "that the sexual excitation of the child flows from diverse sources." In addition to the excitations inherently associated with the erotogenic zones, Freud contends that "sexual excitation originates with the organism, as it were, as a by-product in a great number of processes as soon as they attain a certain intensity." Specifically the sources of sexual excitability, according to Freud, lie in: (a) "A gratification which is experienced in conjunction with other organic processes." (b) Appropriate peripheral stimulation of erotogenic zones. (c) Awakening in connection with other impulses (e. g. looking, showing, cruelty). (d) Rhythmic mechanical shaking of the body. Freud thinks this may explain the fondness of children for swinging, rocking, riding in railway trains, etc. (e) Muscular activities. Freud is not sure whether the pleasure the child derives from muscular activity is in reality sexual excitement or whether the former is the cause of sexual excitability. He calls attention to the fact that many people claim to have experienced their first genital excitement when fighting or wrestling, and at least he is sure it can be said that "the infantile connection between fighting and sexual excitement acts in many persons as a future determinant for the preferred course of their sexual impulse." (f) Intensive affective processes—e. g. a fear of a coming school examination may be accompanied by a sensation which impels touching of the genitals, or by an emission. Freud suggests that "The sexually-exciting influence of some painful affects, such as fear, shuddering, and horror, is felt by a great many people throughout life and readily explains why so many seek opportunities to experience such sensations, provided that certain accessory circumstances (as in fiction reading, the theater) suppress the earnestness of the painful feeling. (g) "Mental application or the concentration of attention on an intellectual accomplishment will result, especially often in youthful persons, but in older persons as well, in a simultaneous sexual excitement."

various degrees, to infantile wishes are called fixations, and they underlie and explain many personality trends; if large amounts of libido are involved in the fixations, neurotic manifestations are likely to develop.

In connection with each of the above stages or periods of development three aspects or phases must be considered, namely (a) Libidinal organization or localization of erotogenic zones; (b) Libidinal aims or modes of pleasure-finding; (c) Libidinal cathexis of objects or love-object finding. For the sake of clarity these various phases of development should be kept in mind, but it should also be emphasized that they are closely interrelated, and their activities are going on concurrently and reciprocally.

The Latency period, Alexander says, represents a restriction of sex instinct, more or less independent of upbringing, due to insufficiency of the sex organs. He is inclined to stress this stage as being particularly important from the traumatic standpoint. It offers, he says, "a point of attack for harmful external influences, particularly for bad upbringing, which may cause an undue intimidation of the sexual strivings." He thinks that the impressions received during the latency period "play quantitatively the greatest role in the causation of the neuroses."

Jones calls attention to the "highly interesting" relationship between the Infancy and Adolescent periods of development—"naturally they are not identical; the physical and mental differences between the child and the adult make this impossible. Nor is the development of the individual in general a simple repetition of the evolution of the race. But in both cases there is a considerable parallelism and the second development is very extensively determined by the nature of the first. The sexual development after puberty, for instance, assumes a multitude of forms, no two individuals being exactly alike in this respect." The main lines of adolescent development, often with astonishing conformity of details, follow those of the early childhood period. "This is the reason why it is impossible either to understand or to remedy any errors" at the puberty period "(together with their complicated consequences in neurotic disorders) without taking into due account the features" of the early period that predetermined the development at adolescence. "All memory of that first phase is usually obliterated during the great wave of repression that accompanies this period of childhood; a part of it was, indeed, not conscious even at the time and can be recovered only by the psycho-analytic opening up of the unconscious."

According to psychoanalysts the various manifestations of "infantile sexuality" are to be explained largely on the theory that during the *Infancy Period* the libido becomes organically localized or centralized; that is, skin or various mucous membrane portions of the body become successively sensitized to certain specific pleasure-evoking stimuli.

First there is diffuse body distribution of the libido. Then it becomes localized in rapid succession in three different somatic areas (erotogenic zones), oral, anal, and genital, each of which lends a characteristic coloring to the activities associated with that particular stage. A further division of erotogenic zone development into six sub-stages was made by Abraham, and psychoanalysts in general seem to attach considerable importance to this contribution. Abraham points out that each sub-stage has an organic basis of its own, which is never entirely surmounted or completely obliterated.

The stages and sub-stages in erotogenic zone development are as follows: (a) Oral-erotic stage—the stage in which libidinal satisfactions are obtained primarily through the mouth zone; the two sub-stages are first, the early oral phase (localization in the lips) and, second, the later oral phase (localization in gums and teeth). (b) Anal-erotic stage—the stage in which sphincter activities are discovered to bring the chief erotic pleasure; the sub-stages are, first, when expulsion is pleasurable, and, second, when retention is pleasurable. Urethral erotism is included in this stage. (c) Genital stage; the two sub-stages are, first, the phallic or early genital, and second, the stage of late genital, or complete genital primacy. This latter stage is not reached until puberty, but the phallic sub-stage is definitely established at the end of the Infancy Period. In the phallic stage the genitals become an erotogenic zone with pleasure possibilities comparable to those of the oral and anal zones. The penis (and clitoris) absorbs to a large extent the erotogenicity of the other zones and Freud speaks of "phallic primacy." The sexual organ

Freud calls attention to the fact that though the erotogenic zones proper are "predestined," other body areas may also carry an erotogenic adaptability and "may become endowed with the excitation of the genitals and raised to an erogenous zone."

Rickman says that psychoanalysts assume a persistently recurring excitability in certain body areas (erotogenic zones) as inherent in erotic instinctual life on the assumption that it follows the general laws of physiological rhythm. As a result of the libidinal charging or cathecting of these body areas the organism orients itself to the outer world to be stimulated. He suggests that the shifting of erotogenicity from one zone to another may be associated with the libidinal deprivations at each stage—that is, on the basis of the pleasure-principle.

Abraham suggests that the biting phase may be brought about in part at least by the fact that the nipple is beginning to be sensed as no longer a part of the self; it is assuming an external position and is felt to be in danger of being lost. Its importance as a source of pleasure makes it desirable that it be drawn back or retained in the self-system.

The passing from the phallic to the complete genital level is conceived of by Abraham as being manifested by the recognition of the genital organs of the heterosexual love-object as only a part of the love-object, that is, there is a capacity for libidinal cathexis of the body of the love-object as a whole.

Abraham also believes that the real or complete genital stage should normally involve a retention of the best social elements of the earlier levels, together with an elimination of characteristics unfavorable to social behavior.

Alexander, from the point of view of the Life and Death instincts, believes that there is normally a gradual disappearance, through "erotization," of destructive and aggressive impulses (death instinct) during the successive pre-genital stages, and that when the genital level is reached, the erotic elements should be present in a relatively high proportion. Alexander also states that the genital level often brings liberation from the sense of guilt, with unambivalent relations to love-objects, especially extrafamilial persons.

becomes as Rickman says, "The seat of the highest physical pleasure" and masturbatory impulses awaken.

During the *Latency Period* there are no new somatic localizations of the libido, but the stimulability of the pregenital and phallic erotogenic zones persists to some extent, especially the latter. Freud says that from about the eighth year to puberty there is developing an increasing capacity for psychic tension as well as pleasurable stimulability, preparing for the behavior of maturity.

Usually it is only with advancement in the *Adolescent* or *Pubertal Period* that the stimulability and peculiar pleasure qualities of the genital zone become all-important. At the same time the stimulability of the pregenital zones is re-awakened, but they now play a different rôle. At least some of them are "utilized to furnish a certain amount of pleasure through their own proper excitation," which, instead of becoming an end itself as during the Infancy Period, now sets in motion the genital apparatus, thus bringing about finally the production of a more intense gratification. Freud speaks of the function of the infantile erotogenic zones as being now to furnish "fore-pleasure" which should normally serve the purpose of stimulating the necessary motor energy for bringing to a conclusion the sexual act, or "end-pleasure."

Rickman maintains that complete intellectual objectivity is not possible unless the genital stage has been reached—that is, if the pleasure requirements of the Id do not find an outlet on the genital level. Furthermore, those who have not attained maturity in object-relationship, with corresponding genital organization, are liable to traumatism from lesser shocks than better developed individuals.

Abraham says that a complete capacity for love—which involves a psychosexual adaptation to the object—is achieved only when the libido has reached the genital stage. Genital erotism is always accompanied by friendly attitudes toward the love-object. Rickman says that if the genital stage is completely reached sadism is impossible.

As a possible part of infantile sexuality which up to the present has perhaps not been sufficiently emphasized, libido attached to skin and movements of the body may be considered; Sadger long ago referred to "muscle erotism," perhaps more correctly to be spoken of as muscle and joint pleasures, and of "skin erotism." Abraham supports his observations and cites cases of erotic pleasure in movement. He says also that in various cases of street and locomotor anxiety in neurotics he has been able to trace this back to a fixation on muscle erotism.

The eye corresponds to an erotogenic zone in voyeurism and exhibitionism, the skin takes on the same quality in sadism and masochism.

The "sexual aim" is defined by Freud not as purpose, but as "the action towards which the sexual impulse strives." Psychoanalysts when they use this term are always stressing the fact that the early sexual impulses are predominantly toward physical or somatic satisfaction, that is, are bent upon securing an appropriate method of bringing about temporary relief of feelings of sensitivity or irritation in any particular erotogenic zone. The various activities or modes by which sexual satisfaction is achieved are commonly spoken of as the sexual aims.

The sexual instinct is broken up during the *Infancy Period* into what Freud calls "component" or partial impulses, each of which strives independently for satisfaction. The specific ways or modes by which these impulses find their gratification constitute the sexual aims, which, at a later stage in the development, should merge or consolidate into one predominant trend or aim. The various forms of sexual satisfaction (relief of somatic irritability) which come to be desired are believed to be discovered by the child in connection with his experiences of the gratification of other organic needs (nutritional and excretory). These satisfactions are mainly under the control of the erotogenic zones, though some of the impulses manifest themselves independently, and "only later enter into intimate relationship with the sexual life." Infantile sexual aims or modes of pleasure-finding are relatively independent of an object, that is, are largely autoerotic. Specifically, they are: Sucking, biting, touching, rubbing, defecating, urinating, looking (or voyeurism), showing (or exhibitionism), rudimentary forms of fetishism, rhythmical and muscular activities, and the aggressive and passive enjoyment of cruelty (sadism and masochism).

The phallic stage of the Infancy Period is characterized by the spontaneous awakening of sexual curiosity, associated with sexual excitation. The aim, or mode of gratification becomes inquiry and investigation which is commonly met by rebuff on the part of adults. The child (with or without rebuff) compensates for his

Freud says, "The aim of an instinct (impulse) is in every instance satisfaction, which can only be obtained by abolishing the condition of stimulation in the source of the instinct. But although this remains invariably the final goal of every instinct (impulse) there may yet be different ways leading to the same goal, so that an instinct may be found to have various nearer or intermediate aims, capable of combination or interchange. Experience permits us also to speak of instincts which are inhibited in respect of their aim, in cases where an inhibition or deflection has occurred."

(We feel that immense difficulty might be spared the student of psychoanalytic literature if a more logical and consistent use were made of the terms "sexual" and "aim." The difficulties surrounding these terms seem to be (1) Freud has recently extended the term sexual to include sublimated expressions of libidinal energy, yet, at the same time, the word is still retained in its former limited sense to describe the activities of the Infancy period which are quite definitely regarded as being for the sole purpose of achieving sensual and somatic satisfactions. (2) A second complication arises out of the use of the word "aim." The above quotation from Freud illustrates the confusion which may arise regarding this term. Though he speaks of "aim" as synonymous with "way" he certainly seems to imply that it may also be interpreted in the sense of "goal."

We would suggest, in the interests of clarity, the substitution of the word "mode" for "aim," leaving the word "goal" to be employed in its usual significance. Instead of "sexual aims" we could then speak of "sexual modes" of attaining the sexual goal during the Infancy period and of "desexualized (or sublimated) modes" of obtaining the same sexual goal during later stages of development. The word "aim-inhibited" could not then be interpreted, as it frequently is, to mean "goal-inhibited," but rather to indicate a change in mode of pleasure-finding. It would have its meaning limited to sublimated activities.)

lack of knowledge by certain sexual theories and phantasies which bring about relief of excitation. Freud believes these to be of a typical nature, the basis for which is phylogenetic inheritance. These phantasies must inevitably be largely repressed, and they have been discovered to have a far-reaching effect on later development.

Freud is convinced "that no child—none at least who is mentally sound, still less one who is mentally gifted—can avoid being occupied with sexual problems in the years *before* puberty." Freud believes that he has been able to establish the fact of typical sexual theories "that children produce spontaneously in early childhood-years under the influence of the components of the sexual instincts." Though he admits that certain fairly common situations (e. g. birth of another child) may play a part in stimulating the sexual curiosity, nevertheless the theories which the child evolves are inherently only one form of satisfaction of the infantile sexual component impulses. These typical sexual theories, Freud says, though false, yet "contain a bit of the real truth which is explainable on the basis of their innate origin."

Freud points out that the pleasure-giving motor activity which comes to be associated with each erotogenic zone is naturally and inevitably discovered by the child through the fact that it arises in connection with some other universally common body function. The desire is aroused for a repetition of this previously experienced gratification; nutritional activities lead the way to sucking pleasures; feces retention and passage through the anus leads to desires for pleasurable irritation of the anal zone; genital activities are discovered to be sexually pleasure-producing in connection with the voiding of urine and the washing and rubbing of the genitals by adults.

As a possible explanation of the combining of sadistic with oral impulses as determining the manifestations of the oral stage, Abraham points out that biting represents the original form taken by the sadistic impulses. This may be due, he thinks, to the fact that in small children the teeth are the only organs they possess sufficiently hard to be able to injure the objects around them; also, the jaw muscles are the infant's most powerful body muscles.

The anal stage is always characterized by sadistic or cruelty impulses, but just what the connection is between anal erotism and sadism does not yet seem to be clear to psychoanalysts. Freud, in *The Three Contributions on the Theory of Sexuality,* seems inclined to believe that sadism developed independently of sexuality but that there was an early connection between them. Abraham points out the close connection of sadism with the muscular system and Freud speaks of its organic source as being in the musculature. Both Freud and Alexander seem to think that sadism may find its explanation in the death instinct.

The close association which is constantly found by psychoanalysts between anal and sadistic impulses, Abraham thinks, may be partially explained by the fact that the sadistic sexual component displays two pleasurable tendencies—one to destroy the object, the other to control it. These two tendencies combine quite naturally with each of the two anal stages, and we get an expulsive destroying phase, followed by a retaining controlling phase—both known as forms of anal sadistic "love."

Alexander speaks of morality as a form of sadism being derived from inhibited aggression against the environment.

93

These sexual theories are as follows:

(1) The theory that the woman has a penis. "It is precisely in that sexual constitution which we must recognize as a normal one that the penis is already in childhood the governing erotogenic zone, the most important autoerotic sexual object, and the estimate of its value is logically reflected in the impossibility of imagining a person similar to the self without this essential part." This attitude is so strong that Freud says it will almost invariably influence the boy's actual perception, and he invents all sorts of comforting fancies to conceal from himself the girl's lack of penis. If there is a fixation on this theory of a woman with a penis, Freud points out that the whole later object-finding will be influenced—the development is bound to be homosexual. With respect to this theory, Freud calls attention to the fact that for the girl the clitoris actually does through its excitability afford a masculine outlet for her sexual activity, the discarding of which forms a special problem for her during puberty.

The anal stage is characterized by conflicts and ambivalences—there is a conflict between a love for a part of the self (feces) and love for the mother; there is conflict between the pleasure felt with passing excrement and the sensation of pleasure when retaining it.

Jones says of the anal sadistic stage that it is "characterized by a curious combination of features. On the one hand, there is the rough, noisy, obstreperous, and often cruel behavior which parents find so trying; on the other, there are various indications, less obtrusive than the others, of interest, curiosity, secret games, and complicated mental attitudes relating to certain bodily needs." (For more on this point see the section on Behavior, Personality and Conduct Formation.)

Freud writes, "This part of the body (penis) so easily excitable and changeable, and so rich in sensation, occupies the boy's interest to a high degree and never ceases to provide new problems for his epistemological impulse. He wants to see the same thing in other people so as to compare it with his own; he behaves as if he had a dim idea that this member might be and should be larger. The driving force which this male portion of his body will generate later at puberty expresses itself in childhood essentially as an impulsion to inquire into things—as sexual curiosity. Many of those deeds of exhibitionism and aggression which children commit and which in later years would be judged without hesitation to be manifestations of sensual passion prove on analysis to be experiments undertaken in the search for sexual knowledge." (For comparable situation in the case of the girl, see Oedipus and Castration complexes.)

Deutsch believes that in the beginning of the phallic stage the clitoris has for the girl the pleasure-giving capacities which the penis has for the boy. As in the case of the boy sexual curiosity becomes associated with clitoris sensations and the girl thus comes to discover her lack of the penis. This fact she at first denies but finally accepts and regards it as a punishment for her masturbation.

(2) The *cloaca* birth theory. Since children are ignorant of the vagina, even though they, as they commonly do, become aware that babies grow in the body of the mother, it is logical for them to conclude that the baby can only be expelled by way of the anal aperture. Freud points out that at that time the child's interests are strongly coprophilic, and no disgust attaches to this birth theory. There are several logical extensions of this theory—namely, that boys and men can have babies just as well as women; also, that a child may be gotten by eating some particular thing.

(3) The sadistic conception of coitus. Freud thinks it is very common for children accidentally to witness parental intercourse, and says they all arrive at the same conclusion, that the love act is an act of violence. The origin of this theory, however, he is inclined to attribute to the child's own sadism and asserts that impulses toward violence and cruel activity, together with penis excitability, often occur when the child is puzzling over sexual questions. Here again, Freud observes, it is not altogether wrong in that it "divines the essence of the sexual act and the 'antagonism' of the sexes which precedes it."

(4) Theories as to what constitutes "being married." Though they may differ concretely, due to the influence of chance observations, these theories are nevertheless fundamentally the result of the child's own impulses and all have in common the idea "that marriage promises pleasurable gratification, and presupposes a disregard for modesty."

Freud says that there are two stages of infantile masturbatory practices. During the sucking stage the child discovers, through the experiences connected with cleanliness and uncleanliness, the capacity for pleasure in the genitals, with desires for repetition. This is the first step towards the establishment of the future primacy of the genital zone.

A second masturbatory stage occurs later on in the Infancy period and manifests itself while the genital apparatus is still undeveloped through the urinary apparatus. Freud thinks that "most of the so-called bladder disturbances of this period are of a sexual nature."

Sexual experiences in connection with adults or other children are emphasized by Freud as bringing about premature arousal of the genital zone and the learning through others of the pleasures of genital satisfaction.

Masturbatory practices should normally disappear with the latency period but frequently continue uninterruptedly until puberty. At puberty there is normally a fresh wave of masturbation associated with sex phantasies, at first centering about the parents.

Freud thinks that the later sexual enlightenment which children inevitably get from one another, but which contains many false ideas, is "burdened with remains of older infantile sexual theories." At puberty there is a fresh impetus in sexual curiosity, but the phantasies and theories now produced, Freud thinks, are significant for pathogenesis only "in that they reawaken the unconscious vestiges of that first period of sexual interest."

"The way in which the child behaves when he receives (sexual) information also has its significance. In many children sexual repression has gone so far that they will not hear anything, and these may also succeed in remaining ignorant until even later (apparently at least) until the knowledge dating from early childhood comes to light in the psychoanalysis of neurotics." Freud asserts that a knowledge of infantile sexual theories is "indispensable for the understanding of the neuroses, where these childish theories are still in operation and have acquired a determining influence upon the form taken by the symptoms."

Freud believes that the rebuff and repression of childish curiosity may have a permanent crippling effect intellectually. "Being good" may become specifically associated with the repression of his "naughty" sexual phantasies and extend to a retardation of all thinking. The deadlock

During the *Latency Period* no new sexual aims (or modes of pleasure-finding) emerge and the old ones largely drop away, so that this period is often referred to in psychoanalytic literature as "aim-inhibited." New interests and activities begin to manifest themselves. These interests are regarded, however, as still related to sexual excitations. Jones emphasizes the fact that they are in reality only other forms of the same interest, or other modes of gratifying the same instinct. This deflection of the libido into new channels is known as sublimation (see Dynamisms), and Freud believes that it is a process, to some extent at least, organically determined, since the infantile cravings cannot be utilized for procreation, which is the goal of a later stage. Freud also speaks of the building up during this period of "psychic dams" which take the form of "loathing, shame, and moral and aesthetic ideation masses" (Reaction-formations). The child's early upbringing is emphasized by Freud as an important factor in the awakening of these inhibiting forces or dams. At the end of the Infancy Period he is believed to internalize the parental restraints and taboos and set up within himself "the social constructions of morality and authority" (Super-ego formation).

During the *Adolescent Period,* co-incident with the physiological changes in the genital apparatus, there is a re-animation of many of the infantile sexual aims, with, at the same time, the emergence of a new aim or mode of gratification—namely, the union of the genitals in the act of copulation. The autoerotic activities of the Infancy Period which formerly served to alleviate sexual excitability should now normally be directed towards the love-object, and serve only to arouse, both in the individual and his object, genital irritability and psychic tension, which in turn aim at relief through the appropriate stimulus necessary to bring about the discharge of nervous excitation, which has added to it, in the male, the discharge of the sexual substance, a new form of pleasure appearing after puberty. There is thus a unification of the sexual aim, and concurrently the significance of the sexual object also increases.

of infantile searching after the truth in sexual matters may show itself later in confused dreams and associations in analysis, and the complaint of never being able to carry anything through.

Sublimation of the looking impulse can be brought about if the interest is turned from the genitals to the form of the body. This, Freud thinks, normally occurs as an intermediary sexual aim and makes possible the directing of a certain amount of the libido in artistic channels. The looking component of the sexual instinct may, however, remain limited to the genitals and either develop into a perversion or, if repressed, remain "as a tormenting desire which in some neurotic cases furnishes the strongest motive power for the formation of symptoms."

The discovery of the infantile sexual impulses and their final place in normal adult sexual life makes it possible to bring the so-called perversions—deviations and aberrations from the adult sexual aim—into relation with normal sexuality. They are to be explained, Freud thinks, as either (a) a lingering at the stage of intermediary or "fore-pleasure" relations to the sexual object, the stage which should normally be passed through rapidly on the way to the definite sexual aim, or (b) "anatomical transgressions" of the bodily regions destined for the sexual union. This is due, Freud says, to the fact that over-estimation of the sexual object, which is inevitable in all object-love, leads to the inclusion of other parts of the body of the love-object and to the infringement upon other parts of the body than the genitals in the striving for the sexual aim. This over-estimation also explains fetishism—the substituting for a normal sexual object of another object "which is related to it but which is totally unfit for the normal sexual aim"—thus involving a relinquishing of the sexual aim. Examples of fetishes are such parts of the body as the foot, the hair, and often inanimate objects such as the clothing, which have been associated with the love-object.

Freud maintains, "Everyday experience has shown that most of these transgressions, at least the milder ones, are seldom wanting as components in the sexual life of normals who look upon them as upon other intimacies. Wherever the conditions are favorable such a perversion may for a long time be substituted by a normal person for the normal sexual aim or it may be placed near it. In no normal person does the normal sexual aim lack some designatable perverse element. . . ."

Abraham says, "In the normal development of his psychosexual life the individual ends by being capable of loving the object. But the road which he traverses, beginning from the autoerotism of his infancy and ending with a complete object-love, still needs to be studied more exactly. This much may be said to be certain: The child's libido is without an object (autoerotic) to begin with. Later it takes its Ego as its first object; and not till after that does it turn towards external objects. Even then it retains the quality of ambivalence for some time; and it is only at a relatively late period of his childhood that the individual is capable of having a completely friendly attitude toward his object."

Object-love emerges during the *Infancy Period* out of a gradually developing need for the inclusion of an extraneous object in order to achieve the sexual aim. Normally the value of the object for this purpose should continue to increase until object-love proper is achieved. Psychoanalysts believe that this development involves three phases which are described in terms of the direction or channel along which the libidinal energy seeks an outlet. These phases are:

(1) *Autoerotic*—a phase in which the libido is directed along one main channel, namely toward the individual's own body at the time when there is no sensing of "I" or "it." Autoerotism is the utilization of local erotic excitability without any accompanying libidinal relation to the self or outer world, neither of which is as yet distinguished as such. This phase sets in when the oral zone is in the ascendancy and is a result of the nursing frustrations. The child is believed to compensate for the loss of the nipple (until then sensed as a part of his own body) by turning for his libidinal satisfactions to such parts of his body as the thumb, toe, etc. Autoerotism preponderates throughout the Infancy Period, other parts of the body being successively discovered to yield satisfactions. Eventually, however, the libidinal energy entirely shifts from the autoerotic channel.

Narcism has been more fully discussed above under Cathexis.

Psychoanalysts refer often to "secondary narcism," which Freud defines as follows: "Narcism which arises when libidinal cathexes are called in away from external objects must be conceived of as a secondary form, superimposed upon the primary one that is obscured by manifold influences."

There is a subtle distinction between autoerotism and narcism. In the former the erotogenic zones have no autonomous character, no abiding relation to any object; the stimulation of one zone does not mean the stimulation of all. When unification of the sexual impulse occurs, the infant takes his own body as the loved object, something has been added to autoerotism to make narcism, namely, unification of impulses and a love-object. Self-love includes an autoerotic element (Rickman).

According to Abraham, the autoerotic stage is contemporary with the oral sucking stage. He says, "This act (sucking) is one of incorporation, but one which does not put an end to the existence of the object. The child is not yet able to distinguish between its own self and the external object. Ego and object are concepts which are incompatible with that level of development. There is as yet no differentiation made between the sucking child and the breast. Moreover, the child has as yet neither feelings of hatred nor of love. Its mental state is consequently free from all manifestations of ambivalence. . . ." The early part of the biting stage when the child considers nothing but his own pleasure is the stage of primary narcism. "He pays no attention whatever to the interests of his object and destroys that object without the least hesitation." This level, Abraham points out, "is only possible on the basis of unrestricted narcism."

(2) *Narcism*—in this phase there is a branching off of a part of the libidinal energy in the direction of the self or Ego. Autoerotic satisfactions lead the way to a re-establishment of the state of self-sufficiency believed to be associated with nursing pleasures (not then sensed by the child as dependent on the will of another) which the loss of the nipple rudely destroys. The discovery of his own body as a source of erotic pleasure brings about for the child the further possibility of finding within the Ego an independence of the outer world which it cannot yet control (primary narcism). The libido now has an object—the self or Ego. This phase continues throughout the Infancy period, and normally persists always, though in a diminished degree.

Strictly speaking, however, external objects do play a certain subsidiary rôle in the achievement of the sexual aim even during the preponderantly autoerotic and narcistic phases of the Infancy Period. The child makes use (both in actuality and phantasy) of many readily accessible substitutes for the various parts of the body associated with his autoerotic pleasures. Also the partial sexual impulses to show, to look, to know, to dominate, necessitate an object for the achievement of their aim. The choice of an object, however, is a matter of relative indifference as yet.

The activities associated with such objects as are necessary for the sexual aims at this time are regarded as rudimentary expressions of object-love. The specific nature of these manifestations of "love" so-called is largely erotogenically determined. For example, in the late Oral stage when sadism is strong, all libidinally cathected objects are gnawed, devoured, incorporated, destroyed; psycho-analysts speak of this as "oral-sadistic love." In the early Anal stage the predominating impulses are to expel, reject, throw away, lose or destroy this object; this is followed in the late Anal stage by attempts to retain, master, and control the object. Such attitudes toward the object are termed "anal-sadistic love." In the Anal stage, too, the child it believed to have impulses to make gifts to others of "the products of his own body to which are given a narcistic over-estimation." Symbolical and sublimated expressions of this trend

The progress from narcism to heterosexual (extrafamilial) object relationships at puberty includes an intermediate homosexual phase, the period of "chums" and "crushes." MacCurdy suggests that this quite normally follows the stage when narcism predominates, because the love-object, in the sense of being of the same sex, is like oneself, and the process is partly one of self-identification. This homosexual phase, he thinks, is useful in developing qualities (such as cooperation service) essential to later heterosexual object-love.

In discussing the question of whether homosexuality or inversion is to be regarded as congenital, Freud is of the opinion that it is quite possible to account for this deviation on the basis of the normal bi-sexual predisposition and the many disturbances which may arise in the sexual instinct during its development. The Oedipus period solution may be a homosexual one. The boy goes through a "very intense but short-lived fixation" on the mother which ends by his identifying himself with her and taking himself as the sexual object. All his future object-finding assumes this narcistic pattern—he seeks other youths for love-objects whom he loves as his mother loved him. (See Oedipus and Castration Complexes.)

Freud also emphasizes the rôle of environmental influences in early or later life in conditioning homosexual trends—war and prison limitations, situations in which heterosexual relations would be dangerous, etc.

Real heterosexual object-love means that the love-object is realized and loved as another distinct personality, not as the reflection of the lover's self. Narcistic and anaclitic object-choices are, however, much more common.

Jones points out that very frequently the fusion of sensual and tender sentiments which ought normally to take place at puberty is incomplete or perhaps does not appear at all. This may be due to circumstances— "inaccessibility or unattractiveness of the new object, enforced abstinence, etc." On the other hand, however, this lack of fusion may be traceable to "undue attraction of the original Imago (for definition of Imago, see Oedipus Complex), to whom the feelings have got inseparably anchored. In the latter case, the most usual result is masturbation to often carry over to maturity and very frequently a striking characteristic of adult love is the tendency to bestow gifts rather than tenderness upon the object of affection—that is, "anal love."

(3) *Alloerotism*—a phase in which the main volume of the libido is directed toward external love-objects. This phase sets in at the phallic stage and the object not only assumes a greater importance for the sexual aim but at the same time the object-choice becomes very definitely narrowed. The child begins to transfer his sexual aims (up to this time achieved through his own body, or involving other children, animals, and various inanimate objects) to the parents, and his autoerotic (masturbatic) activities in order to yield satisfaction are now accompanied by phantasies of sexual gratifications (of a pregenital nature) connected with the parent of the opposite sex. The child is believed to be giving expression to his unconscious desires in many well-known outward manifestations; he touches and intimately watches the parent, and talks openly of marrying and having children by the parent. Feelings of affection for this parent also now develop, together with rivalry and hostility towards the parent of the opposite sex.

This period is supposed to be all-critical for the child. Happy and care-free though they appear to be, all children, psychoanalysts maintain, become unconsciously aware of the "incestuous" nature of their object-love and are thus in varying degrees the prey of inner conflicts, the outcome of which is the great determining influence on all the later personality development and object-choices. The child's play-activities during this period are regarded as largely symbolical expressions of his sexual urges and conflicts. (See Oedipus and Castration Complexes).

During the *Latency Period* though, the libido normally continues to be directed toward the parental love-object, the "incest barrier" continues to grow stronger and the sexual aims gives place to sublimated expressions of affection—tenderness, devotion, and respect. Proximity to the love-object is, however, still always sought. A progressively alloerotic development during this period involves the dropping out of hostility to the parent of the opposite sex and the accompaniment of libidinal phantasies. In these phantasies the actual forbidden object is replaced by new ones, but this is a change only in phantasy and does not represent any progress in the development of the libido." Jones goes on to point out that the actual relations to the opposite sex will also show a double attitude. In the case of the man he will only be able to fall in love with one type of woman, "one who has traits that unconsciously remind him of the Imago, but he finds it impossible to bring sensual thoughts into relation with her and if he marries her he is impotent." At the same time he may be capable of developing "high sexual capacity and pleasure with an inferior woman," a complete stranger, perhaps a prostitute. Jones says that he would like to commend this fact to the attention of social reformers, "for it shows that prostitution is not altogether a mere *faute de mieux*, replaceable, for instance, simply by making early marriage possible." Jones thinks that incestuous fixations may also explain "the frequency with which men marry women of a lower class than their own and of an inferior stamp to themselves."

Adult object-finding is frequently determined by fetishism; the love-object must possess certain colored hair, wear certain clothing, or perhaps even have certain physical blemishes. This is traceable to early impressions in connection with first object-love relationships and is quite normal. It is to be regarded as pathological if there is also a diminution in the striving for the adult sexual aim, or "when the fetich disengages itself from the person and becomes itself a sexual object."

In *The Ego and the Id* Freud speaks of the cathectic processes of the Id as being characterized by indifference, both as respects the path of discharge and also in regard to the object cathected. "It would seem to be characteristic of the Ego to be more particular both about the choice of an object and about the path of discharge."

The object, Freud says, is the most variable thing about an instinct (an impulse or specific urge) and "is not originally connected with it, but becomes attached to it only in consequence of being peculiarly fitted to provide satisfaction. The object is not necessarily an extraneous one: it may be part of the subject's own body. It may be changed any number of times in the course of the vicissitudes the instinct undergoes during life; a highly important part is played by this capacity for displacement the inclusion of this parent in the sublimated affectional love-expressions. There are also beginnings of reaching out toward others in the immediate environment for friendly relations. These attachments are likely in the beginning to be strongly anaclitic in nature; the child will turn first to those who assist it in its helplessness and gratify its self-preservative needs.

With the onset of the *Adolescent Period,* Jones says, "there is added a powerful current of unmistakable sensuality, which always at first attaches itself in the unconscious to the early incestuous objects of affection." The result is marked conflicts, both conscious and unconscious. Jones says that the struggles of the phallic stage were only a "rehearsal" in preparation for the pubertal struggle, when "the individual has to start again at the beginning and go through the drama in a more serious and sometimes tragic fashion." Normal alloerotic development means the abandonment of the revived infantile sexual aims in connection with the parent and the reaching out of the new sexual aim (appearing with the establishment of genital erotogenic primacy) to an accessible object outside the family. The two trends, sensuality and tenderness, should now combine, "and the loved object becomes endowed with the highest possible degree of value."

Emancipation should take place not only from the libidinal attachment to the parent but also from dependence upon parental authority. A fresh wave of narcism, which is normally associated with the beginning of puberty, aids this emancipation (though at the same time if too prolonged it may stand in the way of alloerotic object-seeking). A short phase of homoerotic object-choice following upon the narcism is also believed to be normal at this stage and to lead the way toward extra-familial heterosexual attachments.

Freud wishes it to be very clearly understood that normally "After the stage of heterosexual object-choice has been reached, the homosexual tendencies are not, as might be supposed, done away with or brought to a stop; they are merely deflected from their sexual aim and applied to fresh uses." Sublimated homosexual trends, Freud thinks, have much to do with the development of the

in the instinct. It may happen that the same object may serve for the satisfaction of several instincts simultaneously. . . . A particularly close attachment of the instinct to its object is distinguished by the term fixation: this frequently occurs in very early stages of the instinct's development and so puts an end to its mobility, through the vigorous resistance it sets up against detachment."

The fact that even in normal people there can be so many substitutions, variations and depreciations of the object, points, Freud says, to the independence of the sexual impulses of an object-stimulus. "Under numerous conditions and among a surprising number of individuals the nature and value of the sexual object steps into the background. There is something else in the sexual impulse which is the essential and constant."

Rickman says that a peculiarity of libidinal impulses is the capacity to change the object without altering the aim, for example anal interests may be displayed in any of the following: feces, mud, sand, marbles, coins, negotiable securities. The aim does not change—it remains to manipulate the store or hoard.

Abraham points out that the libidinal attachment to inanimate objects originates in sexuality and is a form of object-love. "To objects we have grown to like through use, or because of their æsthetic value, we obviously have a personal relationship which is quite analogous to sexual attraction. There are many different degrees of this kind of object-love. Many persons have almost no needs in this respect, while others are completely under the dominion of their passion for certain objects." The collector places an excessive value on the object he collects which is comparable to the lover's over-estimation of his sexual object. "A passion for collection is frequently a direct surrogate for a sexual desire; and in that case a delicate symbolism is often concealed behind the choice of objects collected."

Abraham approaches the development of object-love in a somewhat different and very interesting fashion. He speaks of it as being in its early stages "partial love," this phase extending through the latter part of the oral biting sub-stage, the two anal sub-stages, and the phallic sub-stage, and forming a connecting link between the narcistic and alloerotic phases.

social impulses in the sense that they contribute "an erotic factor to friendship and comradeship, to *esprit de corps* and to the love of mankind in general."

Object-love, though it derives fundamentally from the Id, is really much more the concern of the Ego. Since somatic pleasure alone is its aim the Id is rash and indiscriminate in its object-cathexes. The Ego's narcism, its self-preservative, and eventually its morality demands, all combine to modify the blind reckless object-seeking of the Id, and since the choice of love-object is thus "ego-syntonic" it may be said to be the Ego which "loves."

The Ego not only guides the Id toward its object but persuades it also to restrain and modify its aims in regard to the object in conformity with reality. A certain amount of direct gratification is possible through the substitution of other symbolically associated objects. Phantasied gratifications are also resorted to very early by the Ego and offered to the Id in lieu of the unpermissible motor expressions. (See Dynamisms.)

That the pre-genital behavior towards the love-object, indifferent as it is to the welfare of the object, should be designated as "love," is justified by Abraham on the ground that there is a certain sparing of the object as a whole, the destructive violent trends being directed only to a part. This is what he means by his term "partial love," and he thinks the distinction which he makes between the two phases of the biting stage is very sharply marked and of great importance, since "on that later level the individual shows the first signs of having some care for his object. We may also regard such a care, incomplete as it is, as the first beginnings of object-love in a stricter sense since it implies that the individual has begun to conquer his narcissism." It is at this stage that ambivalence towards the object begins to be felt in its most primitive and unmodified form, but Abraham stresses the point that, though the attitude is preponderantly hostile, the friendly tendency which is manifested in the desire to spare the existence (though attacking the integrity) of the object, must not be overlooked. With regard, too, to the biting, devouring impulses themselves, Abraham points out that the desire is really not so much to destroy as to incorporate and keep as part of one's own property.

Phallic love is the last phase of partial love and the hostility is directed towards the genitals of the love-object. Abraham points out that "the genitals are more intensely cathected by narcissistic love than any other part of the subject's own body. Thus everything else in the object can be loved sooner than the genitals." He adds, "On the level of the 'phallic' organization of the libido . . . the last great step in its development has obviously not yet been made. It is not made until the highest level of the libido—that which should alone be called the genital level—is attained."

Genital love recognizes the existence of another individual as such, and loves him in his entirety, whether in a physical or a mental way and without ambivalence. As Rickman says, the object is "dealt with as a whole and in full relationship to its environment." In other words, the achievement of a complete capacity for love involves a psychosexual adaptation to the object. Abraham says that in this stage of "real object-love" "social feelings of a superior kind" regulate the instinctual life of the individual.

DIAGRAM OF DEVELOPMENTAL STAGES

(The Theoretically Normal Development)

A. Libidinal Localization (erotogenic zones)	B. Aim, or Mode of Pleasure-Finding	C. Libidinal Object-Finding		

INFANCY PERIOD

A. Libidinal Localization	B. Aim, or Mode of Pleasure-Finding	Auto-erotism *	Narcism	Allo-erotism
Pregenital Period 1. Oral Stage	*Infantile Sexuality*			
a. early oral	Sucking, swallowing (incorporating) **	at first objectless		Oral object-choice
b. late oral	Biting, devouring (destroying, annihilating)		Primary Narcism	Oral-sadistic object-choice
2. Anal Stage				
a. early anal	Expelling (rejecting) (destroying) — looking, exhibiting, handling, inflicting pain			Anal and anal-sadistic object-choice
b. late anal	Retaining (controlling) (possessing) — submitting to pain			
Early Genital Period (phallic stage)	Touching, rubbing, exhibiting and looking at genitalia, investigating, comparing, questioning, phantasying (tender affection)			Parent object-choice Oedipus-phantasies

LATENCY PERIOD

A. Libidinal Localization	B. Aim, or Mode of Pleasure-Finding	Auto-erotism	Narcism	Allo-erotism
No new zone	Repression Reaction-formation Sublimation Affectional trends	Further decline of auto-erotism	Diminished Narcism	Development of social feelings

ADOLESCENT OR PUBERTAL PERIOD

A. Libidinal Localization	B. Aim, or Mode of Pleasure-Finding	Auto-erotism	Narcism	Allo-erotism
Late Genital Period Revival of zone sensitivity of infancy period	Reactivation of modes or aims of infancy period	Revival of auto-erotism	Fresh wave of Narcism	Revival of Oedipus object-choice
Later, functioning of vaginal zone	Emergence of adult mode of pleasure-finding			Homosexual object-choice
				Heterosexual object-choice

* For meaning of "autoerotism" in Freudian sense the text should be carefully consulted; it is not synonymous with masturbation.

** The words enclosed in parentheses refer to Ego attitudes and trends arising on the basis of Id impulses.

The Ego

The psychoanalyst's recent stressing of the Ego and its functions has necessarily resulted in an interest in Ego development; several attempts have been made to establish its developmental stages. However, these have not yet been worked out in any detail.

Ego development can be considered from various points of view. From the standpoint of adaptation to reality, three stages have been suggested by Freud. Rickman outlines these as: (a) Incorporation of the pleasant, that is, the Ego favors the urges of the Id; at this stage it ignores the unpleasant, it repels most stimuli. (b) Negation of the unpleasant; the Ego has undergone considerable modification, it has become able to tolerate Id excitations, that is, it acts after consideration instead of letting itself be attracted and repelled by stimuli. Through hallucinations of what has been found pleasant there may perhaps be an ignoring of certain impulses or unpleasant presentations. (c) The acceptance of unpleasant ideas. This means that they are admitted to consciousness, but only in connection or coupled with another presentation of something which compensates for, or more or less abolishes the pain.

Freud says that the Ego is the seat of anxiety, and that the development of anxiety is an Ego process originating in the reality principle. There are certain libidinal crises which the Ego views as dangerous and in connection with which certain typical anxiety states arise.

From the point of view of Ego development, the Ego may then be said to pass through three anxiety stages, namely, (a) fear of loss of love, (b) fear of castration, (c) fear of the Super-ego (the latter being associated with the child's entry into social relations). Each of these types of fear is normal for the libidinal stage in which it arises, but, as in the case of the libido, there may be a fixation of the Ego in any one of these anxiety stages with potentialities of neurotic developments. Also, the Ego development will be influenced by the

Ferenczi suggests three stages in the development of the Ego—from the pleasure to the reality-principle:

(1) Introjection period—the child, before it experiences its first deprivations, feels itself to be unconditionally omnipotent. It has only to wish, and fulfilment follows. In its "primal narcistic self-assurance" it knows nothing of the existence of objects outside itself. The self alone exists and includes within it the whole world of experience. The temporary loss and subsequent refinding of the mother's breast leads first to the idea of the mother as an object.

(2) Projection period—taught by experience, the child realizes that there are limitations to its own personal omnipotence. However, it does not give up the idea of omnipotence in general but transfers it to other persons or things, feeling that whenever it makes known to them in any way its needs, they will be supplied. This attempt to modify the external world soon involves as well a certain adaptation to it, a placating of the higher powers.

(3) Objective Judgment or "Reckoning" period—as a result of insight gained through frustrations, there comes the realization that certain things must be absolutely relinquished and omnipotence surrendered. The tendency to ignore or command the surrounding world is replaced by the tendency to reckon with it as a fact, in other words, to affirm its reality. This objectivity involves an oscillation between outer and inner experiences.

Psychoanalysts call attention to the fact that each libidinal localization presents the Ego with a new task of adaptation. The new stimuli may produce a state of helplessness, and anxiety may develop in the transition period. If the Ego is weak or if the libido is relatively strong in any one zone, the result may be a fixation. (See Fixation and Regression.)

methods of defense against anxiety adopted by the Ego, which will have a reciprocal effect upon the Ego itself.

Super-Ego

The "insufficient elucidation" of the origin of the Super-ego has led to considerable discussion of the stages of its development. Freud places the origin of the Super-ego at the end of the phallic stage, related as it is to the Oedipus and Castration situations. Ferenczi speaks of a "physiological forerunner" to the Super-ego as being related to the renunciations brought about by the "thou shalt nots" of sphincter training and commands to cleanliness. Jones suggests that there is a pre-Super-ego stage of development that has so far been very little investigated. Rickman outlines three stages of Super-ego development, a pre-phallic, a phallic, and a post-phallic. He suggests that the Super-ego begins to operate before the third year, before a full establishment of object-relationships. Alexander places the main period of formation of the Super-ego in the Latency stage.

(Other suggestions concerning the development and function of the Super-ego may be derived from our previous section on the Super-ego, and the following section on the Oedipus and Castration Complexes.)

The age at which the Super-ego begins to be formed, Klein thinks, is very early. It is already at work in the second year; it reaches complete development by the beginning of the latency period.

H. Deutsch believes that in the case of the girl the feelings of guilt attached to masturbatory inclinations in the early part of the phallic stage lead to the castration idea and the setting up of the Super-ego.

The later evolution of the Super-ego is, of course, of great significance. As far as we can gather, one or the other of two possibilities can occur: (a) A temperate, not too exacting Super-ego may be set up in the first place, in which case the individual's later development will be normal. (b) On the other hand, Freud gives the impression that the majority of children pass through a period of childhood neurosis, which would seem to imply that an originally overexacting Super-ego may later become modified—perhaps through successive identifications, or the weak and childish Ego may become stronger and more capable of coping with its Super-ego. Rickman seems to think that ideally the Super-ego, which is primitive and archaic in its origin and nature, should give way to the Ego or a more rational conscience.

According to psychoanalysts there are two possibilities of deviation from the normal pattern of psychosexual development, namely, fixation and regression.

Fixation

Fixation may be defined as a halting of some part of the libido during the course of its development at one or another of its somatic positions or zones. In other words, one (or several) of the infantile "sexual aims" or modes of pleasure-finding has not been relinquished, that is, adequately desexualized or sublimated. If fixation involves a love-object it signifies that the Id is clinging to some element of the "incestuous" parent object-cathexis.

Whether or not a fixation will occur depends on constitutional, developmental, and experiential factors.

(1) The constitutional and developmental factors are:
    (a) Some partial or component sexual impulse may develop in advance of the rest, and through its premature independence and pleasure-giving possibilities may become unduly strong, dominating and hard to relinquish.
    (b) The libido may be constitutionally "adhesive" or lacking in plasticity. Normally, Freud says, a libidinal impulse possesses the peculiar characteristic of being capable of modifying (displacing, sublimating) its mode of achieving satisfaction "without materially losing in intensity." But if the libido has a particularly adhesive quality, substitutive outlets will be less readily accepted by the Id.
    (c) A poorly-developed Ego may fail to make any attempt to modify, or to restrain from unmodified expression, even a relatively weak impulse, and the latter, through undue indulgence, may thus gain in strength and dominance.

Rickman explains fixation by means of a diagram in which the path of development is approximately represented by lines and the arrests by dots of various sizes.

A depicts full development—that is, practically all the libido has attained the genital goal; B shows a considerable arrest at an early stage, but some libido concentration at the genital stage; C shows a more scattered distribution; in D there is almost a complete arrest at an early stage.

Freud once defined fixation as being, "a conjunction of impulses with impressions and with the objects connected with these impressions. This conjunction has to be effected very early, is very hard to resolve, and has the effect of bringing the development of the instincts concerned to a standstill."

Jung has called attention to a peculiar "psychic inertia" which characterizes the neurotic constitution. Freud is of the opinion that this is to be explained on the basis of fixation.

According to Rickman, fixation differs from a dynamism. He distinguishes between them as follows: (1) A fixation is an inhibition in the development of the libido; the dynamisms are concerned with changes in libidinal cathexes occurring at any given moment, that is, not with the fate of the libido as a whole but only with certain parts or quantities; (2) a fixation determines the type of mental disorder; a dynamism explains how the changes in libido can bring about the change in the clinical picture, that is, a complicated hypothesis employed to explain the association of observed events which are otherwise inexplicable.

(d) Even though the Ego may attempt in the beginning to handle an urge largely by sublimations, it may be too weak to maintain these or become undesirous of doing so; thus fixation will be the ultimate issue.

(e) The Ego may also contribute to the establishment of a fixation through a fearfulness of undertaking new adaptations to reality. Each successive stage of libidinal development involves new efforts on the part of the Ego to meet environmental demands, since every new mode of pleasure-finding is subject to certain social restrictions. As Alexander says, "every demand for the abandonment of an already achieved stage and its replacement by a new, untried stage means pain."

(2) The experiential or environmental factors are:

(a) Some experience may tend to awaken and stimulate prematurely a sexual component impulse, thus giving it an opportunity to gain a dominating position.

(b) The disappointments and frustrations inevitable at any stage of development may lead either to an undue centering upon the gratifications of the next stage, or a falling back upon and clinging to a preceding more satisfying stage. In either case, the result will be a fixation.

(c) The environment may either offer opportunities for and tolerate indulgence in unmodified expressions of a strong urge, thus encouraging fixation. On the other hand, fixations may be largely prevented through environmental opportunities for sublimation.

The question naturally arises to what extent fixations are compatible with normal development of the personality. Freud says, "Each stage in the development of psychosexuality affords the possibility of the occurrence of a fixation, and thus for the laying down of a disposition to illness (neurosis) in later life." This statement is challenging and seems to call for a very clear elucidation.

Psychoanalysts contend that definite fixation points can be established for the different psychoses and neuroses, that is, they are the explanation of the "choice of neurosis." Rickman says "paranoia reveals the fixation as regards object-relationship somewhere between the narcistic and the homosexual, dementia praecox at the autoerotic stage of object-relation development." Abraham says it is of "radical importance" to distinguish the fixation point as explaining the symptoms of melancholia and obsessional neurosis. The melancholic has an oral sadistic attitude towards his object (incorporating); the obsessional neurotic has an ambivalent attitude. In hysteria there is a regression to the phallic stage or Oedipus fixation.

Abraham says, "According to the psychoanalytic view, the fixation points that have been formed in the course of the development of the libido will determine to what level the libido of the individual will advance, and to what level it will retreat in the event of a neurotic illness."

Abraham cites a case of oral fixation. In boyhood the patient had been unable to wean himself of a love of milk, and up to fifteen he had a peculiar method of sucking it in. As an adult he continued the habit of drinking milk during the night to quiet violent sexual desires. (Abraham points out that in this he resembled neurotic children who wake up crying in the night and are satisfied if they are given milk to suck, or can obtain a substitutive gratification by putting their thumb or finger in their mouths.) His longing to suck milk represented his deepest and most primitive instinct. In addition this patient showed a marked pleasure in eating as an adult, a tendency to overeat, and there was also a strong flow of saliva during sleep. Free association brought out the connecting of cannibalistic ideas with loving. He recalled desires to bite and swallow "skin, hair, clothes, and all," of a nurse to whom he had been much attached. "Even when his libido found new sources of pleasure, the earlier ones showed no diminution of their importance, and this peculiarity persisted in the further development of his instinctual life. It explains the fact that when he was grown up, his libido never achieved uniformity of direction. He could not attain a normal emotional attitude toward other persons and could not advance to object-choice; and at the same time his different erotogenic zones maintained their original independent significance."

It must be remembered that psychoanalysts assume that even in normal individuals some degree of fixation is always present. Also, a fixation, no matter how slight, is always a potential "weak spot," obviously most often adequately taken care of, but which under circumstances of special pressure may lead to trouble. On the other hand, even a strong fixation does not preclude a certain degree of normality, though always accompanied by various indications of instability. That is, though a strong fixation implies a "neurotic predisposition," neurosis may not always be the outcome.

Psychoanalysts do not regard fixations as always equally active. According to the amount of cathexis, the existence of a fixation implies varying degrees of "continuous straining in the direction of consciousness." There is also always the possibility of an increase in the cathexis through the stirring up of associative connections.

The significance of strong fixations lies in the following:

(a) The greater the amount of libido tied up through fixation, the less freely moving libido will remain at the disposal of the individual to be directed toward outer reality, and the more sensitive he will be to traumata.

(b) The very fact of undue fixation may mean that the libido in general lacks plasticity; in such case the unfixated portion of the libido will meet reality in a rigid fashion.

(c) The fixated portion of the libido exercises a constant attraction upon the portion which is moving on to mature development, and thus handicaps this development.

(d) The need for the keeping up of defenses (repression, reaction-formations, etc.) on the part of the Ego means a constant drain upon its energies. Thus it is less able to undertake the task of guiding and modifying the unfixated portion of the libido.

As illustrations of what he means by internal frustrations, Freud gives the following:—"The young man who has hitherto gratified his libido by phantasies issuing in masturbation and now desires to exchange this state of affairs, so closely related to autoerotism, for actual object-choice; the girl who has given all her affection to her father or brother and now would fain exchange the hitherto unconscious incestuous libido-wishes for the conscious wish towards the man who is wooing her; the wife who would be glad to abandon her polygamous inclinations and phantasies of prostitution so as to be a faithful companion to her husband and a blameless mother to her child—all these fall ill in consequence of most laudable endeavours if the earlier fixations of their libido are powerful enough to oppose themselves to the displacement."

T. W. Mitchell calls attention to an analogy made use of by Freud which illuminates the concept of fixation and regression. "If you think of a migrating people who have left large numbers at the stopping places on their way, you will see that the foremost will naturally fall back upon these positions when they are defeated or when they meet with an enemy too strong for them. And, again, the more of their number they leave behind in their progress, the sooner will they be in danger of defeat."

Regression may be defined as the retreating of the freely moving libido to a lower level of development—an earlier somatic position. Freud says, "Fixation and regression are not independent of each other. The stronger the fixations in the process of development prove to be," the more readily will external difficulties be evaded by regression to those fixations, and the less capability will there be to withstand frustrations on the part of reality.

In the case of the strongly fixated individual, whether or not regression occurs depends largely upon the occurrence of external frustrations, that is, the denial of gratifications by reality to the unfixated libido. Internal frustration is even more important according to Freud. By this he means that, due to the attraction of a strong fixation the unfixated libido cannot reach forth freely to the achievement of mature satisfactions. The individual is, as it were, held back from the gratification of certain newly emerging desires by the opposing strength of older firmly entrenched modes of satisfaction.

The healthy, that is relatively unfixated, individual will meet frustration either by holding the libidinal urge in suspension until a suitable substitutive gratification presents itself, or by directing all his energies toward wresting from the outer world the actual satisfaction desired, or, as Freud says, he will "elude the frustration" by means of sublimation.

The strongly fixated individual will react in a different way to frustration, that is by regression. The regressive process is believed to be as follows: The frustrated libido is withdrawn from objects in the real world and "takes refuge in the life of phantasy where it creates new wish-formations and reanimates the vestiges of earlier forgotten ones." This is known as Introversion, which means, Freud says, that the individual "has by no means broken off his erotic relation to persons and things. He still retains them in phantasy." That is, he has not only substituted imaginary for actual objects, but he has also "ceased to direct his motor activities to the

Psychoanalysts admit that there is often considerable difficulty in deciding whether they are dealing with a fixation or a regression.

Regression is sometimes referred to by psychoanalysts as a dynamism in the sense that it affords a possibility of flight from or defense against difficulties associated with the higher levels of development. Alexander points out, however, that regression does not altogether relieve anxiety since "the stage which is being abandoned leaves its mark on the recaptured earlier instinctive tendency." Thus, he says castration anxiety accompanies regression to pre-genital levels and becomes associated with pre-genital gratifications, though the anxiety is relatively less.

Freud says in one connection that the term regression is purely descriptive, referring to the direction which the libido takes when it returns to another level. In another place, however, he refers to regression as a "process."

E. Glover thinks that it is important for the analyst to keep in mind the different stages of development in reconstructing the patient's history, with a view to ascertaining how one stage modified another, how much acceleration, retardation, or regression has occurred. He does not think, however, that anything is gained by making interpretations to the patient in terms of fixation and regression.

Jones says, "At puberty a regression takes place in the direction of infancy . . . and the person lives over again, though on another plane, the development he passed through in the first five years of life." Jones says that he attaches considerable importance to this correlation between adolescence and infancy, "as affording the key to many of the problems of adolescence."

Regression often occurs when there is physical illness, and also at the various periods of psycho-physiological stress. Abraham speaks of the period of involution as bringing with it a decrease of genital erotism and as that in which states of depression break out most frequently. There is a rejection from consciousness of "the perception of this internal alteration. At the same time the libido undergoes a regressive change of a particularly far-reaching nature." Jones refers to the regression which frequently occurs in old age to anal character traits.

attainment of his aims in connection with real objects." This brings about a "damming up" of the libido and paves the way for regression. The increased cathexis of the conscious phantasies reactivates associatively the unconscious phantasies connected with the infantile fixations, that is, the libido now begins to "flow backward" and "to seek out infantile paths." The reanimated infantile wishes strive again for motor discharge, and there occurs what is spoken of as "the return of the repressed."

In the so-called normal individual this "return of the repressed" will manifest itself sporadically in such compromise forms as dreams, symptomatic acts, and the eccentric behavior of what is spoken of as the "neurotic character."

If the pressure is strong, the Ego tolerant, and the environment favorable, adult sex perversions will develop.

If the Ego is weak and still ruled by a primitive intolerant Superego, the old infantile conflict will be renewed; old defenses will be strengthened and new defenses built up. The result will be compromise-formations in the form of neurotic symptoms. The specific form taken by the symptoms depends largely upon the erotogenic level to which the unfixated libido has regressed.

Of the first step toward regression, namely, introversion, Freud writes, "This means that the quantity of libido which is capable of becoming conscious and is directed towards reality, has become diminished, while the part which is unconscious and turned away from reality (and, although it may still nourish phantasies in the person concerned, belongs to the unconscious) is by so much increased. The libido (entirely or in part) has found its way back into regression and has reanimated the infantile imagos."

Jones says that the normal person having withdrawn his love from one individual transfers it to another. The neurotic "introverts it on to unconscious phantasies"; the paraphrenic applies the libido again to the Ego, that is, he replaces object-love by a narcistic identification of himself with the object, and this is really a regression to the original narcistic way in which he fell in love.

According to H. Deutsch regression plays a part in the normal development of the girl. During the phallic stage she passes through two phases—first, a phase of clitoris pleasure and masturbatory activities which is brought to an end by her discovery that she lacks a penis. This lack she regards as a punishment for masturbation. Second, there is a giving up of clitoris activity and a regression to anal tendencies together with identification with the mother and cloacal phantasies ("the anal child"). The recognition of the penis-lack in the first phase involves a distinct narcistic wound. The clitoris renunciation and the associated narcistic wound mobilizes what Deutsch considers a normal regressive phenomenon.

Rank points out the possibilities of regression which may occur as related to the successive biological experiences of birth, weaning, learning to walk, and leaving the parental home. He claims always to obtain regressive phantasies pointing to the birth trauma in his analyses.

Jones calls attention to the fact that in dreams there is regression in another sense of the word; that is, in the dream the "underlying thoughts" revert "from their ideational form to the raw material of all thought—to sense imagery."

SECTION THREE

OEDIPUS AND CASTRATION COMPLEXES

OEDIPUS AND CASTRATION COMPLEXES

THE OEDIPUS COMPLEX

Using the terms Oedipus Complex, Parental Complex, and Family Romance, Freud and other psychoanalysts greatly emphasize an unconscious development of desire and a conflict concerning it which they insist arises in the unconscious phantasy life of a child during an early stage (the phallic stage) of development. The essence of the Oedipus Complex is libidinal striving taking the form of unconscious desire for sexual satisfaction with the parent of the opposite sex.

In this connection it must be remembered that whole dramas and conflicts can be developed and lived out in unconscious phantasies and can be handled by the unconscious Ego. To the Super-ego a phantasy, unconscious or conscious, has all the significance of an act and is thus capable of arousing a sense of guilt and a fear of punishment in the unconscious Ego. The immediate significance of this is that the Oedipus Complex, and the Castration Complex which is directly connected with it, may exist entirely in the Ucs and be coped with completely without ever entering consciousness. In other words, it is not the actual relationship to the parents which is dynamic, but rather a phenomenon arising spontaneously in the unconscious instinctual phantasy life.

The term, Oedipus complex, has been adopted from the Greek myth, concerning the life and fate of Oedipus which was the subject of trage-dies by Sophocles and other Greek dramatists. But really, the original story does not at all fit the Oedipus situation as developed in the theory of the psychoanalysts. Oedipus, deserted in infancy by his parents and brought up by foster parents, meets his own father on the road and kills him without any knowledge that he was his own father and long before a later love relationship developed between Oedipus and his own mother. Also this love grew as between strangers, neither mother nor son real-izing their relationship. But the whole chain of events was predicted and follows the line of "fate," so often dwelled on in Greek drama.

Earlier psychoanalysts used the term Electra complex when referring to the girl-father love-relationship, again taking over a term from a Greek myth. But this usage seems to have been discontinued and now the term Oedipus complex is employed for the love-relationships of chil-dren of both sexes with actual parents, parent-imagos, or other mem-bers of the family as they may become for the child a parent-surrogate.

The force of the Oedipus complex rests not only in its natural uni-versal occurrence, but also in the usual taboo against incest among primitive as well as civilized people. Alexander says that the prohibition against incest remains active in the unconscious of the adult, and that this is the crux of the psychoanalytic theory, as is also the fact that the entire incest conflict later completely disappears from consciousness. He says, "The submergence of conscious moral inhibitions into the uncon-scious is a readily ascertainable fact."

Jones says of the Oedipus complex that it is "the most characteristic and important finding in all psychoanalysis, and against it is directed the whole strength of the individual's resistance as well as the external criticism of psychoanalysts. It is hardly an exaggeration to say that what-ever manifold form this resistance may take, and whatever aspect of psychoanalysis is being criticized, it is the Oedipus that is finally re-sponsible."

Thus the real basis of the parent complex is found not only in the universal parent-child situation and the experiences which are bound up with it as a result of infantile libidinal strivings, but it also has deeper roots in racial experiences which are carried over in the life of the young individual as inherited ideas. The theory of phylogenesis is thoroughly involved in the psychoanalytic notion of the development of the Oedipus Complex. Freud states that the unconscious psychic life of the child appears to recapitulate the evolution of the species. "In the soul-life of present-day children the same archaic moments still prevail which generally prevailed at the time of primitive civilization."

From their theory and from their analytic findings it comes about that immense stress has been laid by psychoanalysts on the Oedipus situation. They believe that evidences of the complex are to be discovered in every case analyzed, and contend that it is practically a universal experience. Indeed, it is believed to be a necessary stage in normal development; Freud calls it "a general human characteristic decreed by fate." He insists on the danger of underestimating rather than overestimating its importance in all personality development. Jones says, "All other conclusions of psycho-analytical theory are grouped around this complex, and by the truth of this finding psycho-analysis stands or falls."

The Oedipus Complex finds part of its conscious expression in the child's desire for various forms of physical intimacy with the parent, bodily contacts, caresses, sleeping with the parent, etc. On the unconscious side the libido is represented by a direct incest motive; the unconscious strivings are primitive in this respect, as in all others, and are for direct sexual satisfaction.

Out of this situation inevitably develops the sensing, both conscious and unconscious, of the parent of the same sex as standing in the way of desired gratification. Hostile impulses grow and are manifested more or less openly in such ways as expressions of joy at the parent's absence, the lack of wish for his or her return, the conscious phantasy or even openly expressed desire for sole possession of the parent. In the unconscious, the child is believed to

Freud contends that mythology and history, "the tangible record of the ideas which permeate the fancy of primitive man" support his phylogenetic theory of the Oedipus and Castration complexes.

Rank has shown how much of imaginative literature is constructed about the incest theme.

For Alexander the Oedipus complex is the most demanding of all traumatic situations. Its surmounting involves the twofold problem—first, the sublimation of the erotic relation to the mother, second, the transference of part of the freed libido on to the father, so the purely hostile attitude to him acquires an erotic component. After sublimation is effected, there will be simultaneous sublimated love for both parents and continued sublimation or distributions over a number of love-objects.

Alexander finds in Freud's recent instinct classification theories a new angle from which to approach the resolution of the Oedipus complex. He explains or reinterprets this phenomenon on the basis of instinct fusion and defusion, q. v. The aggressive impulses felt toward the parent of the same sex arise, he thinks, out of the death or destructive instinct, and their overcoming is by a process of fusion with the Eros or life instinct (erotization). He speaks also of the desirability of sublimating these destructive tendencies.

Alexander points out the danger of the aggressive feeling against the father being turned back on the self and becoming a self-destroying tendency of abnormal strength. The normal person, he says, has at his disposal outwardly directed destruction impulses which in the neurotic are directed against his own instinctual urges in the form of conscience inhibitions and need for punishment. Both symptoms and other self-punishment processes, he points out, permit the maintenance of Oedipus tendencies, combative as well as erotic.

have phantasies of killing or injuring (perhaps castrating) the rival parent and taking his or her place with the loved parent.

In the case of the *boy,* the Oedipus Complex in its simplest form arises from what is spoken of as an "anaclitic" origin. That is, a previously formed attachment to the mother as nurse, protector, etc. results naturally at the phallic stage in her becoming the love-object, now that impulses more specifically sexual begin to emerge. While this libidinal object-cathexis of the mother (or mother-imago) is evolving, another all-important element of the so-called Oedipus situation begins to emerge. The boy's primary identification with the father now becomes centered upon taking the father's place with the mother and thus the latter is felt to be an obstacle. The hostility, both conscious and unconscious, which then begins to arise toward him in this one respect results in ambivalence and conflict.

The Oedipus situation, however, is seldom as simple as stated above. Freud admits that it is very difficult to obtain a clear view of the facts in connection with the earliest object-choices and identifications and still more difficult to describe them intelligibly. This is due to "the complicating element introduced by bi-sexuality," constitutionally innate in all children. On the whole, he thinks it is always well to assume (at least in all cases of neuroses) the existence of what he calls the "complete Oedipus." By this he means that there will be present at the same time both a positive and a negative (or inverted) Oedipus situation; that is, the boy will combine (with various degrees of cathexis) a father identification and mother object-love with a mother identification and father object-love. The amount of cathexis distributed to either the positive or the negative situation depends partly upon the relative strength of the innate masculine or feminine disposition in the boy and also upon experiential factors.

With regard to the dissolution of the Oedipus complex, Freud has expressed two apparently contradictory views in the same volume: (a) "Normally an Oedipus complex should be abandoned or thoroughly changed simultaneously with the termination of early sex life." "As a rule, this transformation is not thorough enough; therefore, during the period of puberty the Oedipus complex may be revived, in which case it is liable to induce dire results." (b) "At puberty, the impulses and object-relations of a child's early years become reanimated and amongst them the emotional ties of the Oedipus complex." (*The Problem of Lay Analyses.*)

Freud is quite sure from clinical findings (including analyses of children) that the child unconsciously desires much more than mere demonstrations of parental affection. Some form of sensual gratification corresponding to the limitations of his "infantile sexuality" is also necessary to him. The usual culmination of the child's (even of the boy's) unconscious Oedipus wish is to give birth to a baby in some vague manner.

With regard to the actually incestuous nature of the child's unconscious desires Freud is willing to admit that the child never surmises the real facts as to the actual physical sex relations, but this ignorance, he thinks, is mitigated by vague deductions based on impressions and observations. Also it is not until puberty that full-blown unconscious incest desires are experienced. At neither stage of development will conscious conflicts arise unless the child becomes aware of the directly sexual aim connected with his "love" for the parent.

To Jung the Oedipus is really a Possession Complex. He gives the very simple explanation that in the early stage of undifferentiated sex both the boy and the girl want the mother, who is felt as a source of delight, and desire to be rid of the father. The element of eroticism gradually increases, however, and the girl begins to develop a typical affection for the father with a corresponding jealous attitude toward the mother.

The Oedipus Complex is regarded as "such an important thing that the manner in which one enters and leaves it cannot be without its effects." According to Freud's later theories (*The Passing of the Oedipus Complex*) this complex succumbs in the boy to castration fear, that is, his attention and interest become narcistically centered upon the penis and there develop in his Ucs fears of being robbed of it by the father. The castration complex by its threatening attitude "literally smashes to pieces the Oedipus Complex."

For the boy the normal dissolution of the Oedipus Complex is as follows: The unconscious Ego under pressure of castration fear renounces or represses one part of the "incestuous" strivings, desexualizes or sublimates another part, while the rest of the libidinal stream moves on to its final zone-localization at the late genital (or pubertal) stage of development. The boy should now (at the end of the Infancy Period) feel for the mother only sublimated love or tender affection. The hostility toward the father should drop out with the relinquishing of the rivalry between them and there follows an intensification of the primary identification with the father. Concurrently there should be a breaking-up of the Inverted Oedipus through sublimation of the incestuous (homosexual) father-love and a weakening of the primary mother-identification. This outcome consolidates the boy's masculinity. During the Latency Period, the sublimated or desexualized affection should be extended first to the father and gradually to others in the immediate environment beside the parents.

The above is the normal passing of the Oedipus Complex. It may be, however, that the Id will cling very tenaciously to its "incestuous" aims and that the unconscious Ego may fail in its attempts at sublimation. In such a case, fixations will occur and an undue amount of repression will be demanded. This, of course, prepares the way for later neurotic developments. Should the primary identification with the mother involved in the Inverted Oedipus be strengthened instead of weakened, homosexual trends are likely to develop.

At puberty, even in the normal individual, there is a re-enactment

134

Jung sees in Freud's incest desire only a symbolic expression on the infantile level of the desire to return to the original source of life, to the arms of the mother for rest, or to the maternal womb for rebirth. In this sense, according to Hinkle, the Oedipus finds an important place in Jung's philosophy. "The conflict of man lies in the struggle between these two states—the lure of the desire for oneness with the mother versus the desire and need for separate life and development."

Rank agrees with Jung's concept of the Oedipus complex as a "rebirth phantasy," but, in working out this complicated situation (for the boy alone), bases the unconscious sexual wish upon his birth trauma anxiety theory. The mother's body, specifically her genital apparatus, was an object surcharged at his birth with anxiety and fear for the child. The latter now unconsciously senses the opportunity to transform the original source of pain to a source of pleasure, but any attempt to do this is doomed to failure, not only on account of the immaturity of the child, but also "chiefly because the attempt is made upon the primal object itself, with which the entire anxiety and repression of the primal trauma is directly connected."

In one of his more recent writings, Freud says, "As regards what precedes the Oedipus complex in boys, we are far from complete clarity. We know that this prehistoric period includes an identification of an affectionate sort with the boy's father, an identification which is still free from any sense of rivalry in regard to his mother."

Freud believes that masturbation "is attached to the Oedipus complex and serves as a discharge for the sexual excitation belonging to it." He is not clear, however, as to whether the masturbation "has this character from the first, or whether, on the other hand, it makes its first appearance spontaneously as an 'organ activity' and is only brought into relation with the Oedipus complex at some later date." On the whole, he is inclined to think that this second possibility is the more probable.

Whether enuresis sometimes may not be a result of masturbation, and parental attempts at its suppression regarded by boys as a threat of castration, Freud says is also a doubtful question.

of the Oedipus drama. Again there should remain only sublimated or tender affection for the parents. The rest of the libido, its sexual and desexualized aims merging together, should begin to be directed to an exogamous love-object, and "emancipation" from the parent thus be established. Fixations, however, in greater or lesser degree, are likely to occur and influence both later object-choice and the mental health in general.

In the case of the *girl* the development of the Oedipus situation is quite different. Freud says that from his experience he is inclined to believe that it is "far simpler, less equivocal" than in the case of the boy. At the same time, however, he admits that the elements entering into the rise and fall of the Oedipus Complex in the girl are very shadowy and vague. Rather tentatively he suggests that the Oedipus development may take the following pattern: Her sexual curiosity leads the girl to the discovery of the anatomical differences between herself and her little brothers and boy playmates and "penis envy" develops. Normally she then comes to regard her lack of a penis as castration and her Oedipus Complex begins to develop. This means that having, as in the case of the boy, taken the mother as her love-object the girl's libido must now slip into a new position and take the father as love-object. Phylogenetic factors may bring this about, but it is also believed that the girl's new object-love is the result of an attempt at compensation for the loss of the penis, which is possible because in the unconscious "penis" has symbolically the same value as "child." Thus the girl's Oedipus Complex culminates "in a desire which is long cherished to be given a child by her father as a present, to bear him a child." At the same time feelings of hostility and rivalry develop toward the mother, leading to ambivalence and conflict.

The dissolution of the Oedipus in the girl takes place much more slowly and gradually than in the case of the boy. Freud thinks that it comes about partly because the wish for a child is never fulfilled and partly because of external intimidation in connection with masturbation (threats of loss of love). However, both the wish for

Analysis has revealed that the observations of parental coitus are often responsible for the child's first sexual excitation, and may act as "a starting point for the child's whole sexual development." Freud says that masturbation "together with the two attitudes in the Oedipus complex, later on become attached to this impression, the child having subsequently interpreted its meaning." He is willing to admit, however, that, though a common experience, the observation of coitus is not a universal occurrence, and "so at this point we are faced with the problem of 'primal phantasies.'"

Freud concludes, "Thus, the history of what precedes the Oedipus complex, even in boys, raises all these questions to be sifted and explained; and there is the further problem of whether we are to suppose that the process invariably follows the same course, or whether a great variety of different preliminary stages may not converge upon the same final situation." (*Anatomical Distinction Between the Sexes.*)

Rickman describes the Oedipus complex as being in full force at the phallic stage. It follows the anal-sadistic organization of which ambivalence is such an outstanding characteristic, and thus "inherits an already established fusion of Ego and libidinal impulses toward each parent." The boy experiences erotic genital desires for the mother which cannot come to expression because of the interference of the father. He is unable to put up a fight because of (1) affectionate feelings for the father, (2) physical weakness, (3) fear of danger to his genitals if he gives any expression to his erotic desire for the mother. The conflict must be solved "in such a way that the Ego may undergo as little danger as possible and yet afford the libido as much gratification as possible. The way out of the difficulty involves alterations in object relationship to father and mother and in libido organization."

When the father is perceived to be an obstacle, the full Oedipus complex has developed. The outcome is determined by the relative strength of the masculine and feminine disposition.

The relation to the mother suffers only one change—the renunciation of the phallic mode of pleasure-finding. This is not the same as the complete deflection of libido because some gratification is possible through aim-inhibited relationships. When the mature genital aim emerges, there is liberty given but it must be exogamous.

a penis (Castration Complex) and the wish for a child continue "powerfully charged with libido in the unconscious and help to prepare the woman's nature for its subsequent sex rôle."

H. Deutsch out of her experience in analysis of women believes she has been able to clarify the various steps in the development and decline of the girl's Oedipus Complex. The girl, according to her, passes through two phallic phases; in the first, there is clitoris pleasure and masturbatory practices, but when she discovers her lack of penis she interprets this as punishment for masturbation and develops a sense of guilt. During the second phase there is a transference of this sense of guilt to the incestuous wishes which have developed in connection with the father, and it is this which brings about for the girl the dissolution of her Oedipus Complex.

Freud says the Oedipus Complex is "nuclear" for personality development. On the manner of its dissolving, more than on anything else, depends the determination of later normality or neuroticism. "If the Ego does not achieve much more than a repression of the complex, then the latter persists unconsciously in the Id and will express itself later in some pathogenic effect." Alexander says that an Oedipus fixation, namely, an unsatisfactorily resolved Oedipus, means that the individual "will treat every subsequent love relation as if it were the old incest wish." Then a sense of guilt will attach itself to normal adult sexual expression, causing excessive instinct-restrictions and inhibitions, and, in extreme cases, symptom-formation.

Much normal cultural and creative activity is traceable, according to psychoanalysts, to the Oedipus Complex and it is also, they claim, through formation of the Super-ego the final source of all religion and morality. Such sexual and social aberrations as homosexual and some criminal trends also have their origin in this all-critical experience.

The Oedipus experience results, among other things, in the establishment of what Freud calls "conditions of love," that is, the future choice of an object, and the behavior with respect to the object will always be determined to some extent by certain

Klein believes she has sufficient data to establish the existence of a femininity phase in the early sexual development, which, in the boy, becomes a Femininity Complex (or Inferiority Complex). This occurs at the anal-sadistic level and its favorable issue is of great importance for the later development.

The boy is believed during his femininity phase to feel frustrated, just as does the girl during her masculinity phase, because of the lack of a special organ. He identifies with the mother and covets the vagina and breasts as organs of receptivity and bounty. He also equates feces with child, and desires to have children. His anal sadism and destructive tendencies become predominantly directed towards the organs of conception, pregnancy and parturition; he wants to rob the mother of the womb and its contents, viz. children and the penis of the father which he believes to be in the womb. As a result of the hostile impulses towards the mother he fears punishment (mutilation and dismemberment) from her, and interprets the anal frustrations in this way. "In terms of psychic reality the mother is already the castrator" and the way is also paved for the Castration Complex.

This dread of the mother as castrator may seriously interfere with the normal development of the boy's Oedipus situation. The outcome largely depends on the strength of the constitutional genitality. The struggle between the genital and pre-genital positions of the libido may end in regression to or fixation in pre-genital sadism and mother identification and will show itself later in an attitude of marked rivalry towards women, a blending of envy and hatred. Klein points out that the establishment of the genital position of the libido prompts to rivalry with men but this is not normally of the asocial nature which it shows in connection with women.

The boy's desire for a child may, with the awakening of his epistemophilic impulse (and also because of the recognition which he realizes the girl gives to his superior possession of a penis), lead to a compensatory displacement resulting in a narcistic over-valuation of the penis and an attitude of intellectual rivalry with women.

"A tendency to excess in the direction of aggression which very frequently occurs has its source in the femininity-complex." That is, as Klein says, such aggressive tendencies are rooted in the dread of the mother, though in part also they may be conditioned by over-compensatory attempts to mask sexual ignorance and anxiety, and may also be a unconscious impressions left by the experience. Normally, there will remain only a few traces which point unmistakably to a parental prototype behind the object-choice and behavior; Freud gives as an example of this the preference often shown by younger men for mature women. However, as he says, there are many "strange ways" of loving, and the peculiar conditions of love which underlie them, and to which they owe their characteristics, can always be derived from a fixation in some phase of the Oedipus situation. In this connection, he has established for the man several types of object relationship. These are:

1. The need for "an injured third party" type of object-choice—the man always chooses a woman to whom some other man (brother, husband, lover) has a right of possession. This relates back to the child's concept of the mother as belonging inseparably to the father, and at the same time "the unique, the irreplaceable one." With this type, Freud says, there will often be a series of object-choices, each one of which is really a mother surrogate. The urgent desire in the unconscious "for some irreplaceable thing often resolves itself into an endless series in actuality—endless for the very reason that the satisfaction longed for is in spite of all never found in the surrogate."

2. The need for the "light woman" type of object-choice—that is, for a woman who is "more or less sexually discredited, whose fidelity and loyalty admit of some doubt." Lovers of this type always demand that feelings of jealousy shall be associated with their object-love. The lover himself must fulfill certain conditions of love in his attitude towards his object—he must want to rescue her. This type of object relationship can be traced back, Freud thinks, to an unconscious fixation on the mother first as the ideal and personification of non-sexual purity, with subsequent destruction of this illusion through sexual enlightenment. Or during his Oedipus experience, the boy regards the mother as having been unfaithful to him because of what she has granted to the father. During puberty his revived unconscious Oedipus phantasies center about

protest against the feminine rôle which castration would involve. Klein also speaks of possibilities for sublimation of the "desire for a child and the feminine component which play so essential a part in men's work."

Klein points out that the femininity phase is bound, through the mother-identification, to have some effect upon the Super-ego formation in the boy. Like the girl he will make "both cruelly primitive and kindly identifications. But he passes through this phase to resume . . . identification with the father. However much the maternal side makes itself felt in the formation of the super-ego, it is yet the paternal super-ego which from the beginning is the decisive influence for the man. He too sets before himself a figure of an exalted character upon which to model himself, but, because the boy is 'made in the image' of his ideal, it is not unattainable. This circumstance contributes to the more sustained and objective creative work of the male."

Of the "penis-envy" phase in girls Freud writes, "From the analyses of many neurotic women we have learned that women go through an early phase in which they envy their brothers the token of maleness and feel themselves handicapped and ill-treated on account of the lack of it (really, on account of its diminished form). . . . During this early phase little girls often make no secret of their envy of the favorite brother and the animosity it gives rise to against him; they even try to urinate standing upright like the brother, thus asserting the equality with him that they claim."

Of the part played by the Oedipus complex in bringing about a neurosis, Freud writes, "Distinct traces are probably to be found in most people of an early partiality . . . on the part of a daughter for her father or on the part of a son for his mother; but it must be assumed to be more intense from the very first in the case of those children whose constitution marks them down for a neurosis, who develop prematurely and have a craving for love."

the mother's infidelity; "the lover with whom the mother commits the act of unfaithfulness almost invariably bears the features of the boy himself, or to be more correct, of the idealized image he forms of himself as brought to equality with his father by growing to manhood." His later choice of a woman inclined to fickleness and unfaithfulness is due to the fact that these propensities bring her into dangerous situations, "so it is natural that the lover should do all he can to protect her by watching over her virtue and opposing her evil ways."

The Boy

"In psychoanalytic literature the term Castration Complex implies a network of unconscious thoughts and strivings, in the centre of which is the idea of having been deprived, or the expectation of becoming deprived, of the (male) genitals. This complex is a general one, probably universal, but the intensity of its effects varies." (Stärcke.)

The idea of the Castration Complex appeared in Freudian literature as early as 1908 particularly as the result of the study of the phobia of a five-year-old boy. Since then much water has passed under the mill and the grinding out of ideas concerning the Castration Complex still goes on. It has come to be recognized as a very complicated process. The idea began with the discovery that the neurotic's recollections always included experiences of threats of sexual injury. The subsequent discovery that some neurotic patients had definitely suffered as the result of this complex even when they had experienced no actual castration threat, suggested to Freud that the origin of the intimidation must be traceable largely to phantasy life.

Further light has been thrown on the whole process by the finding that the complex arises in the phallic stage when, as a matter of normal development, there is intense conscious and unconscious interest in the sex organs. Finally, Freud has come to view the Castration Complex as of universal occurrence and vitally bound up with the Oedipus, which it follows and brings to an end. This view has led him to postulate racial experiences as carried over in vague memories of fears which are part of the equipment of the primitive unconscious mental life of every individual. So sensitized is the individual at this phallic period to ideas of possible sexual injury that, even if there are no actual threats, "the child constructs this danger for itself out of the slightest hints, which will never be wanting." Why the child phantasies such threats is another story. But at any rate, the incidence and the

The use of the term castration complex is another example of rather extravagant terminology. Castration really means, of course, removal of the testicles without injury to the penis. The idea embodied in the castration complex theory is very largely that of injury, mutilation, and deprivation of the penis itself. It is exactly that organ, and not the testicles, upon which attention is centered in the phallic stage and which is a subject of the more recently developed notion of the importance of sex differences as observed in childhood. It would almost seem as if the terms mutilation or deprivation complex were more meaningful and less startling.

Alexander points out how pre-genital experiences of the individual become an affective preparation for castration anxiety. "The expectation of castration is only one manifestation of an expectation of a general narcistic wound. It is the deposit of an ontogenetic experience—that every pleasure has its outcome in loss, in pain." Birth, he says, entails the loss of the mother's body (actually a part of the child's own body) and also the loss of the foetal membranes. At the moment of birth a pleasure condition and a pleasure-giving organ are lost for the first time in life and are replaced by a painful condition. Then follows the loss of the pleasure-giving nipple (Stärcke's oral primal castration), later the loss of the pleasure-giving stool (Freud's anal primal castration). Finally, masturbatory pleasure is followed by fear of loss of penis. Thus, Alexander thinks there is no need for invoking phylogenetic phantasies in explanation of the castration complex.

Stärcke believes that at their deepest level the actual unconscious castration phantasies center about the withdrawal of the nipple. He says, "It is in the situation of being suckled that there lies a real basis for the wishes, strivings and dispositions that are comprised under the term Castration Complex." In the practically universal situation of the child at the breast "a penis-like part of the body is taken from another person, given to the child as his own (a situation with which are associated pleasurable sensations) and then taken away from the child, causing 'pain.'"

solution of the Castration Complex belongs to normal development.

The great emphasis which is being laid at present upon the Castration Complex by psychoanalysts is quite in line with Freud's more recent tendency to stress anatomical sex differences in early childhood, and the tremendous psychic significance which the possession or lack of possession of a penis has for both sexes during the phallic stage. The libidinal localization in, and consequent stimulation of, the genitals, which occurs at the stage of phallic primacy, becomes the driving force which "expresses itself in childhood essentially as an impulsion to inquire into things"—as sexual curiosity. That is, Freud believes that the epistemophilic impulses are now largely occupied with the new center of sexual sensations, the penis, and that the boy's interest is concentrated upon this organ. He says, "From all one hears in analyses one could not guess that the male genitals consist of anything more than the penis." This penis preoccupation is the basis of the term, "phallic primacy" so-called because it is believed that for both sexes at this stage of childhood development "only one kind of genital organ comes into account—the male."

Freud maintains that at the stage of phallic primacy every little boy in his Ucs "is beset with fears of having his father rob him of his sex organs, and that this fear of being castrated is of the greatest influence in connection with the general development of his character and sexual tendencies in later life."

The activation of the Castration Complex, Freud is inclined to believe, is to be found to a large extent in the privation, injuring, or punishment threats made by adults in connection with the boy's masturbatory practices. This childhood experience, though of course not universal, psychoanalysts think they are justified from their findings in claiming to be very common. However, Freud thinks that these threats are not taken seriously by the boy, until, as a result of his epistemophilic impulses, he makes investigations which lead to the discovery that his much-prized penis, "so easily excitable and changeable, so rich in sensation," is not "one

The child senses the nipple as a detachable part of his own body which has to be renounced temporarily at each nursing, and permanently at the weaning, and this becomes the "primitive castration" which accounts for the universal occurrence of the castration complex.

The fact that the castration complex is always associated with phantasies and fears of genital deficiency, Stärcke thinks, can be explained as due to displacement, partially at least, of loss in the mouth zone, to the genitals; perhaps also genital feeling is aroused during the sucking, analogous to that during kissing. The nipple also strongly resembles the penis in several respects, and is thus easily identified with it. The narcistic value which the child later attaches to the penis is, according to Stärcke, to be attributed to this identification with the nipple which "is perceived as the centre of one's own personality, and an injury to it is felt as a severe injury to the ego itself."

Freud says, "It has quite correctly been pointed out that the child acquires the idea of a narcistic wound or deprivation of a part of its body by the experience of the loss of the nipple after suckling and of the daily production of its feces, even already by its separation from the womb of the mother at birth. Nevertheless, the castration complex should be a term reserved for the occasion when the idea of such deprivations comes to be associated with the loss of the male organ."

Regarding the relation of defecation to the castration complex, Freud says, "Defecation brings about in the child the first differentiation between a narcistic and an object-loving attitude." He goes on to say, "Another part of the connection is far more clearly recognized in the man; it is established when the child's sexual investigation has discovered the absence of the penis in the woman. The penis is therewith looked upon as a part of the body that can be detached, analogous to excrement, which was the first part of the body the infant had to renounce. The old anal defiance thus enters into the constitution of the castration complex."

According to Freud the anal stage has an important bearing upon the Oedipus and castration complexes. "The handing over of feces for the sake of (out of love for) someone else becomes a prototype of castration; it is the first occasion upon which an individual gives up a piece of his own body (it is as such that feces are invariably treated by children)

147

of the possessions common to all creatures who are like himself."
This discovery may come about through the very common experience of the accidental sight of the genitals of a little sister or
girl playmate, and this experience "forces him to believe in the
reality of the threat which he has hitherto laughed at." The boy's
first reaction to the absence of a penis in the girl is to turn away
from or deny the fact, or to take comfort in imagining that her
penis is small and will grow. He comes gradually "to the conclusion, so fraught with emotion, that at least it had been there
and had at some time been taken away. The absence of a penis is
thought to be the result of castration, and then the boy is faced
with the task of dealing with the thought of a castration in relation to himself."

The Castration Complex, psychoanalysts claim, may have very
far reaching effects on later object-choice. Freud says there will be
one or the other (or a combination or both) of two reactions,
which, if they become fixed, "will permanently determine the
boy's relation to women; horror at the mutilated creature or tri-
umphant contempt for her." He also says, "We know, too, to
what a degree depreciation of women, loathing of women, and
(consequently) a disposition to homosexuality, are derived from
a final conviction of women's lack of a penis."

The universality which psychoanalysts are inclined to claim for
the Castration Complex involves the taking into account of another
factor which has an important share in its evolution. As with the
Oedipus Complex, Freud has no hesitancy in invoking phylogenetic phantasies as accounting, in part at least, for the Castration Complex, though it is doubtful whether all psychoanalysts
are ready to adhere to this theory. That is, the boy is supposed
to go through a phase in his individual development in which
in his unconscious Ego he recapitulates the racial experience of
fear of mutilation by the father, or father-surrogate, on account of
unconscious incest wishes toward the mother. From this point of
view, actual experiences with the parents are less important than

148

in order to gain the favor of some person whom he loves. So that a person's love for his own penis, which is in other respects narcistic, is not without an element of anal-erotism. 'Feces,' 'child,' and 'penis' thus form a unity, an unconscious concept—the concept, namely, of a little thing (*das Kleine*) that can become separated from one's body. Along these paths of association the libidinal cathexis may become displaced or intensified in ways which are pathologically important and which are revealed by analysis."

De Groot believes that castration is feared by the boy because of both his positive and negative Oedipus attitudes—that is, because of both the inadmissible incest wish and the adopting of the feminine rôle in relation to the father. The boy has to renounce love relations with both parents.

The same author suggests that not only is the boy's renunciation of his Oedipus desires a victory for his narcism, the wish to retain "a highly prized bodily organ," but he also unconsciously (phylogenetically) realizes that his renunciation of the mother is really only a temporary one. If he gives up the penis, the possession of the mother, or mother substitute, becomes forever impossible. There is a very violent inner struggle and the boy holds tenaciously to his first love-object. He submits temporarily to the father's superior strength, since by doing so it is possible for him later to wage a more successful fight with his rival and return to his first love-object or her substitute.

Freud points out the actual castration threats may have what he calls a "deferred effect." They can have no significance for the child until he has reached the stage in his development when the penis has great narcistic value. The actual threats of castration, too, eventually fit themselves into a "phylogenetic schema," Freud contends. Very frequently the castration threats are made by the mother or nurse, yet in the end it is from the father that the child comes to fear castration. This Freud thinks points to a triumph of hereditary over accidental experience. "In man's prehistory it was unquestionably the father who practised castration as a punishment and who later softened it down into circumcision."

the unconscious representation of parental behavior and prohibitions. Freud has recently postulated that the anxiety aroused in the unconscious Ego in connection with Id impulses is due to its perception of three different successive danger situations (see Dynamisms—Introduction). The second of these is the danger of castration. He says, "When the boy feels the powerful father as his rival for the mother, becomes aware of his aggressive inclinations against him and his sexual intentions toward the mother, he has the right to fear him, and the fear of punishment can through phylogenetic strengthening be expressed as castration fear."

The significance of the Castration Complex lies in the indelible impression which it leaves upon the child's personality. His fear of narcistic wounding leads him to borrow, as it were, strength from the father to stamp out the unpermissible incestuous urge, and Freud calls this a most "momentous loan." Through identification with the father, he sets up within himself the latter's prohibitions. In other words, the castration fear is internalized and the boy submits now to self-imposed restraints; thus his narcism is preserved both through retention of the penis and the feeling of no longer submitting himself to external authority.

The Ego differentiation thus established is known as the Superego, upon the character of which depends the whole future fate of the individual. In its weakness, the Ego, to tide itself over a crisis, calls to its aid this new power. It may find, however, that it has created for itself an exacting and tyrannical master, whom it must thenceforth endeavor to appease. In such a case, neurotic trends are likely to develop.

In regard to the boy's reaction to his discovery of the girl's lack of a penis, Freud says, "It should not be presumed, however, that the child instantly and readily makes a generalization of its perception that many women possess no penis." He assumes that the absence of a penis is due to a punishment. "On the contrary, the child imagines that only unworthy female persons have thus sacrificed their genital organ, such persons as have probably been guilty of the same forbidden impulses as he himself. Women who are regarded with respect, such as the mother, retain the penis long after this date. Not yet is being a woman the same thing to the child as having no penis." Later, when the child becomes curious about the origin and birth of children and divines that only women can bear children, the mother, too, becomes deprived of a penis. At the same time quite complicated theories are constructed to account for the exchange of a penis in return for a child. The real female genitals, however, do not seem to be discovered. "As we know, the baby is supposed to live in the mother's body (bowels) and to be born through the bowel passage. These last theories take us up to the end of the period of infantile sexuality or beyond."

Stärcke points out that the threat of castration, which Freud thinks occurs so commonly, may have been expressed in many forms (warnings of insanity, illness, punishment, etc.) or may have been simply a prohibition against masturbation. His explanation of the specific dread of castration is that, "In consequence of the talion expectation, any threat will tend to be realized in the child's phantasy at the spot in connection with which he feels a sense of sin. And, as the threat is probably always uttered on account of genital manipulations, the expectation of punishment is localized to the genitals and hands."

Flügel believes from his dream analyses that a very strong castration complex may express itself in what he calls polyphallic symbolism; that is, for the absence of the penis there is substituted a plurality of phallic objects. He interprets this polyphallic dream content as not only an attempt by means of "representation through the opposite" to avoid the censor, but as also evidence of an over-compensatory wish-fulfilment.

"Unfortunately we can describe this state of things only as it concerns the male child; the corresponding processes in the little girl are not sufficiently known to us." "Nevertheless," Freud continues, "we know that the female child is extremely sensitive about the lack of a sex organ equal to that of the male child. Accordingly, the girl comes to consider herself inferior to the boy, developing a condition of "penis-envy" from which may be traced a whole chain of reactions characteristic of the female." And again he says, "As we learn from our psychoanalytic work, all women feel that they have been injured in their infancy and that through no fault of their own they have been slighted and robbed of a part of their body; and the bitterness of many a daughter towards her mother has as its ultimate cause the reproach that the mother has brought her into the world as a woman instead of a man."

Abraham likewise claims that psychoanalysis reveals very frequently the repressed wish in women to be male. Also, direct observation of young girls "shows unequivocally that at a certain stage of development they feel at a disadvantage as regards the male sex by their poverty in external genitals." He is inclined to assume that the wish is common to all women and in a large number has not been successfully sublimated.

In both boys and girls the Castration Complex is intricately bound up with the Oedipus, but the relation between the complexes presents a fundamental contrast in the two sexes. Freud says, "Whereas in boys the Oedipus complex succumbs to the Castration Complex, in girls it is made possible and led up to by the Castration Complex." In the boy, the Castration Complex having "smashed to pieces" the Oedipus complex, normally drops out and Super-ego formation takes its place. The reversal of the order of these two complexes in the case of the girl presents many complexities, and various psychoanalysts have attempted explanation of the problems involved.

The origin of the Castration Complex in the girl (frequently

He also thinks that polyphallic symbolism and its close relation to the castration complex is very evident in mythology. Flügel suggests that an example of polyphallic compensation in actual behavior may be polygamous and promiscuous tendencies in women—the need for a multiplicity of lovers.

In considering the fact that the relation between the castration complex and the Oedipus situation is fundamentally different in boys and girls, Freud points out that this is comprehensible when we remember "that the castration complex always operates in the sense dictated by its subject matter; it inhibits and limits masculinity and encourages femininity. The difference between the sexual development of men and women at the stage we have been considering is an intelligible consequence of the anatomical distinction between their genitals, and of the mental situation involved in it; it corresponds to the difference between a castration that has been carried out and one that has been merely threatened."

The fact that in the girl the castration complex precedes the Oedipus, and that thus the explanation of the dissolution of the latter complex and the formation of a feminine Super-ego is less evident than in the case of the boy, has created a difficult problem for Freud. As a result, perhaps, of his depreciatory remarks concerning the feminine Super-ego, many women analysts have evidently felt called upon to defend their sex, and recent psychoanalytic literature contains many interesting—often perhaps far-fetched—attempts to clarify the complexities surrounding feminine infantile development and Super-ego formation.

L. De Groot (who admits that her findings are based upon the study of only two cases and so may not be typical of the evolution of women) believes she has discovered both a positive and negative Oedipus phase through both of which the girl normally passes. Up to the phallic stage her development is similar to the boy's and the mother is the love-object. With the observation of the boy's larger penis, the girl's narcism is wounded; she is forced to renounce her love longings—both the love-object and "the active conquering tendency of her love aim." Thus, the girl's castration complex deals a death blow to her negative Oedipus phase and ushers in the positive Oedipus. Castration is an accomplished called the Masculinity Complex) Freud ascribes to the "momentous discovery" of her lack of a penis, which discovery, he says, "it is the lot of little girls to make." Penis-envy almost invariably sets in at once, which if not recovered from "may put great difficulty in the way of regular development towards femininity."

According to Freud, the girl may react to her penis deprivation either by fixation on the hope of some day obtaining a penis "in spite of everything and so of becoming like a man," or by "denial," a refusal to accept the fact of being castrated, a clinging to the conviction that she does possess a penis. Of the first reaction Freud says, "It may persist to an incredibly late age and may become a motive for the strangest, and otherwise unaccountable, actions." Of the "denial" process he says that it is not uncommon or very dangerous in the mental life of children. If persisted in, it results in the woman's being "compelled to behave as though she were a man" in many ways. (For further discussion of both these types of reaction, see Behavior, Personality and Conduct Formation.)

There may be other important and far reaching effects of penis-envy for the girl. Freud says, "After a woman has become aware of the wound to her narcism, she develops, like a scar, a sense of inferiority. When she has passed beyond her first attempt at explaining her lack of penis as being a punishment personal to herself and has realized that that sex character is a universal one, she begins to share the contempt felt by men for a sex which is the lesser in so important a respect, and, so far at least as maintaining this judgment is concerned, she clings obstinately to being like a man."

The character-quality of jealousy, Freud thinks, plays a much greater part in women than in men and this may be because in women, "it is enormously re-enforced from the direction of displaced penis-envy."

Another consequence of penis-envy is "a loosening of the girl's relation with her mother as a love-object," since the mother apparently is held responsible for the lack of a penis. This unconscious development very frequently expresses itself in jealousy

fact for the girl; she is normally bound to recognize this at some time and abandon her negative Oedipus and its accompanying masturbation. She makes an identification with her mother, takes the enemy father for love-object, and develops a wish for a child, attaching the same narcistic value to the desired child as the boy does to the penis. She has now adopted the positive Oedipus attitude. Thus, in opposition to Freud, De Groot thinks that the castration complex in girls is a secondary formation and derives its great psychic significance from the preceding negative Oedipus.

De Groot thinks that many peculiarities in the mental life of women can be explained on the above basis. A complete femininity development may be disturbed either by the girl's inability to give up her mother completely and thus forming a weak attachment to the father; or she may have made an energetic attempt to substitute the father for the mother as love-object, but been disappointed in him and returned to the earlier or negative Oedipus position. De Groot suggests that woman's greater tendency to jealousy is perhaps to be explained through the fact that she never can succeed in securing her first love-object, while the man has a later possibility of doing so through a mother substitute. De Groot thinks that the wholly feminine woman does not know object-love in the true sense of the word. She can only let herself be loved. A fixation in the negative Oedipus phase or a regression thereto, since it is an attempt to deny castration, involves the refraining from masturbation and other forms of sexual gratification, and this perhaps often explains frigidity in the marriage relationship.

of another child "on the ground that the mother is fonder of it than of her, which serves as a reason for her giving up her affectionate relation to the mother." This prepares the way for the Oedipus development in the girl which becomes a *fait accompli* with the displacement of the penis wish upon the desire for a child. "With this object in view, she takes her father as a love-object. Her mother becomes the object of her jealousy. The girl has turned into a little woman."

One of the most important effects of the discovery of clitoris inferiority is shown, Freud thinks, in the rôle which masturbation plays in women. On the whole, he says, they are less tolerant of this form of outlet than men, and from his analyses he has discovered "that in girls soon after the first sign of penis-envy, an intense current of feeling against masturbation makes its appearance, which cannot be attributed exclusively to the educational influence of the persons in charge of the child." This fact, he thinks, is to be explained through "the narcistic soreness which is bound up with penis-envy, the girl's reflection that after all this is a point on which she cannot compete with boys, and that it will therefore be best for her to give up the idea of doing so." Freud concludes, "Thus the little girl's recognition of the anatomical distinction between the sexes forces her away from masculinity and masculine masturbation on to new lines which lead to the development of femininity." He points out that this repressive impulse may not succeed, and the conflict with this form of autoerotism may thus persist into adult life.

Freud recently admits that his findings with regard to the Castration Complex in women are based on only a "handful of cases" and may not turn out to be typical.

Klein thinks that the girl's early sexual development can be shown to closely parallel the boy's. According to her, both boy and girl turn from the mother at weaning, passing through what she terms femininity phase, which, for the girl, becomes the first step towards the Oedipus attitude. Anal deprivations reinforce the hostility to the mother and the turning towards the father. The culmination comes with the phallic stage when the girl, like the boy, becomes aware of a new source of erotic satisfaction through the sensations experienced in the vagina and genital apparatus, which bring into play their receptivity. The receptivity aim of the oral stage having been disappointed by the mother, the girl now turns definitely to the father, and his caresses are construed as a seduction. The mother is regarded as the hated, and hating, rival.

The discovery of the lack of a penis Klein believes to be coincident with the awakening of the epistemophilic impulse. The increased hatred of the mother, who is blamed by the girl for this state of affairs, adds another powerful motive to possess the father.

As the result of her identifications with the mother made in connection with the femininity and Oedipus complexes the girl's Super-ego is predominantly of maternal origin. Through her projection of her own hostility upon the mother, as well as the punishment interpretation which her sense of guilt for her sadistic and Oedipus desires leads her to make of the anal and penis deprivations, the girl comes to view the mother as the enemy and would-be destroyer of her womanhood. Her anxiety in this respect is increased by her uncertainty regarding her internal organs. (The boy who is in plain possession of his penis does not share this uncertainty.) Thus the girl's Oedipus impulses are checked by anxiety over her womanhood, just as the boy is influenced by concern over his manhood. Penis-envy is really an underlying anxiety regarding her womanhood which leads on the part of the girl to an exaggeration of the value of the penis.

Klein believes the pride and joy in the feminine rôle is a normal phase of the girl's development, but the anticipation of motherhood becomes so bound up with uncertainties due to Oedipus frustrations and guilt feelings that it is apt to be repressed and a depreciation of womanhood result. A fixation in this phase will have a marked influence on the woman's later relations with men. Oedipus frustrations on the part of the father may cause regression to the mother as love-object and lead to

DEVELOPMENT AND EFFECTS OF OEDIPUS AND CASTRATION COMPLEXES

IN BOY

NARCISM (primary)—Complete self or Ego-love; Primary narcism continues and plays an important rôle in Oedipus and Castration situations and their developments.

$$\downarrow$$

EARLY OBJECT-RELATIONSHIPS—Self-preservative and narcistic object-cathexes; destructive object-cathexes; object-cathexes associated with primarily autoerotic infantile pleasure-finding; beginnings of identification with father (perhaps also with mother, since sex differences not perceived as yet).

$$\downarrow$$

OEDIPUS COMPLEX—Masturbatory impulses accompanied by phantasies of sexual intimacies with mother (or mother-imago); boy turns to mother either because of (a) anaclitic object-choice or (b) through mother's special affection for son (vs. daughter). Development of unconscious "incestuous" object-love. Fourfold pattern of Oedipus development possible:—

Simple (positive) Oedipus—incestuous mother-love; development of feelings of rivalry and hostility towards father, desires to get rid of him (castration wishes, death wishes), ambivalence conflict. Or complicated with underlying minor elements of father object-love (passive desires) and mother-hostility and jealousy—ambivalent feelings.

Simple (negative) Inverted Oedipus—father object-love (passive desires) and mother-hostility and jealousy—ambivalence. Or complicated with underlying minor elements of father rivalry and hostility, and mother object-love.

(Many possibilities of complications and variations in picture due to ambivalence, bisexuality, narcistic identifications.)

$$\downarrow$$

158

many oscillations between identifications with the father and over-compensatory object-love for him. Unless hate develops, Klein says, there will be later a feeling of gratitude to the husband for having fulfilled the desires for a child.

The girl's repudiation of masturbation, Klein believes, may be due partly to the fact that the practice is not as adequate an outlet for her Oedipus excitations as it is for the boy.

Van Ophuijsen, who admits basing his conclusions on a small sequence of cases, is inclined to distinguish between what he calls the Masculinity Complex in women and the castration complex on the grounds of the relative absence in the former of guilt feelings. In the Masculinity Complex the feelings are predominantly of having been ill-treated, with consequent violent embitterment, and attempts to protest against, and to make up for, the lack of penis. Also he believes that there is always present a conviction that a penis will eventually develop.

"The origin of the Masculinity Complex is, of course, to be traced to the sight of a male organ, belonging either to the father or to the brother, or some other man; and in the history of most women patients, and without exception in those with a strongly marked Masculinity Complex, there is found the memory of such an observation and of the comparison of the patient's own body with that of man."

In addition to the identification which the girl makes, after the trauma of seeing a male organ, with the father or brother there are also other factors which Van Ophuijsen thinks nourish the Masculinity Complex. During his analytic work he says he has received a strong impression "of the intimate connection between the Masculinity Complex, infantile masturbation of the clitoris and urethral erotism." The urethral erotism (which Freud has remarked to be closely connected with ambition) strengthens the penis-envy; the discovery of clitoris sensation and masturbatory gratifications brings reassurance and a sense of having realized her penis expectations—the conviction of being an exception to other women.

CASTRATION COMPLEX—Narcistic over-evaluation of penis—unconscious fears of being robbed of organ by father. Origin of castration fear—(a) phylogenetic inheritance of primitive incest-taboo; (b) in connection with masturbation actual punishment threats later (when girl's lack of penis discovered) interpreted as castration threats; (c) justifiable fear that strong father will revenge self on rival; (d) projection of own aggressive (death) wishes on to father. In case of Inverted Oedipus boy fears punishment for passive (homosexual) wishes toward father.

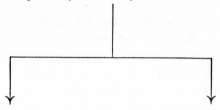

DISSOLUTION OF OEDIPUS COMPLEX—Heterosexual normal solution —because of castration and Super-ego fears part of incestuous mother-love sublimated; part renounced or repressed; intensified identification (primary) with father, dropping out of hostility, extension to him of sublimated love. Boy's masculinity consolidated.

Homosexual solution—overstrong identification (secondary) with mother; seeking love-objects resembling the self. If Inverted Oedipus is present in marked degree, intensified identification (primary) with mother, and seeking of male love-objects.

SUPER-EGO FORMATION—Dropping out of Castration Complex; castration fear internalized through identifications (primary and secondary) with prohibiting parents. Super-ego built up preponderantly on one or the other parent, according to boys' sexual disposition. Normal development—if incestuous urge not over-strong, or if Ego strong enough to make adequate sublimation of a strong urge, temperate Super-ego will be set up, that is, many symbolical and substitutive outlets will be permissible. Some *sense of guilt,* but limited to desires for unmodified expression.

In opposition to Van Ophuijsen, Stärcke says that he considers as effects of the castration complex "those cases in which the feeling of guilt is not perceived as such but is projected on to the surroundings and contributes towards the intensity of the feeling of hate against them and is expressed by a marked feeling of having been unjustly treated, together with that of embitterment."

With regard to penis-envy, Jones thinks there are two stages—an autoerotic and an alloerotic. The former refers to the wish to possess a penis as the boy does, that is, for urinary, exhibitionistic, scoptophilic, and masturbatory activities. The alloerotic (or post-Oedipus) penis-envy signifies the desire to share the penis in coitus with the father (which may reactivate regressively the primary penis-envy). Jones thinks this is the type most often found clinically, but he also maintains that no woman escapes the early penis-envy stage.

K. Horney contends that the belief in "penis-envy" has evolved as the result of a too exclusively masculine orientation. This predominantly masculine cultural milieu is bound, she thinks, to affect the viewpoint of a little girl. On the other hand, Horney thinks that biologically the girl has in the capacity for motherhood "a quite indisputable and by no means negligible physiological superiority." She claims there is sufficient data for believing that "the unconscious of the male psyche clearly reflects intense envy of motherhood, pregnancy, childhood. (Groddeck also speaks of this.) She suggests that the "tremendous strength in men of the impulse to creation" is simply over-compensation for their feelings of biological creative inferiority.

Horney says, "Every little girl who has not been intimidated displays penis-envy frankly and without embarrassment." Analyses of adult women also confirm the fact that penis-envy "operates as a factor of enormous dynamic power."

It is, however, a secondary or regressive penis-envy to which Horney refers. She thinks that regularly when the girl renounces the father in the Oedipus situation, she recoils from the feminine rôle altogether and reverts to penis-envy. The girl, she says, fears vaginal injury just as the boy fears castration—so takes flight into the fictitious male rôle. Phantasies of being a man secure her against libidinal wishes in connection

Neurotic solution—inadequate sublimation; strong fixation on incestuous desires toward mother, (or, in Inverted Oedipus, toward father),—strong repression. All future object-finding subject to inhibitions and conflicts.

Neurotic Super-ego formation —weak Ego, unable to sublimate will bring to its aid strong relentless Super-ego. Intolerant critical Super-ego induces undue *sense of guilt* in Ego, and desires to placate by accepting punishment, thus *need for punishment* develops.

LATER OBJECT-CHOICE—Normally revival at adolescence of Oedipus complex. Emancipation from parents; Exogamous object-seeking.
Neurotic development—parental fixations.

LATER SUPER-EGO ALTERATION—Normally Ego should become stronger, and Super-ego should be modified, less arbitrary, less dominating.
Neurotic development—persistence of overexacting Super-ego, sense of guilt, and need for punishment.

with the father. Uncertain, vague fears of vaginal injury are replaced by concrete castration fear. The Oedipus complex becomes the motive for flight from the male rôle.

H. Deutsch believes that the Masculine Complex in the woman plays a much greater rôle than does the Feminine Complex in man. She thinks that identification with the father is an important factor in the formation of the Masculine Complex.

Jones, in an attempt to explain the dissolution of the Oedipus complex in the girl, criticizes the term "castration" which he thinks "has in some respects hindered our appreciation of the fundamental conflicts." He agrees with K. Horney that the whole matter has been approached too much from the male point of view, with perhaps "a danger of importing into the one, considerations with which we are already familiar in the other." He argues that in the case of both the boy and the girl the issue is the same, namely, the dread of a total loss or deprivation of sexual gratification. In the boy's unconscious this deprivation dread becomes concretely a castration dread. For the girl the concrete dread becomes fear of separation from the father through the mother, also fear of the father's disapproval of her desires, and of being rebuffed by him.

The question arises, can deprivation engender a sense of guilt? Jones thinks that it can, since environmental frustration of the child's desires for immediate sexual gratification may not only be interpreted by him as a permanent deprivation but also as a hostile punishing attitude on the part of the parent.

The Oedipus situation, according to Jones, is fundamentally the same for both the boy and the girl, namely, the choice between renunciation of either the sexual object or their own sexual characteristics (manhood or womanhood).

DEVELOPMENT AND EFFECTS OF OEDIPUS AND CASTRATION COMPLEXES

IN GIRL

NARCISM (primary)—The same development as in boy.

EARLY OBJECT-RELATIONSHIPS—The same development and rôle as in boy.

CASTRATION COMPLEX (or Masculine Complex)—Two-fold development: (a) lack of penis interpreted as punishment may develop contempt for her own sex and envy of opposite sex—("penis envy"), feelings of inferiority; (b) denial of lack of penis, hope of obtaining one; (c) castration accepted; gives up masculinity; begins to substitute compensatory desire for a child.

OEDIPUS COMPLEX—Turns away from mother who is held responsible for lack of penis; turns toward father as love-object, desires child, perhaps as gift, through him. Developmental pattern less complicated and equivocal than in boy.

DISSOLUTION OF OEDIPUS COMPLEX— Takes place slowly and gradually, due largely to disappointment at non-fulfillment of wish for a child.
Heterosexual normal solution— intensified identification with mother, consolidating of femininity. Relinquishing of part of "incestuous" desires towards father. Development of sublimated love for him.

SUPER-EGO FORMATION—Genesis of Super-ego formation in girl not so clear as in case of boy. Fears of loss of love may take place of castration fears which boy has.

H. Sachs claims that he has repeatedly found in his analysis of normal women "passionate oral desires directed toward the father." This regression to the oral level, without relinquishment of the Oedipus object, he says, is "often an exceedingly profound process and may be of crucial importance in the development of female character." He has come to believe that these oral desires (tendency to incorporate the father orally when frustration of vaginal satisfaction occurs) are a regular stage of development in the case of girls.

The line of development, he says, is invariably the same—first, the girl accepts the fact of castration, so finds clitoris masturbation unsatisfactory; second, she is frustrated in her genital desires, the object of which is the father, or the child she wants him to give her; third, she makes a final effort to cling to the Oedipus complex, that is, to her fixation to her father, and so she transfers to him the oral desires which were originally gratified at the mother's breast. This solution of the Oedipus complex, Sachs thinks, has an influence on the character of the Super-ego. The fact that the girl introjects the frustrating father means that she achieves gratification of her desire to receive him into herself and in this way manages to detach herself from the real father. No true Super-ego, Sachs says, can be formed until there has been frustration, and final renunciation of the father. A highly developed Super-ego and marked tendencies to self-denial and renunciation will be the result of this solution.

Frustration does not always destroy the girl's Oedipus complex. In this case she remains throughout life fixated on the father and an independent impersonal Super-ego is not formed. The Super-ego may be often highly developed and powerful but simply copied from the father.

Sachs points out that one essential difference in the formation of the male and female Super-ego is due to the fact that the origin of the male Super-ego is in the threat of castration—something menacing about it; the woman's Super-ego is based on the ideal of a renunciation. The boy's Oedipus complex is shattered by the menace of castration—the girl endeavors to cling to the father, either through her desire for a child or by oral regression.

SECTION FOUR

CONSTITUTIONAL PATTERN AND EARLY EXPERIENCES

CONSTITUTIONAL PATTERN AND EARLY EXPERIENCES

CONSTITUTIONAL FACTORS

Psychoanalysts believe that through their study of the neurotic they have been able to throw considerable light upon the psychic constitutional pattern or the "structural plan," as Von Uexküll calls it, of the normal human individual. For the formation of personality this structural plan is most important in its reactive interrelationships with the environmental situation up to the end of the so-called Infancy Period; from then on, the behavior and personality development of both the normal and neurotic individual tend to follow and repeat infantile prototypes.

Thus for psychoanalysts, the evolution of the human personality is dependent upon a constitutionally inherent psychic pattern of development specific for and common to the human individual. By virtue of this pattern, certain elements of environmental experience are selected out and reacted to because they have special values for the human being, values either pleasurable or traumatic.

Briefly recapitulated, the "structural plan" of the mental life of the young child is characterized, psychoanalysts believe, by the following features:

(1) One of the outstanding characteristics of the young child is his erotic stimulability. A large part of his behavior is to be attributed to his desires (conscious and unconscious) to secure libidinal gratification.

(2) The young child is essentially self-loving and filled with the sense of his own importance; underlying much of his behavior is the effort to preserve his "omnipotence," or to compensate for inevitable feelings of psychic helplessness.

(3) Impulses of aggressiveness, destructiveness, and hostility form a part of the instinctual life of the young child. These impulses happen to be directed towards those persons to whom his affection is chiefly given, simply because they form the most immediate and frustrating parts of his environment.

(4) Through his helplessness the child craves to be loved (nourished, cared for, erotically stimulated) rather than to give love.

(5) The young child accepts the frustrations of reality reluctantly; if they are too alien and hostile he tends to take flight into his own inner world of phantasy.

(6) As his Ego comes to recognize and side with the claims of reality (parental demands) and to set them up within itself (Super-ego formation) much of the child's behavior becomes motivated by an unconscious sense of guilt which becomes attached to his erotic and aggressive impulses.

(7) If the unacceptable impulses are too strong to be relinquished or exchanged, the relatively weak and immature Ego defends itself against them; repression of the ideas to which the impulses are attached is resorted to. It is this tendency of the Id to cling tenaciously, and of the Ego to repress, which lays the foundation for neurotic development.

Alongside their discoveries regarding the spontaneous development of the human individual in early childhood psychoanalysts also have placed emphasis on certain universal and typical situations inherent in the family life and parent-child relationship which arise in sequence and keep step with the various stages of development through which the child is passing. These situations, since they offer unique opportunities for pleasure and are also invariably followed by frustration or pain, become intricately interwoven with the child's inner life and leave their imprint on all phases of later personality development.

But these universal and typical situations and the modifying influences which they exert upon constitutional tendencies can be understood only by keeping well in mind the "structural plan" of the young child according to which he acts selectively upon his environment and seizes upon and receives impressions from those phases or aspects of the external world which produce, as it were, deep, reverberatory responses from within.

The typical *early situations* through which all children pass and which according to psychoanalysts are so significant for future development can be summarized under the heads of the child's helplessness, parental love, and parental training. Expanding these somewhat they are: (a) The long drawn out physical and psychic helplessness of the child places it at the mercy of external and internal stimuli and thus its dependence on objects is greatly intensified. (b) Parental care and tenderness inevitably tend to stimulate the child's erotic life. Freud speaks of the inexhaustible source of sexual excitation and gratification of erogenous zones which the mother especially supplies to the child as she "pats it, kisses it, and rocks it." The father kisses and fondles the child and this, too, is believed to excite it erotically. (c) Parental training and prohibitions come into play. The child "loves" those who excite him libidinally; then these loved objects begin to thwart his demands for pleasure. As Sadger points out, in the child-parent re-

The satisfactions of intra-uterine existence and the rude destruction of this blissful state by the process of birth have both been emphasized in some quarters as more significant than any other childhood experience for future healthy or neurotic development. The great protagonist of the birth trauma theory is Rank, who claims that his psychoanalytic experience has convinced him that prenatal existence is normally supremely pleasurable and the experience of birth a tremendous psychic shock. With birth there comes not only a cataclysmic change both in environment and modes of functioning (change of temperature, light, noise, handling by adults, bathing, etc.), but also the former security and freedom from effort and disturbance is lost and feelings of helplessness and anxiety arise. Rank maintains that traumatic potentialities are always present in the birth situation through the severing of the physical and psychical attachment to the warming, nourishing, protecting mother. The deepest levels of the individual never accept this severance, and the whole later existence is reaction to extra-uterine suffering and loneliness, an attempt to make the whole world a substitution for the womb. Instead of adaptively substituting, that is, reacting off (abreacting) the trauma of birth, the neurotic individual endeavors to maintain the mother-attachment through various dependency devices.

The process of birth represents a change from a highly pleasurable to an extremely painful situation (pressure and the struggle for oxygen). This constitutes the primal anxiety, since it is the first content of perception; it is believed to remain operative throughout the whole life. This primal anxiety is not purely physiological, but is also psychically anchored, and has the effect, Rank thinks, of preventing the striving back tendency of the libido. The fixed impression of the primal anxiety blots out the memory of the former (prenatal) pleasure state and prevents regression. Man could not bear this painful separation from the primal object and the happiness herewith associated and would be constantly harking back to it were it not that he is checked in his regressive tendencies by the threatening repetition of the primal anxiety of birth.

All later pleasure-seeking impulses have as their final goal, according to Rank, the re-establishment of the prenatal pleasure state. Sphincter training resentment on the part of the child is really the putting forth lationship the libido is being constantly stimulated and constantly frustrated.

The specific *early experiences* which inevitably condition the development and weave themselves into the "structural plan" center about the experience of birth and the various stages of libidinal development. These have been already dealt with to some extent in other sections (see Developmental Stages) but a further brief summarization seems to be of value in this connection.

(1) *Pre-natal existence and the birth-trauma.* Freud in one of his most recent writings refers to intra-uterine security and stresses the birth experience as producing a sense of physical and psychic helplessness. This is important because through it the dangers of the outer world become of greater importance, "and the value of the object which can alone protect from these dangers and re-place the lost intra-uterine life is greatly enhanced." The need for love is created which Freud says "will nevermore leave the human individual." Birth, since it is the first dangerous situation through which the child must pass, establishes a physiological anxiety pattern which the Ego makes use of in later danger situations to give the "pain signal" to the Id.

Most psychoanalysts are not inclined to lay much stress on the birth trauma from the emotional point of view. Freud points out that there is as yet no recognition of the mother as an object, so seve-rance from her can have no emotional import.

(2) *Nursing pleasure and the weaning trauma.* Freud thinks that the nursing situation replaces for the child the biological foetal situation. Various views are advanced by different analysts with regard to the importance of the weaning trauma. A good deal of stress is laid on the fact that the child is mortified through loss of his feelings of power and mastery. It is suggested that the child feels a narcistic wound through a sense of desertion. Abraham lays emphasis on the disappointment which the child suffers at the hands of the mother which may show itself in a persistence of ambivalent and hostile attitudes towards the mother. Alexander thinks that weaning prepares "an affective component" for the

of a claim to the earliest intra-uterine freedom. Thumb-sucking is an attempt to replace the mother's body by the child's own. Toe-sucking re-establishes the intra-uterine position of the body. Masturbation perhaps prepares for the sublimest substitution for reunion with the mother, the sexual act.

With regard to the birth trauma Freud is willing to admit that "the act of parturition appears to be the first individual anxiety experienced to give the characteristic traits of the expression of an anxiety affect" (motor innervations of the respiratory organs and the heart), but he warns against an over-estimation of this connection. He feels that "it is unjustified to assume that in every outbreak of anxiety something occurs in the soul life which reproduces the birth situation." Freud criticizes Rank's emphasis on the birth trauma from several points of view:

(1) The danger from birth has as yet no psychic content—"we certainly may not presuppose that the fetus has any kind of knowledge that it is in danger of annihilation." All that the fetus perceives, he thinks, is "a wholesale disturbance in the economy of its narcistic libido." A series of unpleasant situations arise through the fact that "large quantities of excitations" penetrate the fetus. Thus Freud thinks that far too little is actually known of the psychic comprehension of a new-born child for us to be certain just what is later recalled and how it is recalled.

(2) Rank's explanation of child phobias (fear of small animals as they vanish into or emerge from holes) as based on a birth impression, Freud attacks on the ground "that it rests on a presupposition that the infant has definite sense impressions, especially those of a visual nature" at birth, and he says "it is not credible that the child at birth has anything beyond tactile and general sensibility."

(3) Certain typical cases of child fear, Freud points out, are quite inconsistent with Rank's theory. He asks, why does the child not enjoy darkness and solitude as a restoration of the intra-uterine situation?

Freud gives Rank credit for his discovery of the association between fear reaction to the birth-danger and later danger situations and their fear reactions. However, he opposes Rank's theory that according to the severity of the trauma, there is variation in the amount of fear reaction and that "the initial volume of the fear development should determine whether the individual will or will not acquire mastery—whether he is to become normal or neurotic." This theory, he says, is "vulnerable in a castration complex. Stärcke stresses weaning as more significant from the point of view of castration than the later Castration Complex of Freud. Though the actual content of the Castration Complex is closely bound up with anxiety regarding the penis, Stärcke believes that the Complex itself has its origin in the Oral Stage, when the child feels the nipple as part of itself. The taking away of the nipple is thus sensed as castration and since this is a universal occurrence the universality of the Castration Complex is accounted for.

(3) *Defecation pleasures and sphincter-training trauma.* Psychoanalysts believe that the infant in the beginning of his existence gets a great deal of pleasure from contact with his own warm excretions. The passing of the excretions also is believed to be pleasant both because of the erotic stimulation and the relief of tension which follows. Training in control teaches the child the pleasure of retention and postponement of the act. It is also believed that he has interest in handling the product, which he regards as a part of himself.

Anal deprivations of these several kinds, are also viewed by some psychoanalysts as castrations and blows to narcism. Freud, however, regards such deprivations (as well as in the birth and weaning traumas) chiefly as intensifying of the child's feelings of biological and psychic helplessness. By helplessness is meant the child's feeling of being overwhelmed with excitations for which he has inadequate means of discharge.

(4) *Genital-stimulation pleasures (Oedipus phantasies) and their prohibitions.* At the phallic stage the child is believed to get his chief sexual pleasure through penis (and clitoris) touching and rubbing. The parents inadvertently provide many opportunities for pleasure of this sort. Powdering and cleansing manipulations on the part of the mother, assistance in urinating on the part of the father, provide sexual gratification which the child interprets as a proof of love, perhaps a "seduction," and which may bring about fixations and homosexual trends in the child. Interference with masturbatory activities, the inevitable disappointments in

high degree" since (a) it is not known just what is meant by abreaction, indeed Freud has given up the use of this term, together with the idea of catharsis, (b) "emphasis of the variable strength of the birth trauma leaves no room for justifiable etiological claim of the hereditary constitution," (c) phylogenetic factors are left out of consideration, (d) "there have been no good studies as to whether severe and protracted labor coincides unmistakably with the development of neurosis, and if children thus born show the phenomena of early infantile fears longer or more strongly than others." Freud points out that Rank's theory is accessible to experimental testing, but "as long as such a trial has never yet been actually undertaken, it is impossible to judge of the value."

On the whole, Freud has come to the conclusion that though Rank's contribution may be of definite value, it by no means offers the solution of the foundation of neurosis; the demand for a "uniform final cause of nervousness still remains unsatisfied."

Ferenczi says, "The more I observe, the more I realize that none of the developments and changes which life brings finds the individual so well prepared as for birth." Physiological preparation, reflexes, and the intuition of the parents, he thinks, go to make this transition as smooth as possible. Birth is really a sort of triumph for the child, and as such, must assert an influence on his whole life.

Alexander agrees that the birth trauma may be an important pathogenic factor but thinks that as yet Rank's claim has been unsubstantiated by any empirical data. Ferenczi explains the birth phantasies which Rank claims to get in his analyses as being really coitus phantasies.

Kenworthy points out that security may be one of the most significant of the pleasures of intra-uterine existence, establishing later security-seeking patterns. The fact that the birth trauma is apt to be more excessive with the first born child, or if there has been maternal emotional and physical instability during pregnancy, is, she thinks, to be taken into account. She claims that it has been noted that the Caesarian section child is less sensitized.

Oral and anal deprivations produce a feeling of helplessness, Freud says, because the need arises to replace old modes of gratification by new ones which the child has not yet learned to master.

regard to Oedipus hopes and the hostility and conflicts arising therefrom all combine to make this a most crucial experience in the child's development and, at least so Freud believes, constitutes a nucleus for neurosis.

(5) *Discovery of anatomical sex differences.* Freud believes that this discovery is inevitably made by every child and brings to a head the Castration Complex in both boy and girl.

(6) *Various degrees of parental rebuff of sexual curiosity.* Freud speaks of the limitations set to the child's sex quest by his elders as leading to an inferiority complex. The child takes refuge in his own sexual theories which he comes to feel as taboo and so represses. The repression of sexual curiosity may have an effect on intellectual curiosity in general. The early feeling of not knowing may intensify the child's sense of helplessness.

Klein thinks that oral and anal frustrations become the prototypes of all later frustrations. They signify punishment and thus later frustrations come to be regarded in the same light and are more keenly felt.

Sadger thinks that the sadism of early ambivalence can be accounted for through the fact that the child "loves" those who excite him sexually and that then these loved objects proceed to thwart his demands for pleasure. Hate and love must then from the very outset be directed toward the parent. The fiercest feelings of hate are roused with the suppression of masturbation.

Freud calls attention to the fact that since the Oedipus desires are so completely unrealized by the parents the inevitable frustrations which are associated with them have little to do with actual parental behavior.

Klein stresses what she calls the "tremendous questioning impulse," for the most part unconscious, thus unable to express itself in words and so remaining unanswered. This early feeling of not knowing, accentuates feelings of incapacity and intensifies the castration complex in both sexes. At the same time there is a failure to understand words and speech, and feelings of hate are likely to develop. This not-knowing complex may leave traces, Klein thinks, in later inhibitions regarding learning (incapacity to learn foreign languages), hostility to foreigners, direct disturbances in speech. The connection between the epistemophilic impulse and sadism is very important for the whole mental development.

Freud points out that the discovery of sex differences for the girl is traumatic because she accepts the boy's estimation of his penis. She develops a great interest in the boy's organ, tries to urinate like the boy and openly expresses the wish to be a boy. Klein contends that the girl feels more uncertainty than the boy regarding her sexual organs and their purpose. This together with other impressions associated with the Oedipus situation may seriously damage her later maternal capacity.

Alexander speaks of "the uncanny sense of expectation" which, he says, is often felt by neurotics and also by healthy individuals, "that an indefinite vague misfortune will follow just when great success has been achieved, or when life seems for a moment to have granted perfect happiness." This feeling is to be traced to the deep imprint of early affective experiences.

In spite of the importance now attached by psychoanalysts to constitutional factors and universal typical experiences closely associated with them, the accidental or fortuitous experience also plays a significant rôle in the establishing of fixations and conditioning of personality trends. Apart from the specific content which they lend to the individual phantasies, chance environmental situations largely in connection with family life may be all-decisive for personality formation (a) through premature arousal of some component sexual impulse, or (b) through reawakening an old fixation into activity and thus aiding in an early regressive process, or (c) through reinforcing some existing constitutional trend, or (d) through stimulating a greater intensity of repression.

For the sake of making as clear as possible the exact significance which psychoanalysts attach to the chance environmental situation some concrete example have been culled from psychoanalytic literature. Incidentally, this illustrative material may throw light on other fundamental psychoanalytic concepts. The most frequently referred-to accidental situations seem to be the following:

(a) Seduction experiences. These may be brought about in various ways. Freud includes such sensations as may be brought about inadvertently by the mother or nurse in cleansing the child's genitalia. Experimental activities with other children may also bring about pleasurable sensations and desires for repetition. Such experiences may have a marked affect upon the sexual aim, for example a boy who submits to the touching of his genitalia by another child may acquire a passive homosexual trend. Sexual curiosity may also be awakened prematurely by such experiences.

(b) Observations of parental intercourse ("primal scene"). Most infants sleep in their parents' room or in a room close to them and may very easily either observe the act itself or over-hear various sounds. The result of this may be a sym-

In one of Freud's best-known cases (the Wolf-man) observation of the primal scene was found to have a strongly conditioning influence on the development. It was also established that this experience took place at the age of a year and a half. Freud discusses whether a child of this age could actually perceive all the details of such a complicated process and preserve them so accurately in his unconscious. He explains this on the theory of "deferred action," that is, the impressions are not understood or adequately reacted to until a later experience revives them and makes them significant. This he thinks is also the case in connection with castration threats. The boy does not take them seriously at first and they have no real significance until he makes the accidental discovery of the girl's lack of a penis (see Oedipus and Castration Complexes).

Other early environmental situations of relatively infrequent occurrence are mentioned by various psychoanalysts:

Anal-erotic or castration complex trends in the mother—Abraham points out how the mother's obvious disgust at the sight of the boy's penis may injure his narcism and may intensify the development of his castration fears. A mother's excessive interest in the boy's defecation may alter his libidinal orientation and lead to a regression from genital to anal aims thus impelling to passivity and the taking of the father for the love-object.

An observation of animal coitus may lead to sexual enlightenment and resentment of parental evasions.

Father's tendency to "affectionate abuse" (making playful threats, to gobble up child, etc.) may play a part in later phobia formation.

Overhearing conversation of adults, especially if carried on with an air of secrecy and mystery, may intensify the child's "not-knowing" complex.

Lack of tender response, feelings of not being loved may make it difficult for the child to discard his aggressive impulses. Abraham points out that the illegitimate who has no examples of love finds it especially difficult to develop social feeling.

Quarrels between parents and unhappy marital relations, Freud says, stimulate the child's emotional life and lead it to experience "intensities of love, hate, and jealousy." This situation, he says, determines "the severest predispositions for disturbed sexual developments or neurotic diseases in children."

pathetic premature arousal of excitement in the child, or the father's action may be construed as sadistic—the posture perhaps being associated with fighting in play with other children. This sadistic conception of coitus may have a marked influence on the child's sexual theories and also affect later martial relationships. A more cruel Super-ego may also develop.

(c) Castration threats. These may take many forms and usually, Freud says, come from women who strengthen their authority by saying that the father or the doctor will "cut it off." Sometimes the threat is made that the hand will be cut off and this may condition various inhibitions with respect to manual activities. The slightest hints, however, are sufficient to make the child construct for itself the castration danger. (See Oedipus and Castration Complexes.)

The above situations recur so frequently in analyses that they either must be regarded as typical and universal for neurotics or phylogenetic origins must be invoked to explain them.

(d) Coming of another child. The conditioning possibilities of this experience are many. A few examples are the following: Seeing another child suckled may revive early pleasure impressions and assist regressive trends; the Oedipus complex may be set in motion prematurely; Oedipus disappointments and disillusionments may be reinforced; the mother may be felt to be faithless and the temporary separation from her as well as the more permanent diminution in her care and attention may both increase the fixation upon her and at the same time stimulate repression; sexual curiosity may be stimulated prematurely and attempts be made to figure out just where the rival came from and how such a happening may be prevented in the future; parental rebuffs of the curiosity thus awakened may intensify the already developed Oedipus hostility; hostility to the new baby (shown in unfriendly criticisms, wishes for its disappear-

Any situation which tends to depreciate the parents as love-objects, according to Anna Freud, brings the child into the danger of both losing and depreciating his Super-ego, and is the origin, she thinks, of many anti-social and character abnormalities.

Though Freud takes such a firm stand on phylogenesis, his followers are in many cases inclined to look to ontogenesis as the only source of all unconscious phantasy-formations. Stärcke contends that weaning is quite sufficient to account for later penis-loss dread. He says that he is firmly convinced that all unconscious phantasies are "ultimately repetitions of the early situations"; they only appear peculiar and divorced from reality, he thinks, because of the difference between infantile and adult thought.

Alexander thinks that the affective experiences associated with birth and with oral and anal deprivations easily prepare the child to anticipate the loss of the penis. That is, his previous impressions that pleasure is always followed by pain—loss of part of himself (womb, nipple, feces) lead to similar expectations in regard to genital pleasure activities.

M. Klein lays great stress on the real experience. With regard to seduction she claims that practically all children go through varied forms of sexual relations in their play with each other. Through displacement the unconscious phantasies often involve adults. There is also a further significance; the other child may be looked upon as a substitute for the parent and thus a sense of having actually realized incestuous coitus may be acquired. This, Klein thinks, reinforces the normal anxiety attaching to the Oedipus Complex, and thus more intense repression and a stronger sense of guilt may be brought about. She suggests that the difference between a criminal and neurotic development may hinge on the real experience.

Abraham and Freud both point out how experiences of seduction may actually establish the fixation on this specific mode of pleasure-finding. The repetition compulsion principle and the need for punishment are also significant in this connection.

ance, perhaps even aggressive attacks) may lead to conflict and repression.

(e) Excessive tenderness and over-indulgence on the part of parents. Freud calls attention to cases in which the mother is affectionally or sexually unsatisfied by her husband and makes her child her love-object, pouring out boundless tendernesses and caresses upon it. This has great significance for later neurotic development since the child is apt to become insatiable in his demands for love and unable to renounce or be satisfied with a normal degree of it in later life. Sexual precocity may also be stimulated, for example, the child who is habitually taken into bed with its parents is certain to be stimulated erotically. In the case of the girl the mother's over-tenderness may easily bring about a fixation upon her and thus establish homosexual trends.

(f) Parental punishments. Severe punishment on the part of the parent can give an excuse or rationalization for hostile unconscious Oedipus impulses. Sometimes the offenses for which chastisement is given by the parent may have the unconscious significance for the child of a love overture and the punishment may then be interpreted as a rebuff and so stimulate repression. Being whipped, Freud says, is often a narcistic trauma, the child is "cast down from his throne of imaginary omnipotence." Punishment may often strengthen masochistic trends, or may serve as a gratification of feeling of need for punishment. The origin of "beating phantasies," which Freud thinks are so common, is also partially traceable to some early impression of a similar nature.

(g) Absence or death of a parent. When the father is frequently away from home the boy has opportunities for many uninterfered-with expressions of his Oedipus impulses regarding the mother; the limitations necessitated by the father's return may increase the hostility to him. The lack of a father may hinder the boy in working through his castration

184

In 1909 Freud declared that he believed it to be extremely probable that a child's education could "exercise a powerful influence for good or for evil" as far as a neurotic predisposition was concerned. However, he concluded that "what that education is to aim at and at what point it is to be brought to bear seem at present to be very doubtful questions."

Certain as they are of the significance of their findings in respect to early child life and its importance for later development, psychoanalysts are still reluctant to lay down specific rules for child-rearing. This noncommittal attitude is quite comprehensible when it is remembered that because of the peculiarities of his "structural plan" the child will seize upon and be influenced by just the phases or aspects of his environment which correspond to his inner needs of the moment. For example, a very mild punishment may be viewed unconsciously as a severe narcistic blow, or a rebuff of Oedipus hopes, or a satisfaction of masochistic trends and thus bring about a mental reaction of an exaggerated nature of which the parent will be completely unaware.

Ferenczi is inclined to think that there can be such a thing as a too-well brought up child. In his clinical work he has found that patients whose phantasy life he has had to stimulate artificially (see Therapy), were individuals who as children had had their childish naughtinesses nipped in the bud and had "lacked every opportunity to observe, much less to experience, in their surroundings anything sexual." They were so well brought up that their infantile sexual impulses had simply not had "the opportunity to get angry in the world of reality." According to Ferenczi the infantile phantasies of children in such an environment fall under the "primal repression" and so never reach consciousness. (See Dynamisms—Repression.) He maintains that a little sexual traumatism "not only does not damage but actually promotes later normality, particularly the normal activity of phantasy." On the other hand, he is careful to point out that the actual experiences "ought not to exceed a certain optimum; too much, too early, or too strong may bring about repression and with it a poverty of phantasy."

Ferenczi also speaks of the possibility of "over-successful" sphincter training leading to a lack of courage which he finds in neurotics to face the inevitable tension or pain associated with pregenital erotism. He also thinks that children make prohibitory identifications with the parents anxieties, and may result in a great tendency to an excessive fixation on the mother (who is apt to make the boy a substitute for the husband). Ferenczi claims that sons who grow up without a father are seldom normal in their sexual life, are inclined to be neurotic or homosexual. Death of a father may bring about excessive remorse for hostile death wishes and the need for punishment and atonement may persist throughout all later relationships.

(h) The presence or absence of brothers and sisters or playmates. Many opportunities are afforded for narcistic wounding through parental preferences. Opportunities for sexual experiment and enlightenment may influence sexual theories of the child. Opportunities for the discovery of anatomical sex differences will influence the development of the Castration Complex. Lack of playmates as outlets for erotic impulses may intensify the fixation on the mother or lead to excessive day dreaming trends. Freud says that spending a great deal of time with other children clearly enters into a child's normal development.

It seems to us that any student of psychoanalytic literature should have very clearly in mind the evolution of Freud's concept of the significance for normal and neurotic development of real experiences in early childhood. For the sake of clarifying the discrepancies which would seem to exist between Freud's earlier and more recent writings we trace briefly the historical development of his thought in this connection.

(1) In the beginning of his work Freud came to the conclusion that on the basis of his clinical findings he was justified in assuming an accidental infantile seduction experience or trauma as the starting point of neurotic development. By seduction he meant not only cases of assault on the part of adults but genital stimulation and coitus activities of various sorts both on the part of adults and other children. For a time his whole stress was laid on this early accidental traumatic experience.

(2) By degrees he came to believe that the uniformity with which his patients were able to recall memories of seduction was due to unconscious defense phantasies. The real experience, common to all children,

and thus "a severe sphincter-morality" may be set up "which can only be contravened at the cost of bitter self reproaches and punishment by conscience." Ferenczi calls attention to bad ways of weaning and prohibitions against obscene words as having possible pathogenic results.

Abraham points out that the forcing of a habit upon a child before he is psychically ready for it (that is, when he begins to transfer his narcism to objects) may mean that the child will respond through fear rather than love. His inner narcistic fixation will remain and there will be a permanent disturbance of the capacity to love.

Alexander believes that both excessive indulgence of the child's sexuality as well as severity and drastic intimidation on the part of the parent may both lead to pathogenic repression. He points out that spoiling makes sublimation superfluous and tends ultimately towards greater repression since infantile wishes must be finally abandoned. Drastic intimidation also hinders sublimation, since fear attaches to even the sublimated forms. In other words a cruel Super-ego is set up in either case; in the first instance, since punishment is not to be expected from the indulgent father, the sense of guilt associated with the Oedipus hostility to the father must be taken care of by self-punishment. In the case of the kind father, too, the sense of guilt may be intensified from the fact that his actual conduct gives no opportunity, as in the second instance, for rationalization of Oedipus hostility.

With regard to the stories told or read to children Freud points out that the child's unconscious phantasies may receive reinforcement from various well-known fairy tales. The story of Red-Riding Hood, for instance, may interest the child primarily because the children are taken from the wolf's body and this stimulates sexual curiosity. In one case (the Wolf-man) Freud claims that the hearing of stories from the New Testament opened up avenues of sublimation.

Freud is firmly convinced that sexual instruction and enlightenment should be given the child "at each stage of its inquiries." He warns against a home atmosphere of secrecy and mystery and says it is "important that children should never get the idea that one wants to make more of a secret of the facts of sexual life than of any other matter not

was simply autoerotic activities (masturbation), which might have come about quite spontaneously. At puberty the child tries to efface all recollection of his former autoerotism and so evolves phantasies of seduction which exalt the earlier memories to the level of object-love. At puberty also there is a tendency to sexualize earlier trivial experiences and this together with the fact that the masturbation may frequently have been stimulated by caresses and punishments would also explain the child's tendency to associate objects with his autoerotic activities. The traumatic element was thus deprived of importance and the stress laid upon the infantile sexuality.

(3) The emphasis thus shifted from accidental external factors to constitutional (which Freud declared he had never quite ignored), but at the same time the importance for unconscious phantasies of universal experiences inevitable in the family life of the child began to be seen. Fixations involving traumatic possibilities became significant.

(4) The question at issue was finally not whether the critical experiences were actual or phantasied but how did the child respond to them. Did he make efforts to banish from consciousness the memories of intolerable experiences? That is, did he resort to repression and cling to his fixations? The emphasis fell now upon repression or defense.

(5) Freud has now reached the place where he is inclined to lay much stress on phylogenetic inheritance as accounting for the origin and development of typical unconscious phantasies which come to light in neurotics. There are three experiences the memories of which are found to be constantly revived by neurotic patients, namely, seduction, coitus observations (primal scene), and castration fears. Though real experiences of this nature are quite possible and probably very frequent, Freud is convinced that even if the real event does not occur it will be "evolved out of hints and elaborated by phantasy." Thus for Freud the "structural plan" of the human individual, both normal and neurotic, includes an inherent store of unconscious experiences.

suited to their understanding." Progressive enlightenment, taking the period of the child's development into consideration, would prevent too intense curiosity and inevitable repression.

Ferenczi points out that the child can come to terms with all other external objects sooner than he can with his fellow creatures. One great difference between other objects of the external world and people is that the former never lie. For a long time the child is deprived of discovering errors in the statements of his parents because "they impress him so much from the beginning with their real and supposed omnipotence that he does not dare to doubt them"; also he is often prohibited from making efforts to convince himself of the correctness of adults' statements. Ferenczi contends that "innate tendency and educational influences co-operate" to bring about an attitude of blind belief on the part of the child.

The child's adaptation to adults is rendered still more difficult from the fact that their demands are not consistent and uniform. They will reward and acclaim manifestations of intelligence on the part of the child as long as these do not concern "sexual and religious questions or the authoritative position of the adults." The crippling effect of this is seen later in the type of personality which always succumbs to the influence of other persons or which displays a tendency to general inhibition of thought and to credulity.

SECTION FIVE

DYNAMICS AND DYNAMISMS

DYNAMICS AND DYNAMISMS

GENERAL DISCUSSION

The dynamics and dynamisms (ordinarily called mechanisms) of mental life as discovered and set forth by psychoanalysts are closely bound up with their theories of infantile sexuality. It is in connection with the handling of the early component sexual impulses that the various dynamisms, which all through the individual's existence unconsciously play a tremendously important part in mental life, are first developed and utilized.

Mental dynamisms can be best understood by keeping in mind as clearly as possible the parts or functions assigned by Freud to the Id, Ego, and Super-ego in the play and interplay of psychic life. His conception of the Id is a bundle of incoherent, unorganized cravings predominantly sexual (that is, on the level of organ gratification) and aggressive, and which demand various forms of motor discharge for complete satisfaction. Strivings of the Id brook no delay; they are bent upon immediate rash gratification, that is, prevention and relief of an over-amount of excitation, or "pain."

It must be remembered that in the beginning there is very little differentiation between the Id and the Ego; the Ego develops out of and continues to merge into the Id. What little organization the embryonic Ego takes on is devoted to securing outlets for the Id. Like the Id it is predominantly pleasure-loving, that is, receptive of Id strivings, and concerned very little with the possible consequences involved in their gratification. Ego and Id for a time tread the primrose path together.

From the very beginning, of course, the environment presents obstacles to primitive and immediate satisfactions. The Id and the

We strongly urge the adoption of the term "dynamism" in place of the more commonly used word "mechanism." We have long felt certain incongruities in the employment of the latter term and one of us, at an academic meeting of scientific people, heard some forceful criticisms and even amusement expressed concerning the taking over of the term "mechanisms," as in "mental mechanisms," by psychiatrists. Then, too, we note an occasional tendency on the part of psychoanalysts themselves to speak of dynamisms. An equation might be set up—Mechanics: Mechanisms:: Dynamics: Dynamisms. It is perfectly clear that mechanics cannot be under consideration in discussing mental life, while as for a mechanism, that, properly speaking, is the arrangement of the parts of a machine—a combination of objects not necessarily doing anything. To be sure, a mechanism is sometimes spoken of as a mechanical operation or action. Now psychiatry, and especially psychoanalysis, is particularly interested in the dynamics of mental life, in "moving forces and the laws which relate to them." Then, as a physicist might formulate it, a dynamism is a specific force operating in a specific manner or direction. This exactly fits the conception of displacement, repression, sublimation and the other specific processes by means of which the Ucs operates.

The whole subject of mental dynamics is tremendously important for the understanding of personality, as may be seen particularly in the discussion of various dynamisms. Since it cannot be emphasized too strongly that psychoanalysis has very largely busied itself with the consideration of what it calls the *fundamental urges,* by that meaning primitive, unmodified, primal, infantile, unsocialized desires and wishes, the methods by which these are taken care of become correspondingly significant.

elementary Ego attempt to avoid the "pain" of frustration and over-excitation by various adaptive devices and disguises, all of which strive to bring about motor discharge (that is, action) on the primitive organ-pleasure level. These dynamisms all continue to play a part in later adult mental life.

The Id is too incoherent and unorganized for any foresight or realization of the dangers which its blind strivings for immediate and unmodified impulse discharge are bound to bring about. The Id does not learn from experience. Throughout life its ultimate goal remains unchanged, namely, unmodified, even though disguised, libidinal satisfactions. Never of its own volition will it renounce its organ-pleasure aims, or attempt substitutive, that is, desexualized gratification.

The demands of reality and its own self-preservative needs force upon the gradually developing Ego a certain degree of separation from the Id. Freud, however, makes it very clear that there is no inherent opposition between the Ego and the Id. The Ego's great urge is for unity and harmony; thus, as it matures its chief task becomes to transform and desexualize some part of the libidinal energy, by which it serves both its own purposes and at the same time assists in preventing over-tension in the Id.

Throughout its dealings with the Id the Ego's own narcism must always be reckoned with. In the beginning narcistic gratifications are closely tied up with organ-pleasure and the Ego is thus receptive of the Id strivings. Freud seems to think that this association always continues to some extent. On the other hand, according to the extent to which the Ego comes to side with objective reality (or what it senses as reality), its narcism becomes associated with efforts to modify Id strivings or to deny them discharge.

Freud has recently concluded that the Ego's contacts with reality lead it to become aware of three typical danger situations which arise at different stages of the child's early development, and all of which threaten "pain," or a continuous state of helpless over-stimulation. These three danger situations are, (a) danger of loss of

love (which arises in the pre-genital stages), (b) danger of castration (which arises in the phallic stage), and (c) danger of loss of Super-ego approval (which arises at latency). Freud points out that the Ego is quite justified in fearing these dangers, but as a part of its development these fears should normally be left behind. The neurotic Ego acts as if these early danger situations still exist.

The more developed Ego may not be strong enough to exert itself positively and constructively as an ally of the Id when it senses the dangers threatening it. Then it may become panicky and employ various forms of defense, some of which are more like flight than attack and all of which are efforts to prevent or inhibit the discharge of the Id excitations. The utilization of defense dynamisms means that the Ego no longer feels itself in harmony with the Id, regards it to some degree as an enemy and refuses, at least partially, to act as mediator between the Id and reality. But a very sharp sundering of the Ego and the Id points to pathological developments.

All defense dynamisms are to be found in a moderate degree at work in the normal individual. Their excessive use, however, means that relatively little psychic energy is left for the molding of outer reality, that is, for bringing about situations favorable for the quantum of both direct and modified libidinal gratifications which the human organism normally demands. Freud admits that to some extent passion should be stifled and restrained; that is, that the autoplastic change of the individual has its place. Nevertheless, he points out, the supreme achievement of the Ego is to know when it is the part of wisdom to face and fight the world, that is, to make an alloplastic adaption. This, of course, implies that the Ego can discriminate well between inner and objective reality.

The average Ego is inclined somewhat to confound inner reality, that is, it fails to abandon completely its old fears. Also, normally the Id may cling to some one of its infantile desires or their derivatives (fixation). As a result both normal and neurotic

development is largely a compromise between Ego fears, denials and defenses, and Id strivings. The rôle of Super-ego as the chief incitor to defensive measures must, however, not be forgotten.

THE DYNAMISMS

The very specific processes by which the unconscious Ego attempts to take care of, or to defend itself against, Id urges, desires, wishes, are properly to be discussed under the head of dynamisms.

Dynamisms are various unconscious devices for the mastering of inner stimuli, that is, for eliminating or reducing tension. They are processes conceived as existing as a result of the activity of the pleasure and reality principles. Freud speaks of them as making paths which will ultimately put an end to or avoid "pain." Dynamisms are used by both normal individuals and neurotics, only the degree to which they are employed characterizing the two groups.

Dynamisms can be thought of as fulfilling any one of three functions: first, they may provide other than the original avenues for discharge of libido that has not been desexualized; second, they may bring about deflected and desexualized discharge in harmony with Ego standards; third, they may serve as barriers or "defenses" which partially or completely hold back unmodified libido from discharge. In psychoanalytic literature, however, these distinctions of classification are not widely adhered to. Earlier all dynamisms were viewed as defenses and still are so regarded by some psychoanalysts. But recently Freud has greatly clarified the concept of defense, apparently regarding only certain dynamisms as working specifically in this way.

Freud in *Inhibition, Symptom, and Anxiety* speaks of only five defense dynamisms—regression, repression, isolation, undoing, and reaction-formation; it is not clear that the term "defense" should be applied only to these; it appears to us that several other dynamisms, in part at least, have what he calls the "rebuffing tendency," which seems to be the essence of the defense process.

We have not included regression under dynamisms since it seems so clearly a characteristic of libidinal activity. As we have pointed out elsewhere (see Developmental Stages), Freud earlier conceived of regression as a libidinal property. In his later work he justifies regarding it as a dynamism since the Ego can call to its aid this (and other) Id "contrivances."

The established dynamisms of psychoanalysis are:
1. Displacement
2. Transference
3. Symbolization
4. Condensation
5. Unconscious phantasy
6. Repression
7. Reaction-formation (Reversal-formation)
8. Projection
9. Isolation
10. Undoing
11. Conversion
12. Introjection
13. Identification
14. Sublimation
15. Rationalization
16. Idealization
17. Dream-work

1. Displacement

Displacement is a term which is used with two meanings:

(a) Displacement is a process by which one idea may surrender to another the whole volume of its cathexis. This dynamism was first discovered in the study of dreams, and then was found to be a dominant characteristic in the obsessional neuroses where there is displacement of affect from that which is actually important to a triviality which may thus take on the coloring of great and urgent significance. But such displacement may also occur under the conditions of quite normal mental life. Jones says that in any case displacement means the replacement in the affective life of one idea by another which is more satisfactory or acceptable.

"The concept of displacement is based on the assumption that an affect has a certain autonomy."

Freud speaks of the displacement of object-choice as being frequent in dreams, where there occurs a looseness in the association which brings about far-fetched incongruities.

Jones emphasizes the fact that displacement plays a large part in every-day life where there is direction away from forbidden thoughts to socially acceptable activities; its function is to evade a painful complex, "associations between the primary and secondary conceptions is often of an exceedingly superficial order."

Jones (*Papers on Psycho-Analysis*) gives many trenchant illustrations of displacement as it occurs in the exaggeration of dreams and among neurotics, and also as it occurs in ordinary life.

Abraham mentions that the phenomenon of fetishism is due to a combination of partial repression and displacement. The latter is represented by the replacement of the idea and affect originally associated with one object by another, a shoe, for example, taking over the interest of the genitals, or underclothing taking over some of the values of the body or the skin.

An illustration of displacement in this sense is when self-reproach is associated with a conscious ideational content which does not in itself justify the intensity of the affect, as when self-reproach about a repressed sexual experience becomes attached in consciousness to a trivial dishonesty. This is brought about through "mistaken associations"—the substitute idea is suitable in some way or another for the displacing process, but only through superficial unconscious carrying over of some idea. It is this superficial associating quality of the process which renders conscious logical mental life powerless to deal with the situation.

(b) Freud has also used the term displacement in connection with the Id seeking only for gratification of its urges. It is very ready to utilize one pathway of discharge instead of another in order to prevent its own deprivation. Displacement in this sense appears to be merely the shifting or swerving of sexual instinctual energy from one pathway to another—the Id not being particular in its choice of a path, in contrast to the Ego standards which are implied in the concept of displacement first given.

An illustration of this is when the component instinct voyeurism meeting environmental frustration turns into exhibitionism, another component instinct.

The type of displacement given in the illustration under (a) is frequently seen in dementia praecox, Abraham says. The sense of guilt takes the form of delusion of having sinned, which is displaced with the sinfulness to some ideas of less original affective import, a phenomenon so exaggerated that it constitutes mental abnormality.

Erotogenic zone development normally involves displacement in the meaning given under (b). But when discharge on one zone is unacceptable to the Ego and gratification is attempted through another zone, displacement in the sense of that given under (a) has occurred. In psychoanalytic literature there is often reference to "displacement from below upward," meaning sometimes displacement from the genital to the oral zone, a concrete example of what Jones calls the "over-emphasis of the upper part of the body in general, interest in the lower half being repressed."

Critical reading of the literature leaves one with the feeling that the term displacement has been used in more than one sense; sometimes undoubtedly being employed in an ordinary and sometimes with a technical meaning. Under (a) displacement appears as somewhat of a defense dynamism. The second usage of the term indicates merely the shifting of instinctual energy from one pathway of discharge to another, the displacement occurring without any obstacle being in the way. If there were not this ready mobility fixation would occur.

2. *Transference*

Transference signifies shifting of feelings of love (erotic ta-thexes) from one object or person to another. The Id can also transfer its destructive cathexes, but the term transference has been used thus far in psychoanalytic literature strictly in reference to the erotic impulses.

In its simplest form transference connotes the tendency of the various sexual component instincts, and also of the sexual instinct in its completely matured form, to change the object any number of times. A capacity for transference, that is, for achieving sexual aim through various objects, is necessary for mental health. Inability to transfer involves object fixation.

In the beginning the Id transfers readily to any object which would give it some degree of satisfaction and would continue to do so, but the Ego attitudes very early enter into the situation. The Ego either accepts the Id's choices or being obliged to be more discriminatory with regard to reality adaptation, attempts to modify them in harmony with reality, or sets itself in opposition to and attempts to inhibit them.

Although many psychoanalysts use the term transference in the broader sense given here, Freud wishes to confine the use of the word to the physician-patient relationship established in psychoanalytic therapy. (For fuller discussion of transference, see Therapy.)

Freud himself insisting on confining the use of the term transference to the psychoanalytic therapeutic situation seems to utilize the word displacement for transference as here defined.

Transference is a form of displacement, the latter being the broader term, since it includes not only object, but aim or mode of pleasure-finding.

An illustration of transference of object-choice on the Id level is when the thumb takes the place of the nipple, and some other object replaces the thumb—the mode of pleasure-finding, sucking, remaining the same.

The transferences that lead to neurotic difficulties only occur when there has been some degree of fixation.

The phenomenon of transference is illuminated in Freud's remarkable essay on *Mourning and Melancholia.* In the former, when the love-object is lost, even though the "libido-position" is never willingly abandoned, bit by bit and with great expanse of energy "reality gains the day." "When the work of mourning is completed the Ego becomes free and uninhibited again." Other purposes and interests may be developed. In melancholia no such normal transference takes place. After perhaps a real loss or psychic injury the object-cathexis is abandoned, but the free libido is "withdrawn into the Ego and not united to another object." "Thus the shadow of the object fell upon the Ego." But this essay as a whole should be read for appreciation of other dynamisms that enter into the situation.

3. Symbolization

Symbolization according to psychoanalytic usage is an unconscious process built up on association and similarity whereby one object comes to represent or stand for (symbolize) another object, through some part, quality, or aspect which the two have in common. But the essence of symbolization is in the displacement of emotional values from one object to another. The resemblance is generally so slight or superficial that the conscious mind would overlook it. The recognition of the identity is so peculiar to and characteristic of the childish, primitive mental processes of the unconscious mind that the resemblances are foreign to the conceptions or perceptions of the conscious Ego. Symbolization is utilized as a dynamism only in the interests of wish-fulfilment—some urge is thereby given disguised gratification. In this sense it is very normal, but it also plays a big part in compromise formation.

Jones points out that symbolism differs from all other forms of indirect representation in two respects, and that these are the two cardinal characteristics of the process: (1) the process is completely unconscious, that is, incapable of becoming conscious; (2) the libidinal cathexis of the symbolized idea "has not, in so far as the symbolism is concerned, proved capable of that modification in quality denoted by the term 'sublimation.' "

Through the historical approach to the study of the human mind we learn that symbolization is a psychological principle evidently based upon the structural make-up or the configurative tendencies of mental life. Symbolization has a rich setting in folk-lore and in the practices of primitive peoples, with continuance of many specific connotations through the ages so that Groddeck says, "Man is at the mercy of the symbol and individual symbolism is predetermined by a common heritage of symbols." Stereotypy in symbolism is due to certain uniformities of development of human minds; thus symbolism is representative of fundamental and perennial interests of mankind. (Ernest Jones, in *Psychoanalysis,* has an especially good chapter on The Theory of Symbolism.)

It is upon the background of this principle that symbolizing has developed as a dynamism. One member of the resemblance couple or pair remains part of a complex in the unconscious. It is on account of this that many symbols, without the associations dug up through psycho-analytical process, seem so far-fetched.

In symbolization the individual is quite unaware of the meaning of the symbol he has employed; indeed, he is often unaware of the fact that he has employed one at all. To his conscious mind the symbol is not a symbol; it is reality in and of itself.

Sexual symbols, on account of the interest inherent in sexual functions, etc., and on account of the accompanying common taboos and repressions, comprise the vast majority of all symbols. It is said that there are more symbols for the male sex organ than for all other symbolized material. Freud states that the number of things that find symbolic representation in dreams is not great. Jones thinks the total number of ideas symbolized is very limited, perhaps about a hundred, representing the most primitive ideas and interests, which retain their original importance in the Ucs throughout life. They may be grouped as ideas concerning the self, immediate blood relatives, the phenomena of birth, of love, of death. The number of symbols themselves mount into the thousands. (But see discussions of symbolization under Dream-work and Dream-formation.)

4. Condensation

Condensation is a process by which an idea "may appropriate the whole cathexis of several other ideas."

This process is especially outstanding in dreams. As an example of condensation, Jones points out that a person in a dream "may be constituted by the fusion of the memories of several different actual persons," either by combining different traits of each person involved, or "by making prominent the traits common to different persons and neglecting the ones not common to them."

Condensation also takes place as part of the process of conversion-hysteria where an area of innervation appears to absorb the whole cathexis.

In phantasy life several phantasies may be expressed simultaneously by means of the same material through the process of condensation.

Brill defines Condensation as a fusion of events, pictures, and elements of speech.

Jung points out how unconscious satisfaction can be secured through the symbolical nature and content of certain occupations.

We may remember that unconscious mental processes are unverbalized. The thought-life of primitive peoples is of a similar kind and hence resembles phantasy. The universality of typical phantasies (also typical dreams and typical symptoms) and the fact that they cannot be given historical or associative interpretations during analysis, but, as Mitchell says, "can be understood only in the light of knowledge of the meaning of symbols which has been obtained from other sources" has inclined Freud to the view that the typical characteristics of phantasies "common to large numbers of people are derived from the experience of the race and can be explained only as a racial inheritance"— that is, these "primal phantasies" are of phylogenetic origin.

5. Unconscious Phantasy

Unconscious Phantasy is composed of images or representations existing in or elaborated in the unconscious mental life and, as such, is free from the restraints of reality. In considering phantasying from the psychoanalytic point of view, it is necessary to keep in mind that complicated, even organized, psychical processes may take place without coming into consciousness. Perhaps it is enough to say in proof of this that even a moderate amount of psychoanalysis brings out the fact that definite formulations of wishes have been elaborated in the mind while the individual has been unaware of them.

Great importance is attached by psychoanalysts to early phantasy life, such as occurs perhaps between the ages of three and five years. It begins with even some earlier vague ideas or wishes. According to Freud these take on more or less typical forms, quite regardless of the specific environment or real experiences of the child. For example, both the Oedipus and castration situations which must be passed through by all children are really based on phantasy rather than reality. The father and mother imagos need resemble only to a slight degree the real parental persons. (The term Imago, or image, earlier more current in psychoanalytic literature, is used to indicate a specific holding or building up within the unconscious mind of a representation or idealization of reality, most commonly as related to personalities, for example, the "mother imago.") The very common unconscious sense of guilt also is tied up with and part of phantasying. Freud states that the unconscious phantasies of children can scarcely be distinguished from the processes of conscious thought.

The student of recent psychoanalytic theory hardly needs to be more than reminded of the fact that if unconscious phantasies are the product of organized mental processes they must be developed in the unconscious Ego.

At one place Freud introduces the subject of phantasy-making with comments on the general tendency in mental life to economies; sources of pleasure are held on to and with difficulty renounced. With the introduction of the reality-principle phantasy as a mode of thought activity was split off.

Psychoanalysts believe that in children there are many typical unconscious phantasies the reactions to which are observable not only in dreams but in the child's questionings. Some of these unconscious phantasies concern themselves with the theories about the origin of babies and their methods of birth. Freud thinks that among the unconscious phantasies probably of all human beings "there is one which is seldom absent"—that of watching parents in sexual intercourse, though the nature of the physical act is not known and may be merely thought to be that of kissing or lying in bed together.

Freud points out that autoerotism makes possible the retention for some time of phantasy in place of satisfaction through the sexual object. Both autoerotism and the satisfactions of phantasy life make for delay on the part of the sexual instincts in subordinating themselves to the reality-principle.

In her work with children Klein goes on the assumption that the conscious phantasies which children reproduce in abundance are to be taken as more or less modified re-representations of unconscious phantasies, and the child's symbolic play activities are also to be interpreted in this way. Klein claims that when she interprets the child's phantasies and play behavior in terms of phylogenetic unconscious phantasies she is able to establish a contact with the child's unconscious. The fact that the child reacts favorably to her interpretations, she thinks, establishes the fact that in his play and phantasy activities he is abreacting.

Psychoanalysts speak of both conscious and unconscious phantasies. (For conscious and preconscious phantasies, see Phantasy-formation.) Freud says that unconscious phantasies "have either always been unconscious and formed in the unconscious, or more often, they were once conscious phantasies, day-dreaming" which have been repressed into the unconscious.

Psychoanalytic knowledge of unconscious phantasies has come through clinical experiences, studies of dreams, and through the more recent development of child analysis. Investigation seems to prove that the unconscious phantasies of young children (the primal phantasies of Freud) center not only about the Oedipus and castration complexes, but also about the phenomena of birth, notions of procreation, assault or seduction, and as particularly emphasized by Rank, about the bliss of intrauterine existence.

While Freud at first emphasized that childish phantasies of these types (and sometimes allied experiences) form the bases of neurosis, he came later to believe that such phantasies were common to normal children. Since they are universal and typical they must be obtained from some source and probably are to be explained partly through the fact of the racial inheritance of ideas. They are the common phylogenetic possession of every individual by which he "reaches beyond his own life into the experiences of antiquity" and fills in the "gaps of individual truth with prehistoric truth."

An illustration from her cases is that of the little girl who when analysed at less than three years of age was carrying out an obsessional ceremonial with a toy elephant regularly placed by the bed of a doll tucked in to go to sleep. The play phantasy was that the elephant would prevent the doll-child from getting up and going into its parents' bedroom and injuring them or taking something from them. But this was based on a deeper phantasy, according to Klein, developed before the child was two years old when she had wished to usurp her mother's place with her father and "to steal away the child with which her mother was pregnant" and to injure both parents. In her play phantasy the elephant was really the father who prevented such things—it was the Superego.

Anna Freud (*Technic of Child Analysis*) hardly agrees with Klein's conclusions and thinks that much of the conscious phantasy and play content of the child might be accounted for by its actual observations and experiences.

Psychoanalysts have discovered that symptoms can be traced back to repressed phantasies, as well as to memories of actual experiences. Mitchell says, "although phantasies have no material reality, they have psychical reality, and in the field of the neuroses psychical reality is all-important."

In the transference neurosis the relation to reality is not really broken off. Imaginary objects—a combination of memories and phantasy—are substituted for the real object. If these phantasies become, as Freud says, "over-luxuriant, and over-powerful" the necessary conditions for an outbreak of neurosis are established. Varendonck neatly says that hysterical symptoms are directly dependent, not upon actual memories, but upon the phantasies built upon the basis of memories.

Later unconscious phantasies, continuing as they do in both normal and neurotic individuals, arise on the basis of unrelinquished ideas or wishes. The wishes are renounced in so far as actual gratification is concerned, but enough libido remains attached to them to give rise to phantasies which continue in a state of repression. (Whether or not earlier unconscious phantasies are considered all to partake of this same nature is not clear; we find no statement on the point.)

With the onset of adolescence, unconscious phantasies concern themselves particularly with the revival of the Oedipus complex— "the family romance," as Freud sometimes calls it. About the same time some aspects of this give rise to the well-known rescue or "saving-life" conscious phantasies—they are displaced from the parent on to some other person and thus can enter consciousness.

Helene Deutsch (*Psychoanalyse der Weiblichen Sexualfunktionen*) pays special attention to the unconscious phantasies of the adolescent girl: (a) the parthenogenetic phantasy, so named from the biological analogy, the essence of which is the desire to produce a child all by herself, (b) the street girl phantasy, which is concerned with the desire to give herself to many men, (c) the assault or rape phantasy, perhaps not so common.

In the background of neurotic illness psychoanalysts frequently find a "wish for illness" which must be developed in the form of an unconscious phantasy since the patient is certainly unaware of it and, of course, would repudiate it. The existence of this phantasy does not seem so extraordinary when we realize the definite gain (particularly the epinosic gain of Freud) that accrues to the individual in some sense. The motives for being ill on an economic basis and for the sake of gaining attention are well-recognized by physicians, but there are deeper psychical motives founded on unconscious conflicts and their phantasied solutions which are only to be ascertained by psychoanalysis. On account of these deep phantasies resistance to treatment is frequently to be observed.

If the question of the extent of unconscious phantasy life is raised, it may be interesting to regard the other dynamisms as specific ways in which phantasies develop. Projection, introjection and identification, for example, have been described as phantasy processes.

Another point not altogether clear is whether in the common animal phobias of children unconscious phantasy is involved. It is Freud's idea that large animals are unconscious representatives of the father of whom the child has unconscious fear. An animal phobia, Freud says, by its obstinacy to conscious influences betrays its origin in the unconscious.

The same question arises concerning the death wishes of the unconscious, of which Freud speaks. The death phantasies so common in children are more conscious and more directly in the nature of a wish fulfilment.

Apropos of the "saving life" phantasy, Freud thinks that the underlying unconscious meaning varies according to the sex of the rescuer. In the male, saving the mother means giving her a child; in the female, saving a life means begetting a child, etc. (For other points on his paper, *A Special Type of Object Choice* should be consulted.)

H. Deutsch thinks that unconscious adolescent phantasies are common for all girls, normal and neurotic. These begin at about the time of puberty and increase in intensity, until with maturity there comes possibility of sex satisfaction in reality.

The analysis of dreams affords one of the best evidences of unconscious mental activity that sometimes amounts to unconscious phantasying, repressed material being utilized in dreams. (See Dream Formation.) Still more striking is the way in which the existence of unconscious phantasies comes to light in the study of neuroses. Freud speaks of the "illusory strength" of instinct which terrifies the neurotic as being due to the uninhibited development of it in phantasy. Unconscious repressed phantasies are recognized as "preliminary phases in the formation of both dreams and symptoms." Hysterical symptoms are based on unconscious phantasies made manifest largely by their conversion into physical phenomena.

In the analysis of neurotic patients it has been found that the same phantasies occur repeatedly and center oftenest about seduction, the castration and Oedipus ideas, and the witnessing of parental intercourse. Freud has concluded that "childhood experiences of this kind are in some way necessarily required by the neurosis . . . if they can be found in real events, well and good; but if reality has not supplied them, they will be evolved out of hints and elaborated by phantasy." Freud is even inclined to think that these phantasy experiences are sometimes in direct opposition to the actual experiences.

Her interpretation of the parthenogenetic phantasy makes it have its roots in the Oedipus and castration complexes and contain several wish fulfilments; it satisfies one phase of the wish and guilt feeling rooted in the Oedipus in that it denies the wish for a child by the father; the castration wound and penis loss are compensated for by the phantasy assertion, "What man can do, I can do, too." Sublimated, the phantasy expresses itself in a striving for independence in intellectual production of a masculine kind. It is characteristic of women who over-value the masculine rôle and assume it by striving for intellectual goals which they consider belong to men. Sometimes this unconscious phantasy is carried out by taking as a possible father the first man who presents himself.

The "street girl" phantasy arises also in the Oedipus and castration situations and gives the outward expression of disappointment, "I will go as a prostitute on the street and give myself to every man. If my father will not have me, I will throw myself at anyone." There enters also an element of wish for revenge for supposed castration, a tendency to take from all men something belonging to their body only to despise it through not giving it any love value.

The so-called rape phantasy is rooted in the idea that the sex act is a matter of violence against woman by man. It minimizes the guilt feeling, since one is not responsible for what is done by violence; in this way there can be wish fulfilment without conscience. This phantasy evidences itself in the fear of robbers and in pathological lying where there is false accusation of rape.

It has been pointed out that one of the most extraordinary evidences of unconscious phantasies is to be found in the women's wards of hospitals for mental patients where one can often observe even the most refined women giving vent to sexual and other taboo ideas that certainly could not have been part of their conscious mental life or experiences.

6. Repression

Repression is the exclusion of painful and unpleasant material from consciousness and from motor expression.

The proof that Repression is a widely and powerfully operative mental process was discovered through psychoanalytic procedure. When therapeutic aid is given the Ego vast amounts of material unknown to consciousness can be drawn up from the Ucs. Not only repressed ideas then become known, but also the fact that strong impulses were connected with them. Some of the ideas, it is found, were recognized as having appeared in consciousness earlier and had been thrust down into the unconscious by the process which Freud names Repression.

A first question may well be, what is repressed? The answer to this requires consideration of the content of consciousness. Ideas which form the main content are carriers of instinct-strivings. Freud speaks of this combination of idea with striving or impulse as an "instinct-presentation," by this meaning an idea or group of ideas which has cathexis from the mental energy pertaining to an instinct and hence derived from the Id. "An instinct (an instinct-striving) can never be an object of consciousness—only the idea that represents the instinct." "If the instinct did not attach itself to an idea or manifest itself as an affective state we should know nothing about it."

When Freud says that Repression is essentially a process affecting ideas this must be understood in connection with other statements made by him. "The essence of the process of Repression lies in preventing the ideational presentation of an instinct (impulse) from becoming conscious." "To suppress the development of affect is the true aim of Repression." As will be seen later the result of Repression may be different as it influences the fate of either ideas or the strivings (perceived in consciousness as effects, emotions, or feelings) which were connected with them.

Repression keeps from consciousness both material that never was conscious (primal Repression), as well as pushes conscious or preconscious material into the unconscious Ego or the Id (after-

Students of the important topic of Repression should prepare themselves by reading first the historical aspects of the development of the concept, such as appear in the earlier *Collected Papers* of Freud, and in particular should digest well his papers on *Repression* and *The Unconscious* which appeared in 1915. Then they may well pass on to certain illuminating passages in *The Problem of Lay-Analyses* and finally study with great care the horizon-enlarging monograph, *Hemmung, Symptom und Angst.*

(No careful student of psychoanalytic literature can doubt the difficulty which we have experienced in attempting to organize and elucidate the theory of the process of Repression. We have taken the best statements we could find and have largely dealt only with the conceptions of the founder of psychoanalysis. No little confusion exists because of loose terminology and of the introduction of the later topographic and economic theories. The latter, however, have for us pointed the way to clearer understanding than would have been possible from the earlier statements concerning Repression. Freud insists on the extraordinary intricacy of the factors of Repression which have to be taken into consideration. It was the difficulty of explaining these factors in terms of the Ucs and the Cs which drove him to his newer theories of the Ego–Id–Super-ego relationship. Certain confusions in the writings of other psychoanalysts are obvious. If we ourselves are wholly correct in every detail it will be a surprise to us, but the only way to future consistency in up-building psychoanalytic theory is through such an organized presentation of this part of the structure).

Repression is such a foundation-stone in the structure of psychoanalytic theory and practice that, Freud states, "it is possible to take Repression as a center and to bring all the elements of psychoanalytic theory into relation with it." Every student can readily see that it is one of the unique discoveries of psychoanalysis.

expulsion). Freud speaks of the latter as Repression proper. He makes it plain that most Repressions with which psychoanalysts have to do are cases of this after-expulsion which pre-supposes the existence of primal or archaic repressions which are exerting their influence on the newer situation.

Since, according to psychoanalytic theory, there is denial of entry into consciousness of some archaic ideas attached to instinct-strivings, we must ask then at what age or stage of development Repression begins to take place. The answer seems to be that since Repression is a function of the Ego, it is only with the gradual development of the Ego that any Repression at all occurs and that the evidences of Repression, at least the intensive evidences, such as outbursts of anxiety, only show themselves after there is differentiation of the Super-ego. But Freud expresses himself as unable to judge whether the appearance of the Super-ego creates the border between primal Repression and after-expulsion. In emphasizing the fact that too little is as yet known of the background factors of Repression, Freud states that it is easy to fall into the danger of over-estimating the rôle of the Super-ego in Repression.

Why does Repression occur? So far as primal Repression is concerned, Freud suggests that excessive strength of excitation from an instinct-stimulus and weaknesses of protection against the stimulus may be the first occasion for a Repression. At later stages of development there is resistance on the part of the Ego to an instinctual impulse which may cause mental conflict or struggle between instinct and resistance to instinct even in the fullest light of consciousness. Repression proceeds from the Ego either through its own perception of pain or "perchance in the service of the Super-ego." The Ego defensive activity ensuing is sometimes spoken of as an attempt at flight by the Ego. The resistance—the opposition to the instinct-presentation, the impulse of which has been incited by the Id—results from operation of the pleasure-pain principle. When, in its combination of idea plus impulse, the instinct-presentation causes much more pain than pleasure, the Ego can use one of its methods of defense against it. If it employs

Freud demonstrates the mobility of his own mental processes by the growth of his ideas concerning Repression. Earlier it played a greater part in his conceptions of what took place when the individual in his mental life felt himself endangered. But since through further researches and development of theory other dynamisms have come to light, there has been "contraction of the notion of Repression." Freud now regards Repression as only one of the defense technics which the Ego utilizes. It is only a single representative of the defenses which the Ego uses to protect itself against impulse claims on the part of the Id.

Concerning the content of consciousness, which is a main consideration for understanding the theory of Repression, it should be stated that according to the Freudian theory instinct-impulses or strivings can only find representation in consciousness in the form of emotion, feelings, or affects. Conversely, for emotions, feelings, and affects to be unconscious is out of the question. It is of the essence of an emotion that it should enter consciousness. "There are no unconscious affects in the sense in which there are unconscious ideas." It appears then that with Repression emotions, feelings, and affects are turned back to become again merely instinct strivings.

In the present stage of the development of psychoanalytic theory, the process of Repression must be conceived of in terms of Super-ego Ego and Id functions as well as of the conscious and unconscious realms of mental life. While the point does not seem to be explicitly made, yet it would seem that Repression may take place through the activities of both the conscious and unconscious Ego. Hence, Repression is not merely a matter of thrusting material out of the Cs or Pcs—the conscious Ego may repress into the unconscious Ego, or if the thrust is strong enough into the Id, and the unconscious Ego may repress into the Id. But we are obliged to state that even Freud makes no clear statement about this whole matter.

It should be noted that Repression is not the only means of dealing with an impulse perceived by the Ego to be dangerous or unpleasant. In particular, Freud recently emphasizes the use which the Ego makes of Regression for the same purpose; not that Regression does away with the eventual need of Repression. Then also Isolation, Undoing, and Reaction-formation are directly utilizable.

Repression the Ego protects itself by refusing to entertain in its own organization the pain-producing idea. Repression is not essentially a result of tension being raised to an unbearable degree; it is rather the result of the growth of the power of avoiding relative pain as set over against relative pleasure; the pleasure of certain instinct-gratifications may simply be irreconcilable with other claims and purposes. Nor does Repression mean that satisfaction to an impulse is denied when it is repressed.

In speaking of fear and anxiety, Freud recently states that it is only in the organization of the Ego that fear can develop, and that processes frequently are set going in the Id which give rise to fear on the part of the Ego. This leads to the probable fact that the earliest Repressions together with the majority of the later ones are motivated through the Ego's fear of individual strivings in the Id.

What happens when Repression takes place? In primal Repression the particular ideational content persists unaltered with the instinct qualities remaining attached to it. Even primal Repression demands continuous effort to guarantee its persistence, and anticathexis in the Ego is the only source of energy utilizable for maintaining primal Repression.

An outlay of energy is necessary for all Repression, primal or later. The Ego has to set up a counter-charge to inhibit portions of the Id, and this, very naturally, to some extent impoverishes the Ego. Even what takes place when there is after-expulsion, a thrusting of an idea out of consciousness or preconsciousness, requires anticathexis.

In later Repression a severance takes place between the impulse and the idea to which it belongs and "each then fulfills its separate destiny." It is necessary to follow up the fate of each quite separately. The idea, repressed into the unconscious Ego or the Id remains as an unconscious formation. "The idea then remains without cathexis, or receives cathexis from the Ucs, or retains the unconscious (archaic?) cathexis which it previously had." Thus the repressed idea may be very capable of action and may make re-

In one place Freud says, "Repression is a preliminary phase of condemnation," but when he expresses himself more clearly he makes a sharp differentiation between Repression and Condemnation, making the latter a conscious, rational process. Thus Repression is merely a "forerunner of the later normal condemning judgment," in the sense, evidently, of occurring for the most part in an early stage of development.

The Ego, in its repressive faculty, works sometimes at the behest of the Super-ego—the unconscious conscience—as well as under the influence of the reality principle, the activities of libidinal urges not fitting in with the standards and requirements either of the Super-ego (the individual's ideals) or of the socialized world.

It may be argued that in any final sense the dynamics of Repression are hedonic in character. Reich says that external frustration and the anxiety it produces sets the process of Repression in motion, and inner frustration, or the functioning of the Super-ego, maintains it.

In conversation, the specific inquiry has been made by us concerning the possibility of successful Repression. Many leaders among the psychoanalysts assert its frequency; Alexander, for instance, insists that in all of us an enormous amount of Repression has been carried out successfully from a practical standpoint.

In writings widely separated by the passage of time Freud speaks of the repressed being "free as a bird" away from Ego control and that repression does not withhold from consciousness "all the derivatives of what was primarily repressed." If the derivatives, owing to the process of distortion or an account of a number of intermediate associations, are sufficiently removed from the repressed instinct-presentation, they have free access to consciousness. Repression acts in a highly specific manner in each instance; "every single derivative of the repressed may have its peculiar fate."

newed attempts to penetrate consciousness. Not only the original archaic instinct-impulse may remain attached to the idea, but also other impulses in or derived from the Id may be gathered to it. Repression does not hinder the idea from further activities, from "putting forth derivatives and instituting connections." There is an "attraction exercised by what was originally repressed upon everything with which it can establish a connection." This explains the "unchecked and luxuriant" development of parts of an instinct-presentation withdrawn by Repression from conscious influence.

The fate of the instinctual impulse, formerly connected with the repressed idea, is not so clear. The older conception that it simply was thrust down into the Ucs, and remained there indefinitely and unchanged has been much altered. It would seem that by circuitous routes and associations it may obtain various forms of discharge and substitute-gratifications, such as are to be found in symptom-formation.

The charge of impulse in the instinct-presentation finds proportionate expression according to its quantity and has its fate either in complete repression, or it "appears in the guise of an affect of a particular qualitative tone," or it becomes anxiety. Writing evidently of the second of these three possibilities, Freud suggests, "it is quite possible that the cathexis withdrawn from the idea is the very one used for anti-cathexis."

Taking it altogether it appears that the fate of the instinct-impulse is more important, at least it frequently is, than the fate of the repressed idea. Freud made much of the somewhat round-about process by which fear and anxiety arise as the result of Repression—and this is only when the impulse part of the instinct-presentation is not successfully repressed. But this was an earlier concept that recently has been completely changed by Freud. It now appears that anxiety or fear precedes and is the cause of Repression.

At this point a very important general fact should be distinctly understood. That successful Repression does very frequently take place is often indicated or connoted in psychoanalytic literature.

In spite of his picturesque phrasing, Freud does not cover the point concerning the part played by the unconscious Ego in the drama of Repression. Even recently he writes frequently of Repression merely as into the Ucs, and this, of course, includes the unconscious Ego. He leaves us with very little information about the relative degree of organization of the conscious and unconscious Ego. If, as we suspect, Repression may be into the unconscious Ego as well as into the Id we have little inkling of what "the laws that reign in the realm of the Ucs" are in that region, as over against the laws of the Ucs reigning in the Id.

An important matter to consider is that through the diversified possibilities of the process of Repression one may have some of the best qualities of personality and character arising as the result of repression. As Freud puts it, through the study of Repression it becomes comprehensible that even the preferred ideals of life may have their origin in the same perceptions and experiences which concerned materials or affairs greatly abhorred. Many illustrations could be given of this by any careful student of human life, but Freud merely offers in connection with this statement a slight observation concerning the origin of a fetish. In such a case the original instinct was split in two, one part undergoing Repression while the remainder undergoes idealization.

Jones holds that primal Repression is more important for personality-formation than the Repression of material which was once in consciousness. The cultural process (the activity of the Reality-principle) is early and constantly making for Repression in the developing individual and often both emotional values and ideas are under ban. The early unconscious material that has to be repressed is made up predominantly of infantile sexual phantasies and wishes based on pleasurable sexual experiences.

Therapeutic interest is naturally claimed almost entirely by cases of unsuccessful Repression. It may be unfortunate for psychology but Freud thinks that the process of successful Repression will, for the most part, elude study. When the Ego, making the pain signal, attains its objective of repressing the instinct-presentation, or what is most essential, repressing in particular the instinct-stimulus, "we learn nothing of how this is brought about."

The Ego not only initiates Repression as the result of perceptions of danger from without and unpleasant situations arising within itself, but is also considerably affected itself by the Repression which it carries out. Through deeper Repression the Ego injures the Id, but in doing so renounces some of its own sovereignty. Notwithstanding its own supposed weakness in its relation to the Id it demonstrates its own power over the Id when it gives "the signal of pain." In the case of any Repression the Ego must weaken itself to a certain extent by the persistent outlay of energy which continued Repression evidently often requires.

With regard to the material more deeply repressed the Ego closes itself against the Id while it remains accessible to the influence of the Super-ego. But it is on account of "the tormenting criticism of the Super-ego" concerning the matter of Repression that sometimes a sense of guilt arises in the Ego.

The amount of alteration which the Ego undergoes as the result of Repression depends naturally upon the amount of resistance to the re-appearance of what has been repressed, and also upon the amount of strength the repressed may have acquired from Id sources.

Sometimes coming to the aid of the repressive process there is reaction-formation in the Ego. This constitutes an alteration of the Ego. This may be perceived in the psychoanalytic attempt at therapy when the fact of resistance comes to light as a strengthening of "the antithesis of the repressing impulse-direction." The resistance then presupposes the phenomenon of counter-investment. In some instances there is such an antithetical development of sympathy, conscientiousness, purity.

Writing of the fate of the repressed, evidently as concerns any single idea or impulse, Freud says that one possibility is that "in the form of an unrecognizable substitute the isolated urge penetrates to the Ego and to consciousness, presenting itself in what is known as a symptom." This return of the repressed is seen very strikingly in the obsessions and in paranoia, as well as in other symptom-formation.

Further proof of the process of Repression is found in the direct results of psychoanalytic therapy. As Freud states it, when, during the analysis, aid is furnished to the Ego enabling it to abolish its Repressions, it regains power to some extent over the Id and then can allow "the impulses to run their course as if the old danger-situations no longer existed."

Concerning the period of life at which Repressions mainly take place, Alexander definitely says that most Repressions take place in childhood; the adult does not condemn everything which he repressed as a child. "The general reactions of the child's Ego (relatively undeveloped as compared with the instincts) to a great part of the claims of instinct, especially to certain aggressive and genital sexual tendencies, is defence (Repression)." "Thus the Ego protects itself not only against the painful consequences of an eventual instinct satisfaction (disappointment and painful experiences) but also against the anxiety which would develop in connection with the becoming conscious of the instinct representatives and memory pictures of previously miscarried attempts."

The repressions of later life are only possible in regard to derivatives or other connections of the primordial repressions which take place in infancy.

In order to get the full meaning of the significance and process of Repression it is necessary to piece together not only a great deal that Freud has set forth in different places but also the illuminating additions that other authors have made to the theory.

7. Reaction-Formation

Reaction-formation, sometimes called Reversal-formation is the development in the Ego of conscious socialized attitudes and interests which are the antithesis of certain infantile unsocialized trends which continue to persist in the unconscious. That is, there is only an apparent conformity to the reality principle. Freud speaks of reaction-formations being "deceptive," "insecure and constantly threatened by the impulse which lurks in the unconscious."

Reaction-formation is a defense dynamism which is frequently employed as an auxiliary to repression. Freud speaks of it as an erection of "barriers" or "dams." In ambivalence conflicts especially the Ego is apt to resort to an intensification of conscious love in order to suppress the hatred. The two attitudes, Freud points out, often exist side by side in the child until the attempt of the hostility to penetrate into consciousness may "give an impetus to an excess of devotion."

Like all other defense dynamisms reaction-formation is only significant for pathogenesis when the anti-cathexis or counter-investment made by the Ego takes an exaggerated form. In moderation reaction-formation trends have a social value, but in regard to personality-formation it must be remembered that the Ego alteration is after all only a seeming one, serving to conceal underlying opposing impulses, which may have played a much larger rôle in the development than is apparent on the surface. Freud suggests that there is a certain hypocrisy about reaction-formation.

Some illustrations of the workings of reaction-formation may be given: a hostile wish against the parent may show itself in excessive anxiety about him; in the case of an animal phobia the feared object has been originally a source of pleasure; an otherwise unaccountable disgust reaction to being kissed in adult life may be traceable to association with an originally pleasurable sexual activity which was suppressed by the formation of repulsion.

Jones calls reaction-formation a "correlative of sublimation" and points out that through reaction-formation a practical equilibrium may be attained which is of considerable stability. Such personalities, he says, "have what is popularly called a reserve of mental and moral force with which they can meet disappointments, difficulties, and emergencies of various kinds in life . . . their capacity for readjustment to radically new situations is fairly elastic."

In approaching the study of personality it should be pointed out that psychoanalysts claim that it is possible to distinguish between personality characteristics which are the result of reaction-formation and those which follow upon sublimation. It is obviously important not to misinterpret estimable behavior trends (such as philanthropy or strong love of justice), which in some cases are genuine sublimation, but which in other cases may indicate exactly the opposite underlying behavior tendencies. For example, a fundamentally cruel child may develop an exaggerated sympathy and tenderness with over-sensitivity and horror for pain and suffering.

Where there is sublimation there is resolution of conflicts; in reaction-formation this is not the case, and as the psychoanalysts put it, there is always danger of a "return of the repressed."

Reaction-formations are clearly observable in compulsion neurosis, and Freud points out that these characteristics are exaggerations of normal ones developed in the latency period. The "anal character" is largely built up through reaction-formations, shame and disgust arising on the basis of intense anal interests.

The relation of reaction-formation to repression is, according to Freud, a protective one, the latter reaction involving a "counter-fixation." This counter-fixation becomes tangible when there is a strengthening of the situation which is the antithesis to the direction of the repressed impulse and may show itself, for example, in sympathy, conscientiousness, purity.

One of the outstanding characteristics of the so-called "anal character" is orderliness. This is believed to be a reaction-formation against the infantile execretory interests and activities.

8. *Projection*

Projection is a defensive process under sway of the pleasure principle whereby the Ego thrusts forth on the external world unconscious wishes and ideas which, if allowed to penetrate into consciousness, would be painful to the Ego.

Freud explains the dynamism of projection as follows: The organism orients itself in the beginning by means of both inner and outer perceptions. External reality is recognized as a perception which can be avoided or altered by motor activity. Inner perceptions, it is discovered, cannot be thus made to disappear and the individual wishes "to be equipped with a similar weapon against the often merciless claims of his instincts." Accordingly, he displaces outward or projects all that becomes troublesome from within. This externalization of an internal menace makes possible either attack or flight, just as in the case of a real external danger.

Projection is one of the first defensive or protective measures employed by the young child, according to Ferenczi. When he first attempts to adapt to reality the child makes efforts to preserve his own narcism. His realization that omnipotence does not dwell within himself leads him to ascribe it to the persons about him who minister to his desires and obey, as he interprets it, his magic gestures and words. Thus, while relinquishing his own all-powerfulness he projects it upon others.

Reaction-formation may be considered a compromise-formation since it is pointed out by certain psychoanalytic writers that the development of the estimable characteristic not only serves as a cover or concealment for the undesirable wish, but may also offer an opportunity for its indirect expression. Rado points out that in the case of exaggerated tenderness of a mother for her child, not only is ambivalence atoned for, but also through maternal over-tenderness and solicitude (tormenting love) sadistic desires may gain an outlet.

Freud (The Ego and the Id) speaks of the Super-ego as representing "an energetic reaction-formation against Id choices."

Alexander speaks of the important part played by the Ego in the process of projection. The Ego yields to the Id to the point of falsifying perceptions of the real world and of reshaping reality in harmony with Id tendencies. Projection thus resembles the paranoic process, which Alexander says is "nothing else than a disavowal or falsification of inner and external reality."

Alexander gives an instance of what he calls the "paranoid mechanism"—the projection of a conflict. A man with dishonest tendencies becomes tremendously concerned with keeping a close watch on others, customers and employees, to see that they do not rob his employer. A double projection is involved; the Ego-ideal and the repressed part of the personality are both externalized and the conflict fought through on the outside.

Both Freud and Ferenczi point out that projection is a very common process in the normal individual. Freud speaks of it as the common tendency to refer the causes of certain of one's own unpleasant sensations to the external world, instead of regarding them as belonging to one's self, as is commonly done when others are under consideration. For example, the doubt of another person's love may easily be a projection of the individual's own unconscious doubt of his love for that person.

The "tu quoque arguments" of children are cited by Freud as a good instance of normal projection, and as pointing also to its primitiveness as a defense dynamism. The making of the same reproach against someone else as a method of defending oneself has, he says, "something undeniably automatic" about it. Thus projection is really a conscious protective thought or phantasy regarding another which acts as a "cloak" for unconscious thoughts "which are anxious to escape from criticism and consciousness."

The neurotic tends to use the dynamism of projection much more than the normal person, but its fullest development is seen in paranoia. In this mental ailment the ideas of being hated and persecuted, which psychoanalysts believe very regularly have their origin in an unconscious homosexual love for the "persecutor," represent a complete change of affect. Thus unconscious feelings of love are perceived externally as hostile intentions on the part of the unconsciously loved object. Freud gives the formula: Beginning with unconscious homosexual wish-phantasies which arouse internal objections, the patient changes his unconscious, "I love him" to "I hate him." Then projecting the latter, there arises the concept, "He hates me." The final form is, "I do not love him —because he persecutes me."

This discovery by Freud of the dynamic and underlying mental content of the baffling mental disease, paranoia, a discovery which has been confirmed by many others, constitutes one of the most significant contributions of psychoanalysis to psychiatry.

Ferenczi says of the paranoiac that instead of acknowledging certain forms of love and hate in himself he believes that these feelings which, if he allowed them to become conscious, would be unbearable for his self-regard "are whispered in his ear by invisible spirits, or he reads them in the countenances or the movements of his fellowmen."

9. Isolation

Isolation is a process by which the memories of unpleasant impressions or experiences are deprived of their affective cathexis, "so that what remains in consciousness is nothing but an ideational content which is perfectly colorless and is judged to be unimportant."

Isolation—a newly-discovered dynamism—has also been defined as a technique the purpose of which is "to loosen the contents of consciousness from their connections, separate the individual elements and thus conceal their meaning."

Isolation is a dynamism which manifests itself in connection with the frustrating experience (exciting cause) leading to the outbreak of a neurosis. The experience is not forgotten, it is simply retained in consciousness without any affect being attached to it, or any association being established between it and the neurotic symptom which has sprung out of it. Isolation also takes place in the "motor sphere," and the unconscious "interrupting" or holding apart of associations is strengthened by the interpolating of a pause "in which nothing is to happen, no perception is made, no action carried out."

This dynamism of Isolation underlies obsessive ceremonials. These, as Freud points out, are quite worthless in themselves, but they have a protective value in that they take the place of actions which might restore old associations, that is, they perform an isolating function.

E. Glover describes both Isolation and Undoing as dynamisms "which operate with a view to surrounding any impulse-presentation with a thought- or action-vacuum." He speaks of the work of analysis in the case of the obsessional neurosis as the "placing thought-bridges over the defensive vacuum-belts."

Isolation is a newly discovered dynamism, which (together with that of Undoing) is discussed for the first time in Freud's *Hemmung, Symptom, und Angst*. The concept seems somewhat obscure, and Freud himself says it is a process "the technic of which we cannot yet give."

In an attempt to clarify the process of Isolation, Freud points out that since "it seeks to hinder associations" and combinations of ideas, "it follows one of the oldest and most fundamental commands of compulsion neurosis, the taboo of contact." Bodily contact or the touching of the object is the goal both of the destructive and erotic impulses, and this explains why the avoidance of contact plays so predominant a part in the obsessional neurosis. This taboo of contact becomes the prototype for the process of Isolation, and when the obsessional neurotic "isolates even an impression or an activity through a pause he gives us to understand symbolically that he will not allow the thought of it to come into associative contact with other thoughts."

Freud thinks that Isolation as a normal Ego function is evidenced in ordinary concentration of thought. Indifferent, irrelevant, and unsuitable impressions which are making a simultaneous claim upon the attention with that to which we wish to give our entire thought and energy are held apart or aloof and not allowed to disturb the main task.

10. Undoing

Undoing is the unconscious attempt, through a symbolical act, to abolish or will out of existence a past experience or impression, the consequences of which have been painful to the Ego.

Freud speaks of Undoing as being essentially a "rebuffing." He also calls it an attempt to "blow away," or to use a "negative magic." He thinks it is a process which originates "in the animistic situation to the external world" and that it underlies various folk customs and religious ceremonials, as well as obsessional ceremonials.

Undoing is more radical in its aim than Repression. Repression strives for annihilation of the impulse to repeat a pleasurable infantile experience. Undoing aims at the abolition of the experience itself, that is, its purpose is to wipe out the past.

11. Conversion

Conversion signifies the symbolic expression by means of physical manifestations (motor and sensory) of both repressed instinctual wishes and the defense set up against them.

Conversion is a dynamism specially typical of hysteria. Hysterical symptoms mean that repression has been unsuccessful, and, as Ferenczi says, "the effective energy of what is repressed radiates into the bodily sphere."

Freud describes hysterical conversion as "an excessive innervation (in typical cases a somatic innervation) sometimes of a sensory, sometimes of a motor character, either as an excitation or as an inhibition." This innervation is a substitute formation for the ideational content of an instinct presentation, the latter being completely withdrawn from consciousness.

Freud thinks that Undoing "has a large field of application and extends far back." He also declares that there is a very clear distinction between the two processes of Isolation and Undoing. Isolation, he says, is a sort of foresight or attempt to prevent the repetition of something unpleasant, and these precautionary measures he speaks of as "rational." In the case of Undoing the abolitions are "irrational or magical in nature."

As manifested normally the process of Undoing is in evidence when there is "a resolution to treat an event as if it had not yet happened," that is, not to concern oneself either with the event or its consequences. Neurotic Undoing attempts to abolish even the remote past, and Freud says that it is a dynamism "of the first rank" in symptom-formation.

According to Jones the direction taken by the discharging energy in hysterical conversion is determined by the existence of preformed associations "such as the usual physical accompaniments of emotion." The dynamism also makes use sometimes "of an abnormal somatic reaction already preformed on an organic basis." Asthma, he says, is a good example of this.

Ferenczi points out that hysterics go further than obsessional neurotics; the latter can tolerate a harmless thought-substitute, but the hysteric creates a symbol for his repressed impulses in his physical body. This he speaks of as "materialization phenomenon," "the realization of a wish as though by magic out of the material in the body and its disposal." It is a plastic representation, though in a primitive form, "just as the artist molds the material of his conception."

The disposition to hysterogenesis, Ferenczi says, implies an "autoplastic fixation," on a very primitive level; that is, no endeavor is made to adapt to reality by modification of the external world, there is simply a modification of one's own body.

The "mysterious leap" from mental to bodily excitation presupposes what Freud calls a "somatic compliance"; that is, the symptom becomes located in some particular organ because of what Ferenczi calls "a special suitability or tendency of the organ concerned to combine with the excitation masses liberated from the repressed material."

The form which hysterical symptoms take is believed to be due partly to this somatic compliance and partly to the fact that they are disguised and distorted expressions of the fulfilment of sexual, and for the most part perverted, wishes on the genital level. Identification is also largely responsible for the form taken by hysterical symptoms, and explains what often appears to be imitation of the ailment of another person.

An example of hysterical-conversion, or "the representation of unconscious phantasies in bodily terms" is paralysis of the arm, which can signify both an intended aggression and the defensive struggle against it in the Ego.

Ferenczi points out that the predisposing factor to hysteria is found by Freud to be the disturbance of the normal sexual development "at the stage when complete primacy of the genital zone had already been reached." Hysterical symptoms, he says, are the displacement of genital impulses on to apparently indifferent parts of the body, or in other words, "conversion-hysteria genitalizes those parts of the body at which the symptoms are manifested." This means that a regressive process is at work; the displacement is from below upwards, and Ferenczi believes that the pregenital autoerotisms become charged with genital sexuality. This shows itself in the tendency of hysterical symptoms to manifest themselves in connection with the throat and bowels. In other words, hysterical conversion symptoms are expressions of genital object-love clothed in the form of autoerotism.

Part of mental energy under normal conditions is conducted off by way of physical innervation. This becomes hysterical conversion whenever there is an exaggeration; there is a far more intense emotional expression which finds outlets by new paths.

The psychoneurosis, hysteria, offers a wealth of examples of conversions. Some constitutional peculiarity may be betokened by the "unusual degree of readiness of the physical response."

Concerning constitutional or other personality characteristics as the background of conversion (hysterical) phenomena, Freud says that the hysterical predisposition consists in "an immense sexual desire and a very exaggerated sexual rejection." The outlet is found through the symptoms which do not banish the libidinous strivings.

Freud's conception is that "Psychoanalysis removes the symptoms of hysteria on the supposition that they are the substitutes—the transcriptions as it were—for a series of emotionally accentuated psychic processes, wishes, and desires, to which a passage for their discharge through the conscious psychic activities has been cut off by a special process (repression)."

12. Introjection

Introjection signifies the incorporation by the Ego of "objects presenting themselves, in so far as they are sources of pleasure." Freud points out that in the beginning the Ego, in so far as it is auto-erotic, has no need of the outside world, but that through its self-preservative needs it is forced to a recognition of objects.

The concept and term "introjection" was first introduced by Ferenczi to describe the first stage in adaptation to reality "in which the Ego alone exists and includes in itself the whole world of experience." He also speaks of introjection as a process by which the object is "psychically assimilated."

Jones defines introjection as the unconscious tendency to incorporate the environment into one's own personality.

13. Identification

Identification is the unconscious molding of a person's own Ego after the fashion of one that has been taken as a model.

There are two forms of identification, namely, primary and secondary. Primary identification is the earliest expression of an emotional tie with another person. It is a form of object-choice which precedes later libidinal object cathexes. It arises in the oral stage and in the beginning object-identifications can scarcely be distinguished in their outward expressions from object-love.

The distinction between identification (primary and secondary) and object-love lies, according to Freud, in the difference between what one would unconsciously like *to be* and what one would like *to have*. In the former case the object is taken as the ideal or model, and the imitation is either a sweeping one, or limited and partial.

It seems to us that psychoanalysts make very little distinction between the concept of introjection and that of identification. Many times in their literature we find the terms used interchangeably. Freud, in one place, speaks of identification, and in the very next sentence writes "this introjection." The examples which Jones gives of introjection seem equally appropriate for identification. M. Klein speaks of the "introjection of identifications." Ferenczi says quite clearly "introjection, i. e. identification."

Yet it seems that there must be a distinction, even if a very subtle one. Identification, we are told, is based on the desire to be the object, and the object is regarded as a model. Introjection seems to arise out of the desire to have or retain (incorporate) an object which has been lost, or is in danger of being lost. Abraham says that introjection is an unconscious consoling or compensating for the loss. It is as if the Ego said to itself, "My loved object is not gone, for now I carry it within myself, and can never lose it."

Abraham speaks of two forms of introjection both of which may explain the self-reproach of the melancholiac. Either the introjected object becomes the Ego-ideal and the merciless self-criticism emanates from the introjected object, or "the content of these self-reproaches is ultimately a merciless criticism of the introjected object" by the Ego. This suggests that the distinction between identification and introjection may perhaps have some connection with that between primary and secondary identification. (See Identification.) The whole matter, however, seems quite obscure.

Abraham explains introjection as an oral process, its physical prototype being the swallowing reflex.

Introjection is peculiarly a dynamism of dementia praecox; the environment is blended with the personality, with a consequent swelling and indefiniteness of the individuality, the loss of reality varying with the completeness of the process.

Projection is the typical mental dynamism of the paranoid personality who invests the external world with his own unpleasurable ideas and feelings. It is pointed out by Jones that this means a "shrinking" of the Ego.

Primary identification shows itself when a little boy exhibits a special interest in his father, expresses wishes to grow up like him, wants to take his place in many ways. Freud points out that this behavior has nothing to do with a homosexual object-cathexis of the father, that it is typically masculine and prepares the way for object-love and the Oedipus Complex. As the latter matures, the object-identification with the father becomes focused on the specific desire to take his place with the mother sexually. A hostile element now creeps into the relation and the father is viewed as a rival to be got out of the way. Ambivalence thus develops. Freud is inclined to think that this is "inherent in the identification from the beginning." The normal solution of the Oedipus conflict, namely, the formation of the Super-ego and the consolidation of the boy's masculinity, is largely the result of primary identification.

Secondary identification—the replacing of an object-cathexis by a substitute object set up within the Ego, or in other words the Ego itself becomes the Id's libidinal-object. Freud admits that the process by which this is achieved is "insufficiently known" and "hard to describe." He says, however, that it is a method by which the Ego can obtain control over the Id. It assumes the features of the abandoned love-object and forces itself upon the Id as a substitute. It tries to make good to the Id the loss of its external object, or in other words, it may be said to make use of its power of adapting to reality by offering the Id a more suitable love-object.

Freud makes several attempts to clarify the concept of secondary identification. It may be, he says, "a derivative of the first oral phase of the organization of the libido, in which the object that we long for and prize is assimilated by eating, and is in that way annihilated as such." Again he suggests that by undertaking this "introjection" the Ego "makes it easier for an object to be given up or renders that process possible." It may be, indeed, that identification "is the sole condition under which the Id can give up its objects."

The changing of object-libido into narcistic libido implies an abandonment of sexual aims (desexualization). It also implies a

Kovacs, in discussing the psychological processes involved in "aesthetic sympathy" (aesthetic appreciation?), for example, the emotions aroused by any creative work of art, describes introjection·as the identification which the onlooker, the listener, the reader, etc. makes with the object of his attention. The artist, on the other hand, projects as he attempts to embody in his creation his own emotions.

Abraham says of introjection that it is "a far commoner psychological process than has hitherto been supposed." The introjection of a lost object occurs in both healthy mourning and melancholia. In the former case it is a way of recalling the object to life by setting it up in the Ego. In melancholia there is a radical disturbance of the libidinal relations to the object, a severe ambivalence, and a way of escape is sought through introjection or by turning against the self the hostility felt toward the object.

Freud points out that partial identification plays a rôle in hysterical symptom-formation. A girl who is passing through her Oedipus Complex may give outward expression to the unconscious identification she has made with her mother by developing a cough like the mother's. This serves also as a punishment for the incestuous love wishes toward the father.

Identification may arise where there is no emotional tie with the person imitated. This, too, enters into symptom-formation. The person copied is in a situation in which the identifying person would unconsciously like to be, or the two Egos concerned have repressed the same wish. There is a certain unconscious sensing of a common quality shared with another person. This sort of identification underlies sympathy very often, according to Freud. Such partial identification, if the common quality shared is important, may lead to the development of an emotional tie between the two persons concerned.

regression, that is, from object-love to narcism. This regression is perhaps made possible through the fact that the original object-choice was of the narcistic type. Normally, secondary identification, Freud says, should be followed by other processes, notably sublimation.

Identification, both primary and secondary, has a great share in determining the development of the Ego and "contributes materially towards building up what is called its 'character.'" It is a very common and typical process in the very early stages of development, and the identifications made in these early years are "profound and lasting." The first and most important identification is the primary one made with the parents.

Identification is often partial and limited, that is, it may only borrow a single characteristic. Freud thinks, however, that in many cases identification is the root of male homosexuality. This means that it takes place on an "ample scale" since the Ego is re-molded in one of its most important features, that is, its sexual character. The boy does not actually abandon his tie with the mother, but "transforms himself into her," and seeks for love-objects resembling himself.

Secondary identification, if not employed too frequently and extensively, seems to be a normal method for dealing with abandoned object-cathexes. However, Freud points out that if identifications are "too numerous, unduly intense, and incompatible with one another" the result may be pathological, that is, the Ego may become disrupted, and conflicts arise between its different parts. Freud speaks of "a varying capacity for resistance to identification." He suggests that cases of multiple personality may be explained on a basis of several profound and mutually incompatible identifications co-existing within the Ego.

Freud speaks of identification as "oral mastery of the object." He calls attention to the primitive belief that attributes of animals eaten survive as part of the character of the persons who eat them—one of the roots of cannibalism. Identification underlies both the totem feast and Holy Communion.

The "rescue phantasy," Freud thinks, is a good example of a complete identification. The boy's impulses of love, gratitude, sensuality, defiance, self-assertiveness, and independence are "all gratified in the wish to be the father of himself." (See phantasy-formation.)

Freud suggests that the concept of identification may have some bearing on empathy, which he defines as an "intellectual understanding of what is inherently foreign to our own Ego in other people."

Psychoanalysts speak of a "borrowed" sense of guilt by which they mean the product of an identification, and which, Freud says, may be "the sole remaining trace of an abandoned love-relation." This borrowed sense of guilt may be significant as intensifying a sense of guilt already individually acquired.

The symptoms of melancholia are believed to be explained on the basis of identification. The abandoned love-object has been loved with great ambivalence and the Ego has attempted to solve the ambivalence conflict by internalizing or introjecting the object. This means that the melancholiac saves his erotic cathexis from annihilation by taking his own Ego as a substitute love-object. At the same time, he can find outlet for the hate-element and torment of the original external object through his illness. The actual symptoms arise from the fact that the alteration brought about in the Ego through identification arouses the criticism of the Super-ego. This explains patience heaping self-reproaches upon himself.

The concept of identification, Freud thinks, does away with any need for postulating a "herd instinct," as underlying social and group phenomena. The origin of group feeling, he thinks, is to be traced to jealousy and hostility. The elder child in the nursery is jealous of his successors and has impulses to get rid of them, but he becomes conscious that his hostility cannot be maintained without damage to himself, that is, loss of love on the part of the parents. Thus, he is finally forced to unite with his brothers and sisters, that is, identify himself with them in respect to the tie with, and the favors desired from, the parents. Identification is followed by reaction-formation and thus instead of claims arising out of rivalry, justice and equal treatment for all are demanded.

Later adult group formation can be explained in a similar fashion. The libidinal tie with the leader takes the place of that with the parent and the various individuals comprising the group subordinate their rivalry by means of identification based on the common libidinal relationship to the leader. The identification between members of a group can also be explained in the sense that the leader becomes for each individual the substitute for his Ego-ideal, which makes for a sense of oneness on the basis of a quality shared in common.

Ferenczi views identification as a method of making oneself independent of the object. Alexander, speaking of the identification of the child with its parents (that is, the assimilation of their demands into his conscious Ego), says it is for the purpose of escaping conflict.

Identification may be the precursor of libidinal ties. Freud speaks of the "desexualized, sublimated, homosexual love for other men which springs from work in common."

14. Sublimation

Sublimation is the exchange of infantile sexual aims for interests or modes of pleasure-finding which are no longer directly sexual although psychically related, and which are on a higher social level. The terms "desexualized" and "aim-inhibited" are used throughout psychoanalytic literature to describe sublimated activities. Sublimation is fundamentally an unconscious process.

Freud points out that in sublimation a few of the original sexual aims are also preserved, e. g. desire for proximity with and for sight of the love-object. Sublimated aims are of varying stability and can always be transformed back into their original sexual aims, if environmental difficulties become too strong.

Sublimation is the healthy and constructive way of dealing with a part of the infantile sexual urges as they arise at successive stages of development. For example, after the Oedipus Complex has been resolved the child should be tied to the parents only by aim-inhibited or "tender" feelings.

According to Freud's most recent conceptions, sublimation is the work of the Ego, which comes to the assistance of the Id by draining off some of the libido and thus lowering Id over-tensions. The work of sublimation may be undertaken by the Ego either when outer obstacles to direct sexual satisfaction present themselves, or to satisfy the Ego's own narcism (which may be closely bound up with sexual frustrations) or at the behests of the Super-ego.

Freud is inclined to believe that sublimation is always preceded and made possible by identification. Through the latter process the Ego gets control of some of the object-libido and then "goes on to give it another aim."

The relation of sublimation to the choice of profession or employment, Jones claims, is more important than external factors and opportunities. The latter are often but the pretext for the expression of some primary submerged striving.

Psychoanalysts admit that complete sublimation is difficult to achieve, and, since the capacity for it varies, some degree of sublimation will commonly be accompanied by repression.

Alexander, in discussing sublimation, takes into account the factor of individual differences. He thinks it is certain that restrictions on the impulses may affect different individuals with different degrees of intensity, and to a certain extent at different stages in their development.

Freud says a certain amount of direct sexual satisfaction is absolutely necessary for most persons. Sublimation succeeds with the minority, and with them only intermittently. The sexual instinct, he says, is characterized by special stubbornness.

Ferenczi, in discussing pedagogical methods, says ". . . it is the concern of education to tame and mitigate the asocial instincts, to 'domesticate' children. We have two adjuvants towards this objective, repression and sublimation."

Jung questions whether sexual energy can ever be voluntarily transferred into a sublimation. He says, "It does not lie in our power to transfer disposable energy at pleasure to a rationally chosen subject."

Alexander, who lays much emphasis on the Eros and death urges, and the constant fusion and defusion which exists between them, makes much of the fact that sublimation, or desexualization, sets free some of the instinct to destroy. There is a delusion of the erotic component and an inevitable liberation of a quantum of the Death urge. "To find a place for this nascent quantum of destruction instincts is the problem, the solution of which is the most difficult task in the life of contemporary human beings." Alexander points out that there is danger, both of an aggressive attitude towards the environment, or a turning inward of the destructive trends, and the formation of an oversevere Super-ego.

An example from the well-known case of the Wolf-man may help to clarify these concepts. The boy in question had an excessive love for his father, and a strong sense of guilt accompanied his homosexual trends. An external situation made possible what Freud calls "an ideal sublimation." His mother made him acquainted with religious doctrines and New Testament stories. The fact that his birthday was on Christmas day made it very easy for him to identify himself with Christ. In this way he could love his father by loving God, since the Deity had become a father surrogate. His desexualized libido found many opportunities for expression in ways "laid down by religion" and these expressions "were not haunted by that sense of guilt" which had attached itself to his sensual love for his father. Thus it was possible for him "to drain off his deepest sexual current," his homosexuality.

At the same time, as Freud points out, certain more obvious masochistic tendencies "found an incomparable sublimation without much renunciation" because of his identification with Christ who was ill-treated by the divine Father.

Sublimation is not a defense. The Ego is really acting as the ally of the Id, though at the same time it is serving its own interests. Defense may exist alongside with sublimation; part of the libido may be sublimated and part of it repressed, but Freud says clearly that sublimation is "a way out which does not involve repression."

Sublimated love creates more permanent ties than sensual love. Sexual impulses which are uninhibited in their aim "suffer great reduction through the discharge of energy every time the sexual aim is attained." In order to last, sensual love must either be combined with sublimated tender components or transformed into these.

Psychoanalysts speak of the "capacity for sublimation," and signs of this capacity at a very early stage of development are looked upon as indicative of good mental structure and balance.

Jones points out that sublimation is not a matter of transforming for other purposes a diffuse energy, but an accurate and specific

In discussing sublimation, Alexander states that the process represents a legitimate activity directed outwards, with an aim lying outside the personality, and secondly it has a social quality. It is a normal modification of impulses not adapted to reality. These profoundly modified impulses become attached, Alexander says, to other impulses which are Ego-syntonic, "and in this good company get by the censorship." In contrast, the neurotic supplants outwardly directed activity by bodily changes which have a purely subjective significance (hysteria), or by commonplace activities which do not essentially get beyond the bounds of the personality, or by purely psychological quantities of imaginative activity. Neurotic activity does not produce changes in the environment. The content of the instinctive urge remains unaltered with the neurotic —merely cloaked and disguised from consciousness—an alteration of the self rather than in the environment. In sublimation real fulfilment is not sacrificed, but the aims or goals of the impulses change so that fulfilment no longer meets with resistance from the environment. Neurotic restrictions inhibit the activity of the striving; normal restriction or sublimation changes its content.

Since an actual gratification of the original urge is involved in sublimation, Alexander discusses the question of why no sense of guilt attaches to the process. Social achievement, he thinks, can allay the sense of guilt, that is, it has the same economic function in the healthy person as suffering has in the neurotic.

Jones draws a distinction between sublimation and idealization; the former is a process that concerns the impulse while the latter concerns the object. Idealism, he points out, may be simply a hiding place for narcism and may be accompanied by very incomplete sublimation and strong repression.

The term sublimation has been used by psychoanalysts entirely in connection with infantile autoerotic and alloerotic impulses. Sublimation of aggressive and narcistic impulses is, however, occasionally referred to—for example, baseball pitching may be a sublimation, both of the early autoerotic urethral pleasure and also of early narcistic satisfaction through urethral prowess.

transfer of energy from one given field to another. That is, as development goes on, each specific later interest really gratifies a specific primary desire, or sexual instinct component.

In Freud's later writing, he suggests that the process of sublimation is always through the agency of the Ego which changes sexual object libido in accordance with narcistic interests. Thus the specific goals or sublimated activities will vary somewhat according to individual differences; nevertheless, the range of selection for each individual is comparatively small. Jones, in his chapter on *Sublimating Processes,* says, "Experience teaches that there is a considerable stereotypy in the forms that sublimation of a given tendency take, and as there are only a quite limited number of such primary tendencies, it follows that the results of sublimation must show a considerable resemblance in a large number of individuals."

What is done by way of handling frustration always involves the problem of just what quantity of libido "the particular Ego in question can control, that is, can hold in suspension, sublimate, or make direct use of."

In this connection Freud enters into a discussion of libidinal abstinence and the practical possibilities of sublimation. Quite aside from the fact that there are individual differences both in the amount of libidinal gratification necessary for satisfaction and in the plasticity of the libido (readiness to exchange one mode of attaining satisfaction for another, to accept one object as substitute for another) Freud is nevertheless convinced that "the measure of unsatisfied libido which the average human being can stand is limited . . . sublimation can, moreover, never account for more than a certain small fraction of the libido, and finally, most people possess the capacity for sublimation only to a very slight degree." Such considerations must be kept in mind, Freud says, if we are to understand the significance for the causation of neuroses of the restrictions which culture imposes upon the facilities for (libidinal) satisfaction."

Jones distinguishes between sublimation and reaction-formation as follows: "In contradistinction to sublimations, where the energy is not only derived from the repressed impulse but flows in the same direction as it, that of reaction-formations is derived from the opposing ego forces and is aimed in exactly the opposite direction. They might, indeed, be described by the more static metaphor of barriers erected as dams against the repressed impulses. The contrast between them and sublimations may be illustrated by a couple of examples. The primitive tendency to self-display (of the person) may be sublimated into a taking pleasure in self-prominence, either physically or in oratory or, more indirectly still, as in the many varieties of fame-seeking, or, on the other hand, it may lead to the reaction of modesty, shame, and the like. The primitive pleasure all children take in dirt may be sublimated into painting, sculpture work, or cooking, or it may lead to the reaction of cleanliness, tidiness (dirt is matter in the wrong place!), and similar traits."

15. Rationalization

Rationalization is a process which arises out of the need for accounting or justifying to the self for certain feelings, ideas, or behavior. Jones explains this as "the necessity everyone feels to have what may be called a theory of life, and particularly a theory of himself." As rational creatures we feel that we ought to be able to account to ourselves for our conduct and opinions, and all our mental processes "are unconsciously manipulated and revised to that end." In other words, rationalization is the work of the unconscious Ego by which it evades the recognition of irrational and inconsistent behavior which really arises on the basis of unconscious urges. It can be seen that the Ego's narcism is always largely involved in the process of rationalization.

Freud points out that in rationalization the Ego is really in a sense defending the Id. The Ego pretends that the Id is showing obedience to the mandates of reality "even when in fact it is remaining obdurate and immovable." The Ego by rationalization "throws a disguise" over the Id's refusal to adapt to reality and also over its opposition to the Super-ego.

Jones was the first to introduce the term "rationalization" into psychoanalytic literature. It has been accepted by Freud and has come into very general use with all psychoanalysts.

Jones gives as examples of rationalization the tendency to explain queer mistakes and slips of the tongue as "chance" and "accidental." One of the best instances of evasion, he claims, is the arguments advanced by an individual to defend the particular form of religious belief which he has adopted. A man, he says, who during his adolescence has joined some sect either because he was brought up in it or because some of his friends did so is later likely to become convinced that he is a member of this religious sect because of the truth of its doctrine. He does not want to admit that the real reason for his adherence is because of his father's adherence.

Secondary elaboration in dreams is, Jones thinks, very closely allied to the process of rationalization.

16. Idealization

Idealization is a process which is possible both in the sphere of object-libido and Ego-libido.

In the case of object-love, idealization shows itself in what Freud calls "sexual over-estimation," which he says "is the origin of the peculiar state of being in love." While this state exists the love-object enjoys a certain amount of freedom from criticism and all its qualities are given a higher value than those of persons who are not love-objects. In other words, the object is treated as one's own Ego. Rationalization enters into the process of idealization and the Ego spares itself the realization of the actual situation, namely, that "spiritual merits" have been lent to the love-object because of its sensual attraction, and believes that the sensual attraction exists because of the spiritual merits.

Idealization as it concerns the Ego-libido has to do with the process of setting up an Ego-ideal or Super-ego. This is a normal process and takes care of a certain amount of Ego-libido which is not carried over into object cathexes and which otherwise might lead to a surplus of narcism. Some of the self-love which in childhood is directed to the Ego (primary narcism) is transferred or displaced on to a substitute which now instead of the infantile Ego is looked upon as "the possessor of all perfections." The child is reluctant to give up a once-pleasurable gratification; he does not willingly relinquish his early narcistic perfection. As he develops, however, his narcism is bound to be disturbed by the admonitions and criticisms of adults which awaken his own self-criticism. Accordingly, "he seeks to recover the early perfection thus wrested from him in the new form of an Ego-ideal."

Idealization in the sense of a formation of an Ego-ideal, Freud says, must be clearly distinguished from sublimation. The displacement of primary narcism on to an Ego-ideal does not by any means imply that success in sublimating sexual impulses has been achieved. As Freud points out, although the Ego-ideal demands sublimation it cannot enforce this: "sublimation remains a special process which may be prompted by the ideal, but the execution of which is entirely independent of any such incitement."

Idealization as it concerns the love-object is to be distinguished from sublimation. In the latter process the sexual aim is deflected and the accent falls on this deflection. In the case of idealization, the process concerns the object rather than the aim, and "without any alteration in its nature" the love-object "is aggrandized and exalted in the mind."

Identification must also be distinguished from idealization. Though the former may often be based on admiration of the object, it also involves a partial alteration in the Ego after the model of the object. In the case of idealization the object is retained, and there is, Freud says, "a hyper-cathexis of it by the Ego and at the Ego's expense." In other words, there is "an impoverishment of the Ego in respect of libido" in favor of the love-object.

Freud points out that in the neurotic there exists a high degree of tension between the development of his Ego-ideal and the extent to which he has been able to achieve sublimation of his libidinal impulses. He speaks of the difficulty in convincing the idealist "of the inexpediency of the hiding place found by his libido."

The formation of a narcistic Ego-ideal drains off, according to Freud, "large quantities of libido which is essentially homosexual" and the maintenance of this idea gives it outlet and gratification for homosexual trends.

17. Dream-Work

Dream-work is a name given by Freud to a special process, a combining of dynamisms, by which latent dream thoughts are converted into the manifest content of the dream.

Every dream has a double content, one manifest and one latent. The manifest content is all that is directly known to and recalled by the dreamer; in many ways it appears absurd and confused. Psychoanalysis, by free association, discovers the latent content, an underlying mental structure of which the manifest dream is nothing more than "a distorted, abbreviated, and misunderstood translation, and usually a translation into visual images."

The dynamisms, most of which plainly are forms of distortion, which enter into dream-work are:

(a) Displacement.

(b) Condensation.

(c) Symbolization—this dynamism, found in other spheres of mental activity, is very active in dream-work as the result of censorship "directed against the unacceptable of the unconscious wish-impulses."

(d) Dramatization—the manifest dream mainly depicts a situation or action, and, because it involves much more visualization than verbalization, may be said to resemble a theatrical production. This necessitates the employment of certain characteristics of unconscious thinking; namely, pictorial thinking or presentation, and the rapid wiping out of one scene by another, mere visual sequences standing in the place of logical causal connections.

(e) Secondary Elaboration—the filling out of details as the dream becomes apprehended in consciousness. (This seems to be partly the work of the dream, and partly to be due to the effort of consciousness to know the dream.) The dream has to be remodeled in order to bring it into harmony with other conscious mental processes; it must be modified in order to make it comprehensible. This inevitably leads to further distortion which continues after waking, so the longer the period which elapses, the more altered the original dream becomes.

Dream-work, it will be noted, is *merely* the operation of dynamisms. Its results, as Jones points out, involve no intellectual operation.

Freud's censor, which has been the subject of so much discussion, is a function of the Ego, he explains. It is a resistance phenomenon. In the relaxation of sleep, the repressive resistance of the Ego is reduced, but not done away with. Some of it still exists in the shape of what Freud calls "censorship," preventing the unconscious impulse from expressing itself in forms which it otherwise might take. The censor is so severe in dreams that much distortion takes place. Latent dream thoughts are transformed and softened "so as to make the forbidden meaning of the dream unrecognizable." Freud shows that dreams are constructed like neurotic symptoms—"they are compromises between the demands of a repressed impulse and the resistance of a censoring force in the Ego." They are both built up from the same origins, in their manifest content they are equally unintelligible, and they stand equally in need of interpretation.

It is certainly very difficult to distinguish how much of the displacement takes place relatively in the recital of the dream to the analyst, or as an accompaniment of secondary elaboration, or in the actual dream-process. The psychology of testimony appears to be here involved. It is hard to know how accurately the recounting of a dream, even with the aid of notes immediately made, a procedure nowadays much deprecated, corresponds to the dream as it actually occurred.

Symbolism plays an important rôle in dream-work. Jones states that dream symbolism differs from other symbolism in being exclusively sexual. The reason for this, he says, is still unknown.

We gather, particularly from conversation with H. Deutsch, that more recently psychoanalysts have altered their earlier view concerning the number of symbols having general or universal interpretative value. They are inclined now to believe that the meaning of the symbol cannot be known without the individual's associations called forth through analysis in the individual case. It is still maintained that there are a few general symbols, but even for these the significance is not unvarying. For example, as Deutsch says, in dreams water is a general symbol of rebirth, yet it may be found frequently with quite different significance in the dreams of persons who, having crossed the ocean, are far from home, family, and familiar surroundings, their dreams then hav-

Freud gives the relationships between the manifest dream elements and the latent unconscious dream-thought as (a) that of the part to the whole, (b) that of the illusion, (c) that of imagery to the more abstract thought of unconscious dream-life, (d) that of symbolic representation.

(For further discussion of dreams, see Dream-Formation.)

ing emotional values that accrue from their immediate life situation.

Visual dramatization, common to the majority of dreams, Freud points out, is similar to the pictorial mode of thought characteristic of the Ucs and of early and primitive life, and as such is regressive.

Jones suggests that secondary elaboration is closely allied to rationalization. The possibilities of changes in presenting unconscious thinking in terms of conscious mental processes are obviously many. For example, since the dream consists of a series of pictures, any attempt to translate these into words inevitably involves certain inaccuracies and elaborations. Then too, the "timelessness" of the dream-processes, characteristic of all unconscious thinking, must be expressed, to satisfy the demands of logic, in the temporal concepts of conscious thinking.

A very curious occasional phenomenon of dream-work has recently been discovered by Alexander and receives the name of "Paired Dreams." A dream significant of punishment precedes a dream of the same night representing gratification of some unconscious wish. The two dreams seem to stand for the idea that if the price is already paid, the dreamer is free to indulge himself. The unconscious need for punishment here receives expression.

SECTION SIX

<hr>

BEHAVIOR—PERSONALITY FORMATION —CONDUCT

Section VI

BEHAVIOR—PERSONALITY FORMATION—
CONDUCT

From almost the first beginnings of his studies Freud was naturally led into making many discoveries pertaining to human behavior, to the formation of personality and conduct trends that seemed only incidentally, if at all, related to the disease process that primarily was under observation. This accumulation of knowledge has grown vastly; Freud and others of the psychoanalytic school through their researches have by this time gathered a great mass of information that bears on the genetics of behavior tendencies and personality formation. Some matters, such as the behavior of the mind in phantasy formation, dream life, and symptomatic acts, have received much attention and we shall deal with them in this section as certain general modes of mental behavior. Personality formation, often called character formation, also has been a subject of much consideration as well as some specific forms of behavior that, because of their moral implication, are properly designated as conduct. These and certain other matters that have been more or less studied by psychoanalysts are introduced under the various topical headings of this section. There is certainly no claim.on the part of psychoanalysts that the last word has been said about many forms of human behavior, using this term in its general sense, indeed it is specifically stated that there are matters enough ahead concerning human behavior to occupy psychoanalytic thought and research for generations to come, but the published material has great value and is worth close scrutiny.

We see great advantages in using the terminology which is now generally accepted by the great group of sociologists and social psychologists —there is a constant need for psychoanalysts to correlate their conceptions with those prevalent in other fields of contemporary thought. Appreciations and fair-minded discussion will be obtained in no other way. Hence we have adhered to the following definitions and usage:

Behavior: The sum total of responses to stimuli, internal and external.

Personality: The habitual patterns of behavior of the individual in terms of physical and mental activities and attitudes, particularly as these have social connotations.

Conduct: That behavior of the individual which has more or less definite "moral" implications.

The term "character" may be, and often is, loosely used. Certainly in English-speaking countries it always has moral or definitely social implications; it is not equivalent to the concept personality.

The development of psychoanalysis in its contributions to the understanding of human behavior is much in line with the growth of other sciences. In the medical sciences, for example, the start was with the grossly pathological and there was very gradual leading up to physiology, the science dealing with the normal physical organism. And it ever remains that as a matter of methodology, the more normal workings of a complex organism are best to be studied and understood when some of its parts or functions are out of gear, side-tracked, or working aberrationally.

It is ever to be remembered that the great interest of psychoanalysis is always in the historico-genetic study of the background of human behavior. Whether more general researches, such as those of anthropology or sociology, occupy attention, or modification of behavior is the aim, as in analysis of the individual's mental life, the psychoanalyst contends that accretions to scientific knowledge require the method that alone can lead to fundamental understandings, namely, their own method of tracing the psycho-biological evolution of the individual from his very earliest beginnings.

In studying human behavior as being manifestations of mental life it is to be remembered that the various dynamisms work in combination as the so-called specific *formations,* all of which may be regarded and are variously designated as Compromise-formation or Substitute-formation. Our discussion of behavior will proceed under the heads of:

Phantasy-formation—Day-dreaming
Dream-formation
Symptomatic-acts formation
Personality-formation
Conduct-formation
Symptom-formation

It hardly needs be reiterated that for the psychoanalyst the great fundamentals for understanding human behavior are the divisions of mental life into the Cs and the Ucs, the activation and effects of the work of the various dynamisms, and the tripartite division of the human personality into Id, Ego, and Super-ego or Ego-ideal. As Schroeder states, psychoanalysis insists upon the discovery of unconscious, subjective determinants of conduct and thought. Ever recurring is "the influence of the habitual infantile and childish unconscious mentation." An all-important psychoanalytic formulation is, "The predominant emotional tones and values with which we come away from our earliest pre-adolescent meeting with sex problems will be the dominant emotional tones and values which we bring to every other problem in life." Any considerable fear, shame or guilt will, for example, often promote the tendency to evasion of human responsibility. There may even be the creation of a general aversion to many of the concrete facts of existence and a relative unconsciousness of objectives. "From this need for escaping some realities also comes some idealistic philosophies, metaphysics, theologies, and other world moralities."

Phantasy-formation on the conscious level or day-dreaming is freely wandering thought. Phantasy-making, Freud says, is a thought process which has been "kept free from reality-testing, and remains subordinated to the pleasure-principle alone." Conscious phantasies are a refuge; they offer opportunities for flight. Phantasy-making may thus be regarded as a "defense" in the sense that the Ego tolerates phantasies of gratification when actual motor discharge would be unacceptable. Relinquished sources of pleasure and abandoned paths of gratification are permitted to continue and exist in phantasy, in forms free from the demands of reality.

Freud makes the point that phantasy-making begins in the games of children, and is later continued in day-dreams. The difference between these two forms of phantasying seems to lie in the fact that in games the child borrows objects from the real world to help in giving expression to his desires, while in day-dreaming all dependence on real objects is abandoned. Normally the life of phantasy in a growing individual should gradually be brought into a closer relation with the facts of reality.

Freud draws attention to the fact that the adult always makes a great secret of his day-dreaming, he is ashamed of it, while the child is quite open in his play activities. This, he thinks, is to be explained by the child's great wish to be grown up; his play imitates adult activities, and there is nothing to be ashamed of in this. The day-dreamer on the other hand, has a certain realization that day-dreaming is a form of play and that he is not supposed to be a child any longer; also some of his phantasies spring from repressed wishes and are thus to be carefully guarded.

Freud discusses the rôle of phantasy-making in poetic and artistic creation. The artist, having withdrawn from an unsatisfying reality into the world of the imagination, knows, unlike the neurotic, how to find the way back from it and once more to get a firm hold on reality. Creations of art and literature are in the nature of compromises since they are obliged to avoid any open conflict with the

Psychoanalysts, although they have done comparatively little research in normal mental life along this line, have found much reason for being interested in phantasies on the more conscious levels (preconscious and conscious), and exceedingly suggestive contributions have been made concerning the significance of phantasies. In many of Freud's writings there is abundant reference to the nature and import of phantasy-life; Anna Freud deals with this topic from the standpoint of her special work (*The Technic of Child Analysis*) and Klein also; Rank and Jung—and also Freud—have been greatly intrigued by the similarity between neurotic phantasy and myth; Jones has made important contributions. The only systematic work on conscious phantasies is the notable volume by Varendonck, *The Psychology of Day-Dreams,* to which Freud has furnished a short but trenchant introduction.

We have adopted the plan of discussing phantasy-formation "on the conscious level" as over against unconscious phantasying; phantasies which exist wholly or in part in the Pcs are readily brought up into consciousness and thus are utterly different from unconscious phantasies. The preconscious phantasy is closely allied to the conscious. Besides, there are the points given below made by Freud against separating day-dreaming into conscious and preconscious.

Quite clear definition of conscious as distinguishable from unconscious phantasies has not as yet been forthcoming; perhaps it is not possible. Here, again, loose terminology beclouds. However, the following generalizations and specific statements tend to clarify the issue. Varendonck takes his stand that there are preconscious and conscious phantasies and calls them both day-dreaming. Freud, in his introduction, objects to Varendonck's dichotomy because he does not think that it serves any good purpose and leads away from the important differentiating characteristics of two kinds of thinking which otherwise Varendonck himself continually emphasizes: Phantasy as freely wandering thought is in this respect entirely in opposition to "intentionally directed reflection." "Day-dreams are thought-structures which have been elaborated without the intervention of the will, but under the direction of affective elements," Varendonck says in summary.

forces of repression, but they differ from the asocial, narcistic products of more abnormal phantasy life in that they are calculated
to arouse interest in other people and are able to invoke and gratify
similar unconscious wishes in others. In literature an author has the
chance to express his phantasies without any feeling of shame about
having them.

Phantasies have many of the characteristics of dreams, particularly because of ready dramatization exhibited and their general
visual character. Symbolism is sometimes exhibited, particularly
in childhood phantasy, as various writers have shown. Normally
the life of phantasy is more coherent than that of dreams and in
later periods of life is brought into closer relation to reality. Jones
thinks there is a marked difference in this last regard, as shown first
during the period of transition from infancy to later childhood,
and then when adolescence flows into adult life. The phantasies of
childhood are obviously more egocentric; there is a progression
from preoccupation with the self to a greater interest and love for
the outer world, an unfolding of the personality is characterized by
phantasy.

The psychoanalytically discovered characteristics of conscious
phantasy-formation are of great interest, especially since, as Freud
says, the part played by day-dreams in our psychic life has not yet
been fully recognized and investigated.

Varendonck says that day-dreaming "gives the illusion that
wishes and aspirations have been fulfilled; it thinks obstacles
away; it transforms impossibilities into possibilities and realities."
It is, "a search for pleasurable representations and an avoidance of
everything likely to cause pain." When it responds "to the mood of
the moment, or to some craving or other, it does not need to
take reality into consideration." Anything may achieve expression
in phantasy even if contrary to conscious wishes. "The most re-
spectable man may become aware . . . of undesired and undesirable tendencies." And since the strongest repression on which
civilization has imposed is upon our primordial sexual instincts
"it is not surprising, nor a token of bad morality, that in day-

Bleuler introduced the term "autistic thinking" for indulging in reveries or ruminations; this is phantasy or day-dreaming as opposed to logical, realistic, directed thinking. Freud thinks autistic thinking cannot be fairly used as a term synonymous with preconscious thinking, because day-dreaming does not owe its peculiarities to the fact that it "proceeds mostly preconsciously"—its forms are not changed when it is a conscious phenomenon. And even directed thought "may be achieved without the co-operation of consciousness"; it may be achieved preconsciously.

The student may find in the literature many examples of conscious phantasies based on repressed wishes and indeed with only a little effort at self-analysis they may be dug up from one's own mental life. But in spite of the high individualization of conscious phantasies psychoanalysts have discovered that some very curious phantasies turn up again and again in different patients. Some examples are the following:

Freud has written an article about the "beating phantasy"—a day-dream which others, too, have found in their patients. The content of this phantasy is that someone is beaten or is being beaten, usually "a child is being beaten," and the phantasy is particularly found in girls. Analysis shows that it has autoerotic significance; it is "invariably charged with a high degree of pleasure"; it has sadistic-masochistic components since the phantasy often turns into the day-dreamer's being beaten; it is based on the Oedipus situation: because the beater is often the father, or the father-substitute, a sense of guilt is involved, and, finally, it is only because an unconscious phantasy is distorted that this phantasy arises at all.

One most curious unconscious phantasy, well-known to psychoanalysts, is that of anal rape, occurring in girls or women and sometimes caused by or connected with the giving of enemas in early childhood. As Jones says, a variable amount of sadism is revealed in this phantasy, which may or may not pass over into conscious beating phantasies.

dreaming we constantly meet with the sexual and its perversions."

The qualities of phantasy as related to time are expressed by Freud thus: Phantasy hovers between the past, present, and future; it is connected with some idea of the present which has the power to arouse desire. Thence it wanders back to memories of an early experience in which a wish was fulfilled. Then comes creation of a situation representing future fulfilment of the wish.

The two principal groups of phantasies are egoistic and erotic, Freud states. Unsatisfied unconscious wishes form the driving power of phantasy. In day-dreaming the Ego tolerates wishes and thoughts, even of killing, that directed reflection would never condone. The content of phantasy proves that it is affective thinking escaping from a censorship that is stringent in its repression. In this way phantasy may be considered, as Varendonck says, as a safety valve for the abreaction of strong affects. Maeder speaks of day-dreaming as an appeasing function.

All are agreed that day-dreaming is common even in normal mental life; it is particularly manifested through absentmindedness and periods of distraction; it plays its part in invention, inspiration, and wit.

But when it is remembered that, as Varendonck points out, "a certain amount of madness is normal to our phantasies," some criterion of normalcy must be determined. For one thing it is a question of estrangement from reality. The neurotic is a victim of his phantasies, often without being aware of it, as is so readily shown in hysteria and the compulsions; the normal day-dreamer never loses his sense of reality, he can return to directed thinking whenever he chooses. Then, as Federn maintains, abnormal phantasy is analogous to sexual fore-pleasure in the sense that it does not go on to completion. It represents satisfaction obtained entirely in a mental state or activity that desires no fulfilment in the experiences of reality or further activity.

Saving or rescue phantasies are common, their content being that some-one is saved from a dangerous situation by the person who phantasies. Freud says that the meaning of such phantasied saving depends on whether the day-dream is framed by a man or a woman, and again this rests on the unconscious phantasy of "the family romance," the Oedipus conflict. Underneath, the male identifies himself with his father and saves somebody who represents the mother, the saving meaning giving her a son like himself. If a boy rescues his father it signifies his defiance of him, he repays the father for all that he has done for him.

Another extraordinary type of phantasy which has received as yet too little attention at the hands of psychoanalysts is the king-slave phantasy, in which the individual phantasies himself perhaps as now king, now slave, bound to service even by invisible golden chains.

Screen phantasies, or screen memories, are spoken of as being utilized to cover up deeper contents of mental life. The meaning of the term is clear.

Freud has spoken of a "common girlish phantasy" which he has met with in governesses and nurses where the mistress of the house is made to disappear, her place being taken by the one who does the day-dream-ing. This is developed on the basis of a repressed Oedipus conflict.

Sachs makes some comparisons between phantasy-formation and artistic creations. They show similarities because both are free from the conditions of reality, both offer compensations for lacks, both concern themselves sometimes with pain and tragedy. In the last they may both express masochistic trends, often because of a deeply rooted sense of guilt which finds satisfaction only through suffering. Phantasies show differ-ences from art productions in that while the main personage in the day-dream is the self and has meaning only for the self, the creations of art even when they may be centered about personal interests must have meaning for many. Then, the day-dream is formless and a mixture of words and pictures intended only for immediate pleasure, but the work of art must have form, unity, and clarity. Though the day-dream is often the first step in art creation, it has to be worked into form through the personality of the artist, so the artist must have gifts for self-expression which the day-dreamer does not need.

Unconscious phantasies, which arise on the basis of unrelinquished infantile wishes, are to be distinguished from conscious phantasies and day-dreams of the infantile type. "The point has been made that adult phantasies of the conscious type are of great diversity and strongly individual, but no such individual peculiarities are found in the unconscious phantasies." Like dreams they tend to have certain typical forms.

Concerning the difference between childish and adult conscious phantasies Jones writes brilliantly: "A young man or woman will often weave an elaborate fiction in which they (themselves) do not recognizably appear, but with children the hero is hardly disguised, if at all. Then, as a rule with children we miss the note of yearning or aspiration, that reaching out to something beyond the individual self, an endeavor even to attain to the infinite, with which we are familiar particularly in late adolescence. It may assume manifold forms here—religious, artistic, poetical, or purely social—but in all of them the characteristic marks are the feeling that the self is incomplete or even unsatisfactory, and the intense desire to get into contact with something—an idea or a being—outside the self. With this goes usually a much greater development of altruism, and the . . . development of a higher capacity for loving and the desire to love, as distinct from the older desire to be loved which is such a prominent feature of childhood."

Federn calls attention to a rather interesting fact, namely that many people fall asleep under the influence of wish-phantasies; the Ego then regresses to a childish state. He also suggests that an explanation of the greater difficulty that is found with advancing years in the ability to go to sleep is caused by the increasing disability to free oneself from the sense of reality.

A phenomenon very hard to classify is that of the *déjà vu*—a transitory illusion in which there is a feeling of familiarity on experiencing something new—for example, a new scene—Freud explains as the result of an analogy between two situations, the analogy not becoming conscious because of conflict and repression associated with the earlier experience. This then involves identification, the common situational element being unrecognized by the individual. One might consider either identification or displacement the underlying dynamism. Ferenczi, in stating that the *déjà vu* is explained by Freud as due to forgotten or repressed daydreams that dealt with a similar situation, adds his observation that he was able in many cases to trace this phenomenon back to nocturnal dreams from the previous or from a long-past night.

Freud also speaks of the *déjà raconté,* another form of *fausse reconnaissance* which sometimes makes its appearance at the close of a psychoanalytic treatment, "much to the physician's satisfaction." After the repressed is brought up and accepted by the patient against all resistances, and the patient has rehabilitated it, as it were, "the patient may say: 'Now I feel as though I had known it all the time.'"

A different phenomenon is seen in the case of "ideas of reference," where projection is the dynamism involved. Here others are supposed falsely to be noticing or speaking about the person, when in reality, the individual is projecting on to the external world his own self-criticism.

The significance of dreaming as such a frequent phenomenon of human behavior has been a matter of great concern for the psychoanalysts. First as to the general significance of dreams: Freud has discovered, he believes, that the general purpose of dreaming is to ward off external or internal stimuli which would tend to arouse the sleeper and thus secure sleep against interruption. External stimuli are warded off by being given a different interpretation and setting in the mental life which is always active in sleep, while "internal stimuli, caused by the pressure of instincts, are given free play by the sleeper and allowed to find satisfaction." The kernel of the dream is wish-fulfilment, imaginary gratification of repressed wishes.

The unconscious wish makes use of the nocturnal relaxation of repression in order to push its way into consciousness, but the resistance of the Ego is not entirely surrendered. Some of it remains in the form of a censorship of dreams and forbids the unconscious to express itself in the forms which it would otherwise assume. This alteration and softening process is the explanation of dream distortion, the most striking characteristic of the manifest dream. "A dream is the disguised fulfilment of a repressed wish; it is a compromise between the demands of a repressed impulse and the resistance of a censoring force in the Ego."

Next, concerning the interpretation of dreams it seems certain that this throws great light on personality-formation, whether or not dream-life is effective in producing personality characteristics. The method of psychoanalytic free association as applied to dream-life shows wishes, fears, hopes, and much other material that is buried in the Ucs. As Freud says, "Whenever we sleep we cast off our hard-won morality like a garment, only to put it on again next morning. This divestiture is naturally unattended by any danger because we are paralyzed, condemned to inactivity by the state of sleep."

The psychoanalytic literature on dreams is vast; it contains much interesting and challenging material that cannot possibly be reviewed here. We would earnestly recommend the reading of Freud's first book, *Die Traumdeutung*, 1900, or later editions (translation, *The Interpretation of Dreams*), which it is to be hoped may be revised some day to bring it in line with the later developments of psychoanalytic theory; the chapters on dreams in *A General Introduction to Psychoanalysis;* and the succinctly stated paragraphs on dream-life in *The Problem of Lay-Analyses.* For the more technical aspects of the interpretation of dreams, many parts of Freud's *Collected Papers* should be consulted. Second only to the works of Freud, it seems to us, are the contributions on dream-life by Ernest Jones, see particularly his *Papers on Psycho-Analysis,* later articles contributed by him to the periodicals, and even his few pages on dreams, a clearly stated summary, in the little popularized presentation, *Psycho-Analysis,* 1928. And there are many other notable contributions which may be found listed in Rickman's *Index.*

The significance of dreams was, of course, no new discovery of psychoanalysis; it is a matter of age-old knowledge. Even the fact and interpretation of dream-symbolism, as Freud says, long antedated psychoanalysis. Freud and his co-workers have simply affirmed what was known before, and through the technic of psychoanalysis have evolved better understandings of symbolism as it appears in dreams.

Freud feels that one of the strong points of psychoanalysis is that it has rescued the problem of dreams—"disguised expressions of highly significant underlying psychical processes"—and their possible meaning from the realm of superstition or scientific indifference and given them "a fresh scale of values in scientific thought."

The interpretation of dreams as carried out by the psychoanalysts requires not only infinite patience but immense skill, and the ingenuity displayed by eminent psychoanalysts is truly remarkable. In running through the work of Jones on dream-interpretation we find that recognition is required of opposites, distortions, reversals, absurdities which are distortions welcomed by resistance, transpositions, twistings, modifications, transformations, references, representatives, symbolizations, fusions, combinations, allusions, hidden connections and motivations, contradictions, substitutions, displacements, reminiscences, wishes—superficial as against deeper, expediences, conjurings up, inversions, repressions, elaborations, interchanges.

The latent dream-thoughts (see Dream-work) contain the meaning of the dream, while its manifest content is simply a make-believe, a façade, which can only serve as a starting point for the association technic of psychoanalysis. The analyst's interpretation is based upon what is revealed as the latent content of the dream.

"When the latent dream-thoughts that are revealed by the analysis of a dream are examined, one of them is found to stand out from among the rest, which are intelligible and well-known to the dreamer. These latter thoughts are residues of waking life (the day's residues, as they are called technically); but the isolated thought is found to be an impulse in the form of a wish" which is foreign to the waking life of the dreamer. The wish is the actual constructor of the dream; it provides the energy for its production and makes use of residues from waking life, nearly always from the preceding day, as material.

In general, psychoanalysts insist that dream-analysis is one of their most potent weapons for penetrating into the Ucs and thus for revealing and understanding underlying factors in personality-formation, normal as well as abnormal. Dream-interpretation gives access to forgotten mental material of childhood; infantile amnesia is largely overcome, Freud maintains, in connection with the interpretation of dreams.

Dream-interpretation proves to have a double value. The analyzed dream reveals the fulfilment of a repressed wish, but also, as the continuation of some fore-conscious activity of the day before, it gives a clue to conscious mental content. In the latter there may be subject matter giving expression to a determination, to a warning, to a reflection, or to the fulfilment of a wish.

Freud stated earlier that a recent or conscious wish is inadequate to cause a dream unless associated with a repressed unconscious wish, but a current wish may arouse deeper and older repressed thoughts. This explains why "the day's residues" appear in connection with older material discoverable in the latent content of the dream.

Freud in one place states that, "It is always a strict law of dream-interpretation that an explanation must be found for every detail."

We hesitate much to enter into discussion of typical symbols of dream-life because there appears to be a definite change of opinion among psychoanalysts concerning this whole matter. It now seems that every symbol has to be interpreted in and for itself, and particularly as related to the dreamer's own mental content. There certainly are frequent typical dreams of "falling, flying, floating, swimming, of being hemmed in, of nakedness" etc.—these typical dreams "yield first one and then another interpretation for the different patients, without resulting in an explanation of their motives and typical recurrence."

Anent the persistent statements that Freud ascribes sexual meaning to all dreams, we note his own definite assertion (*Lay-Analyses*) that he has never maintained this. "It is easy to see that hunger, thirst, or the need to excrete, can produce dreams of satisfaction just as well as any repressed sexual or egoistic impulse."

Those who wish to consult what was written years ago by Freud and one of his leading followers concerning the interpretation of symbols as they appear in dreams should read Freud's *Introduction to Psychoanalysis* and Jones' articles on symbolism and dreams in his *Papers on Psycho-Analysis*. Jones stated that the number of symbols encountered in practice can certainly be counted by thousands while the number of ideas thus symbolized is very limited. "All symbols represent ideas of the self and the immediate blood relatives, or of the phenomena of birth, love, and death." There are less than a hundred of these ideas. The vast majority of all symbols, Jones says, belong to the field of sexual symbolism and there are probably more symbols of the male organ than all other symbols put together.

One way of looking at the significance of dreams is that they take care, as Brill says, of what otherwise would develop into neurotic trends; in this sense they afford normal outlets.

MacCurdy strongly insists that the mood of the day is often influenced by dreams of the night before. His conception is that the dream process must be completed, that since in sleep we regress to the primitive type and content of infantile thinking, an adult type and content of thought must be developed before fully waking to face the world, otherwise the succeeding day will show more or less psychic disturbance.

There is a marked difference between the dreams of the young child and the adult. In the former the manifest and latent dream content is identical and represents plainly the imaginary fulfilment of an ungratified wish. The fact that repression is stronger in the adult determines the disguised or distorted form of the dream. The child dreams always of fulfilment of unsatisfied wishes aroused the preceding day. The latent dream thought is always associated with impressions of the preceding day and appears as the fulfilling of the unsatisfied wish.

Freud much earlier found that all dreams of the same night are concerned in one way or another with different aspects of the same subject. Reich corroborated this to the extent of finding "paired-dreams" but thought them too isolated to permit of the phenomenon being made the basis of any generalization. Alexander later made a very definite discovery that there were paired-dreams in which a punishment dream precedes, permitting subsequent appearance of dreams "containing unusually apparent wish fulfilments." "After these punitive demands have been satisfied, there were no longer any inhibiting forces to obstruct the fulfilment of wishes." In this way even a particularly clear and undisguised incest and pollution dream may follow a punitive dream—the Super-ego thus furnishing antecedent absolution and opening the way for the indulgence. Alexander suggests that this is analogous to the situation in which a child provokes punishment from its elders in order that it may sin freely, or it is similar to the principle operative in the manic-depressive situation.

Jones, in particular, enters into the question of how and to what extent dreams may influence waking life. He thinks that it is probable that many of our waking processes are affected by preceding dreams to a greater extent than is generally recognized; he gives some instances. He thinks that it is not only conduct but also moods and beliefs that can be traced to dreams. But such a tracing is only a step towards the elucidation of the phenomenon. The most that the dream can do is sometimes to give to an underlying mental process its particular form. The deeper meaning is to be ascertained through analysis of the dream itself.

Freud's conception of dream interpretation has been termed the reductive or causal-reductive method; it reduces the dream to its component reminiscences and the instinctive processes that underlie them. Thus it deals essentially with the past, with repressed infantile wishes. Jung, breaking away from the Freudian school, conceived of dream interpretation as a constructive or productive method. It has also been called the prospective or forward-looking method, inasmuch as the dream is thought to be dealing with the present problem looking ahead to a solution of it. Adler, in parting ways with Freud, deals very little with the unconscious and frankly says he concerns himself very little with it. For him the dream reflects the future in the sense of dealing with the life goal of the individual.

Jung's view of dreams is that they may not only be wish fulfilment representations but may also throw light upon the present problem of the dreamer's life and be of great practical value to him. Besides this, dreams represent the collective unconscious of the human race to some degree, the inheritance of past experience and "world images," and as such have direct relationship to racial myths. The fact that symbols appearing in dreams are frequently of an archetypal character, such as are common to various peoples, is held by Jung to be a conclusive argument for the primordial nature of dream life.

W. H. R. Rivers, following somewhat the same lines, suggested as an alternative to Freud's formula the working hypothesis that the dream is the solution or attempted solution of a conflict which finds expression in ways characteristic of different levels of early experience; it is an attempt to solve the conflict by such means as are available during sleep.

Perhaps we may dare here mention as a partial critique and as an alternative method to that of psychoanalysis the work of Havelock Ellis on dreams, especially as he elaborates it in *The Synthesis of Dreams* (Volume 7, *Studies in the Psychology of Sex*). Then, presenting particularly the theory of the relation of dreams and of dream symbols to physical stimuli, the work of Lydiard Horton and his inventorial method of dream analysis is to be considered. (See various articles in the *Journal of Abnormal Psychology*, 1914–1920.)

The behavior peculiarities of everyday life, ordinarily regarded as normal enough mannerisms, errors, slips, forgettings and what not, have come under the close scrutiny of psychoanalysts through their discovery of the latent meanings of these manifestations in the course of their analysis of patients. Symptomatic or faulty acts have the appearance of being unmotivated, unintentional, and insignificant, but through psychoanalytic procedure many of them can be shown to be determined by unconscious motives.

According to Freud the actions which may properly be placed in this category must fulfill three conditions:

(a) They must not exceed a certain measure, that is, they must be generally agreed upon as "within normal limits."

(b) They must be merely temporary disturbances. That is, the same action must ordinarily be performed correctly. If corrected by others there must be immediate recognition of the fact that the act has been performed incorrectly.

(c) There is frequently a failure on the part of the individual performing the act to realize he has done so, but if the action is perceived or brought to the attention by others there must be no perception of any motivation, and the individual must attempt to explain it as due to "inattention" or as an "accident."

It is self-evident from the tremendous number of peculiarities that are observable in the everyday life of all people that the organization of them and the determination of their significances according to psychoanalytic thought must be no easy task. However, the subject affords immensely interesting reading material. The chief sources to consult are Freud's *Psychopathology of Everyday Life* and Brill's *Introduction to Psychoanalysis*. The latter has made some of the most interesting observations which have appeared in the literature, observations backed up often by hours and hours of search for correct interpretation. Jones, too, has a good chapter on this subject appearing in his *Papers*.

It should be noted that the term "symptomatic acts" is used by Freud and also Jones in connection only with what we have termed "manneristic" acts. In view of the fact, however, that both erroneous and manneristic acts are regarded as compromise-formations and therefore resembling symptoms in their relation to repression, we feel justified in speaking of both groups as symptomatic.

Examples of erroneous acts are: (a) slips of the tongue and pen, such as use of the wrong word, use of the opposite word to the one consciously intended (e. g. "selfish" for "unselfish" when making a funeral eulogy), compounding syllables to produce a new, or partially new, word, transposing words, etc; (b) ignorance and omission of, or making an incorrect substitution for, a name or fact when the correct name or fact is particularly needed, such name or fact having been previously well-known; (c) holding beliefs, and perhaps making emphatic statements based on these, which both before and afterwards are recognized as false; (d) failure to carry out instructions comprehended when given; failure to perform a commission willingly undertaken; (e) making a promise which the individual is consciously reluctant to make, but has the conscious intention of keeping, only to discover later that he had himself previously made it impossible in some way to keep this promise; (f) misplacing, losing or destroying in some way a consciously valued object (e. g. dropping and breaking a dish when the conscious intention is not to break it); (g) such "awkward" acts as injuring one's self or stumbling over a clearly visible object in the case of an individual who is habitually graceful and well-poised.

Symptomatic acts originate on the basis of the same unconscious repressed material as do symptoms, and, like them, are compromise-formations. They are a way out for the non-neurotic or so-called normal individual, and comprise a large group of mental phenomena, which are not only "meaningful" for the study of normal personality, but also emphasize the fact, so insisted upon by psychoanalysts, that there is no sharp line of demarcation between the mental life of normal and neurotic individuals.

There are apparently two distinct groups of symptomatic acts, namely:

(1) Acts carried out erroneously—that is, the individual consciously intended to perform them correctly. Freud speaks of these as "errors," and says they are "the result of the mutual interference of two different intentions," the interfering intention being unconscious and having a very definite relation to the conscious one with which it interferes. Such erroneous acts are either (a) very inconspicuous, requiring only such trivial excuses as "a mistake," "a slip," "a *faux pas*," or (b) more striking and leading to pronounced inconvenience or embarrassment to either the self or others, but nevertheless necessitating only such perfunctory and conventional excuses as "an accident," "didn't think," "just happened," etc.

(2) "Manneristic" acts—that is, apparently aimless movements, gestures, postures, more or less habitual or characteristic and made automatically "without attending to them, or as if in a moment of distraction." These acts differ from "errors" in that they arise independently of other conscious acts.

The speech blunder of blending parts of two words together Freud terms "contamination" and says that it is the beginning of the process of condensation. He admits other explanations such as Wundt's "contact effect of a sound" or the influence of preceding or anticipated sounds upon a word, but he is convinced that there is almost invariably an additional disturbing element in the Ucs which comes to light through the speech blunder.

Freud thinks that some forms of speech blunder can be traced to a colliding of the consciously intended word with unconscious impulses to obscenity. In support of this he calls attention to the purposive disfigurement or distortion of words and phrases by vulgar people which serve the purpose of hinting at obscene expressions.

The very common shame reaction to having attention called to one's mistakes in speaking and the anger associated with inability to recall a name and the surprise "at the tenaciousness of an apparently indifferent memory" invariably mean that an unconscious factor has contributed to the disturbance.

With regard to the falsification or distortion of names, Freud points out that when this is done intentionally it always amounts to an insult. Few people, he says, "can avoid feeling a tinge of resentment when they find that their name has been forgotten. . . . They instinctively realize that if they had made a greater impression on the person's mind he would certainly have remembered them again, for the name is an integral part of the personality."

The rôle of self-criticism is often very significant in speech blunders, that is, there is "an internal contradiction against one's own utterance." In such cases, Freud says, the blunder itself "lays bare the inner dishonesty."

An illustration is the forgetting of a proper name when greeting an old acquaintance, or when performing an introduction, etc. Freud thinks this is one of the most common of symptomatic acts, and is to be traced back to what he calls a "self-reference" complex, that is, the name which it is temporarily impossible to recall would revive some unpleasant narcistic blow, probably having to do in some way with personal, family or professional affairs. Another example of forgetting which originates in

285

Psychoanalysts are convinced that all acts of the above nature have frequently, and perhaps always, a deeper unconscious significance. Even though the justification given for the act seems good, Freud thinks that the possibility of its having an unconscious origin should never be dismissed. Close observation, he says, will almost inevitably show that those actions "about which consciousness knows nothing or wishes to know nothing" really give expression to repressed complexes.

It is obvious that an indirect and unchallenged outlet is offered through the medium of erroneous actions to the aggressive impulses associated with ambivalence; manneristic actions afford a symbolical and innocuous outlet for erotic impulses; minor acts of self-injury give opportunity for an expression both of destructive impulses and the forces opposed to them. Self-injuring and self-inconveniencing acts may also, as in the case of symptoms, be motivated by and serve to appease secondarily an unconscious sense of guilt and need for punishment. Thus from the point of view of personality study symptomatic acts are of the greatest importance. No matter how trivial the act may appear, analysis of it may reveal fundamental trends.

repression is the failure to remember to carry out a project or promise at the proper time, recalling it later when it is impossible to carry it out.

Freud contends that a certain group of awkward, seemingly-accidental movements are really strongly dominated by some unconscious intention, "and they accomplish their aim with a certainty that cannot be generally credited to conscious arbitrary motions." These awkward movements result in some form of damage to objects, and Freud says that the indifference with which we accept this damage to something we consciously value may certainly be taken as proof of the existence of an unconscious purpose in the awkward act.

In the case of breakages on the part of domestics Freud thinks that these, too, may be traced to unconscious factors such as hostility to objects which have no aesthetic value for persons of this class, and which may also be a source of a great deal of work for them. The dexterity in handling delicate objects which is often acquired by clumsy people may be due, Freud thinks, to identification with the owners of the objects.

Examples of "manneristic" acts are: toying or trifling with parts of the body or clothing or with objects within reach (e. g. scribbling with pencil while listening to conversation, jingling coins in pocket; Freud points out that in the last mentioned instance the individual often does not hear the sound he is producing and is astonished and incredulous when his attention is called to it); humming of melodies while thinking or doing something else.

Symptomatic acts differ from symptoms in that they are confined "to the least important psychic activities, while everything that can lay claim to a higher psychic value remains free from disturbance." Symptoms, on the other hand, "appear in the most important individual and social activities in a manner to disturb the functions of nourishment and sexual relations, professional and social life."

Freud's emphasis on the unconscious motivation of all seemingly arbitrary actions is quite in keeping with the firm stand he takes on strict psychic determinism in connection with his therapeutic free association technique. He has no hesitation in declaring that there is no such thing as free choice even in such trivial matters as thinking of a name or a number. (See chapter on Determinism—*Psychopathology of Everyday Life*.)

Symptomatic-act formation involves some, but not all, of the dynamisms operative in producing symptoms. In addition to the initial repression, a significant rôle is played by symbolization, displacement and rationalization. The last dynamism, of course, must be constantly active in connection with the explanations or justifications which the individual feels the need to advance either for his own consumption or that of others. Identification (primary) must also be reckoned with in many cases of manneristic acts, which very frequently owe their origin, in part at least, to similar manifestations in others.

It seems clear that psychoanalysts regard as peculiar to symptomatic-act formation a certain unconscious process which might be described as a temporary non-receptivity or insensitivity to external and internal sensory impressions and perceptions. This process takes such specific forms as not-hearing, not-seeing, not-feeling, not-thinking, not-knowing, not-recalling (or forgetting). There may be also hearing, seeing, etc. substitutively or erroneously; in general, the process seems to aim at shutting out from conscious awareness objects or impressions (actual or remembered) in order to afford an outlet in a disguise acceptable to the Ego for a repressed wish. For example, the misplacing (that is, putting a thing in a different place and then forgetting where it was put) of a consciously valued object may be due to an unconscious dislike for it, or to an unconscious dislike for a person who has been associated with it in some way, or to a displacement upon this particular object through symbolic association of the unpleasant affect attaching to another more strongly cathected object.

Much is made by psychoanalysts of manneristic or symbolic acts as they occur during the analytic session. Freud says, "Of equal significance to the physician, and worthy of his observation is everything that one does with his clothing often without noticing it." Every slight negligence or change in the customary attire (e. g. an unfastened button, etc.) "means to express something that the wearer of the apparel does not wish to say directly." The proof of the interpretation made by the analyst of such trifling acts is supported, Freud says, by the fact that the ideas which come to the surface when the patient's attention is directed to the act are in harmony with other material being brought to light during the analysis.

Jones draws attention to the fact that a manneristic or symbolic action is sometimes quite a complicated one and performed only in certain specific situations.

Freud points out that symbolic actions are always carried out more completely the more there is conscious absorption in something else. A great deal of symbolism of this kind, he thinks, occurs in everyday life and passes by quite unnoticed. This is associated, he thinks, with a universal urge to confess.

Both Freud and Ferenczi are of the opinion that symbolic acts are often "pantomimic announcements" of the desire to masturbate. Ferenczi therefore also thinks that there is probably a close connection between acts of this nature and certain forms of *tic convulsif*.

Freud calls attention to the significance which the paranoiac attaches to trivial details of behavior in other people and which usually escape the normal person. Though the paranoiac makes interpretations of such details in an excessively far-reaching manner, nevertheless Freud thinks that he really sees more clearly certain minor aspects of behavior than does the ordinary healthy individual.

Not-recalling or not-knowing is, so psychoanalysts believe, a very common method of shutting out pain-evoking stimuli. That is, the "forgetting" in which they are especially interested is of the nature of transient lapses of memory in regard to impressions and facts that are at other times easily recalled, and is always an evidence of repression. Conscious embarrassment and annoyance is always associated with forgetfulness of this type.

Freud describes two other varieties of forgetting, both of which are a form of substitutive recalling. One of these is false recollection. In the case of name forgetting, for example, the individual who strives to recall an escaped name often finds other substitutive names (immediately recognized as false) forcing themselves into consciousness. This phenomenon Freud explains as due to displacement, the incorrect substitutive name standing in direct association with the forgotten name.

Freud makes it clear when discussing the forgetting of proper names, that he is not contradicting the conditions of memory reproduction and forgetting assumed by other psychologists. He has only, he says, added another motive to "the factors long recognized as positive in the forgetting of names." He even goes so far as to say that the relations and dispositions assumed by other psychologists "are indispensable also in our case in order to make it possible for the repressed element to associatively gain control over the desired name and take it along into the repression." The repression might not have been possible in the case of another name "having more favorable conditions of reproduction." In the case of proper names, at least, Freud seems inclined to take account of a constitutional tendency to forgetting or faulty recollection as re-inforcing a repressive process.

Repression may also be responsible for forgetting in the sense that there may be a "disturbance of thought through an inner contradiction emanating from the repression."

When faulty recollection occurs in connection with impressions and these find credence Freud says they "may be designated as delusions of memory." He points out that though disturbances of memory have been frequently noted as having a significance for various pathological syndromes, "there is no reference whatever to its being motivated."

Freud speaks of two forms of screen memories, namely, interposing and contemporaneous. In the former the concealed memory lies chronologically beyond the screen memory; in the latter the concealing memory is connected with the impression it conceals not only through its content but also through contiguity of time.

The other variety of forgetting or substitutive recalling, Freud terms "screen-memories." He found in analytic treatment that many of the recollections of early childhood were of a relatively unimportant and accidental nature, and became convinced finally that these indifferent impressions of the childhood period played the part of a concealing memory in consciousness, owing their existence simply to an association with an earlier experience against the direct reproduction of which there are resistances. Thus displacement is again at work.

Freud rules out as insufficient explanation for symptomatic acts the factors of fatigue, excitement, absent-mindedness, and distraction of attention. Such factors, he says, only act by way of facilitation of the unconscious dynamisms which are at work. The question must always be answered, why did the act take this or that specific form? e. g., why the forgetting of one particular name? why the particular form of gesture, accident, etc.?

It seems clear, though psychoanalysts do not expressly designate it as such, that a specific dynamic process is at work in, and peculiar to, symptomatic-act formation. *Desensitization* suggests itself as an appropriate name for this dynamism, since the Ego suffers a temporary contraction of one or several of its sensory functions, and by so doing aids the Id to camouflage and further distort some derivative of an infantile hostile or sexual impulse. Thus motor discharge is afforded, and at the same time the Ego is withdrawn from danger and the need for undertaking new defenses.

Temporary forgetting of impressions may be regarded as a dulling or desensitizing of inner perceptive powers, and thus as having a value similar to failures in actual perception for the bringing about of impulse distortion and motor discharge.

It is to be pointed out that desensitization may frequently underlie and produce such overt phenomena as distraction of attention, absent-mindedness, etc., whether or not this behavior is accompanied by, and used as an excuse for, actual "blunders" or "mistakes." It will of course be readily admitted that, even occurring by themselves, lack of attention, failure to hear, etc. afford an easily acceptable outlet for the discharge of unconscious hostility. (A. M. Bowers.)

Behavior which forms into habitual patterns having special personal and social significances has come to have great interest for psychoanalysts; their discoveries have challenged their interest in personality-formation. And here again it is upon the historical aspects, the psycho-biological development, of personality that special light has been thrown. For our presentation we may offer first one given classification of developed personality types, the only one that apparently has been formulated. Next we shall review certain developmental beginnings, as such, of personality-formation, and in the course of this review many discrete personality characteristics will come to be mentioned. Finally we shall take up certain specific personality-formations and their implications for group and educational situations.

Alexander maintains that in psychoanalysis we have a psychology that for the first time deserves the designation of being a science of the mind. Former schools of psychology dealt with abstractions, such as perceptions, feelings, etc., but psychoanalysis deals with the factual elements of the psychic content. In unprejudiced fashion Freud has investigated the real motives and strivings of his fellowmen.

A difficulty is found in investigating personality-formation because, as Freud states, "the process of character-formation is less transparent and less accessible to analysis than is neurosis because either repression is not at work at all or it easily attains its aim." It is perhaps on account of this difficulty or perhaps because the time is not yet ripe for it that there has not been as yet much attempt on the part of psychoanalysts to organize or classify in the field of personality studies. Yet knowledge of many elements that go to form personality has been gained through studies of more or less pathological material. And outside of the psychoanalytic procedure with individuals, psychoanalytic observations and investigations of a great deal that may be regarded as the best products of our civilization throw much light upon the development of human behavior trends.

Ferenczi comments on the psychoanalytic viewpoint from which it appears that basic mental attitudes and mental activity patterns represent the transformation of infantile psycho-physical states or organic dispositions. It is not merely the infantile impulses and their repression, sublimation, etc., which are responsible for later mental attitudes and trends, but the idea seems to be that physical sensations which have to do with muscle innervations and their control are the forerunners or prototypes of later mental reaction patterns. For example, as will be shown later, the pleasure in feces-retention may presage, through being transferred to other love-objects, a general attitude of possessiveness; a fixation at the biting stage of oral erotism may be the forerunner of later hostile destructive tendency with regard to love-objects.

The building up of personality, according to psychoanalytic theory, is matter of control by the Ego of fundamental urges partly as the result of its own perceptions of reality and partly under the influence of the Super-ego. All cultural strivings are to be accredited to the normal repressive tendencies under the influence of the Super-ego. It is through this inhibiting activity that various asocial urges are hindered or sublimated and the demands of social adjustment met. The domestication under pressure of the Super-ego of aggressive and certain sexual strivings makes for social serviceability which finds expression in industry, art, science, and religion.

Personality-formation is largely a matter of Ego-identifications which take the place of abandoned Id cathexes but, Freud says, the part played by the Super-ego in personality-formation must always be reckoned with. Although the Super-ego "is amenable to every later influence, it preserves throughout life the character given to it by its derivation from the father-complex, namely, the capacity to stand apart from the Ego and to rule it. It is a memorial of the former weakness and dependence of the Ego, and the mature Ego remains subject to its domination." The later fear of conscience has its origin in the Ego's dread of the Super-ego.

Alexander has been particularly interested in setting forth the psychoanalytically understood welding of elements that come together to form the developed personality and we shall follow his lead in discussing personality types. As the result of the working of the different forces that go to produce personality, there are to be described, Alexander believes, four principal types of personality or "character."

Abraham says, "If we consider the problems of character-formation from the one large unifying point of view which psychoanalysis affords us, from that of infantile sexuality, then it is obvious how everything weaves itself into a whole, into the characterological sphere."

Concerning the matter of the permanence of personality characteristics, a matter always of great interest to students of personality-formation, we may note what Freud says about the development of splendid personality characteristics in adult life as related to bad behavior in childhood. He says that even those who have been the most pronounced egoists may through reaction-formation become the most helpful and sacrificing members of a community; even great friends of humanity and of animals have been evolved from little sadists and animal-tormentors. Both love and hate as twin opposites are present in all of us, and "it might be said that we owe the fairest flowers of our love-life to the reaction against the hostile impulse."

Reaction-formation is a very common way for the child to adapt to social norms. This, Abraham thinks, never succeeds completely. He says "we invariably find the opposite extreme more or less strongly developed." Reaction-formations are really over-compensations (examples are exaggerated orderliness and pedantry) and behind them there is apt to be hidden an obstinate holding fast to original impulses. Obedient children (and adults) may be concealing, Abraham says, "underlying rebellious impulses."

1. *The Normal Personality*—In this there is a harmonious working together of the forces of the Id, Ego, and Super-ego. The original urges are not unhealthily inhibited, but rather are domesticated in the service of the individual and society. Nor does the Super-ego create too much blocking of urges; its influence in normal personality is confined to insistence upon unpermissible urges being transformed into socially valuable activities.

The normal character is defined by E. Glover as an organized series of behavior reactions which secure equilibrium between Id tendencies and surrender to reality. These reactions begin in the period of infantile sexuality and form a continuous series of adaptations. There are few so-called normal personalities whose life is not interwoven with habit-formation of the most insignificant kind which point to constant gratification of the Id.

Freud speaks of the stable character that is contrasted with vacillation resulting from the presence of many fixations. When in the development of instinctual life there are many fixations constant ambivalence is produced.

E. Glover speaks of normal character-reactions as being not only a safety valve for Id tensions, but as forming a first line of defense when repression endangers the personality. In both sublimation and reaction-formation there is desexualization, Glover says. And in the case of reaction-formation the desexualization does not differ from an act of repression, indeed, reaction-formation plays a definite rôle in repression. Thus the social reactions of sympathy and humanity oppose themselves to the cruel urges of the Id.

Alexander thinks that contributions of psychoanalysis to study of the non-neurotic individual has so far been unfortunately neglected. He asks, since all normal as well as abnormal actions are at bottom modified expressions of the Id and since all sublimations originate from the Oedipus complex, how it is that the normal man has no sense of guilt, either about his impulse life or his sublimations. Some light may be shed on this problem: (1) With the attainment of the genital stage, the relation to exogamous objects of the unsublimated impulse life indicates "approval in the deepest strata of the conscience." (2) Genitality also brings with it social efficacy—social deeds silence the sense of guilt. In the healthy subject these take the place of pain or suffering in the neurotic. "While the neurotic pays in coin having a narcistic value, from which while suffering he can extract masochistic pleasure, the socially directed act is an active performance which can do good."

Psychological types of personality: Psychoanalysts are in distinct disagreement with Jung's conception of psychological types. Freud defines introversion as a substituting for actual objects phantasies of these objects. This means that the erotic relation has not been broken off but the individual "has ceased to direct his motor activities to the attainment of his aims in connection with real objects." Freud goes on to say quite clearly "it is only to this condition of the libido that we may legitimately apply the term *introversion* of the libido which is used by Jung indiscriminately."

Abraham claims that his experiences with patients have uniformly shown that an attitude of hostility to objects can be broken up during analysis, which goes to prove, he thinks, that it is not "a manifestation of a rigid psychological type." His explanation of introversion "in Jung's sense" is "an infantile clinging to the pleasure in anal retention."

2. *The Inhibited Personality*—Alexander says that in this there is the influence of an overstrenuous, overmoral Super-ego which produces an unliberated shy type of personality. Only a quantitative difference distinguishes this from the "neurotic character."

Freud has recently undertaken to discuss the dynamics of inhibited behavior, found so frequently in the so-called normal individual and manifesting itself in minor disturbances of common activities in the sexual, the nutritional, the locomotor, and occupational spheres. These disturbances take such specific forms as lack of pleasure in sex activity, loss of appetite, disinclination for walking or feelings of weakness when walking, diminished desire for work or poor execution and fatigue associated with its performance.

Inhibitions are not defenses, but they are closely connected with defense, since they aid in withdrawing the Ego from danger-situations. The Ego unconsciously renounces, or submits to restrictions upon, various motor functionings proper to it in order either (1) to obviate the need for undertaking new or increased defenses, or (2) in order to have at its disposal more energy to employ in meeting the demands for fresh defenses.

In the first case, some special activity or the bodily organs associated with the performance of the activity may through symbolical association become erotized, that is, may take on the significance of a derivative of some repressed infantile phantasy and thus likewise demand repression. Instead, however, of undertaking this new repression the Ego renounces the questionable activity and thus, as Freud says, avoids a conflict with the Id.

Freud suggests that another motivation of inhibition-formation may be "in the service of self-punishment." This, he says, frequently occurs in connection with professional activities. Some particular line of work through which the individual derives a special pleasure (either through a sense of expertness or the recognition of others) may be also bringing some form of erotic gratification "disapproved of by the more strict Super-ego." By developing a certain clumsiness of performance or lack of satisfac-

Alexander says, "All manifestations of neurotic inhibition rest upon the schematic procedure of the Super-ego." This can be understood only by remembering that Alexander looks upon the Super-ego as the repressing faculty. Thus an over-severe Super-ego may exclude from consciousness "and therefore from access to the motor apparatus" many forms of outlet which would be by no means ego-dystonic, namely, unacceptable to the Ego. In other words, "over-repression" on the part of the Super-ego may inhibit perfectly natural and justifiable outlets (sublimated or otherwise) for sexual impulses. This underlies many inhibitions associated with speech and gesture.

Abraham thinks that certain forms of neurotic inhibition are due to the fact that there has not been a successful displacement of libido to the genital zone. If genital libido is lacking there will be not only inhibition associated with the procreative act itself, but also "we invariably find a lack of productivity and initiative in other forms of behavior."

Freud points out that inhibitions serve the same purpose as do symptoms in withdrawing the Ego from danger situations. He also states that an inhibition may arise through the displacement of an unconscious "counter-will" from one conscious resolve to another. He gives as an example a case reported by Brill of a woman who had always enjoyed letter writing and who suddenly found herself greatly disinclined to carry on her correspondence. She found she had to make a very great effort before she could bring herself to write a letter. This was due to the fact that she had received one particular letter which necessitated a very unequivocal reply. She was undecided what to say so did not answer the letter at all, and this indecision was unconsciously transferred to other letters, bringing about an inhibition to letter writing in general.

Ferenczi says that the doubting mania of the obsessional neurotic "is characterized by inhibition of the power of judgment; belief and disbelief come into play here simultaneously, or immediately after each other with equal intensity, and prevent the formation either of a conviction or of a refusal of a statement, that is, of any judgment whatsoever."

tion in something which had previously been highly pleasurable the individual satisfies his need for punishment and avoids a conflict with the Super-ego.

Inhibitions are sometimes to be explained as Ego-retrenchments in the service of defense, when, through regression, a sexual phantasy begins to take on a stronger cathexis and to demand motor discharge. Thus, inhibitions may obviate the need for symptom-formation.

Freud makes it very clear that there is a marked distinction to be drawn between inhibitions and symptoms. He says, "These do not flourish on the same soil." Symptoms "signify indications of disease processes," while inhibitions have "a special relationship to function," and do not "necessarily indicate something pathological."

Jones points out how inhibitions may arise if the Super-ego "fails to develop freely." The childish attitude of over-morality may persist and may become directed also "against remote derivatives of the forbidden impulse" resulting in the becoming forbidden of "all sorts of quite innocent acts, even those such as walking, eating, and so on." This appears to consciousness "simply as an incapacity," which can often be remedied by tracing it to its source, namely, "the burden of irrational guilt."

Jones thinks that inhibitions of interest may be the explanation in many cases of what appears to be intellectual incapacity. The aversion for or the inability to comprehend some study in the school curriculum may be simply because it has some symbolical association with a primary unconscious idea and the child avoids an activity which will bring about Super-ego condemnation and thus necessitate the undertaking of new defenses. He says, "The difference between one geometrical figure and another, between the spelling of one word and another, and still more in such gross matters as the difference between the feeling for one language and another may strike quite different roots in the unconscious and dictate all sorts of preferences and distastes."

The same writer draws attention to a "general inhibition of thought," a sort of "affective feeblemindedness," which he says Freud has frequently pointed out occurs in adults who as children were exposed to a parental attitude which demanded suppression of all doubt and curiosity in respect to sexual and religious matters. Such intellectually inhibited individuals have not been able to achieve, Ferenczi says, the partial surrender of judgment demanded of them and have reacted by a tendency to an all-embracing credulity and submissiveness to authority.

Freud and Jones give as examples of symbolic association causing erotization of parts of the body—in these cases the fingers—instances where there is disinclination for playing on the piano or organ because this symbolized for the patient his own autoerotic desires.

Both Abraham and Freud make mention of walking inhibitions. Abraham says he has repeatedly observed a fear of walking too quickly which is based on a symbolical association with some repressed erotic pleasure which might "run away" with the individual. Abraham also draws attention to the fact that, since in the normal person pleasure in movement is associated with object-finding, locomotor inhibitions may be due in many cases to an incestuous fixation, a "dread of attaining their libidinal aim."

Abraham traces many of the reactions of women to the sexual act (e. g. vaginismus, frigidity, lack of orgasm) to the castration complex. The sexual inhibitions arise even when the woman consciously is willing to assume the female rôle because of the unconscious desire to take revenge on the man by arousing his expectations and then disappointing him. This may extend itself to a more general personality characteristic, namely "to excite expectations of a pleasant nature in their environment and then not fulfil them." Abraham draws attention to the fact that many women only obtain normal sexual satisfaction after they have had a child. The castration "wound" has been healed in the compensatory way desired in childhood, i. e. by the "gift" of a child.

Freud refers to the fact that general inhibition is very characteristic of depressive states, especially of melancholy. He thinks his theories of inhibition-formation should be a beginning towards the better understanding of these states.

3. *The Neurotic Personality*—The term "neurotic character" is employed by psychoanalysts to designate those individuals who, as Alexander says, "suffer from no very definite symptoms of illness, but whose behavior in life is in the highest degree impulsive and frequently even compulsive; they are unusually subject to the domination of their unconscious instinctual tendencies" which shows itself in senseless, irrational behavior. Again he says, "the unconscious is always victorious and seizes its satisfaction at the expense of the most elementary interests of the Ego. . . ."

The "neurotic character" is regarded by both Jones and Alexander as standing between the neurosis and the healthy personality. Jones says that in the case of such people there has been an imperfect transformation of the early infantile impulses and conflicts into personality characteristics; the characteristics peculiar to the "neurotic character" he speaks of as "still betraying evidences of unconscious characteristics" as well as of their unconscious origin. They are "manifestations intermediate between normal character traits and neurotic symptoms." Alexander speaks of a "life inter-woven with neurosis"; Jones says the neurosis is, as it were, "built into the character." Thus it is more difficult to eradicate than the symptom since it is not felt as foreign to the personality.

Alexander says of "neurotic characters" that they are often regarded as weak-willed people and frequently their careers are tragic. A not uncommon final fate is death by suicide.

Extreme examples of the "neurotic character" are found in typical cases of adventurers and swindlers. They display both anti-social compulsions and uncontrolled activities that greatly endanger their own interests. Their behavior "eludes the vigilance of the censorship" by ascribing the calamitous consequences to fate. In a sense they are thus both the offender and the judge.

Alexander points out the difference between a perversion and the behavior of the "neurotic character," namely, the perverse satisfaction is accepted by the Ego, while the illogicality of the "neurotic character" is not recognized as a satisfaction by the Ego. This distinction also holds good for neurotic symptoms which, as Alexander says, are "all characteristically isolated as far as possible from the rest of the person's life," that is, are felt as Ego-dystonic.

Alexander speaks of two types of "neurotic character"—the criminal type and the oversensitive conscience type. Both are perpetually driven to injure themselves in life, and if this outlet is denied them, they are apt to produce neurotic symptoms.

The misery which the "neurotic character" often creates for others must be taken into account, Alexander says, as affording him some satisfaction.

The "neurotic character" Alexander thinks, makes use of a dynamic process similar to that of work in the manic-depressive cycle and paired-dreams. In all three instances there is an alternation of impulse-satisfaction and atonement.

Reich thinks the "neurotic character" is more serious than neurosis. Ferenczi speaks of it as a private psychosis which is tolerated by the Ego. Opinions differ in regard to therapy.

No special dynamisms are made use of by the "neurotic character." Alexander says there is perhaps some repression, but not enough to hinder direct gratifications in reality. On the whole, people of this type are "suffering from a deficiency of defense reactions." The sense of guilt, however, is present but is taken care of not by "the symbolic overcompensations" or self-punishment of the neurotic, but by a perpetual compulsion to self-injury through the environment. That is, satisfaction is attained by a specific way of living. The "neurotic character" lives out his impulses, and at the same time manages to get himself punished, as it were, by the cruelty of fate or chance.

Though they differ concerning the specific personality peculiarities which distinguish the "neurotic character," psychoanalysts seem to be in agreement on one point, namely, the uniform tendency of this type of individual to embroil the environment in his fight against his sense of guilt. In the neurotic the need for punishment is satisfied by the formation of symptoms; in the healthy individual this satisfaction is obtained through the embarrassment and inconvenience resultant upon trivial everyday blunders. The "neurotic character" achieves the needed atonement or penance by committing his irrational acts as it were compulsively "at the most important and decisive moment of his life."

Alexander discusses in detail a case of "neurotic character" which he analyzed. He claims that he was able to trace this development back to the castration complex which "stood as the central point in the whole character-formation." As a result of the treatment the man's personality showed a complete change and there were also certain external changes; his expression, his manner, his handwriting, and above all his gait altered conspicuously.

As a boy this patient had stealing tendencies—he stole money from his father's pockets, also he stole pens, pencils, and money from two cleverer schoolmates, whom he both envied and liked. He stole only from his father and these two friends. He had many hairbreadth escapes brought about by his own blunders and faulty actions. (These were recalled associatively. Alexander is not sure whether these recollections were factual or phantasies—he does not think it matters.)

At the time of his father's death when he was six, he had a very remorseful reaction and a desire to atone to the father for "all that I have done against you."

As a man he displayed certain peculiar personality characteristics and trends; he was inclined to establish a father-son relationship with his business employers, worked with intense energy and self-sacrifice for them; he was meticulously overconscientious and honorable in business; he was keen to detect dishonesty in others, especially his subordinates. He was constantly lending money to his friends and being defrauded and exploited by them. He was constantly putting himself in positions where there were great temptations to dishonesty. He had a sense of guilt over every acquisition of money, and managed to lose it in some way.

Alexander points out that though money played such a significant part for this man, his personality characteristics and behavior arise on the basis not of anal-erotism but of the castration complex. They are to be accounted for on the basis not of the feces-money equation, but on the money-penis equation. Another important point to be noticed is the fact that object-transference figures conspicuously (the childhood stealing from two boy friends only, the loaning money later only to friends—all these being father representatives); had anal erotism been the basis of the personality formation, the specific persons from whom he stole or to whom he lent money would not have mattered.

307

4. *The Criminal Character*—The criminal character shows itself for the most part in defective powers of moral inhibition resulting from an incorrect or neglected educational upbringing. The anti-social tendencies, which in the normal individual are inhibited through the influence of the Super-ego not only appear in consciousness but definitely lead to criminal acts. (For other discussion of the criminal character see Delinquency and Criminality.)

Staub goes somewhat further than Alexander and includes under the head of the criminal character all cases of chronic or professional criminality—those individuals who with full consciousness enter into criminality. He agrees with Abraham, Aichhorn, and Adler that in the great majority of cases such individuals have suffered from the want of love and satisfaction of pleasure during their early childhood experiences.

According to E. Glover, the "neurotic character" is best understood and described in terms of behavior. He thinks that the study of it is a useful way of approaching the study of the normal individual.

Glover distinguishes between neurosis and the "neurotic character" on the basis of autoplastic (in the neurosis) *versus* alloplastic methods of tension discharge. Then, as in the case of the psychotic, the "neurotic character" is deficient in a sense of reality. These differ however in that the latter makes social situations and conventions fit in with his ideas, while the psychotic gets his distorted notions of reality by projection.

Both Alexander and Staub believe that later educational measures and those satisfactions which are aimed at the better building up of an Ego-ideal can do much towards character development in these cases. Analytic experience shows clearly that there is very little reason to believe in the inheritance of anti-social character peculiarities.

Psychoanalysts are convinced that, on the basis of their empirical observations, they have been able to demonstrate conclusively that a close connection exists between the various aspects of personality-formation and the different states of libidinal and psycho-sexual development. With regard to personality-formation in general, Abraham emphasizes the fact that psychoanalysis does not set up norms. It looks on normal personality development as representing in a social sense merely "a relative success in over-coming the more primitive types of mental structure."

The form the libidinal impulses take in early childhood is, psychoanalysts believe, the permanent basis for all later development, both normal and abnormal. Jones says, "Wishes and interests of later acquirement are chiefly significant in so far as they ally themselves with those of childhood life. . . ." Even though an interest may appear to spring up suddenly in later adult life as the response to some external stimulus, it is actually to be traced to a deep unconscious trend persisting from early childhood. Psychoanalysts maintain that "the main traits of character are permanently determined for good or ill before the end of the fifth year of life."

The growth of psychoanalytic thought as it developed conceptions of personality-formation is of interest. The fact that infantile sexuality is predominantly important not only for later symptom-formation, but also for normal adult personality-formation was brought to light through Freud's discovery that in cases of obsessional neurosis there was also to be found a more or less regularly co-existing triad of strongly marked personality characteristics. He termed this group first the "obsessional character," but later (when the association between obsessional neurosis and a constitutionally strong infantile anal-erotism was established), called it the "anal character."

For those who are interested in the psychoanalytic theories of personality-formation we give the following references: Jones—*Papers on Psycho-Analysis,* Anal-Erotic Character Traits; Abraham—*Selected Papers on Psychoanalysis,* Contribution to the Theory of the Anal Character, The Influence of Oral Eroticism on Character Formation, Character Formation on the Genital Level; Freud—*Collected Papers,* Vol. II, Character and Anal Erotism, Vol. III, Anal Erotism and the Castration Complex.

We have desired to use consistently the term "personality" because "character" as correctly used denotes moral issues, but we have felt obliged in many places to retain the psychoanalytic term "character" because it is so generally used. We accept the criticism of social psychologists concerning the use of the word "trait." Nobody seems to know what a trait is, so it appears to us better to use "characteristic."

Psychoanalytic therapeutic efforts have been extended to include "character analysis." Abraham says that this is one of the most difficult pieces of work the analyst can undertake but that it has undoubtedly been in some cases the most repaying. Nevertheless, at present, he says, psychoanalysts are not in a position to make any judgments regarding the results of personality analysis.

Varied opinions have been expressed by different analysts; some have said that it is very doubtful whether personality characteristics as a whole can be changed by psychoanalytic procedure even though certain specific problems are solved for the patient. Somewhat in contradiction to other of his statements, Abraham in one place writes that no achievement in personality-formation is ever regarded as necessarily permanent, since the theory is that it "is dependent upon the general position of the libido, and that this dependence exists at every age." Thus, even in later years personality characteristics may alter.

The goal of personality-formation, according to Abraham, seems to be largely a matter of balance, the avoidance of over-accentuating characteristics of any sort. A well-balanced personality, for example, should be able to steer between over-obstinacy and over-suggestibility. The sense of justice should not degenerate into excessive punctiliousness over trifles (obsessional "fairness"). Ordinary friendly feelings should be distinguished from pathologically exaggerated over-kindness. Impulses should be controlled, not completely disavowed.

Freud's subsequent investigations into the "anal character" led him to the conclusion that it developed systematically in the case of such individuals who, as children, had shown marked and long-continuing anal interests and peculiarities. When these eventually drop out they leave in their stead certain specific personality traces.

His conviction of the truth of his observations led Freud to postulate a theory which has had very far-reaching consequences for psychoanalytic therapy and thought. What, he asks, is the fate of that portion of the anal-erotic libido which does not pass on to establish mature genital development? He has concluded that, in addition to possible fixation and repression and the consequent establishment of a neurotic predisposition, an important part of the constitutionally strong anal-erotism is "absorbed by transformation" into personality-characteristics.

This transformation process is brought about by various mental dynamisms—those playing the most conspicuous part being reaction-formation, symbolization, identification, and sublimation. (For more detailed discussion see below.)

The oral and anal stage had first to be assumed on the basis of the data obtained from pathological sources. Abraham admits that these developmental processes are hardly accessible to the direct observation in children—especially in normal conditions. The development in the first year of life takes place so quietly that generally no obvious manifestations of the changes that are occurring can be observed.

Various observations have been brought forward by psychoanalysts in proof of the oral and anal personality development theory. In corroboration of his "anal character" Freud claims that psychoanalytic experience has shown that the triad of personality characteristics as so constituted is noticeably absent in some individuals "who have retained the erotogenic quality of the anal zone into adult life, as for example, certain homosexuals." The close connection between the two interests of money and defecation is confirmed, Freud says, by a phenomenon frequently observed by psychoanalysts, namely, that "obdurate cases of so-called chronic constipation in neurotics" can only be cured by inducing the patient to bring into consciousness his "money complex."

Abraham points out that during analysis some definite changes in personality characteristics frequently occur which can be shown to be directly dependent upon progressive and regressive movements of the libido. Jones calls attention to the frequent appearance in old people of anal characteristics, heretofore not exhibited or at least in a less pronounced form, which he claims represent the waning of sexual vigor and libidinal regression.

Part of Ferenczi's "active therapy" consists in a regulation of anal and urethral functions by which he attempts to bring about a reactivation of anal and urethral erotism. Following this there is a release of associated material clearly related with pregenital erotism, and this is accompanied by a dropping out of anal personality characteristics. Ferenczi is so sure of the close association between pregenital erotism and personality-formation that he suggests making the approach to "character analysis" by means of active measures directly calculated to reactivate anal-, urethral-, and oral-erotic interests.

Freud's discovery of the so-called "anal character" stimulated Abraham to intensive work upon the personality characteristics associated with melancholia, which psychoanalysts have agreed upon as having its roots in oral erotism. As a result of his investigations, Abraham claimed to be able to establish an "oral character" also deriving from this early stage. He says, "the first, and therefore perhaps the most important, step the individual makes towards attaining a normal attitude in his final social and sexual relationships consists in dealing successfully with his oral erotism." In fact he claims that the entire later behavior, choice of profession, and hobbies, may be "rooted in oral erotism."

Great varieties and differences may exist within the realm of oral character formation, but Abraham believes that the most important differences are dependent upon whether a "feature of character has developed on the basis of the earlier or the later oral stage; whether, in other words, it is the expression of an unconscious tendency to suck or to bite."

With regard to the sucking stage, Abraham points out that the pleasure obtained is to a great extent "pleasure in taking," in being given something. This "taking" type of satisfaction influences very noticeably the later personality reaction-patterns which evolve as a result of the management, successful or otherwise, of oral erotic impulses and deprivations.

Abraham claims to have discovered two types of personality development definitely derived from the sucking stage:

(1) If the sucking pleasure is marked and undisturbed the whole attitude toward life is apt to be an optimistic one. If there has been abnormal indulgences on the part of the mother, then in addition to the optimistic attitude, there may be a tendency to carefree indifference and inactivity, perhaps even no attempt to gain a livelihood. The whole general attitude in the case of such individuals is one of expectation that some kind person (a mother-representative) will care for them, that the mother's breast will "flow for them eternally." Generosity is also frequently

With regard to oral personality-formation, Abraham points out that oral characteristics are very frequently re-enforced by or combined with anal traits; also that oral impulses are much more capable of being expressed acceptably in their original form than are anal impulses and so have much less need for sublimations and reaction-formations.

Abraham thinks that the mouth does not lose its significance as an erotogenic zone, either in neurotics or in many normals. This is shown in various sucking habits (tongue, cheeks, lips); eating habits—preference for fluids and sweets, interest in dieting; certain forms of kissing. Sucking erotism can become a dominant influence on adult conduct. Abraham says there are " a great many people who have to pay a certain permanent tribute to their oral zone." This results in various compromise forms of behavior—for example, there are people who can only concentrate on their work if they allow themselves a certain amount of oral erotic gratification at the same time, finger in mouth, biting nails, gnawing pencils.

Bitter, biting speech may be a sublimated form of oral impulses to bite and devour the object. "A milder form of aggression has appeared though the mouth is still utilized as the organ of it."

brought about, according to Abraham, by an identification with the bounteous mother.

(2) Failure to achieve gratification in the sucking period may result in a later asking or demanding social attitude (either modest or aggressive), a tendency to cling to others, a dislike of being alone. Impatience is a marked characteristic of this type.

The fundamentally pessimistic type of individual (heretofore attributed to anal sources) Abraham thinks can be traced back to a disappointment of oral desires. This type he describes as showing a consistently apprehensive attitude towards life, a tendency to make the worst of everything and to find undue difficulty in the simplest undertaking.

The biting stage of oral erotism also leaves its definite mark on later personality development in many cases. Disappointments in this primitive sadistic stage are apt to bring about regressive trends to the sucking stage, which means that the child begins his personality development "under the influence of an abnormally pronounced ambivalence of feeling" as concerns instinctual impulses and friendly-hostile object-relationships. Such a beginning, Abraham says, accounts for the development of pronounced attitudes of hostility and dislike and also for the presence of abnormally developed envy.

Ambivalence underlies fundamentally all character traits derived from the second oral or biting stage, and distinguishes them very definitely from those derived from the first stage, which is marked by intense cravings but no tendency to destroy the object. According to his observations, Abraham says, "this fundamental difference extends to the smallest details of a person's behavior."

The "anal character" was the first to be discovered and investigated and its specific characteristics as well as the dynamisms mainly involved in their formation have been worked out in much greater detail than those associated with the "oral character." Jones declares that the anal character is one of the most astonishing of Freud's findings, and "certainly the one that has evoked the liveliest incredulity, repugnance and opposition." That this should be so, he says "merely illustrates the remoteness of the unconscious from the conscious mind, for of the truth of the statement itself no one who has undertaken any serious psychoanalytical study can have any doubt."

Freud's cardinal triad of anal characteristics comprises (a) orderliness (bodily cleanliness, reliability, conscientiousness in performance of petty duties)—in an over-accentuated form, pedantry; (b) parsimony, which may become avarice; (c) obstinacy, which may become defiance and perhaps also include irascibility and vindictiveness. These three personality qualities are found regularly together, the last two forming a constant element. For the sake of a clearer understanding of the whole psychoanalytic theory of personality formation a somewhat detailed, but by no means exhaustive, discussion of the various forms of anal interest and the processes by which they are transformed into anal personality-formation seems to be justified.

The fundamental premise must be kept in mind—namely that the child in whom anal erotism is constitutionally strong derives great pleasure, both autoerotic and narcissistic, from the various activities associated with the excretory processes, and that he feels with equal intensity the deprivations inevitably associated with sphincter training and with the strong taboos imposed by his environment on all direct modes of expression of his anal-erotic interests.

T. W. Mitchell, commenting on the importance of anal erotism says, "The part it plays in the formation of character is one of the most astonishing discoveries of psychoanalysis. Probably no one ever encounters psychoanalytic teaching on this matter for the first time without regarding it as false and preposterous; and yet no one who has carefully investigated a case of obsessional neurosis can ever doubt its truth."

Discussing anal interests Hinkle says the real problem of personality trends lies deeper in the structure of the human being than even these primary functions. The attitude which the child takes toward sphincter training will be exhibited with regard to other frustrations and interferences on the part of adults as well, and is at bottom dependent upon his psychological type as discovered by Jung.

The fundamental relationship which has been found to exist between sadism and anal erotism must be taken into account in deriving character traits from the anal stage. Other components of the sexual instinct may also be involved.

Abraham in proof of the close association between sadistic and anal impulses cites instances in his experiences with neurotics when an explosive bowel evacuation has been a substitute for a discharge of anger or rage or has accompanied it.

Orderliness may be the result both of reaction-formation against anal impulses or sublimation of sadistic trends. If deriving from the latter it is an expression of a desire for domination, for exerting power over things, forcing them into a system, and forcing other people into this system.

Abraham points out that there is often a certain ambivalence with respect to orderliness and cleanliness, for example, an individual may be clean and neat with respect to his own person but have no interest in keeping his home tidy.

Generally speaking, these are two aspects of anal-erotism to be remembered when tracing back to its source any specific "anal character" constituent. These, according to Jones, are (a) pleasure in the act—twofold, expulsion and retention; (b) pleasure in the product. He claims that, though certain "anal character" constituents may be derived from both these aspects of anal erotism, the form of the future personality-characteristic is largely determined by whichever aspect of the original interest predominated. It makes for clarity, he thinks, to keep in mind the distinction between these two aspects of anal-erotism.

The aim of sphincter-training, according to Jones and Abraham, is twofold, namely (a) not to soil, and (b) to perform regularly. The former involves the renunciation of coprophilia, and the latter the giving up to a great extent of autoerotic and narcistic pleasures. The child may meet these demands by either compliance, which is normal, over-compliance or defiance, and underlying these reactions various dynamisms are believed to be at work.

The normal meeting of these demands is through identification (primary) with the requirements of those who train the child. It is an effort to avoid narcistic wounding—the setting up of self-prohibitions as opposed to outside authority. As Abraham puts it, "In favorable cases the child succeeds in making a virtue out of necessity," his original self-satisfaction "is replaced by gratification in his achievement, in 'being good,' in its parents praise." Obedience and submissiveness in relationships with others, also cleanliness and orderliness in personal matters are the outcome of this process of identification.

Reaction-formation, reversal-formation, is a very common way out for the child, but this seems to be regarded by psychoanalysts generally as a less desirable form of adaptation than identification. Abraham, for example, points out that the former process never succeeds completely, that we "invariably find the opposite extreme more or less strongly developed." It is felt that, since they are apt to be exaggerated and also to conceal an antithetical

Over-cleanliness may take the form known as the "purity complex," that is, agony at the thought of anything being stained or soiled. The passion for tidying and arranging symmetrically are other reaction-formations.

Ferenczi speaks of "stool pedantry" which he thinks explains a good deal of neurotic constipation, and is really a clinging to a primary form of pleasure.

Anal pride or desire for uniqueness may express itself in what Abraham and Jones speak of as the "reversal type." Such individuals have a tendency to act in great and small things in an opposite way to others, to wear different clothes, etc. Such mistakes as reversal of letters in writing, tendency to revert right and left are also believed to have an anal erotic derivation. Obstinacy is closely associated with this reversal tendency.

Anal defiance is also shown in the tendency to self-will with regard to the demands or requests of others, a desire to impose one's own system on others, to keep others dependent. This desire to preserve one's own right of decision is often associated with a willingness to accommodate when no request is made. This all harks back to defecation-patterns; the child became constipated when a demand is made that he perform, yielded at a time agreeable to himself, postponed evacuation as a protection against his mother's "shall."

If when the child resisted defecation demands he was given enemas and purges by the parents another type of personality may develop. Abraham describes such individuals as inactive, lacking initiative, and productivity, intellectual activity being replaced by brooding. They want a kind father or mother constantly at hand to remove every difficulty. During the analytic treatment they find difficulty in giving free association—want the physician to do all the work.

Certain work and activity patterns are believed to be correlates of early defecation patterns, for example, thoroughness, persistence, and general energy, inactivity, brooding, delay, postponement of work with final complete absorption and obsession and rapid productivity, irritation when disturbed in work, shrinking from beginning work because unable to leave off.

primitive impulse, there is a certain instability about personality trends built up through this dynamism. Over-compliance, over-yieldingness and over-gentleness, also over-cleanliness and pedantry point to reaction-formation, and outbursts of refractoriness on the part of usually very good, polite and obedient children can be explained on this basis.

Anal retention is believed to be a narcistic expression of defiance at the interference of adults with sphincter activities. This early narcistic self-determination is believed to persist in the form of a general ego attitude of obstinacy as displayed in social relations.

Parsimony as an anal-erotic trait can only be understood by taking into account the underlying process of symbolization. The unconscious identifying of feces, gifts, and money influences many later social relations involving money. Freud makes it very clear that it is not the normal "rational" interest in money (which he defines as "entirely free from libidinal influences" and as regulated by the demands of reality) which is to be traced back to excremental pleasure. Money as it plays a rôle in the anal character, "has been withdrawn from conscious control" and has attracted to itself "the psychical interest which was originally proper to . . . the product of the anal zone."

A general Ego attitude of possessiveness and proprietorship is an outstanding characteristic of object-relationships as found with the anal character. This is to be traced back to the original psychic pleasure in retention. Anal love also expresses itself largely in the bestowing of gifts rather than tenderness upon the love-object. This may be carried over into social relations at large in acts of philanthropy, benefaction, and patronage. The possessiveness of anal love shows itself clearly in the collector; the objects collected are associated symbolically with excrement.

Sublimation plays a large part in taking care of infantile coprophilic interests and impulses which are, of course, especially taboo with adults. Later interests in painting, sculpture, cooking, metal molding, and carpentry are believed to be traceable to coprophilic pleasure in smearing and molding. The choice of

Abraham claims that there are certain facial evidences of the anal character. The "anal physiognomy" is characterized, he says, by a morose expression, constant tension of the nostril line with a slight lifting of the upper lip, the impression being given of constant sniffing.

Ferenczi has traced the development from feces to symbolization in money as follows: Feces, mud pies, sand, pebbles, marbles, buttons, jewels, coins. He admits that the value attached to such things by adults conditions these unconscious equations. That is, as Abraham says, "The child first takes pleasure in substance that is soft and yielding, then in hard and granular material, and finally in small solid objects with a clean and shining surface. In the Ucs, these objects all remain equivalent to excrement."

Freud points out that the close association which psychoanalysts believe exists in the Ucs is corroborated in myths and dreams.

The pleasure taken in expulsion is largely autoerotic, but Abraham thinks that sadistic impulses may also find expression through this medium. Retention, besides affording autoerotic satisfaction is also believed to be closely bound up with the child's narcism—his self-esteem, his feelings of power and omnipotence. Anal (and urethral) exploits and rivalry are typical of this period of development. It is also believed that the child attaches an over-value to the product which he regards as part of himself, and that enforced surrender of it is likely to be felt as a narcistic blow. On the other hand, through the child's unconscious equating of feces and gifts, his willing compliance with adult demands shows, according to Freud, that object-love has got the better of narcism. It is also claimed that the markedly anal-erotic child would, if allowed to do so, take great pleasure in smelling, touching, moulding, smearing and hoarding the product, and that these coprophilic interests condition very strongly his adult interests and choice of occupation.

occupations and professions is thus largely dependent upon the process of sublimation of anal interests, but Jones is careful to say that this and other dynamisms are not the only factors which are operative in determining the choice, though "extensive experience of the tenacity, vigor, and durability of such unconscious factors forces one to estimate their importance much more highly than is generally done."

Abraham emphasizes very strongly that what seems to be at first glance identical character traits in two individuals really, on closer observation, can be seen to present slight differences; these differences are traceable to the libidinal level from which the personality characteristic has been derived. For example, oral parsimony differs from the anal variety in that it involves an inhibition of the craving for objects and shows itself rather in a haunting fear of losing the smallest part of what one already possesses.

Abraham also points out certain respects in which the oral and anal character are the direct antithesis of each other. He contrasts oral impatience, haste, and restlessness with anal perseverance and persistence; also the anal conservative attitude toward innovations with the oral accessibility to new ideas. The bright sociable individual who has been gratified in the early oral stage is also to be contrasted with the hostile malicious individual whose characteristics in this respect are to be traced back to the biting stage, and with the morose, aloof, reticent individual whose trends are derived from the anal stage.

The obstinacy due to anal retention expresses itself in various concrete forms: (a) resentment at being thwarted—which may lead to later individualism and sensitivity at all interference, chronic irritability and bad temper, vindictive desire for revenge, insisting on own rights, advice taken badly; (b) sensitivity to encroachments on one's own power—this shows itself in refusal to accommodate to the arrangements of others, demanding that others do the accommodating, interest in drawing up rules and regulations for others; (c) self-willed independence—this is expressed in a difficulty in deputing work to others, a conviction of being able to do everything better than other people, a conviction of uniqueness (showing itself perhaps in pretentiousness, arrogance, and the despising of the activities and possessions of others), a pride in possessing what others do not possess.

Certain specific parsimony or avarice patterns are found in connection with the anal character; for example, (a) avarice in regard to certain things combined with liberality in regard to others. A grudging attitude connected with the giving or lending of certain things is believed to be tied up with copro symbols, that is, books, time, food, are believed to be identical with money in the unconscious. (b) The saving of small sums and the spending of large; the tendency to forget small debts—this indicates a pronounced anal character. (c) Dislike for waste and efforts to make use of it; time-saving devices—carrying on two occupations at the same time.

In general the later social behavior of an individual is determined, according to Abraham, by the degree in which it combines personality features which are to be traced back to oral and anal elements of pleasure in incorporation, expulsion, and retention. "If the pleasure in getting or taking is brought into the most favorable relation possible with the pleasure in possession as well as with that in giving up, then an exceedingly important step has been made in laying the foundation of the individual's social relations."

Urethral personality-formation—very little seems to have been discovered as yet as to the specific characteristics deriving from urethral erotism. Freud speaks of the "burning" ambition found to be closely associated with childish enuresis.

Hitschmann claims that both ambition and predilection for play and working with water (for example, excessive bathing and washing) have been empirically deduced from urethral erotism. He also claims that some of the symptoms in obsessional neurosis can be traced to urethral erotism.

Glover mentions ambition, envy, and impatience as all of urethral origin. Abraham derives ambition from oral erotism and thinks it is re-enforced by urethral impulses. He claims to have found that with a certain group of neurotics "there is a particular pleasure value attached to micturition and a strongly accentuated erotogenicity of the urethra."

Frink cites the case of a baseball pitcher who felt that he was getting much the same pleasure in pitching ball as he had in early urinating exploits. Frink attempts to show that all the impulses involved in the childhood urination play could find a sublimated expression or equivalent in baseball pitching. "The curving parabolic course of the ball," he says, corresponds to the stream of urine. "The sense of power and achievement connected with pitching a swift, sharply curving ball" had been bound up earlier with "squirting to long distances a strong stream of urine." The lateral curves produced seemingly at will in the pitched ball corresponds to the waving of the stream of urine from side to side." At the same time, participation in the game gives an opportunity just as in the earlier urination play for the gratification of impulses of rivalry, exhibitionism, and desires for male companionship. Frink claims to have come across an instance of a golfer for whom driving a golf ball had a similar significance.

The genital stage of libidinal development is generally regarded by psychologists as finally and predominantly determinative for personality formation. Those features which are derived primarily from pregenital levels are apt to be developed to an exaggerated degree, according to Abraham, and are thus only incidentally of value for social adaptation. He terms these, "archaic types of character-formation," and stresses the point that, though they can never be "entirely surmounted or completely obliterated" (since their basis is organic), they ought, nevertheless, to be profoundly modified normally when the genital level is attained. That is, the individual in the genital stage should absorb and retain those elements of personality-formation which "conduce to favorable relations between the individual and his objects,"—for example, enterprise and energy from the early oral stage, endurance and perseverance from the anal stage, and from sadistic sources enough aggressiveness to aid in carrying on the struggle for existence. Along with this absorption the traces of more primitive stages which are unfavorable to social adaptation should normally be eliminated, such as anal avarice and distrust, sadistic hostility and destructiveness.

The problem of object-relationship and social attitudes assumes a new aspect at the genital stage. While the handling of autoerotic and narcistic impulses is the basis during the pre-genital stages for later Ego-attitudes and personality trends, at the genital level allo-erotic (homosexual and heterosexual) impulses must be dealt with primarily, since the object now becomes of chief importance for sexual satisfaction.

Abraham calls attention to the fact that oral and genital personality-formations are similar in certain respects. There is a lack of ambivalence in the attitude towards objects deriving both from the early oral and late genital stages. Anal object-love is distinguished by the reaction-formations of over-yieldingness and over-gentleness and thus has a socially useful character to some degree, but is inferior to and must not be confused with real object-love on the genital level.

Both Freud and Abraham stress importance of identification in bringing about changes in adult personality-formation. Abraham claims that women especially assimilate their personality to that of the man with whom they are living, that sometimes personality changes are observable with every change in the love-object. Husbands and wives who have lived a long time together show a tendency to resemble each other in character.

The effect of Oedipus fixations on later object-choices and mating has already been discussed. (See Oedipus and Castration Complexes and Developmental Stages.) Some of the "conditions of love" (really conditionings) then established reveal themselves later in more or less neurotic demands; such as for example: over-strong jealousy of the father at the phallic stage may later lead to the possibility of object-choice in terms of the loved woman belonging to another, that is, she must arouse jealousy. The child's idea that the relationship between the parents is a wrong one from which the mother is to be rescued may lead to later necessity that the loved woman be of a light nature, that is in need of "rescue." If there is over-emphasis on the idea that sex relations are forbidden or matters for extreme secrecy, later love relations may be possible only outside of marriage; while early ambivalent attitudes, coupled with the belief that the mother through relationship with the father has disclaimed respect, may lead to such conditioning that the sexually acceptable woman must be ethically or socially inferior or "degraded," that is, lack of respect becomes a necessity for potency.

329

The fact that the first object desired by the child for genital satisfaction is the parent greatly complicates the situation. The development in the Ucs of the Oedipus and castration complexes produces a deep inner fermentation which, as it emerges on the conscious level, profoundly affects all future object-relationships and social attitudes. The first step should be the achievement of sublimated or aim-inhibited feelings toward the parents, which, if the development continues to be normal, should gradually extend to other persons in the environment, and finally to the community at large. (See Developmental Stages.)

When there is failure in the part of the child to transfer friendly feelings from the parents to others an impress is left upon his personality. Abraham says that "a marked disturbance of his character will be the direct consequence," he later may display sexual impulses unaccompanied by any desires for affectional relations, and may have difficulties in getting the proper feeling-contact with other people.

The genital stage then is important from the point of view of strengthening already initiated social trends, but mainly as establishing real and positive social feelings. The social adaptations made in the pre-genital stage, the result largely, as they are apt to be, of reaction-formations, a structure reared on the foundations of ambivalence and narcism, do not make for real stability of social adjustment. Abraham warns for example against the confusing of a too great yieldingness and gentleness arising out of a reaction-formation to sadistic impulses, with a real transference-love. The character trait of over-kindness, though it may be socially useful, is, he says, in essential respects inferior to full object-love. The distinction seems to be, according to Abraham, that in the pregenital stages the interests of the individual and those of the community run counter to each other, the individual making his adaptations only of necessity, while on the genital level the interests of the individual and the community "both coincide to a great extent."

Important as he regards the castration complex for both neurotic and normal personality development, Abraham protests against Adler's over-evaluation of the "masculine protest" as the essential motivation of all the neuroses. He says, "Our psychoanalytic experiences should constantly remind us of the over-determination of all psychical structures." Abraham is careful to state that in all cases where he found evidences of castration complex he also found "ideas connected with female passive instincts."

Concerning the development of personality characteristics in women, Freud thinks that the castration complex preceding the Oedipus situation in girls raises the problem of Super-ego formation in women. He says "I cannot escape the notion (though I hesitate to give it expression) that for women the level of what is ethically normal is different from what it is in men. Their Super-ego is never so inexorable, so impersonal, so independent of its emotional origins, as we require it to be in men. Character traits which critics of every epoch have brought up against women —that they show less sense of justice than men, that they are less ready to submit to the great necessities of life, that they are more often influenced in their judgments by feelings of affection or hostility—all of these would be amply accounted for by the modification in the formation of their Super-ego which we have already inferred."

The possible relation of the castration complex to homosexual trends in men is suggested by Flügel. "Those to whom the absence of the penis is very abhorrent can seldom become entirely reconciled to a love-object which possesses this defect, and the persistence of homosexual tendencies —at the unconscious level, at least—is, therefore, facilitated."

H. Lampl describes in detail a case in which a strong castration complex (castration anxiety in regard to both father and mother) was the underlying cause of marked masochistic trends, showing themselves in a suffering passive attitude to life and marked over-compensation in his sexual relations. Some of the personality and conduct manifestations enumerated are as follows: The constant feeling that some evil power was working against him, the constant failure in everything he attempted with cursing of fate (Lampl says, "Here he completely overlooked the fact that this was precisely what he meant to happen"), a tendency to

The genital level is relatively unnarcistic and unambivalent. "Generally speaking, we may say that when the child has been able to subdue his Oedipus complex with all its constituents, he has made the most important step toward overcoming his original narcism, and his hostile tendencies; and at the same time he has broken the power of the pleasure principle to dominate the conduct of his life."

Identification (both primary and secondary) plays the chief rôle in personality formation at the early genital stage. The setting up of the Super-ego is the most momentous of all the inner changes through which the child passes for his later personality development. It is out of the childish sense of guilt, Jones says, that there is developed "the adult conscience in which is incorporated all our moral and ethical standards." (There is also, he says, an aesthetic and scientific conscience.) Thus the normal conscience "is the heir of the Oedipus conflict of childhood." It frequently happens, however, "that errors in early development may prevent the normal evolution from taking place. Then there remains an excessive sense of guilt in the unconscious which is infantile and irrational in character and often morbid in its effects."

Distinct traces of the Oedipus and castration complexes linger in the large majority of individuals and the early father-son relationship is believed always to influence to some extent later social attitudes, sympathies, and activities, as expressed in political, economic, and religious affiliations and partisanships. In other words, all later object-relationships both individual and social as well as various forms of belief are really the result of the transference of Oedipus wishes and castration fears to father and mother surrogates.

lose money—to let himself be exploited, together with anxiety about losing money "and thus, as it were, be anally castrated," severe work inhibitions—impossibility of finishing a performance which would be sure to bring him promotion, repeated attempts at rebellion against paternal surrogates, continued dependency in adult life upon his parents (thus maintaining in regard to his parents the nursing relation transferred to money), impotence anxiety shown in dreams of examination failure, of being too late, etc., and in intense anxiety and agitation about public performances. Lampl speaks of this individual as having been too timid to realize the identification with the father. His masochistic attitude to life expressed itself clearly in the fact that his need for punishment was quite separated from an object, that is, "it does not seem to matter from whom the blows of fate come, so long as the blows fall."

Klein agrees with Freud that deflected penis-envy may be the cause of the fact that jealousy plays a greater part in women's than men's lives, but on the other hand she maintains that women possess a great capacity, "which is not based merely on over-compensation," for self-sacrifice and devotion to ethical and social activities. She thinks that the explanation of "how women can run so wide a gamut from the most petty jealousy to the most self-forgetful loving-kindness" lies in the "peculiar conditions of the formation of the feminine Super-ego." The early anal-sadistic identification with the mother means the formation of a "cruel Super-ego after the maternal imago," which may later predominate. But "the more the identification with the mother becomes stabilized on the genital basis, the more will it be characterized by the devoted kindness of an indulgent mother-ideal." If the girl's Oedipus frustrations or her penis-envy lead her to make strong identification with the father there will be established a paternal Super-ego "which sets before her active aims to which she can never fully attain." "The very impossibility of attainment may lend an impetus to her efforts which, combined with the capacity for self-sacrifice which she derives from the maternal Super-ego, gives a woman, in individual instances, the capacity for very exceptional achievements on the intuitive plane and in specific fields."

Klein suggests that women's constant concern for their personal beauty may have its root in the dread of maternal retribution and destruction.

The personality development of many women is believed by psychoanalysts to be profoundly influenced by early penis-envy, or what is sometimes referred to as the masculine complex. (See Oedipus and Castration Complexes.) Abraham has come to the conclusion that traces of the masculine or castration complex are to be found in every woman, and that in a large majority there remains a strong unconscious cathexis of ideas associated with early penis-envy, influencing in many observable ways their relationships with men.

Abraham claims that, though on account of their multiplicity it is difficult to classify later castration complex phenomena, they can nevertheless be divided into two types, namely, (a) wish-fulfilment behavior arising on the basis of desire for physical masculinity, and, (b) behavior prompted by desire for revenge on the man. This revenge type may take part in feminine activities.

Some of the more common manifestations of the castration complex in the normal woman are as follows:

Tendency to direct the object-choice toward the passive effeminate type of man with whom the wife can daily show her superiority.

Great disinclination to follow the lead of any man.

Reluctance to accept help of any kind, even ordinary courtesies, from men.

Open expression of feelings of uselessness because born a woman; these are often associated with refusal both to compete with men and to take part in feminine activities.

Resentment at being kept waiting, in married life this may take the form of revenge of keeping the husband waiting on every occasion.

A frequently expressed desire for great personal beauty or to be wooed by great and important men.

Great horror at the sight of wounds, painful feelings even at the thought of it.

Erotic interest attracted by crippled or mutilated men. Such women have particularly strong feelings of inferiority, and feel an affinity with the man who has lost his "superiority."

Desire for knowledge. Jones mentions in one of his papers a primary instinct for knowledge and differentiates this from the practical problem of how to deal in daily life with external phenomena. He states that it is only in civilized man that this distinction holds and finds that even then it is difficult to separate curiosity from knowledge, from the desire for knowing brought about by life's necessities.

Freud, however, in one of his early writings states that desire for knowledge is an offshoot of the possessive instinct sublimated or raised to the intellectual sphere, while Abraham traces this desire largely to sublimation of scoptophilic impulses. He attributes to this source the impulse toward investigation and interest in observation. Where there is a repression of such sublimation, "the pleasure in looking is changed into an unproductive desire for knowledge which is not applied to real events" but leads to neurotic brooding. A very pronounced interest (found particularly in obsessional neurotics) in all that is dark, that is, mysterious, supernatural, mystical, Abraham attributes to repressed scoptophilia with the special determinant in "pleasurable interest in dark cavities which our knowledge of infantile sexuality has rendered intelligible to us."

Philosophic interests are also related to scoptophilic pleasure. The libido "is no longer directed to the forbidden (incestuous) aim, no longer to that which one must not see, but to that which one cannot see," namely, one's own thoughts. There is thus, also, a regression to infantile narcism.

Abraham enumerates some of the concrete evidences of interests that derive from scoptophilia, including interest in observation of nature, pleasure in seeing things in travel, the impulse toward artistic treatment of visual material. When the exaggerated form exists there may be concentration of attention on objects and processes in the external world, and, associated with this, extraordinarily faithful memory for minute details.

Freud gives the high tree as a frequent symbol of desire for observing. The person on the tree can see everything that is going on below him and cannot himself be seen.

Discussing interest in dark cavities, Abraham relates to this the child's cloacal theory of birth as well as his interest in bowel function.

Abraham thinks neurotic brooding is closely related to philosophic speculation; a very persistent problem with obsessional neurotics is that of the origin of thoughts. The question, "Where shall I go after death?" is, he says, a typical reversal of the question which interested the child, "Where was I before I was born?" The obsessional interest in the origin of thought is only a cover for the early infantile question and a displacement has occurred "of the typical wish of the child to see with its own eyes the act of fecundation and birth."

For the obsessional neurotic sexual ignorance means, "the secret itself has more pleasure value than its disclosure." He may suffer from his ignorance, but he cannot free himself from it. "The question which in fact he wants to ask is not allowed to be answered; the question which takes its place cannot be answered and thus the secret is kept." There is a constant conflict between the desire to investigate and the desire to remain ignorant.

Abraham cites a case illustrating how sublimation of scoptophilia may lead to a pronounced desire for universal scientific knowledge. The man in question found in every branch of science one special problem which interested him and which was due to displacement of a particular sexual problem which had interested him as a child, namely, procreation. In chemistry, he was most interested in the problem of the moment at which a substance was formed or in which two substances united. In the field of palaeontology, he was particularly in the pliocene period, the period in which man first appeared. Here the child's question concerning his own origin has been sublimated to a general interest in the origin of the human race.

The brooding tendency and sexual ignorance are always regularly found together, according to Abraham. The tendency to brood and doubting often exist side by side; the brooder unconsciously endeavors to maintain his ignorance and the doubter to preserve his uncertainty. Then, too, mental preoccupation with abstract things is a way of eluding concrete reality.

Special interest in movement. Pleasure in movement and rhythm is sometimes designated as muscle-erotism. Sadger calls this an independent source of sexual pleasure. There is immediately after birth "a storm of movement and activity." This may seem purposeless, but Landauer thinks that these movements may serve to discharge overexcitation. The fact that the child continues to make movements, he thinks, points to their being pleasurable, hence constituting the earliest pleasure of life.

The pleasure in motion may become associated with the erotic significance of objects. The restless infant may accidentally find an object which satisfies his oral or anal excitability and may come to inhibit the desire for movement. A sense of guilt may become associated with movement erotism which otherwise would have no difficulty in obtaining direct unmodified expression. Movements should be under the control of the Ego or the reality-principle, but they may come under the ban of the Super-ego.

The pleasure in passive movement, when it is overstrong, is sometimes reacted to by certain fears such as a fear of traveling; overexaggeration of the pleasure is found in the great desire which children and some neurotic adults have in traveling about on street cars or railway trains (and nowadays in automobiles). Neurotics show exaggerated signs of such pleasure in walking or rhythmic compulsions which are connected with very definite pleasurable emotions.

Abraham suggests that since all children have the capacity to think visually, lack of visual thinking in an adult may not mean that he is not of the "visual type" but that "there is an inhibition of his scoptophilic instinct resulting from repression."

Abraham thinks that dancing and walking may offer a substitute for sexual gratification "which would otherwise be denied by erotic inhibitions." Walking with some particular person may have symbolic significance of bodily union, as in the case of the girl with marked father fixation who enjoyed walking with him because this "represented a symbolic fulfilment of her incest wish" This prevented her walking with other persons; because of her fixation such an act would signify unfaithfulness to her father.

Pleasure in movement may explain certain mannerisms, such as fingering watch chains, plucking at the hair, etc. Freud states that these and some few other objects are phallic symbols which would account for the particular mannerisms engaged in.

As illustrating inhibition of movement, or pleasures connected with them, Freud points out that in the case of little Hans the earlier pleasures in watching the movement of horses changed into fear and the motion of horses became "an emblem of terror." This was brought about as "obscure impulses to movement" became directed toward the mother during the Oedipus situation.

Pleasure in movements may account for certain forms of play rather than pleasure in play itself or the object of play.

Interest in sports. Abraham thinks that there are two types which may be differentiated with regard to their attitude toward motor performances as shown in interest in sports. They are (a) the inert passive type and (b) the overlively or erethistic type. Both of these, he believes, can be traced back to attitudes toward sexual activity.

The first of these types wants to attain sexual gratification in as easy a way as possible, taking little active part in it. There is pronounced antipathy to all physical exertion including sports. This inertness and passivity is in reality, according to Abraham, a reaction-formation; it has taken the place of a too forcible sadistic impulse. Along with the inertness there may exist a tendency to be quarrelsome, to have spells of anger, and to commit violent acts. Excessive irritability and a paralysis of the normal male pleasure in attack are seen in such cases existing in close proximity. "The frequent juxtaposition of excessive ambition and severe resistance against work is also met with in this group of neurotic persons."

The overlively type is always in a state of haste. Sports are entered into in a hurried, precipitate way. This is explained psychoanalytically as a "fleeing from the unconscious resistance within." All projects must be carried out in feverish haste before resistances break through and compel renunciation. This attitude goes back to a looking upon sexual activity as a troublesome task to be got over as quickly as possible.

Interest in special aspects of art. Jones and others have discussed the origin of interest in painting, modeling and sculpture and have indicated that these are sublimations of anal interests. More recently, J. W. Brown has written on the relationship between design in the plastic arts and certain cardinal psychoanalytic concepts. He believes that from the dynamic point of view, design in art can be traced to the sublimation of libido connected with castration ideas; this indicates that it derives from the genital stage of libido development. Other motives, however, are contributed from the oral and anal stages of development, that is,

340

Brown, in his article, *Psycho-Analysis and Design in the Plastic Arts* (International Journal of Psychoanalysis, Jan. 1929), discusses first the essential qualities in design, and stresses particularly that the arrangement in a definite space achieves a feeling that the design has stability and vitality. There may be either rigid representation or representation through rhythmic line.

Brown then elaborates his theme showing that design is spatial arrangement built upon a circle, ellipse, oval, or pyramid, or any combination of these. Each of these forms has a special meaning, namely, to negate castration fear. In pictures or pure ornament, this negation is attained by using any one of the above forms, the unconscious meaning of which is as follows: circle, ellipse, or oval represent the female genitals; the pyramid represents the penis and is often the basic structure when more than one figure is represented.

"from the pre-genital equivalents of castration which have re-enforced the castration phantasies proper." Thus, sucking is a repetitive act and from this comes the interest in rhythmic repetition which constitutes such an important feature in design. Other contributions come from scoptophilic impulses of the oral stage (seeing the breasts), gratified particularly in design that is dome-shaped. Sublimation of certain anal impulses such as interest in looking at and exhibiting a complete mass, re-enforces genital scoptophilia and exhibitionism, resulting in a desire for continuity, correct placing, and filling of space in design.

In general, Brown believes that pure ornament and design in pictures and other forms of plastic art "represent primarily an attempt to call forth feelings which satisfy certain unconscious wishes connected with the idea of potency as a negation of the idea of castration."

Choice of profession. Jones on the basis of the opportunity that he has had in a large number of cases to trace the impulse that led to profession and occupation, believes that such choice rests on a submerged striving or impulse. He cites as an illustration that the carrying on of the exhibitionistic impulse may develop the career of an actor, orator, or auctioneer. Through sublimation of sadism one may become a distinguished surgeon or successful butcher, according to capacities and opportunities.

Ferenczi believes that discoveries and inventions frequently have a libidinal as well as an egoistic root in pyschic life. He agrees with Spencer's idea that mechanical contrivances are organ-prolongations. Even self-acting machines are organ-projections, a part of the external world is given a soul by human will and works instead of the hands. More primitive machines are an introjection of part of the external world—the sphere of the influence of the Ego is enlarged by them.

The negation of castration fear comes about through the unconscious meaning of the design which signifies (1) the proper relationship of the penis to the body, (2) the woman with a penis, (3) the penis in the mother's genitals, i.e. coitus, (4) the child in the mother's womb. When, for example, the picture presents only the oval, the female genitals are represented, but when within the oval, a pyramid arrangement occurs, the situation represents (3) above.

In sculpture the dome-shaped design is a representation of the mother's breast.

To obtain a clear picture of Brown's thesis with all the detail, the original article, with its illustrations, must be read. It should be added that the author does not claim that these unconscious motives exclude other aesthetic and even intellectual factors.

General Belief Types. Ferenczi describes two very commonly found types of personality, namely, (1) individuals who show a tendency to "blind beliefs," that is, to a credulous acceptance of the scientific statements and explanations of some person in public authority, and (2) individuals with a tendency to "blind disbelief," that is, either to "avoid entirely any scrutiny of facts that contradict too abruptly the established order," or who "endeavor to emphasize the unavoidable weaknesses and incompletenesses of a new point of view in order to drop the whole thing on this account. . . ."

Ferenczi thinks that there is a certain abnormality about both of the above types in the sense of a lack of objectivity. This lack he explains as being due essentially to underlying emotional attitudes which point either to fixations or regressions associated with the individual's development of a sense of reality.

The stages in reality development are, according to Ferenczi: (1) A phase of disillusionment in his own omnipotence which the child passes through when he begins to realize that he cannot gain his desires "merely by vivid wishing" or "magical gestures and word signals." This is followed by the projecting on to the parents (that is, "higher" beings) his own omnipotence together with the feeling of being able to share it with them by various forms of placating behavior; (2) a phase of disillusionment in the power and benevolence of the parents or higher beings. It is recognized by the child that the parents themselves must obey higher powers, and "that these idolized figures often show themselves to be petty, egotistical creatures who consider their own well-being at the price of other people's."

The first phase of disillusionment is the beginning of objectivity in the sense that the child begins to distinguish between the "Ego and the non-Ego." "Only such things are held as 'real' that force themselves independently of the will, often indeed in spite of it, upon the sense perceptions." The second phase of disillusionment Freud calls the scientific phase of the reality sense.

344

The extreme type of "blind disbelief" is seen, according to Ferenczi, in the analysis of hysterics, who, he says, "start the treatment with an exaggerated ecstasy of belief." Later on, he says, it is discovered that these patients were not as convinced as they seemed to be of the correctness of the analyst's explanations, but "had believed them blindly (dogmatically as a matter of doctrine)." This blind acceptance Ferenczi attributes to desire on the part of the Ego "to keep secure the filial love" transferred to the doctor.

Obsessional neurotics show extremes of doubting, "doubting mania." They "immediately oppose the utmost intellectual resistance" to everything the analyst says. Ferenczi thinks this hostile attitude can be traced "to the disillusionment about the truthfulness" and the benevolence "of those in authority, which results in so many people tending to repress their belief and to display only their disbelief."

In discussing the possibility of achieving complete objectivity Freud says that he does not believe that in dealing with "the ultimate things, the great problems of science and of life" it is possible to be impartial. "Every one is under the sway of preferences deeply rooted within into the hands of which he unwittingly plays as he pursues his speculations."

The first stage of the development of the reality sense, that is, the period of disillusionment in one's own omnipotence, corresponds, Ferenczi says, to the religious phase of humanity. "Humanity has learned to renounce the omnipotence of its own wishes but not the idea of omnipotence in general. The latter is simply transferred to other "higher" beings (gods) who benevolently grant man everything so long as certain ceremonies pleasing to them are punctually performed. . . ." The efforts to please the mother or nurse by obeying her demands in respect to cleanliness, etc. have their correlate in pleasing God through "certain prayer formulae."

Those individuals who show a tendency to "blind belief" Ferenczi says have either remained fixated or regressed to a level between the first and second stages of disillusionment, that is, the period when omnipotence and benevolence is ascribed to the parents. The tendency to credulity is often strengthened by the attitude of the parents toward childish curiosity regarding sexual and religious questions. No matter how much they may acclaim the child's precociousness and intelligence in certain respects, he must soon learn that sexual and religious matters are taboo and that the authority of the parents must not be questioned. The child's reaction to this demand for surrender of independent efforts at thought may be a general attitude of submissiveness and suggestibility. Ferenczi says, however, that this overcredulous attitude is often shown through analysis to conceal mockery and scorn.

The type of personality which is associated with a "sticking fast at the doubting stage" shows either (a) a tendency to deprive all authorities equally of·their omnipotence or (b) to continue to reverence them negatively. By this Ferenczi means that the belief in the benevolence of authoritative persons becomes changed into a conviction of their malevolence.

Religious Beliefs. Freud lays great stress on the paternal origins of religion. Psychoanalysis has clearly demonstrated, he thinks, the importance of the father in the idea of God, namely, "that God is in every case modeled after the father, and that our personal relation to God is dependent upon our relation to our physical father, fluctuating and changing with him, and that God at bottom is nothing but an exalted father."

Jones thinks that psychoanalysis throws light on various concepts and doctrines of Christianity. For example, the meaning of sacrifice is essentially "an attempt to allay the sense of guilt arising from the Oedipus complex."

Jones maintains that psychoanalysis has two very special contributions to make on the subject of belief, the first general, the second specific. "The first contribution is the evidence it can

346

At the beginning of his development in a sense of reality the child's first article of belief is "everything is real (that is, effective external to myself), which even when I do not wish it, forces itself upon me as a sense perception." Thus, Ferenczi says, "palpableness," and "visibility" "remain throughout life the basis of all 'proof.'" Later, "in the course of the progressive development of the reality sense logical thought forms are evolved" and "undisputed proof" is regarded as belonging to the laws of logical thought.

Freud contends that the wide-spread religious belief in reward and compensation in a future life for "the renunciation of earthly lusts" in this life is to be explained on the ground of the powerful "endopsychic impression" made by substituting the reality-principle for the pleasure-principle. This substitution, he points out, is "no dethronement of the pleasure-principle but only a safe-guarding of it," that is, a momentary pleasure, the results of which are not assured, is renounced in order to gain a more assured later pleasure. It is the "logical pursuit of this proto-type" which have enabled religions to "effect absolute renunciation of pleasure in this life by means of the promise of compensation in a future life."

Freud suggests that doubts about the existence of the deity may be based on the Oedipus conflict—desire to abolish the father.

Stirrings of religious feelings may be only a repetition of the Oedipus situation and then they will eventually meet the same fate as the original Oedipus conflict. The old struggle is simply renewed on religious ground and so is predestined to meet the same fate.

Conversion, in some cases at least, Freud suggests, may be simply the Oedipus solution of subjection to the will of the father. He admits that all cases of conversion are not so easy to understand.

bring to show the extent to which apparently intellectual operations are influenced by unconscious processes, especially when they concern matters of great personal moment." It is very easy, he says, to build up "a philosophical, spiritual, and intellectual facade," upon unconscious mental processes "which would impose itself as the whole structure."

The second and specific contribution of psychoanalysis has to do with the matter of religious beliefs. Individual analysis and the study of theological and anthropological material in the light of these analyses has added much to an understanding of the "genesis and unconscious correlates" of religious beliefs both in general and in particular. Jones discusses three fundamental factors in religious belief:

(a) *The Fatherhood of God*—Jones follows the same line as Ferenczi in tracing a belief in God to the invariable attributing on the part of the child of "omnipotence, omniscience, and moral perfection" to the father. The ascribing of these qualities to the father proceeds "at least as much from internal necessities as from any external example or suggestion." Disillusionment inevitably follows and the qualities of perfection are abstracted from the father "and incorporated in an intangible figure." Thus, not only reverential religious belief but also "militant atheism" have their roots in the early father-son relationship.

(b) *The idea of sin*—All religion, Jones says, is founded upon "the sense of guilt at not reaching a prescribed standard. Without this idea, religion loses all meaning." This feeling of sin is to be traced back to the two components of the Oedipus complex, namely, rebellion against the father, and the desire for "desecration" of the mother. Jones goes on to distinguish between the rôle played in religion by the unconscious infantile and irrational sense of guilt, persisting in a greater or lesser degree in every one, and the rôle played by the normal "adult conscience." He says that the exact relation of the unconscious and conscious sense of guilt to the idea of sin as embodied in religion is a very delicate one. However, it can be said with assurance "that the lofty sense

Jones calls attention to the fact that, "Over and over again the religious systems of the world have culminated in the worship of a Trinity, which has almost always consisted of the primordial figures of Father, Mother, Son." All the beliefs and legends which have grown up about these three figures, he says, are fundamentally related "to the unconscious conflicts that have to do with the members of the individual human family."

The Protestant and Catholic types of mind, according to Jones, correspond with the particular component of the Oedipus Complex "on which the accent falls."

According to Schroeder, it is the unconscious sense of guilt upon which the revivalist works and is able to induce an acceptance of his scheme of salvation.

Alexander says that in the case of exaggerated illusions of sinfulness these are to be traced to "an insatiable sadism directed toward all persons and all things which has been suppressed in the unconscious." Although this conscious sense of guilt or sin is very distressing, Alexander points out that nevertheless "it contains the fulfillment of a wish—of a repressed wish to be a criminal of the deepest dye, to have incurred more guilt than every one else put together."

The sense of guilt, according to Alexander, is extremely sensitive in children. This explains the silence of many children regarding sexual traumata; they evidently feel that the guilt is not entirely on the part of their seducer. The child is anxiously guarding a pleasure gain.

The unconscious sense of guilt attaching to sexual transgressions frequently become a conscious sense of sin through being displaced on to some less venial transgression, e. g. dishonesty.

of spiritual value attaching to religious feeling and beliefs owes much of its importance to the fact that these at the same time fulfill the deepest cravings of the human mind and afford some appeasement to the unconscious moral tension."

(c) *Belief in immortality*—Jones says that wish-fulfilment plays an important part in this belief. At bottom, "salvation betokens a joyful reunion with the parents against whom the unconscious sinful thoughts were directed." The infantile child-parent relationship involved many "unsatisfactorinesses, hardships, and injustices" and thus heaven is a place where all these will be compensated for and remedied.

Jones sums up by saying that whether or not religious beliefs (savage, mythological, or Christian) are true, "the genesis of them can be adequately accounted for without invoking any external (supernatural) agency."

Schroeder draws attention to different religious manifestations which all have their origin, he says, in the unconscious sense of guilt. These are: a predisposition to interpret certain emotional and ecstatic experiences in terms of the supernatural and spiritual; a tendency shown by some people to glorify their guilt by labeling it religious humility; a tendency to a morbid overstressing of moral righteousness and particularly of sexual orthodoxy. The greater the sense of guilt the more the individual will be inclined to accept doctrines which make it possible to identify himself with superhuman beings and thus lay claim to a spiritual excellence.

Social Beliefs. The early parent-child relationship becomes the prototype, according to Jones, of all later sociological and political relationships, and unconsciously underlies the beliefs and theories therewith associated. For example, an unconscious identification. The acceptance of rulers and governing bodies and the belief in their efficacy is to be traced back to the infantile beliefs in the power and benevolence of the father. The bitterness and resentment at the failure of governing bodies to solve economical and social problems repeat the early disillusionment with and distrust of the father.

Eder points out how identifications with brothers and sisters, or play-mates, for the purpose of combining against the authority of the father, can become the prototype for later identification with fellow workers, fellow countrymen, etc. This explains various patriotic and labor slogans, such as equal rights, justice for all, etc.

Internationalism may be nothing more than a revolt against the father as represented by the state. A rejection of patriotic demands is really a rejection of the paternal commands.

Flügel attempts to show how patriotic enthusiasm may spring from fixation upon the early "rescue phantasy" so commonly found in connection with the Oedipus complex. We regard our native land, he says, "as a great mother who brings into being, nourishes, protects, and cherishes her sons and daughters, and inspires them with respect and love for herself and her traditions, customs, beliefs, and institutions. . . ." In return for this we, as her children, are prepared to work and fight for her, and much of the "horror and disgust which is inspired by the idea of invasion of one's native land by a hostile army is due to the unconscious tendency to regard such an invasion as a desecration and violation of the mother."

351

Superstition. Superstitious beliefs and practices are traceable to the fact that an associative connection has been forged between the act in question and some unconscious idea. Jones says that this unconscious idea is almost always the same in different individuals, since the connection belongs to the group of typical or universal symbols. The feeling or belief that some acts are lucky, others unlucky, is explained on the basis that "the act in the unconscious which is symbolized by the trivial conscious one is one of forbidden pleasure, the bad luck is, in the unconscious, the punishment for this pleasure, the good luck is the enjoyment of the pleasure without punishment." Superstitious ceremonials such as "touching wood" are explained as symbolic secondary "acts of reassurance," or propitiatory acts to avert punishment.

The various superstitions, fears, and taboos associated with the subject of health, Jones says, are to be traced fundamentally to unconscious wish-fulfilments.

Freud has made notable contributions to the understanding of wit, humor, and the comic. Other psychoanalysts have followed Freud in their studies of the same topic. Brill gives a succinct account of the techniques involved in wit, grouping them mainly under the processes of condensation, double-meaning, transposition of words or phrases, similarity of sounds (as in puns), displacements either of words or of psychic accent, absurdity, false logic, representation through opposites, allusion, etc. The most common characteristic obtaining in all of these various forms is condensation. "All the techniques mentioned above have one characteristic, namely, they all show a tendency toward economy of expression."

Wit may be divided into the purposeless or harmless, which has no particular aim other than to produce a feeling of pleasure in the hearer, and into the purposeful, which Brill calls "tendency wit." This term he uses because wit of this type serves two tendencies: (a) it is a hostile joke serving the purpose of aggression or satire; or (b) it serves the purpose of exhibition or exposure. This latter is seen particularly in the obscene or "smutty" joke.

The obscene joke, Brill states, was originally directed toward some person of the opposite sex, even though later, on account of social inhibitions, it may be told to and enjoyed by persons of the same sex. It makes possible gratification of libidinal craving despite hindrances which stand in the way of direct satisfaction. "Owing to the repression brought about by civilization many primary pleasures are now disapproved by the censor and lost, but the human psyche finds renunciation difficult" and wit is a means of regaining what would otherwise be lost.

The wit of hostility or aggression affords a means of making the enemy ridiculous when other ways could not be tolerated on account of conventional restrictions. The pleasure found in this form of wit is produced on one hand by the technique and on the other

Wit may be considered in reference to two persons, the wit producer and the hearer. The mental process aroused by wit in the hearer is usually an imitation of the processes of the wit producer. The outer inhibitions which are overcome in the hearer correspond to the inner inhibitions of the wit producer.

Wit really implies a necessity of three persons, the producer, the person towards whom the "tendency" is directed, and an impersonal hearer. In this respect it differs from the comic which requires but two persons, and from humor, which involves of necessity only one person, the person directly concerned.

Jest, Brill states, is an element of wit the object of which is to bring about the pleasure of play, while at the same time appeasing the protesting reason. This is accomplished through giving sense and meaning to the senseless and absurd combination of words and thoughts. The jest is a means of obtaining gratification by making possible that which reason forbids, through removing inner inhibitions and rendering productive those pleasure sources which would otherwise be inaccessible.

Ferenczi says the joker by profession is generally a somewhat unbalanced character who in his jokes really ventilates his insufficiently censored intellectual and moral imperfections, i. e. his own infantilisms.

by the purpose fulfilled. Ferenczi states that both aggressive and sexual jokes afford cathexis for repressed libido.

Continuing with this line of thought Brill says that wit helps to overcome inner resistances and to remove inhibitions. Sometimes repression is thus evaded, that is, either outer or inner hindrances may be removed. In the one case an existing inhibition is relieved, in the other the formation of a new inhibition is avoided. It is because of this that there is brought about economy of psychic expenditure which results in pleasure. Just as there is in the technique of wit the principle of economy shown in the use of words, so also there is "economy of psychic expenditure in general."

Reviewing briefly the development of wit, Brill states that it begins as play in order to produce pleasure from the free use of words and thoughts. When such senseless play of words and thoughts is not tolerated by reason, the jest or joke is utilized to retain pleasure and to gain new pleasure by use of the absurd. As harmless wit, it allays critical judgment. Finally, in "tendency" wit, it opposes repression, removing inner inhibitions. "The pleasure which wit produces, be it play-pleasure or removal-pleasure can at all time be traced to the economy of psychic expenditure."

Besides the desire to gain pleasure, there are other motives of wit, the most notable being "to show off," an impulse comparable to sexual exhibitionism. "Persons inclined to obscene joking usually conceal a desire to exhibit. Persons having a powerful sadistic component in their sexuality, which is more or less inhibited, are most successful with the wit of aggression." Wit is a social process because the person producing it always wishes to impart it. The hearer may be said to laugh with the amount of psychic energy which is set free by the suspension of inhibitions, "that is, we laugh away, as it were, this amount of psychic energy."

Many of the dynamisms used in wit are those found in dreams, e. g. condensation, displacement. Both are brief, both emerge from the Ucs, both have their roots in infantilism. The main difference

Jones thinks that lack of humor may be due in part to strong repression of the exhibitionist impulse.

Ferenczi writes that the psychological workship of the joke is situated in the Ucs; the scene of the origin of the comic is in the Pcs. "The joker plays with words, and wants to make stupidity and unmannerliness acceptable; the comic person behaves exactly like a clumsy ignorant child; and the humorist too, takes the grandiose phantasies of children as his example."

Jones, also following Freud, groups jokes according to their aim into four classes including not only the harmless ones, the aim of which is to bring pleasure, but separating those with pronounced tendencies into the obscene, the hostile, the cynical, and the skeptical. He compares wit to dreams not only in the similarity of techniques employed, but from the point of view of origin; both are products not of conscious mental processes but of the Ucs. The source of the pleasure is also an unconscious one. In reality, we do not know at what we laugh, we deceive ourselves over the excellence of the joke.

is that the dream is entirely asocial in purpose while wit serves a social purpose.

Brill distinguishes between wit and the comic in several ways. Mainly, wit is made while the comic is found; the main element of the comic is its naïveté. Due to this, ordinary inhibitions become inapplicable, hence laughter is discharged. "It is the person provided with inhibitions who understands the naïve and it is he alone who gains the pleasure produced by the naïve." The laughter expresses a pleasant feeling of superiority attributed to himself by the hearer as he compares himself with the naïve producer of the comic.

Humor stands nearer to the comic than to wit. It is in general the means of obtaining pleasure despite painful effects. "If we are in a situation which causes us to liberate painful affects and motives then urge us to suppress the same in *statu nascendi,* we have the conditions for humor." Thus humor originates through an economy of emotional expenditure.

The pleasure of wit originates from an economy of expenditure in inhibition, that of the comic from an economy of expenditure in thought, and that of humor in an economy of expenditure in feeling.

In a chapter discussing wit, Brill gives many illuminating illustra tions some of which are quoted from Freud's work on the subject.

A highly speculative but brilliant late contribution (1928) by Freud indicates the part that the Super-ego may play in the production of humor. The Ego finds in humor one of its whole series of methods by which suffering may be avoided. Humor liberates inhibitions, as does wit and the comic, but in more dignified and elevating ways. The specific process undertaken by the Ego in the production of humor is the shifting temporarily of a considerable amount of cathexis to the Super-ego, and the latter then appears in the form of a comforter, a protector from suffering. The Super-ego "asseverates the invincibility of the Ego against the real world." Thus there comes the triumph not only of the Ego but also of the pleasure-principle against adversity. However, as Freud says, if this stern master, the Super-ego, turns out to be a comforter we have more to learn about its attributes than was previously recognized.

Experiences and Attitudes in Family Life

The experiences and emotional attitudes developed in family life and the individual's inner mental reactions thereto have proved to be matters of the deepest concern for psychoanalysts. They are referred to almost more frequently than anything else in psychoanalytic literature and have found much place in these pages. Alone of psychoanalytic writers, Flügel has dealt with family relationships as a whole, bringing together a great deal of psychoanalytic thought and the bearings on it of anthropological researches.

In the strictly psychoanalytic portions of his work Flügel takes for main consideration the following: the polarity, love and hate; the constitutional peculiarities of mental life which allow in ambivalent fashion love and hate to be felt towards the same person; the unconscious conflicts which arise therefrom; the ensuing necessity for repression; the fact that the first love-object of the child is necessarily the parent or the parent-substitute; the development of the Oedipus situation; the threat that develops from this.

The first love situation, Flügel shows, is re-enforced by moral suggestions received from outside, even very early in life—love is added to by growth of feelings of gratitude and admiration. Even the Oedipus situation is complicated by these additions. Very early the hate elements of the Oedipus complex, partially on account of these above complications, may through reaction-formation assume a negative form—"in this case usually appearing as morbid and exaggerated, but of course relatively superficial, love for the hated parent; a love which constantly tends to find expression in somewhat forced and unnatural exhibitions of affection." Hatred towards parents of the opposite sex may not only arise from an inverted Oedipus, but "secondarily as a consequence of the natural tendency of this parent to display affection towards the other parent"; from the child's point of view undue attention is given to a sexual rival.

Flügel makes much of a matter which comes frequently to the front in the modern child-guidance clinic. He says that all sorts of considerations make it clear that normal psychic development depends upon the gradual emergence from a condition of dependence or parental authority. Failure in such a development will result in a relatively feeble adult personality. More dangers lie in the direction of too great rather than too little dependence on the efforts and guidance of the parents or their substitutes. However, too sudden or too complete revolt from parental guidance and tradition may be productive of a bias against every kind of authority and convention. A parent-fixation of the Oedipus type may make itself felt in an inability to direct love freely and fully upon any other person of the same sex as the loved parent.

Among the displacements from the parental love-object are some of considerable sociological importance, Flügel states. Parent-substitutes are groups, places, societies and institutions, and he goes on to give illustrations such as *Alma Mater,* Mother Church, Holy Father, etc.

The attitude of parents toward children comes in for considerable attention. Their own heterosexual inclinations lead them to give most affection often to children of the opposite sex. And the favorite child frequently is invested with love that formerly was directed to the favorite parent. It comes about thus that children are sometimes urged to adopt the profession, the mode of life, or the belief of the grandparents. And even in the most devoted parents there remain remnants of jealousy or resentment lurking in the Ucs which may be shown in some degree of hostile feelings toward the child.

In favorable cases of development, the effect of newly unfolding ethical tendencies upon the conflict between the primitive elements of love and hate lead to sublimations and displacements with love set free for bestowal on other persons or things. Although it is frequently possible to trace resemblance between the loved parent and the new object of affection, the resemblances being of various degrees and kinds, Flügel states that the first step is of very great importance, it is the displacement of erotic love from the parent to some other member of the family, particularly a brother or sister.

An exceedingly interesting observation concerned with the setting of the individual in his family life has been made by Freud and Ferenczi. It appears that an individual sometimes actually falls ill because of social advancement, even when the better state of affairs represents "a deeply rooted and long cherished wish" that has come to fulfilment. Cases are cited proving the point. The trouble arises because of internal frustration which only comes into operation when a previously existent external frustration has been removed. The desire for advancement was allowed by the Ego to exist as harmless, so long as it remained in phantasy and seemed remote from fulfilment. The internal frustration turns out to be of the nature of a censuring and punishing tendency. Freud uses for these cases the eloquent phrase, "those wrecked by success."

Ferenczi adds to Freud's observations concerning "those wrecked by success," a group of cases who showed the same symptoms. Three men that he mentioned exchanged a rustic environment for better conditions of town and city life. They then all suffered from sexual impotence; a wave of repression incident to their living under better, or, at least, under more cultured conditions involved to a very marked degree even their sexual life.

But Ferenczi also presents the opposite side of this problem when he speaks of those who are neurotically ill in a good situation of life and who constantly desire to live on a lower level. In some instances there is yearning to change from an aristocratic to a primitive environment. He thinks he sees an echo of this in the tendency to return to nature and in the many stories that are told of affairs between well-to-do girls, even countesses and the like, and coachmen or chauffeurs.

Certain feelings or sentiments are to be explained as reaction-formations against early sexual component impulses, chiefly exhibitionism, scoptophilia, and sadism.

Abraham speaks of the feelings of *shame* which must be learned by the child during his earliest years and which are first confined to embarrassment related to the naked body. This feeling gradually extends itself to social relations in general, conversation, etc. *Disgust,* according to Jones, is a reaction against the early erotic pleasure in handling excrement. This reaction comes more slowly and less completely with some children depending upon the degree of repression.

Abraham says that shame is a part of the normal development in the case of woman. With her, the normal solution of the Oedipus should be a freeing of the libido from the idea of the father and the directing of it to a new love-object—expectancy of a child. This expectant attitude, Abraham says, "is regulated by certain inhibitions (feelings of shame). The normal adult woman becomes reconciled to her own sexual rôle and to that of the man, and in particular to the facts of male and female genitality; she desires passive gratification and longs for a child. Her castration complex thus gives rise to no disturbing effects."

Pity and horror, according to Abraham, are reaction-formations against sadism and masochism.

Sympathy, according to Freud, has a narcistic origin which "is confirmed by the word itself." The child gets an impression that the father or mother has been ill-treated (usually during sexual intercourse) and through identification with them develops feelings of sympathy first for parent-surrogates.

Freud says that the development from egoism to altruism is brought about through the formation of libidinal ties which inevitably limit narcism. This, according to him, is the only basis for the development of community interest.

At this place we would call attention again to the great values that accrue from careful definition of terms, and this applies particularly to usage of terms concerned with the more conative aspects of mental life. We would strongly urge the consistent following of conceptions which psychologists have recently come somewhat to agree on. An affect is a feeling tone, a pain-pleasure accompaniment of an idea or mental representation. It is not the same as an emotion; for example, the emotion of rage may be either painful or pleasurable. An emotion is the bodily expression of or reaction to a mental representation. A feeling or sentiment is a more abstract and subjective mental attitude, perhaps best stated as "an organized system of emotional tendencies centered about some object"—following Shand and McDougall.

Freud says that the transformation of "bad" or egoistic impulses into "good" or altruistic tendencies "is brought about by two co-operating factors, an internal and an external." The external pressure is constantly being replaced by an internal compulsion since "we learn to value being loved as an advantage for which we are willing to sacrifice other advantages."

Freud goes so far as to say that it is quite possible that individuals of today "bring with them as an inherited constitution some degree of a tendency (disposition) towards transmutation of egoistic into social instincts, and this disposition is easily stimulated to achieve that effect." A part of this transformation, however, must be achieved during the life of the individual himself. And Freud warns against attaching "too much importance to the innate part" or the inherited "cultural adaptability." He says, "we run the risk of overestimating the general adaptability to civilization in comparison with those instincts which have remained in their primitive state," and thus of regarding human nature as "better" than it actually is.

Fear. Freud says fear is of a two-fold nature, namely, real fear and neurotic fear, that is, the fear of an impulse claim. With regard to real fear, he thinks that the behavior of small children demonstrates that there is no such thing as "an instinctive perception of externally threatening danger." Thus the fears or phobias of children are to be explained by the fact that certain external dangers have become significant for the Ego through "internalization."

There are three practically universal childhood fears which, Freud says, "may be termed almost normal." These are the fear of being alone, the fear of darkness, and the fear of strangeness, and he explains them as arising on the basis of the unconscious Ego's fear of loss of the protecting object, namely, the mother. In the normal child, these fears should soon be outgrown. The fear of the larger animals such as the horse points to unconscious castration anxiety and may be regarded, if there is no fixation, as normal for that particular phase of development.

The "enigmatic" fear of small animals, fear of thunder, etc. Freud suggests may be "an atrophied residue of a congenital preparation for real dangers which is so distinctly developed in other animals." Such phobias ought normally to drop out; if they persist into later life, Freud says it is because their content has "set itself into association" with impulse claims "and is representative also of internal dangers."

Abraham offers an ingenious explanation of the fear which children frequently display of very small and often quite harmless animals and insects (fly, caterpillar, etc.). He thinks that the fear of the father has been transferred and displaced to these animals because they have "the characteristic of making a sudden appearance, . . . they touch the human body unexpectedly, and disappear with equal rapidity." Small flying or crawling insects and animals "indicate on the one hand the dangerous power of the father, but serve on the other as an expression for the child's ideas of getting rid of him." Individual determinants must, of course, always be taken into account. Abraham cites a case in which a

Freud thinks that many adult phobias or exaggerated fear reactions are due to the fact that an impulse fear has been added to a real fear. Thus in the case, for example, of fear of falling from windows, precipices, etc., "the impulse claim from the gratification of which the Ego shrinks" is masochistic, a desire for self-destruction.

Fear of touching or certain touching inhibitions, Abraham suggests, can be traced originally to sexual pleasure in touching things.

An underlying determinant of topophobia (fear of streets) is, according to Abraham, an unconscious fear of life or of the temptations which beset the individual outside of home. Another determinant of street anxiety is the need for the constant company of particular persons due to fixation upon them; every separation from the love-object means in the Ucs a detachment of the libido from the incestuous fixation. Street anxiety is also another way of exerting power over persons in the environment.

Abraham thinks, however, that none of the above determinants are a sufficient explanation for a street phobia. There is in addition a specific factor in the sexual constitution of individuals suffering from "locomotor anxiety." This factor, he says, is a fixation on the erotic pleasure of bodily movement; the act of walking is accompanied by sexual excitation which is taboo to the Ego.

wasp phobia had its origin in the fact that it had replaced the fear of a tiger because of the similar color, markings, and buzzing. The tiger phobia itself was to be traced to the association made between its roar and the father's "deep threatening voice" when he was angry.

Temper, according to Jones and Abraham, is often to be traced to anal-erotism. Jones says that this is always to be suspected in any one who is the victim of chronic irritability and bad temper.

Hate, has its roots largely in oral and anal ambivalence. With a normal solution of the Oedipus complex, hate should drop out, but ambivalent feelings usually persist to some extent in all adult individuals. Freud says that even those whom we love most deeply are unconsciously "partly strangers, even enemies. With the exception of only a very few situations, there adheres to the tenderest and closest of our affections a vestige of hostility which can excite an unconscious death wish." This, he says, explains the so often observed "exaggeratedly tender care for the well-being of relatives," and also the "entirely unfounded self-reproaches after the death of a loved person."

Dependence, Jones says, "can be defined as a persistent incestuous attachment of the libido, and independence as the disposal of it in some other direction." This "non-incestuous" disposal of the libido may either take the form of object-seeking, or that of sublimation, or both.

Abraham thinks that there is a strong association between the idea of omnipotence and defecation, and that this underlies the phenomena, several times observed by him, of diarrhoea being an equivalent of suppressed outbursts of rage. The over-estimation of the functions of excretion "in the sense of possessing great and even unlimited power to create or destroy every object" offers an explanation of "how an explosive evacuation of the bowels can offer to the unconscious of the neurotic a substitute for a discharge of angry affect. . . ."

Ferenczi says of stage-fright that it is a mistake to think that it occurs as a result of excessive modesty; on the contrary the narcism of those to whom this happens "asks too much of their own performance." They have "fallen into a state of self-observation" and their interest in their own behavior (voice, movements, etc.) "disturbs the normal, automatic, motor, phonetic or oratorical performance."

Jones says that self-confidence in the case of a man is very closely bound up with sexual potency. "It is enough for him to have a suspicion of impotence at a time when he has never put the matter to the test, or fear that at some future time it may come about, for his confidence and his capacity in general to be seriously impaired." Complete sexual impotence is very likely to bring about pre-occupation with "the endeavor to conceal his pitiable state, if not from himself at least from the world around him." The result of this is "an attitude of slinking furtiveness, a constant apprehension of detection, a dread of measuring himself with other men (except in phantasy) or of taking his due place in life, a propensity to suspiciousness in general or specific phobias—in short, a total inability to hold his head erect and look the whole world in the face. . . ."

Inferiority feelings. Freud makes much of the causation of inferiority as derived from the inability to love consequent upon a mental or physical disorder. The main source of the feeling is due to impoverishment of the Ego, resultant upon the withdrawal of an excessively large amount of object libidinal cathexis, that is, to the injury sustained by the Ego through sexual trends that are no longer under control.

In one place, Freud states that the most important contribution to the inferiority complex is derived from a sense of failure to achieve the wishes connected with the Oedipus situation. The irreconcilability of these wishes with reality and the inadequacy of the childhood stage of development lead to a narcistic scar that constitutes the basis of the inferiority feeling. "The sex quest to which the physical development of the child set limits could be brought to no satisfying conclusion"; "hence the plaint in later life, 'I can't do anything, I am never successful.'"

Alexander ascribes feelings of inferiority to the persistence in the Ucs of a father-son conflict. The solution has been attempted by identification with the father and "the conflict is carried on to the Ego system." It "represents a tension between the Ego-ideal and the Ego." It is a narcistic attempt at solution as in melancholia —the sadism of the Ego-ideal is gratified and also the masochism of the Ego. Alexander speaks of the "well-known sadistic-masochistic gain," which he says absorbs the primary aggressive impulses which will otherwise be sublimated and applied in useful occupations.

According to Alexander the "melancholia mechanism" manifests itself in the normal person as a shy, anxious, "inferiority" character, or "melancholic" type of personality; the opposite of this is a "hypomanic" type, that is exuberant, self-confident, unrestrained.

Anesthesia in a woman does not give the sense of inferiority as in the case of man—in fact, the reverse may be often the case, "namely, an exaggerated tendency to narcism, a state of affairs that is partly a cause and partly a result of anesthesia; the woman unable to give what the man most wants attaches in a compensatory way an excessive value to her other charms."

Abraham thinks that the fact that many women only obtain normal sexual sensations after they have had a child (that is, they become "only female in the full sense by the way of maternal feelings") can only be understood in the light of the inferiority resulting from the castration complex. The woman receives now from the husband the "gift" she desired as a little girl from her father, and thus her narcistic wound is at last healed. This makes plain the type of woman who desires a child even against the will of the man and also the opposite type of woman who refuses to bear children, declining a substitute, and to be constantly reminded of her femininity and inferiority by the presence of children.

Freud admits that inferiority may be a reaction sometimes, as Adler maintains, to a realization of some organic weakness, but he points out that Adler does not sufficiently recognize the incidence of splendid achievements accompanying superior organic endowment. Also the study of neurotics shows that in some instances organic inferiority is merely a pretext for a neurosis deriving from other sources of inferiority. There are cases of hysteria in very attractive and beautiful women. In spite of the greater frequency of ugliness and organic infirmities in the lower classes of society, Freud points out that there is not any greater incidence of neurosis among them than there is amongst the more favored classes.

The pedagogy of the future, Ferenczi thinks, will endeavor to become informed of the psychoanalytic discoveries with regard to basic impulses and the social trends which may later emerge from these. This development, he says, must not be left to chance, but "on the basis of a knowledge of the instincts and the possibilities of their conversion" the educator "will himself create the situations necessary for development and thereby guide character formation into proper channels."

But Eder in a review writes, "A great deal of work has to be done before any definite principles can be laid down for the use of psychoanalysis in education—whether in earliest infancy or in the school child: at present psychoanalysts themselves are groping their way."

Low, however, believes that there is already enough to justify considerable application of psychoanalytic theory to education. Some of her contributions are as follows: She believes that teachers should themselves be analyzed. In this way they will acquire the first necessary equipment of the educator, namely, a realization of the unconscious mind and its influence upon consciousness. They must know psychoanalytic principles, the implications of the rôle of the teacher as a parent-substitute, principles of identification, the influence of the repression process, the importance of sublimation, the interdependence of intellectual and emotional factors, the part that phantasy plays in the child's life. In general, psychoanalytic principles alter not only the teacher's attitude but the methods used in teaching and the material or content taught. They enable the teacher to recognize children in need of analysis by the expert and to have a relationship to the normal child through helping him to free and develop the affective life.

Ferenczi emphasizes the importance of the school years which cover the latency period, a period that is of extreme importance "as the time during which character traits are formed and the Ego-ideal built up."

Meng writing on compulsion and freedom in school education insists upon the importance of the first five years for the development of the individual. Among other things the phantasy life of the child must not be interfered with, since phantasy gives so many opportunities for fulfilling the demands of instinctive urges. Play for a child is as important as work for an adult.

Ferenczi states that everyone who wishes to explain or teach anyone anything, becomes a substitute for the father and teacher-imago, and takes upon himself all the disbelief that these personalities formerly roused in the child.

Ferenczi says that Freud has frequently pointed out that the child sometimes achieves merely partial surrender of its own judgment in the face of authority represented by the teacher, but may react to it by a sort of affective feeblemindedness, and that from such are recruited those who succumb early to every energetic personality.

Low discusses the influence in education of the teacher's Ucs. Unless the teacher himself undergoes analysis, he is likely to establish unfavorable relationships between himself and his pupils. "Only the person who is . . . inwardly free can educate others properly." Then, unless there is at least a satisfactory fulfilment of his own more important desires, the teacher will be using his position for personal gratifications. Only through analysis does he understand the meaning of the "parent-child situation" and the ambivalent attitude of the child. Only then is he able to interpret the child's behavior in relation to inferiority sense, guilt feelings, desire for punishment, as they are shown in relation to teacher, his fellows, and his work.

Low says that psychoanalysis also throws light on the problems of special disabilities and of general lack of interests and powers of concentration as these are shown in school life. In general, curiosity which has been repressed owing to guilt and fear may affect many reactions in the whole sphere of learning, knowing, investigating. Conflicts between phantasy wishes and the ideals imposed by the Super-ego may result in an appearance of idleness or apathy. Feelings of guilt may prevent the function of intellectual processes. "They may entirely hinder our ability to comprehend even simple words or to observe what is before our eyes." This is in agreement with the statement of Jones: "Special difficulty that a child may have in acquiring a given subject is often due not, as is usually thought, to any inherent deficiency in this respect, but to inhibitions that originate in a more primary interest with which the subject has become secondarily associated and which has transferred on to the latter its own affects, difficulties, and conflicts."

Low emphasizes the fact that sublimation should play a large rôle in education. "There is an essential relationship between sublimation and education especially during the first half of childhood." This necessitates an accurate and specific transference of energy from one given field of interest to another, but there should not be demand for too great or too speedy sublimation, nor should there be confusion of sublimation with the attempt to develop con-

Some definite mental manifestations of school difficulties given by Low are as follows: (1) Inability to progress beyond a certain stage. (2) Inability to deal with any kind of problem. (3) Inaccurate observation, hearing, or reproduction. This is due to preoccupation combined with curiosity and fear concerning activities of grown-ups, especially the parents, in connection with which guilt feelings are formed. (4) Lack of concentration. This is due to pushing away of a given train of thought by another thought or thoughts. "In all such cases a phantasy life, overt or repressed, is forming the obstacle to attention and concentration, and it is hopeless to seek to alter this situation unless and until the phantasies can be revealed and comprehended." "There is nearly always to be found either a situation of refusal based on a sense of guilt and accompanying fear (that is, the child has withdrawn from efforts and achievements in the reality world, in fear of disappointment or punishment); or the real interest, behind the manifest lack of interest and of attention, is a guilty one—some ungratified, more infantile, preoccupation—which must get an outlet under cover of other activities, disturbing and vitiating the consciously realized interest." (5) Difficulty in speaking or taking part in class recitation. This is due to fear of exposure and to a sense of jealous rivalry. The first is a manifestation of narcism; the exposure fear is often related to early wishes in connection with the own body and the body of the mother. The second is related to the jealousy feelings for the father. (6) Fear of examinations. Here the examination is to the unconscious a "test of personal validity and strong guilt feelings may render such a test a thing of dread terror." (7) Slovenliness and dirtiness of work. This is frequently due to having been forced too early to abandon gratification of instinctual body pleasures, becoming civilized grown-ups with decorous personalities too soon. These abandoned impulses express themselves in indirect form of ink blots and general slovenliness. They are the expression of unconscious revenge wishes for denial of urgent impulses.

Blum explains fear of examination somewhat differently; he says such fear is an outgrowth of the Oedipus situation, castration fear, but the original source is birth fear. Freud says neurotic fear of a test is based on the child's fears of punishment to be given for failure by parents and teachers.

scious substitutive interests; sublimation is an unconscious process. The teacher can make opportunities for sublimation.

Low makes much of phantasy life in children as wish-fulfilment and source of pleasure, as compensation and as expressed in play. Educators must obtain insight into this aspect of the child's life and recognize its importance.

Ferenczi believes that children who are *"too well brought up"* are characterized by a torpidity of phantasy life. The animation of phantasy is in direct relation to those childhood experiences sometimes called "infantile sexual traumata." Children who have been so strongly controlled that they have lacked every opportunity to observe, much less to experience, anything sexual, lack later freedom in phantasy simply because they have not had the "opportunity to get anchored in the world of reality." "We may say, in other words, that a certain amount of infantile sexual experience (that is to say, a little sexual traumatism) not only does not damage but later promotes normality, particularly the normal activity of phantasy."

Jones writes, "It cannot be insisted on too strongly that sublimation is concerned not so much with normal sexual desire in the narrow sense, as with the individual biological components of the instinct, i. e. with the various infantile tendencies that later on form the basis of erotic desire as well as of many other nonsexual interests. This is clearly of cardinal import for education, for it means that sublimation is not a matter of displacing for other purposes a diffuse energy. . . ."

In considering as educational material folk tales and myths from the standpoint of psychoanalysis, Federn remarks on the fact that nowadays it is the fashion to attempt to replace crude mythical stories and folk tales by children's stories presumably more suitable for their upbringing. He thinks that since these tales of old represent the history of the race and so throw the young mind in tune with much that has gone on ages before in history, they are to be preserved for children. Even their gruesomeness and deeds of shame do not destroy the pleasure children derive from the stories. On the contrary, the child seeks in these stories the pleasure of fear, this emotion brings joy in wonderment, it allows satisfaction of primitive wishes. Then, too, through these readings, appreciation is gained of the experiences of the struggles of other ages and of other people, an appreciation that is valuable for the development of cultural and political development. With the gross sexual element of many of these stories eliminated, as it is in present-day literature, they can do no harm.

Meng, discussing sex education from the psychoanalytic standpoint stands entirely for early biological education which may do much to protect childhood, but states that one must avoid giving specific advice about when to acquaint the child with the exact part that his father and mother play in his conception. In every case facts must be given only as the child himself leads up to them.

Coriat, who has contributed more than any one else to the psychoanalytic understanding of the causes of stammering, apparently still holds to his earlier idea that the psychogenesis of this struggle is found in a conflict which centers about results of the resistance to betrayal of certain repressed trends of thought by means of speech. For therapy, the motor symptoms in the speech of the stammerer must also be investigated analytically. Stammering represents an arrest or fixation both on the sucking and biting levels of oral libido. All stammerers display the oral reactions of sucking and biting in their tic-like ways of speech. Stammering is thus really a form of gratification of oral libido—a compulsion dominated by the pleasure-principle.

"The oral libido in stammering is an autoerotic trend which underlies this pathological activity . . . as a regression or unconscious residual from the pregenital phase of development." The repressed is found to refer principally to the Oedipus situation, to certain sexual acts or thoughts, tabooed words, and masochistic phantasies, and also to the pleasure relating to early stages of the organization of the libido. Coriat says that the problem of stammering thus can only be understood by analysis and interpretation of the stages in the Ego and libido development, working through the various phases of pre-genital organization to adult character formation.

But mainly for the purposes of treatment, because stammering is partly a narcistic disorder and thus refractory to treatment, concentrated attention should be placed on the oral libido in order to overcome the regressive tendencies which in stammerers enter into conflict with the Ego. Stammering is a neurosis, says Coriat, in which "fixation of the libido at the developmental phase of oral erotism persists into maturity. In his unconscious and likewise in his conscious motor reactions, the stammerer remains fixed at this primitive biological stage because there is little or no sublimation of the original oral pleasure." But the problem of stammering is very complex and frequently in analysis there is encountered a difficulty in distinguishing the oral-erotic from the anal-erotic component.

Coriat's long experience with the problem of stammering leads him to see that there are several interesting concomitants of this neurosis. For example, the optimism so curiously displayed is a characteristic due to oral fixation; the fluctuations of mood and interest in stammerers may be related in their origin to rhythmic periods of nursing; the motor phenomena hark back to the sucking and biting stages. And the "cures" which depend on speech training alone tend to reinforce the oral-erotic pleasure instead of minimizing or relieving it.

In a review of Coriat's recent little book, representing his most mature thought on the subject, Eder points out the difficulties presented for interpretation of this disorder, which Coriat acknowledges. Eder thinks that as a rule among stammerers inversion of the Oedipus attitude is to be found and thinks there is more to be said in favor of regarding stammering as a conversion-hysteria, noting that stammerers can often speak fluently to themselves or in a certain environment, as Coriat himself says.

Concerning the prevention of stammering, Eder thinks that there is no evidence that any of the bad habits, such as prolonged nursing or thumb-sucking produce stammerers. "Our knowledge of the development of the Ego and of the Super-Ego is all too scanty as yet to warrant a laying down of rules for prevention."

Children's Faults and Difficulties

Naughtiness. Freud brings out an immensely important point when he asks how much of children's naughtiness is due to a preceding sense of guilt. It is easy to perceive often that children are naughty "on purpose to provoke punishment, and are quiet and contented after the chastisement." By bringing naughtiness forward, they force punishments and in that way obtain masochistic satisfactions that are desired. "Later analytic investigation car often find a trace of the guilty feeling which bids them seek for punishment."

Masturbation. A considerable amount of attention is paid in psychoanalytic literature to the subject of masturbation and the gist of psychoanalytic thought concerning it seems to be as follows: Masturbation is to be regarded as a normal phenomenon of human psycho-sexual life. In contrast to what most people believe, it is an extremely common occurrence in infancy and young childhood, exhibiting itself in various forms of physical habits. In the life of young childhood, it reaches its climax at from three to five years, according to the observations of Freud. At or about puberty it is so usual that the vast majority of young people pass through a period of it.

The significance of masturbation from a physical standpoint is very slight, what it means to the individual depends upon what phantasy life is bound up with the practice and what anxieties or other compromise-formations may result. The anxiety or other effects even theoretically can be seen not to be produced by the masturbation itself—getting satisfaction does not produce anxiety.

Even very early in life masturbation is not merely an autoerotic phenomenon. It soon has its concomitants of object-relationships in phantasy life. The masturbation of later years, particularly that of adolescence with all of its richness of phantasy has its significance mainly as it is related to the earlier type of masturbatory

This conception of the causation of some of the naughtiness of children is directly in line with much that recently has been written on the subject of the sense of guilt and the need of punishment; more specifically, it lines up with some of the concepts that are to be found under the head of Delinquency and Criminality.

Klein maintains that criminal tendencies are at work in every child. She thinks these arise on the basis of repressed oral and anal sadistic impulses. These destructive tendencies, she claims, can be *sublimated* for artistic and creative work. Strong sadistic tendencies which are met by an intensely sadistic Super-ego may mean a conflict quite unbearable for a weak Ego and thus lead to strong repression. Another factor is the inability of some children to bear anxiety and feelings of guilt. Klein points out that the child's own sadistic trends are largely responsible for formation of a sadistic Super-ego.

Freud thinks that there is much direct and indirect proof of infantile masturbation, even though parents do not recognize it and deny it.

The reason that psychoanalysts became so much interested in masturbation was that they found it to be the central point of concern with so many neurotics. Freud asked himself early why it should be that so many individuals pass through considerable periods of masturbation without any harm whatever ensuing, and yet in other cases it was found to be such a source of disturbance. That masturbation or its concomitants result in many troubles there can be no doubt, when one studies the origin of various compulsions, symptomatic-acts, and other neurotic behavior. Among the various phenomena of this sort one can note tics, hand washings, excessive embarrassment, hysterical symptoms, etc. Freud noted early that hysterical symptoms hardly ever appear as long as children are masturbating, only when a period of abstinence has set in.

practice. Freud speaks of the masturbation of puberty being a revival of the infantile form with its meanings and portents going back to this period.

The sense of guilt that really makes masturbation important is connected with the phantasy life accompanying it. Freud does not consider the phantasies of pubertal masturbation particularly important, except as they revert back to earlier ones. But the really significant and unconscious phantasy is that connected with infantile masturbation, namely, the Oedipus complex. This forms the basis for anxieties which later may come to be attached to consideration of the act itself. The castration threat that not infrequently is made on account of masturbatory practices may add to the trouble which the Oedipus situation itself involves.

Enuresis. Psychoanalysts have given some attention to the significance of enuresis. Jones says that enuresis frequently acquires the significance of nocturnal masturbation. Abraham agrees that there is a certain pleasure in this emptying of the bladder; in one case he noted that in the dream life connected with enuresis a definite exhibitionist impulse was represented. In older females he has found that they are regularly burdened with strong resistances against their female limitations and in the enuretic process there may persist the infantile desire to urinate in a male position. Thus the castration complex is a determinant of the enuresis.

Pleasure-sucking. Pleasure-sucking, which usually takes the form of thumb-sucking or finger-sucking, can, according to Freud, be looked upon as a sexual activity "which has become detached from nutritive activity, and which has exchanged its external object for one belonging to its own body." Abraham adds that thumb-sucking continued represents a more advanced stage of libidinal development than the prolonged attachment to nutritional sucking or to the pleasures of eating. The oral zone has retained its predominant rôle, to be sure, but in reality and in phantasy the use of the mouth plays its part for sexual purposes.

Jones notes the difference between the results of masturbation in girls and boys. In the former, the common form is clitoris masturbation. Persistence in this is important as leading to sexual anesthesia in marriage; through fixation on the infantile form of sexual pleasure, vaginal sensibility may be prevented. Since in infancy masturbatory practices in both sexes partake of the male form, on account of the clitoris being an analogue of the penis, the girl has a good many more difficulties to overcome in the transitions of her life, and masturbation, as Jones suggests, may come to be bound up with the problems of narcism and homosexuality.

Freud and others have spoken of the relationship which exists between incontinence of the bladder and the idea of fire. Those who earlier were bed wetters are said later on to take an unwonted interest in fires.

Ferenczi calls attention to the fact that many patients who have a tic are, or have been, addicted to enuresis.

Abraham makes a number of interesting observations concerning the dominating influence which pleasure in sucking, as retained into later life, can have for behavior. Some people have to bite or lick their lips when doing hard work, and he thinks that the necessity that some men have for smoking while they are at work is to be accounted for in the same way. There are certain normal expressions of the libido considered quite allowable as attached to the oral zone, such as kissing, but many other practices which represent the same attachment of the libido are unusual and more or less unallowable.

No one interested in childhood habits of thumb sucking, etc., can afford to neglect the research undertaken by Dr. David Levy (American Journal of Psychiatry, May, 1928), a research which in some ways bears upon the psychoanalytic theories of pleasure-sucking.

Peculiar Eating Habits. Freud has called attention to peculiarities of eating as representing the sexual organization of the oral phase of development during which the original attachment of sexual excitation to the nutritional instinct was still in force. Both he and others speak of "cannibalistic ideas" carried over from infancy to later life. Many idiosyncrasies concerning food are due to associations through symbols. Some things seem very desirable and some things nauseating because of unconscious symbolism. Copro-symbols are those which particularly lead to distaste for certain kinds of food.

Evidences of oral erotism are sometimes, according to Glover, found in voracious hunger, compulsion to drink when the stomach is distended, etc., besides in the habits of biting and sucking the fingers.

Exhibitionism and Voyeurism—Childish tendencies to display the body, the sexual organs, the excretory functions before the parents or other children are to be viewed as natural expressions of a component of the sexual instinct. Such manifestations are bound up with the early stages of object-love and some of them may find their place as normal development proceeds in the fore-pleasure associated with the adult sexual activity, and in many sublimated social expressions.

Tendencies to view, scoptophilic interests, are also quite normal expressions of sexual curiosity during the Infancy Period. These may also enter later into fore-pleasure and find various sublimated forms of expression.

Fixation on (also regression to) and the carrying over into adult life of these unmodified forms of sexual activity are sometimes spoken of as perversions.

Ferenczi speaks of examples of exhibitionistic trends as shown in desires to show off one's own children, interest in writing poems, beautiful letters, noticeably plain dress in well-to-do society women.

Abraham says that sublimated exhibitionism is shown in efforts to excel others, that is to draw all eyes on the self. Morbid ambition can provide "a kind of common outlet for repressed sadistic and exhibitionistic trends."

Alexander and Staub present a very interesting exposition of psychoanalytic theory as applied to criminality. They speak of three principal groups of criminals:

1. Neurotic criminals—Those who are enemies of society on the basis of inner mental conflicts between the social and asocial forces within themselves. These conflicts, as in the case of psychoneurotics, arise out of influences which were active in earliest childhood, and the careers of neurotic criminals develop in much the same way as those of psychoneurotics. This is psychological etiology.

2. Normal criminals—Those whose mental life has developed along normal lines, but who identify themselves with criminal prototypes. This is sociological etiology.

3. Pathological criminals—Those whose behavior is organically determined. This is biological etiology.

Staub in a special article on criminality adds somewhat to the types of causation upon which psychoanalysis tends to throw light. The cases of pathological stealing, kleptomania, nearly all of which occur in women and girls, show that such thieving has its root in a specific repressed wish, namely, penis-envy. And even in similar cases among men, the deed symbolically stands for a repressed Oedipus wish to rob the father of his manliness. In such cases, the judicial procedure entirely fails because unpunished kleptomaniacs tend to steal less often than when punishment increases the stimulus to steal. Staub discusses also the adventurer or swindler type, often refined and prepossessing individuals. The roots of the trouble in these cases are to be found in early childhood experiences; as a rule these individuals have come from parents who have given them little affection, or they have been unwelcome members of the family. They have been emotionally undernourished, as Abraham says, they have become enemies of society because they were not loved. Out of their narcism they are vain and luxury-seeking, and seek to create astonishment—not finding normal love-objects satisfactory. Their narcism having been damaged in early childhood, they seek to recompense or revenge themselves.

Criminality from passion, Staub says, represents a momentary outbreak of what really has had a long prior history in the criminal's Ucs. The misdoer has suffered at the hands of the world and this has led to a poor inner adjustment to social requirements. In all cases of passionate crime, there is a faulty moral inhibitory power which has resulted from an unsatisfactory introjection of a good Ego-ideal—paternal authority presented no pattern corresponding to that of good social adjustment. Again, here, the criminal deed is a revenge of the Ucs against the poor type of authority which was experienced in early childhood.

These two authors further suggest a diagnostic scheme of criminality.

I. Chronic criminality.

  1. Criminality conditioned by toxic or other organic pathology.

  2. Criminality conditioned by neurotic tendencies, by the response to unconscious motivation.

    a. Compulsion or symptomatic crime, such as kleptomania, pyromania, pseudologia. In these cases the compulsions appear as something quite foreign to the general trends of the Ego, they are senseless and isolated from the standpoint of the other content of consciousness.

    b. Neurotic criminal activity with participation of the entire personality. The Ego is led to act thus through suffering or through rationalization. In the case of suffering, either a sort of moral freeing of the self is sought, and in that case it is more of a neurotic manifestation, or the suffering is lived out in a phantasy projection of guilt, in which case it is more of a psychotic nature. Rationalization, which occurs with all of us, may lead to criminality through a quantitative difference in falsification of facts, there is overvaluation of the self-righteous motive in order to bring the deed into line with consciousness.

    An extreme case of such neurotic activity is found in the case of criminals who carry out their crimes as the result of a guilt feeling which is based on a real, but relatively harmless earlier breach of social standards. Several dynamic processes are at work which cover up the meaning of the basic process and cause the seeking for suffering.

Staub makes interesting comments on the political criminal. Following Freud, the state and the body politic is to be thought of as a projection of paternal authority. An aggressive attitude toward political authority rests on the basis of an aggressive Oedipus wish. In the Ucs the individual who is against the state is revenging himself upon his father.

On the other hand, the explanation of why political criminals are punished so severely is to be found in the fact that the judge, who is representative of the authority of the state, identifies himself with the state whose integrity he has to preserve; deeds directed against the state are unconsciously regarded as aggressions against his own person. This is the reverse side of the Oedipus drama, one of the matters which psychoanalysis has the task to make clear in order that a rational criminal justice may be developed.

Alexander, writing with Staub, the psychoanalytically minded attorney, states that so far as the future is concerned, it is clear that we shall have to wait for a thoroughly rational justice until such a time as mankind can know itself well enough to throw off its aggressive and sadistic primitive tendencies. A really well-adapted procedure for the treatment of criminals will have to wait for this, if it ever comes about. In the meantime, with better understandings much can be done, much more than is embodied in weak attempts to compromise through altering the criminal code in terms of leniency or supposed reformatory procedures as they are ordinarily conducted. These writers agree with Wittels that criminal punishment gives the chance for human aggressive sadistic tendencies to find expression which they cannot find under the conditions of ordinary social repression. In the law an authorized sadistic expression is possible. When society identifies itself with the law it finds itself satisfaction for its aggressive tendencies. This is to be seen particularly in the carrying out of the death sentence, when, with its published details, it presents a spectacle that has the same psycho-sociological significance as a gladiatorial combat or a bull fight.

3. Criminality conditioned by a criminally inclined Super-ego active in a non-neurotic individual. In these cases the entire personality identifies itself with the criminal activity and one can say that there are anti-social proclivities which stand as assertions of their Ego and Super-ego righteousness. These authors think that many vagabonds, professional criminals, pickpockets, burglars, etc., belong to this group.

4. Although its real existence appears questionable, one can think of a more fundamental type of criminality caused by lack of development of the Super-ego. Individuals whose actions belong in this category must be those who are not at all socialized, those who very directly express fundamental impulses.

II. Accidental criminality.

1. Crimes of so-called negligence, which really represent an unconscious criminal tendency breaking through without in any way laying claim to be directed by the behavior tendencies of the Ego—indeed the Ego rejects entirely the idea of there having been intention to commit a criminal deed.

2. Crimes committed through environmental stresses, namely, situational crimes. The situation causes much stress or suffering that even an ordinarily well-functioning Super-ego is thrown out of functioning—the feeling of justice is so greatly wounded.

Staub elsewhere calls attention to the fact that not only the criminal but also the judge has an Ucs. Called forth during the trial are the judge's unconscious affective motives; his hidden urges appear in the form of the retribution principle of the law. Often it is not the conscious decision of the judge that actually rules, but a sadistic component urge that appears in a correct legal form, however aimless this may be from the standpoint of sociology. Psychoanalysis is just beginning to point out this important fact, which as it may become understood can greatly influence the legal treatment of criminals.

Ferenczi agrees that legal punishment gratifies our own unconscious urge for vengeance and that the feeling for revenge can be explained in no other way than that we "are unconsciously indignant that the criminal dared to do something which we all unconsciously had the greatest inclination to do." "We scorn and avoid the criminal chiefly because our Ucs for good reason is afraid of the infectiousness of the bad example."

Freud tells of finding out by analysis that some patients who had committed such deeds as theft, fraud, and arson had committed these deeds because such things are forbidden and because by carrying them out the doer enjoyed a sense of mental relief. An oppressive sense of guilt was felt, the origin of which was unknown, and after the deed was done the oppression was mitigated. The transgression occurred as the result of a prior sense of guilt. This type of criminal was recognized by Nietzsche and set forth in his, *On the Pale Criminal*. Alexander in his study, *The Need for Punishment and the Death-Instinct,* shows how punishment serves avoidance of pain—the criminal act and the ensuing punishment free the individual from a deep anxiety of conscience and its possible greater pain.

The argument in favor of introducing such a category of psychological causation is that in the long run each type can be more effectively dealt with. The first group of chronic criminals should be regarded as presenting medical problems, the second group is that of the neurotic criminals who require psychoanalytic treatment, and the third, those with a criminally inclined Super-ego represent more of a pedagogical problem. And it goes without saying that all chronic offenders against society should be segregated during the entire time that they show anti-social proclivities.

But if psychoanalysis undertakes consideration of the criminal himself, it must also similarly view society in its development of methods of punishment. The deepest fundamental wish underlying punishment is revenge, although in the present state of the law the revenge motive appears much modified and softened. Secondarily to society has come the idea of expiation or atonement. When the criminal threatens the interests of others he releases a primitive desire for revenge that received its full expression in the talion principle of the earliest criminal law. Society then acted from a tendency which Freud has expressed in the formula: that which a person passively endures he strives to live out afterwards. Atonement appears in modern law through two routes: (a) Society identifies itself with the misdoer, it puts itself in the criminal's place and thinks that atonement ought to be made. (b) Society regards the idea of expiation as a modified sort of revenge.

Aichhorn's studies of young delinquents lead him to say that the delinquent may be thought of as an individual who is controlled by the pleasure-principle as against the reality-principle, but this may not indicate a neurotic trend, rather it often betokens poor training. And in this matter, he follows Freud in considering the importance of the development of the Ego-ideal, the Super-ego, from identifications with the parents, especially the father. The delinquent has an inadequate Ego-ideal and in some instances has identified himself with a criminalistic parent, which identification drives him into anti-social behavior. Aichhorn grants, however, that in some instances delinquency is due to an unconscious sense of guilt developed from the too severe demands of the Super-ego.

Aichhorn insists that the training of the delinquent must be based on ascertained facts about the Ego-ideal, whether it is overstrong or overweak or lacking. Character correction must be aimed at alteration of the Ego-ideal and the educator in this respect must take on the attributes of a father-substitute. The educator of the delinquent must therefore concern himself with the libidinal relationships of early childhood in order to know what unfavorable influences existed for the building up of the Ego-ideal.

Ferenczi speaks of treating nervous patients who besides their ordinary symptoms showed an impulse to criminal acts. Through analysis he found it possible to trace the tendency to unconscious mental driving forces "and to weaken or even completely to annul these tendencies precisely by means of psychoanalytic treatment."

Reich speaks of an "instinct-ridden individual"—a criminal type. "Broadly speaking, they suffer from an ineffective critical faculty, they have practically no conscience, their sexuality is manifest and uncontrolled, the guilt, if present, is anchored in neurotic symptoms or repressed."

The real belief in legal procedure as punishment, according to Freud, Jones, and Ferenczi, has its roots in unconsciously repressed revenge wishes and tendencies. Jones says, "Intolerance of other people's wrong-doing is a sure sign of an uneasy conscience, of the effort it is costing to suppress forbidden unconscious tendencies." The basic problem of punishment is not moral but psychological.

Ferenczi finds much reason for the development of a psychoanalytic criminology. "The conscious confessions of criminals and a statement of the circumstances of the crime, be it ever so complete, will never sufficiently explain why the individual in the given circumstances had to commit just that act." Ordinary investigations into crime leave out of account the driving forces that are the most powerful determinants of all, the tendencies of the unconscious mental life. Nor does the treatment of crime under the law bring to bear any prophylactic measures for guarding against these tendencies. The first step toward a better understanding and procedure is to collect a large amount of criminological psychoanalytic material. This author thinks that a condemned person will have no further reason for concealing the thoughts and associations by means of which his unconscious motives might be brought to light. With the beginning of the treatment the psychoanalytical situation, the so-called transference, will render the offender desirous of being dealt with psychoanalytically. If comparative investigation of similar offenses is carried out, the gaps of criminological determinism may be filled in with solid scientific material. Psychoanalytic insight and its method of treatment may "contribute not a little to render possible the psychic 'rebirth' of criminals and their adaptation to the social order."

The existence of an unconscious urge to confession has been insisted upon by Freud and has been elaborated by Reik. The latter says that the phenomenon is regarded by the analyst as a special form of the "return of the repressed." It signifies that the Super-ego, or conscience comes to expression. The need for confession rests upon a pre-existent feeling of guilt—deep in the soul-life there is a longing for truth. So far as confession of criminality is concerned, the criminal stands in relation to society as the child stands to his father. The child after a misdeed feels the possibility of losing his love-object and confession may bring about the possibility of regaining it. Just so the criminal hopes to rehabilitate himself in his relationships with society. But the urge to confession is to be witnessed not only in the criminal but is also found in art, religion, myth, and the ordinary use of language. The sense of guilt is a universal phenomenon and needs various avenues for confession.

Psychoanalysts believe that in studying stealing it is important to note from whom objects are stolen—for example, are they father-representatives? If object-transference is involved, the stealing can be traced back to the castration complex. Stealing from superiors is symbolic of original penis-envy and active castration wishes.

Alexander and Abraham together came to the conclusion that obsessive stealing is to be traced back "at the deepest unconscious" level to the longing for the first source of pleasure, that is, the mother's breast. Stealing shows that the first refusal of the mother's love, the withdrawal of the nipple, has not been overcome. Alexander points out that if Stärcke's oral castration is accepted, then obsessive stealing may be always traced to an active castration wish.

Female kleptomania seems to be objectless for the most part; there is no object-transference involved, no affective impulse to injure anyone else. Alexander thinks the kleptomaniac's stealing may be traced to penis-envy—"By their thefts they are trying to make good the cosmic injustice of their bodily configuration; their thefts have more of a narcistic tone."

Pyromania, the tendency to incendiarism, is interpreted by several psychoanalysts. Ferenczi mentions it as an urethral-erotic character trait. Many incendiarists were excessive bed-wetters and a sort of ambition develops out of this inferiority, finding exploitation in fire setting.

The psychoanalytic conceptions of the meaning of suicide are based on analyses of cases where suicide was attempted or self-injuries were inflicted. Freud states that "analysis has explained the enigma of suicide" by finding that "probably no one finds the mental energy required to kill himself" unless in doing so he is killing not only himself but also killing an object with whom he has identified himself; he is directing against himself a death-wish which had been directed against another person. Freud goes on to speak of the regular discovery of such unconscious death-wishes in those who have attempted suicide, but this need not strike us as strange since the Ucs of all human beings contains such death-wishes, even against loved ones.

Obsessional suicidal impulses may involve also another process; in some cases the impulse may be the result of a compulsive need for punishment felt as related to the individual's own savage and murderous impulses in the Ucs.

"The tendency to self-destruction exists to a certain degree in many more persons than in those who bring it to completion." "Even where it really comes to suicide the inclination has existed for a long time with less strength or as an unconscious and repressed tendency."

Freud speaks of the curious way in which the suicide chooses special times, means, and opportunities, and tends to explain it by the fact that the Ucs waits for a "motive to take upon itself one part of the causation."

In analyzed cases of attempts at suicide a number of different motives apparently co-operate to make the deed possible. When one considers the amount of narcistic libido which rises up in the form of fear at the menace of death, it seems in great contradiction to the suicidal impulse, but the analysis of melancholia, Freud says, shows that when object-cathexis is withdrawn from the object and turned upon the self, the self is treated as an object; then it becomes possible to launch against the self the animosity relating to an object. In the regression from narcistic object-choice that is seen in melancholia the object is really abolished, but in spite of all proves itself stronger than the Ego's self. In suicide the Ego is overwhelmed by the object, though in a very different way from the contrasting situation of intense love. The tendency to suicide seen in melancholia represents a gratification of sadistic tendencies turned upon the self.

Freud says that some of the means taken to commit suicide represent unconscious sexual wish-fulfilment, thus to poison oneself is the equivalent of becoming pregnant; to drown oneself equals the bearing of a child, etc.

Self-inflicted injuries which are apparently accidental occurrences have received some attention by psychoanalyists, indeed, Freud speaks of "semi-intentional self-inflicted injury." Self-inflicted injuries are considered to be, as a rule, a compromise between the impulse to self-destruction and the forces working against it. In the *Psychopathology of Everyday Life,* Freud gives some remarkable instances where apparently accidental misfortune has become known as half-hearted and perhaps unconscious attempts at suicide. He thinks that "rage against one's own integrity and one's own life can be hidden behind apparently accidental awkwardness and motor insufficiency."

The prostitute is often a person who is seeking vengeance; avenging herself upon every man for her childhood Oedipus disappointment in relation to her father. For prostitution frigidity is necessary; there is unconscious striving to diminish the importance of that part of the body which is used and through this is signified a humiliation of all men, a mass castration of them.

It is only when frigidity exists that a woman can go from man to man as a prostitute does.

In phantasy life, as mentioned under that heading, the prostitution idea may represent a special form of masochism, being the deepest form of humiliation. Jones speaks of the fashion in which prostitutes are found acceptable to men who have married a mother-imago, such men then find it impossible to bring sexual inclinations into their married relationship; they may even find themselves impotent. On the other hand, they are capable of sexual excitement with women of another type for whom they feel no respect or tenderness.

In apposition to the prostitute type, there is the Don Juan type of man who avenges himself on all women for the disappointment which he once received from the first woman who entered into his life.

Freud offers several explanations of the development of homo-sexual trends which he thinks obviate the necessity of invoking hereditary disposition. Bi-sexuality must, of course, always be taken into account and the possibility of a fixation in the inverted Oedipus situation.

Homosexuality, however, may also be traced to the positive Oedipus complex. When at puberty a boy seeks to give up an in-tense fixation on the mother and exchange this love-object for an-other, he may merely identify himself with her instead of going on to desexualized or sublimated object-love and begin to look about for objects on which he can bestow such love and care as he has experienced from his mother and in whom he can rediscover himself. For several years at least one of the conditions of love will be a male object of about the same age that he himself was when the change took place. The process of identification means that there is an inclination toward a narcistic object-choice which is easier to put into effect than a change toward the opposite sex.

Narcism is closely bound up with homosexuality. Freud points out that later homosexual trends are frequently traceable to the high value set by the boy upon the male organ and the inability to tolerate its absence in a love-object. In "childhood he chooses women as his sexual object, so long as he assumes that they too pos-sess what in his eyes is an indispensable part of the body; when he becomes convinced that women have deceived him in this particu-lar, they cease to be acceptable to him as a sexual object. He can-not forego a penis in any one who is to attract him to sexual inter-course, and if circumstances are favorable, he will fix his libido upon the 'woman with a penis,' a youth of feminine appearance."

There is another powerful motive urging toward homosexual object-choice, namely, a regard for the father or fear of him. The rejection of women means the avoidance of rivalry with the father. "Attachment to the mother, narcism, fear of castration—these are the factors . . . found in the psychical etiology of homosexuality."

Freud was the first to show the close association between homosexuality and paranoia. In this case instead of hatred and rivalry being replaced by a love-object relation, the repression of the homosexual love impulses leads through projection to ideas of persecution and hatred emanating from the former love-object.

Freud speaks of the possibility of homosexual urges being drained off by means of a son. Childless marriages may thus contribute to strengthening homosexual tendencies.

In attempting to explain the relation of social feeling to homosexuality, Freud suggests that it is possible that the behavior toward men in general of a man who sees in other men potential love-objects would naturally be different from that of the man who looks upon other men as his rivals in regard to women.

Psychoanalysts believe that in addition to manifest heterosexuality a very considerable measure of latent or unconscious homosexuality exists in all normal people. Psychoanalytic efforts at redirecting homosexual libido have so far not met with any striking success.

Schilder discussing homosexuality says, "It is one of the principles of psychoanalysis that we never find mechanisms in the neurosis which cannot also be found in the normal person. The differences are merely quantitative." There is nothing new in homosexuality, only "something which exaggerates only what can also be found in the sex life of the normal male and female. Activity and passivity are characteristic of every human but . . . we can therefore say that we may understand the psychology of sex only if we consider it under the double aspect of the desire to intrude, the desire to be given to the body into which we intrude." Intruding and being within, being strong and being weak, these are the two poles of every sexual activity.

Another explanation of homosexual development lies in the jealousy felt by a boy toward his brothers, usually older, leading to an exceedingly hostile and aggressive attitude toward them, perhaps culminating in actual death wishes. His powerlessness to satisfy his hostile impulses leads, Freud thinks, to their repression and replacement by love impulses which he can gratify. Thus his rivals become his first homosexual love-objects. This form of homosexuality does not involve a horror of women and so does not exclude a concomitant heterosexuality.

It must be remembered that a homosexual phase is regarded by psychoanalysts as a part of normal development. It is to sublimations of this homosexual libido that Freud is inclined to ascribe the development of many of the social qualities and trends. Altruistic interests and love for humanity at large may have, he thinks, some homosexual origins.

Sachs thinks that in sex perversions the individual does not simply permit himself to express, owing to lack of conscience, what the neurotic represses. He has found the conscience of perverts not less strict but simply working in a different way. Their conscience permits one part only of the forbidden tendencies to be expressed in order to escape from other parts which seem more objectionable to their Super-ego—their Super-ego rejects the Oedipus desires.

The significance of the fetish, according to Freud, is not known to the world at large, and therefore fetishism is not especially prohibited. The fetish object is easily obtainable and sexual gratification by means of it is thus very convenient. The fetishist has no trouble in getting what other men have to woo and exert themselves to obtain. The basis of fetishism is aversion to the real female genitals. The basis of this Freud insists is the original unwelcome perception that the female does not possess a phallus. The fetishist consequently sees an advantage in a substitute for the genital organs of the woman: underclothes suggest the scene of undressing, the last moment in which the woman could still be regarded as having a phallus. Velvet and fur reproduce the pubic hair which ought to have revealed the longed-for penis. This is sometimes complicated by a double attitude on the part of the fetishist; in very subtle cases the fetish becomes the vehicle of both denying and asserting the fact of castration. In this way we may understand something of the unconscious motive of hair snipping. Fetishism may manifest itself in the form of homosexuality which may be derived also from perception of the woman's castrated condition. Finally, Freud thinks that in often very subtle ways the normal prototype of all fetishes is the phallus of the man.

Earlier Freud described fetishism as due to partial repression with compensatory substitute formations.

Abraham says that a process of displacement is involved but it is a question of fixation upon a preliminary sexual aim in the psycho-genesis of future fetishism. For example, coprophilic pleasure and smell may play its part, as in foot fetishism. But then the foot may, too, be a phallic substitute; Glover found in one patient interest manifested in the foot or the shoe as appearing under the skirt and interprets this as phallic symbolism.

Freud suggests that a highly developed sense of smell may play a part in the genesis of neurosis. He says, "I have come to recognize that a tendency to osphresiolagnia which has become extinct since childhood" may play a part in the neurotic predisposition. This, he says, applies particularly to certain forms of fetishism.

Some Special Habits

Smoking. Stärcke thinks that it is probable that feelings of loss continue to exist in the mouth, that is, a certain amount of libido which is set free by the withdrawal of the nipple (and not displaced on the genitals) remains fixated, and that this accounts for certain adult types of oral compensation and gratification. He suggests that people may be divided broadly into two types on this basis: (1) Association with the color and form of the missing organ—smokers; (2) association with the taste of the mother's milk—eaters of sweets. The sucking movements which are involved in both these groups become the exclusive gratification in tobacco chewing and gum chewing.

Abraham thinks that smoking may frequently have the significance of a substitute gratification—a mark of masculinity derived from identification with the father.

Alcoholism. Abraham says that alcohol "acts as a stimulus to the complex of manliness." There is equivalence between sexual potency and intoxicating drink. Thus alcohol may become a surrogate when there are feelings of immaturity and doubt regarding potency in the adolescent and also in the case of the older man who has fears regarding his diminishing potency.

The results of alcohol, according to this writer, lie largely in facilitating sexual transference and in removing the effects of repression. These results may become chronic, in which case the drinker frequently exhibits characteristic excess of feelings, indulges in sentimentality, and loses all the finer feelings which owe their origin to sublimation. Furthermore, continued use of alcohol may reduce actual sexual capacity; a great number of drinkers become impotent. They fail to recognize this causal relationship and continue drinking, identifying the alcohol with sexuality and using it as a surrogate for potency.

Abraham believes that psychoanalytic procedure will prove necessary in the study of alcoholism.

Narcotics. The habit of taking narcotics, according to Abraham, is also related to sexuality. He speaks of drugs evoking sexual excitement in "the hysteric's peculiar constitution."

Ferenczi explains the dislike of cigar and cigarette smoking on the part of certain people as being due to its taking the place of some other erotic enjoyment which the individual looks upon as taboo. He points out that smoking and sexual intercourse are both things that grown-ups only permit themselves and "withhold from their children by means of threats and intimidations."

Abraham is of the opinion that a woman's psycho-sexual constitution drives her far less than the man to turn to alcohol. He points out that alcohol would remove the effects of repression, which is normal for the girl at puberty, and would make her less attractive to the man. In a man, the "grandiose complex," that is, man the begetter, the creator, is deeply rooted.

Abraham claims that alcohol acts on the sexual instinct by removing the resistances and increasing sexual activity. There are many unsolved problems concerning alcoholism, but he is convinced that external factors and heredity are not sufficient to explain drunkenness, it is only possible to investigate the problem if the relationship between alcoholism and sex is borne in mind.

Freud has pointed out that obscene wit "represents an exposure in a psychological sense" and is inseparably associated with the enjoyment of alcohol. Forel has drawn attention to the coarse and repugnant forms which flirting takes under the influence of alcohol.

Abraham speaks of "the well-known jealousy of the drinker" and thinks he is justified through a wide range of experience in associating this with diminishing sexual potency. Since he finds it easier to obtain pleasure through alcohol, the individual in question gives up women, but this state of affairs is very painful to his self-esteem. Therefore he projects his feelings of guilt on to his wife and is convinced that she is being unfaithful.

The idea of the erotic effect of love potions is undoubtedly borrowed from the effect of alcoholic beverages, Abraham points out. Here, as in other myths and customs, intoxication and sexual excitement are identified. The same association is reflected in "drinking one's health" where the drink undoubtedly is the equivalent of or suggests vital force.

Psychoanalysts are firmly convinced that qualitatively there is no sharp cleavage between the normal individual and the neurotic or psychotic. In the case of all three types of individual, there exist repressed Ego-dystonic impulses which are still possessed of energy, and consequently a part of the libido is withdrawn from the control of the Ego.

In support of this contention psychoanalysts point to the rôle played by dreams, symptomatic-acts, inhibitions, and phantasy-life in the so-called normal individual, all of which can be shown to be the result of processes which also play a part in symptom-formation, and which thus refute any idea of absolute mental health or normality. Also, Freud declares that every normal as well as every neurotic person passes inevitably through a neurotic phase during childhood, which goes to show that temporarily, at least, all the factors are present which in the case of the adult neurotic manifest themselves later as full-blown symptom-formation.

Thus, for psychoanalysis the difference between health and neurosis is entirely a quantitative one. Ferenczi says, "Functional psychoses and psychoneuroses are distinguished from normal mental activity only by a matter of degree." As Jones very well states it, "The deviation from the so-called normal is throughout quantitative, not qualitative. Many of the symptoms of neurotic disorders may strike the average person at first sight as being alien to his imagination, but minor parallels for all of them can be found in everyday experience; they are little more than magnifications. And when one penetrates to the causal chain of which they are the final manifestation, one finds oneself at once on familiar ground. Indeed, the deeper one goes in this direction, the closer is the relation to the problems of normal development, and the harder does it become to specify what the essential distinctions between normal and abnormal are."

Regarding the etiology of neurosis, Jones writes, "Formerly these states were explained by the coöperation of two factors—inherited weakness of the nervous constitution, and some current difficulty of which disappointment in love and overwork were the most typical. Between these two, Freud inserted a third—namely, the effect of certain experiences during the early sexual development. He in no way denied the significance of the other two; on the contrary, he has done much to define more nearly the essential nature of them and the exact continuity subsisting among all three."

Wälder says that psychoanalysis has no answer as to the fundamental basis for the development of neurosis. "What is really specific in neurosis eludes us now (since Freud's anxiety theories have been expounded) as much as ever." Wälder defines neurosis as "the automatization of anxiety reaction" but he says it still remains unexplained why some people fall a victim to this automatization, "so remaining in an important part of their being perpetually infantile," and the rest of mankind manage to escape this fate to a degree sufficient for practical purposes.

Freud suggests three main possibilities of disaster: (a) Biological—the long drawn out helplessness and dependence of the child from which comes man's eternal need for love; (b) phylogenetic—the "double thrust" which sexual development imposes on human development; (c) psychological—the differentiation in the mental apparatus brought about through the formation of "institutions which represent the claims of the outer world" (Ego and Super-ego), so that "an external battle-field is extended to within man's mind."

Freud has abandoned entirely his old theory that anxiety follows repression and is a transformation of damned up libido. Now he stresses the fact that the Ego is the seat of anxiety, and that it has power of reproducing automatically a previously experienced fear-affect condition "as a warning of danger and as a means of rousing the pleasure-pain mechanism." Anxiety thus precedes repression.

Briefly, the capacity for enjoyment and accomplishment through reality depends on the relative proportion of the total energy which remains free or bound up in infantile unconscious desires. J. Glover says that the neurotic and healthy individuals are alike in the fact that both have ceased to be conscious of the existence of culturally repudiated inner demands, but in the case of the neurotic these have only been repressed and have failed to find a cultural outlet. The task of maintaining this state of repression renders precarious the whole existence of the neurotic; through his rigidity he is debarred from many of the outlets seized upon by the normal, and thus is more exposed to traumata.

Many perplexing questions at once arise in considering the etiology and development of neurosis. What in general are the factors which contribute to the development of a neurotic predisposition? What is a neurotic predisposition? Why does a neurotic predisposition sometimes lead to neurosis and at other times not? What brings about the various specific forms of symptom-formation, or "choice of a neurosis"?

Freud has recently done much to clarify the above issues by his new conception of the rôle played by anxiety in the neurotic individual, nevertheless, he admits himself still baffled and unable to throw any light "after decades of analytical investigation" upon the *leit motif* of the neurosis.

This new anxiety theory has an important bearing on symptom-formation which is now regarded as a defense against or flight from anxiety. The etiology of neurosis is now closely tied up not only with libidinal fixations, but with Ego fixations also on various phases of anxiety which Freud believes play a part in all early development. He says, "Every danger situation corresponds to a certain period of life or phase of development of the psychic apparatus and seems justified for it." There seem to be three outstanding danger situations, Freud believes, which can bring about "anxiety-fixations"—namely, (1) anxiety about the loss of love, (2) castration anxiety, (3) Super-ego or social anxiety.

Freud points out that normally the fear of loss of love and castration fear should drop out, but, he says, fear of the Super-ego accompanies the individual more or less throughout life. "The neurotic is differentiated from the normal by the fact that he immoderately heightens the reaction to these dangers. Again, no sufficient protection is offered even to adulthood that the original traumatic situations may not return; there should be a limit for every man beyond which his psychic apparatus fails to master the disposal of the importunate amounts of excitation."

Wälder thinks that Freud's anxiety theories also offer "a new approach to the old and obstinate problem of option of neurosis." He writes, "Anxiety about loss of love is particularly characteristic of women; it belongs to the genital phase and seems characteristic of hysteria. Castration anxiety is male; it belongs to the phallic phase and has an unmistakable relation to phobias. Finally, Super-ego is also essentially man's affair; it comes to the fore in the latency period and forms a center of obsessional neurosis."

Alexander is inclined to think that the etiology of neurosis cannot be solved without comparative study of healthy mental life. The question that needs an answer, he says, is why restrictions have led to symptoms rather than sublimation. He thinks the problem of health has received only stepmotherly treatment from psychoanalysis. With regard to neurotic predisposition, Alexander says that perhaps an early resistance on the part of the new born child to extra-uterine existence may determine an excessive tendency to regress to the intra-uterine state, leading later to a psychosis.

411

Freud's great stress is laid now upon (a) the child's contact with the external world before he is fitted to deal with it and (b) his similarly premature contact with the claims of sexual impulse. From the very beginning he realizes his dependence upon objects which will provide him means of libidinal discharge and thus protect him from feelings of helplessness engendered through sexual overexcitations. In the end, his whole conception of, and adaptation to, reality is influenced by his experiences of helplessness and anxiety.

The child's immaturity and helplessness make it impossible for him to become independent of the danger of trauma, which he senses arising either from the loss of the protecting object or the loss of love and benevolence on the part of the object. He turns his attention partly to placating the powerful beings which stand between him and painful or traumatic experiences. At the same time he endeavors to make himself independent of them, or to nullify and deprive of its traumatic value the danger situations which they have it in their power to bring about, by dealing with the sexual excitation itself and attempting to stamp it out or hold it in check. That is, the Ego summons to its aid various defenses, chiefly repression.

Jung views neurosis as the result of a lack of a positive goal or value in life and as really an attempt (unsuccessful) toward a new synthesis of life.

Regarding etiology, Ferenczi writes, "According to the psychoanalytic view no one is completely secure against the too powerful or too prolonged emotional strain of shock, the only significance of temperament being that the individual who is severely taxed from birth is damaged by lesser, and the more robustly constituted by greater shock. Of course psychoanalysis recognizes the possibility that inherited factors can also influence the particular form of neurosis."

Discussing further the constitutional factor, Ferenczi says, "In all neurotics I have been able, after Freud, to demonstrate in an unusual degree the permanent bisexuality of all human beings which was discovered by Fliess. How much of this is to be traced to constitutional factors and how much to infantile experiences, remains in the meantime undecided." Again, Ferenczi writes, "Besides the symptom-forming powers of infantile experiences, Freud had also to call in the constitutional factor to his assistance, only that in place of the far too general and hence uninformative idea of 'disposition' of 'degeneration,'" he put that of an abnormal sexual constitution with a tendency to repressive mechanisms." Through his establishment of the fact of infantile sexuality, Freud was able to lay stress on acquired predisposition, since as Ferenczi says, the period of early childhood thus becomes "preëminently adapted for the reception of impressions and for the fixation of tendencies which education can sublimate for a time, but which obtrude themselves forcibly at the later organic impulse of puberty, and require so powerful a repression that less robust constitutions cannot achieve it without a neurotic illness."

Ferenczi defends Freud against the statement of his critics that he derives the neuroses exclusively from sexual traumatic origins. He says he (Freud) grants the proper significance to constitutional factors. "I must further add that according to him, non-sexual psychic shocks (accidents, fright, tragic events) can also contribute by their traumatic power to a neurosis or even indeed occasion one. In any case, Freud considers the sexual factors as "specific" causes of the neuroses, not only because they are always to be demonstrated in every case, very often

Whether the ultimate issue will be normality or neurosis seems to depend on: (1) Whether the Id is able to disguise or distort the repressed impulses in such a way that they may come into conscious phantasy and neither the nature of the wish nor the nature of the gratification be recognized by the Ego (or Super-ego) for what it really is. (2) Whether an adequate amount of libido is left free for dealing with reality. (3) Whether reality is easy or difficult to deal with. Even a distinctly neurotically disposed individual may escape actual neurosis should he be spared the particular frustrations which in his case would upset the mental equilibrium. On the other hand, the apparently healthy individual may meet with some overwhelming frustration and thereupon develop a neurosis. (4) The Ego's development in the sense of reality. The Ego, in the case of the neurotically predisposed individual clings to the old danger situations and "obsolete conditions of anxiety." (5) Whether the Super-ego is, as Freud says, "amiable," or unduly intolerant of even the most remote derivatives of the infantile repressed wishes.

Neurotic symptom-formation means that the libidinal equilibrium has been disturbed, and the conscious phantasies, until now not too highly cathected to be tolerated by the Ego, receive a greater cathexis. To obviate the unwelcome recognition of the actual nature and the crude infantile origin of these phantasies which are now clamoring for actual motor discharge the Ego, scenting again old danger situations summons new defenses, and "allows itself to fall into symptom-formation."

without the assistance of other causes, but chiefly because they determine qualitatively the symptoms of the illness. And—last, not least—he points to the results of analytic therapy, which cures the neurotic symptom by bringing to light the pathogenic sexual factors, and by overcoming them reëstablishes the balance of the sexual life and of sexual feeling."

The rôle of milieu in neurosis is also discussed by Ferenczi. "Freud compares the inheritance of the neuroses with that of tuberculosis. Just as in inherited tuberculosis a thorough examination often shows that one has to deal with an infection acquired in childhood from a diseased environment and not merely with the congenital organic weakness; in the same way, in the case of children of neurotic parents, we must, along with heredity, attribute great importance also to the abnormal mental impressions to which they have been exposed since early childhood." The early strong tendencies to identification with the parents are of great importance in this connection. Ferenczi says, "Every boy and every girl longs to be father or mother respectively, and we need not be surprised if the children appropriate not only the real or supposed advantages of their parents, but also their peculiarities and neurotic symptoms."

Ferenczi explains the fact that psychoneurosis is more frequent among women as "comprehensible when we consider the difference in degree of the cultural pressure that weighs upon the two sexes. Much is permitted to men in youth that is denied to women, not only in reality but also in phantasy. . . . Society punishes sexual lapses much more strictly in women than in men."

The increased incidence of psychoneuroses in women (especially hysteria) Ferenczi attributes also to "the periodic pulsations in feminine sexuality (puberty, the menses, pregnancies, and parturitions, the climacterium)" which, he points out, "require much more powerful repression on the woman's part than is necessary for the man."

Alexander approaches the subject of the psychogenesis of symptoms from several unique and challenging angles. He thinks that at the bottom of the symptom-formation there is a splitting in two of the Ego function—the unconscious repressing faculty becomes completely at variance with the conscious judgment. The Super-ego, according to

Freud defines the symptoms as "a sign and substitute of a suppressed impulse gratification, the result of a repressive process." The essence of a neurosis lies in the fact that there is a tendency on the part of the Ego to be reconciled with the symptom; in fact the Ego has taken a hand itself in forming a substitute which will not only satisfy the Id, but will also withdraw the Ego from the danger situation (just as in childhood was done by means of repression) and relieve it from the task of undertaking further repressions. The Ego, as it were, compromises with the Id, since its greatest need is for unity and synthesis. The substitute being formed, the Ego "tries to abolish the strangeness and isolation of the symptoms, using for this purpose all possibilities to bind it to itself and . . . to incorporate it into its organization."

The symptom is accepted by the Ego for two reasons. In the first place, it soon discovers that a secondary gain for self-assertion may be derived from the symptom and it becomes gradually more and more valuable and indispensable to it. In the second place, it must be remembered that the Ego is consciously suffering. The substitute which it has joined with the Id to bring about is "strongly blighted" and is "no longer recognizable as a satisfaction. When it is consummated no feeling of pleasure accompanies it. For this reason the consummation has assumed the character of a compulsion." It is clear that this suffering may gratify both masochistic and punishment needs in the Ego. The fact that the Ego is allowing the Id some degree of gratification makes it necessary to placate the Super-ego; this can be done by suffering.

Alexander, though outwardly severe, is inwardly corruptible and in the neurotic there is a secret collusion or pact between the Super-ego and the Id. Thus, forbidden pleasure gratification, by being presented to the Ego as a punishment, is made acceptable. At the same time, the Super-ego itself, which recognizes the latent meaning of the symptom in spite of disguise, is "bribed with suffering."

Alexander also thinks that there is an Ego participation in the neurosis—that is, the Ego is secretly on the side of the Id and prefers to suffer instead of renounce. "The basic characteristic of the neurotic psyche is that it associates inseparably every gratification of desire with the expectation of pain."

Again, he says neurosis is based on two tendencies—the clinging to an infantile instinct gratification and the eliminaton of anxiety by means of self-inflicted suffering. Alexander lays great stress on the fact that the disguising or compromise-formation aspect of the symptom does not sufficiently account for its formation, but the unconscious need for punishment must also be satisfied through the neurotic suffering (or through the formation of ascetic traits of character). "Suffering comes to be a psychic coin by means of which any offense may be expiated"— the Super-ego accepts suffering as payment or bribery.

"The functional relation between neurotic suffering and neurotic satisfaction which mutually condition each other," Alexander contends, is "a characteristic and fundamental phenomenon throughout the entire field of neurotic processes. It leads us to a simple dynamic formula of the neuroses which promises to be of general validity, independent of the individual disease pictures. The principle that the neurotic psyche knows no satisfaction without suffering seems to me one of those fundamental facts which are confirmed in every hour of psychoanalytic practice." Alexander points out how neurosis often vanishes when some outward misfortune occurs.

All neurotic symptoms hark back to the ambivalence inherent in the Oedipus and castration complexes and their content always involves some element of either incestuous or hostile wishes. Thus, the ideation of the symptom comes from the Id's cathexis of various ideas associated with the environment, while the Ego's rôle is to devise a special technique whereby it may remain in ignorance of the true nature of the symptom. This means that it must manage in some way to deal with the pathogenic event which led to the outbreak of the neurosis, and which finds a representation also in the symptom.

Psychoanalysts speak of transference neuroses, meaning thereby hysteria, compulsion neurosis, and the phobias. The significance of the term transference lies in the fact that the conscious phantasies both before and after introversion have to do with objects in the real world. This makes it possible during the analytic treatment to establish the transference, since the physician takes the place of the imaginary object.

In each type of neurosis the Ego brings into play a different defense-dynamism by means of which it withdraws itself from the new danger situation (which it interprets as the past "anachronistic" situation), and thus introduces a characteristic feature differentiating the three types of transference neuroses from each other. In the case of hysteria the Ego produces amnesia for the exciting event, thus protecting itself from any recognition of its part in the symptom-picture. In the compulsion neuroses the technique of isolation is employed to keep the memory of the pathogenic event separated from the affect belonging to it. In the phobias the part played by the Ego is more difficult to determine. It seems to make use of the Id processes of transference and displacement to remove the threatening danger further and further away.

In explaining neurosis from the point of view of the Death and Eros instincts, Alexander suggests that every disease process, both in organic and psychic illness, is "a turning back upon the self of the outwardly directed Death instinct." Symptom-formation must thus be regarded as a part of the healing attempt or manifestation of Eros. The turning in of the Death instinct may be determined by two factors, first, the resistance of the outer world to the combative tendencies; second, the loss of the object or the withdrawal of object-libido, means an inevitable turning inward and de-erotizing of the hate element inherent in the ambivalent object-relationship (as in melancholia). The turning inward of the destructive tendencies may be prevented by a strong and durable object-relationship. In such case a perversion may result instead of a neurosis. "The introverted Death instinct does not lead to an increased sadism in the Super-ego, does not make its appearance as a destructive impulse within the personality, but instead only influences the psychological content of the object-relationship. The masochist stands in a definite fixed relation to his love-object; he loves it feminine-masochistically." In a perversion, the existing object-relationship is modified; in the neuroses the object-relationship is impoverished as a result of the introversion of the libido.

Return of the repressed—this may be brought about (a) associatively —if the content of the unconscious complex is sufficiently stirred by a conscious phantasy or experience; (b) if there is an increase in libidinal cathexis, due either to somatic influences or to external stimuli; (c) if reality becomes too powerful and revives the former "flight" ideation.

Psychoanalysts also claim that the original fixation stage of the libido has a determining influence on the nature of the symptom-content. For example, since in compulsion neurosis regression to the anal-sadistic level of development is characteristic, the impulses which enter into the obsessional thoughts emerging into consciousness are markedly destructive. The horror of the Super-ego at this state of affairs leads to the sense of guilt playing a much larger rôle in the compulsion neurosis than it does in hysteria or the phobias.

Freud's conception of the relationships existing between the Id, Ego and Super-ego have led him to suggest that their siding with or against each other in the event of a frustration "may prove to be the crossroad" where neurosis and psychosis, which he says, "are to all appearances so closely related to each other," may part company. In the transference neuroses when there is reality frustration the Ego takes sides with reality (or reality as represented by the Super-ego) against the Id. In the psychosis there is also frustration by reality, but the Ego here sides with the Id, and allows itself to be drawn away from reality. Psychotic patients, Freud says, cease to perceive actual facts or their traces in memory; they create for themselves a new external world, "following the inclination of the Id." The Ego makes an effort to avoid reality and render it non-existent; it makes itself impenetrable to the outer world. Whether the pathogenic effect of frustration be psychosis or neurosis depends on "whether the Ego remains true to its origin in the external world and restrains the Id there."

Freud also thinks that there is a possibility of another form of conflict, namely, between the Ego and the Super-ego. He places melancholia and mania in this group, which he speaks of as the narcistic neuroses. Alexander writes of the manic-depressive process as follows: "Upon the terror of the Super-ego, upon its rage against the Ego, there follows the outbreak of mania; while the tyranny of the Super-ego in melancholia serves to justify the excesses of the Id in the manic phase."

Jones writes of the neurotic process ". . . current repressed wishes cannot directly produce a neurosis, but do so only by reviving and re-enforcing the wishes that have been repressed in older, unresolved con-flicts. According to Freud, a pathogenetic disappointment or difficulty in readjustment leads first to an introversion or turning inwards of feeling, and the wish that has been baulked seeks some other mode of gratification. It tends to regress back to an older period of life, and thus to become associated with similarly baulked and repressed wishes belonging to older conflicts. It is the combination of those two, the present and the old, that is the characteristic mark of the pathogenesis of neurotic disorders as distinct from other modes of reaction to the difficulties of life."

Freud gives illustrations of narcistic gratification through symptoms. He points out how "the system formations of the compulsive neurotic flatter his self-love through the delusion that he is especially pure and conscientious and is better than other human beings. The delusional formations of paranoia open to the acumen and phantasy of these pa-tients a field of activity which is not readily replaced."

Freud, however, is very anxious to make clear that in spite of the secondary gain which the Ego's urge to synthesis causes it to derive from a symptom, the Ego must not be regarded as primarily involved in the creation of the symptom. He says, "One may also exaggerate the im-portance of this secondary adaptation to the symptom in saying that the Ego has created the symptom in order to derive benefit from it." On the other hand, Freud speaks of symptoms (hysterical) which are a compromise between the requirements for gratification and for punish-ment. He says, "As fulfillment of the demand of the Super-ego, such symptoms have from the first a part in the Ego, while on the other hand they indicate positions of the repressed and of breaches in the Ego or-ganization; they are, so to speak, border stations with mixed invest-ments."

Freud and other analysts often refer to certain personality characteristics as being typical of one or other of the three transference neuroses. In the case of the compulsive or obsessional neurotic Freud points out the following outstanding trends:

(a) A marked degree of superstition. This is found even in highly educated and intellectual persons, though they may at the same time be quite aware of the absurdity of their beliefs. They will avoid the ordinary superstitions such as being afraid of Friday or the number thirteen, but will believe in such things as prophetic dreams and premonitions. Closely associated with this is a tendency to ascribe great influence to their own thoughts, feelings and wishes. Such persons, Freud says, feel a great need to find in their own experiences those events which "will act as props" for their superstitious beliefs, which accounts for the fact that they are so much preoccupied "with the inexplicable coincidences of everyday life. . . ."

(b) The need for uncertainty or doubt. This shows itself in such tendencies as dislike of clocks and watches, managing to keep in ignorance of just those facts which would make decisions necessary. Their predilection for uncertainty leads obsessional neurotics "to turn their thoughts by preference to those subjects upon which all mankind are uncertain," such as length of life, life after death, and memory. Freud speaks of these individuals having a "death-complex," that is, they are "always on the lookout for the death of some one who is of importance to them," usually of someone they love such as one of their parents, or of a rival in order to be enabled to reach a solution of their conflicts. The essential characteristic of obsessional neurotics is the inability to come to a decision, especially in matters of love; they endeavor to postpone every decision.

Speaking of symptom-formation in the compulsive neuroses, Freud says that its general tendency "is to procure more room for substitute gratifications at the expense of renunciation." The result of the Ego's effort to incorporate or assimilate the symptom—that is, derive gratification out of it—is, Freud says, "an extremely restricted Ego"—an Ego filled with indecisions and inhibitions.

With regard to the onset of neurosis, Freud says, that there are four types of exciting cause, namely:—

(a) The denial of libidinal gratification by reality—that is, "the possibility of an outbreak of illness begins only with abstinence."

(b) Reality remains unchanged but there is a frustration and denial of libidinal gratification due to an internal change.

These first two types of falling ill, Freud says, are in sharp contrast. "In the first type an alteration in the external world is prominent; in the second, the accent falls on an internal change." "In the first case the task is one of renouncing a gratification and the person falls ill because of his lack of resistance; in the second case the task is that of exchanging one kind of gratification for another, and the person is wrecked by his rigidity. In the second case the conflict between the endeavor to keep as he is and the other endeavor to alter himself in accordance with new aims and new demands in reality already exists in him; in the first case, the conflict does not begin until the dammed-up libido has chosen other and incompatible possibilities of gratification. The part played by the conflict and the previous fixation of the libido is in the second type incomparably more striking than in the first, for in the first it may well be that undesirable fixations of this kind only reëstablish themselves in consequence of the external frustration."

(c) There is an outbreak of illness owing to an "inhibition of development," and Freud says that in this type "we have to deal with those persons who fall ill as soon as they pass beyond the irresponsible age of childhood." In such cases the libido as a whole has never developed beyond its infantile fixations; "the demands of reality do not suddenly confront an individuality which is wholly or partially matured, but arise out of the bare fact of its having grown older." The incapacity for meeting reality must be stressed here, but there is also a certain amount of conflict or striving to overcome the infantile fixation, "for otherwise

Freud points out the importance for personality characteristics of the different way in which reaction-formation works in the compulsion-neurosis and in hysteria. In hysteria, he says, the reaction-formation "holds tenaciously to a definite object" and thus does not "elevate itself to a general disposition of the Ego." In compulsion neurosis the amount of Ego alteration is unmistakable and shows itself in connection with all object-relationships. In hysteria, there will be excessive tenderness for the fundamentally hated object but no general tendency for love in respect to other objects.

the outcome of the process would never be neurosis but only stationary infantilism."

(d) Some people fall ill because as a result of reaching a certain period in life "the quantity of libido in their mental economy has increased to an extent which by itself suffices to upset the balance of health and establish the conditions for neurosis." These intensifications in libido, Freud says, are well-known to be connected with puberty and the menopause. "The damming-up of the libido is here the primary factor; it becomes pathogenic as the result of the relative frustration coming from the outer world, which would have afforded sufficient gratification to a lesser need in the libido. The dissatisfied and dammed-up libido may now open up the path to regression and excite the same complex as those found in cases of absolute external frustration."

In the case of children's neuroses Freud says that there is no need of an external frustration, or "a flight from some problem which has to be met in real life" to bring about an infantile neurosis. The instinctual trends alone "which the child cannot satisfy and which it is not old enough to master" are all-sufficient. Thus the regressive part of the causation is very insignificant.

According to psychoanalytic experience (which, Freud says, extends among the city children of the white race, subjected to high requirements of culture) child neuroses are "regular episodes of development." In most cases these "are spontaneously thrown off during childhood." In the Latency period ceremonials are very frequent, but only a very slight percentage of these cases develop later a full-blown compulsion neurosis.

SECTION SEVEN

THERAPY

Section VII

THERAPY

In the beginning of his career Freud employed what was known as the cathartic method. At first he used hypnosis but soon abandoned this as unreliable. His aim, however, remained for a time the same, namely, to aid the patient to recall forgotten memories of painful experiences which, at the time they occurred, had not been reacted to with adequate emotion. The production of recollections accompanied by a discharge of pent-up emotion (abreaction, catharsis) was found to be followed by amelioration of neurotic symptoms, though often only transitory.

Freud, however, discovered that two other phenomena which were of great significance, were also occurring. He observed that the degree of effort which he himself had to make to assist the patient in recalling his buried memories varied greatly with different individuals, and he concluded that this must be due to what he termed "resistance" on the part of the patient. This led him to his theory of repression, and he became interested in uncovering these resistances as well as in tracing back or hunting down "complexes." Freud says, "A different view had now to be taken of the task of therapy. Its aim was no longer to "abreact" an affect which had got on to the wrong lines, but to uncover repressions and replace them by acts of judgments which might result either in the acceptance or in the rejection of what had formerly been repudiated." The method of investigation now employed Freud called psychoanalysis.

Freud also noted that a certain type of emotional relationship regularly arose (no matter how incongruous the situation) between the physician and patient, and he came to the conclusion that this element of rapport which he called "transference" was therapeutically of profound significance.

Psychoanalytic therapy employs three forms of technique:

(1) Free association. The patient reclines on a couch, out of sight of the analyst, and tells just what comes into his mind, quite uncensored by consciousness. In devising this technique, Jones says Freud "boldly tested his faith in determinism. . . . Acting on the assumption that something must be directing a train of thought, even when it appeared to be freely wandering, and that this something could only be the influence of unconscious thoughts; he asked his patients to refrain from concentrating on any particular idea and from consciously guiding their thoughts."

E. Glover defines free association as a means by which "powerful drives and affective charges of the unconscious system are allowed to operate in an unhampered way during waking hours." "A selective process is immediately set to work," that is, as soon as the patient begins to tell what is in his mind, willy-nilly there is a distortion effected through the influence of the Ucs.

In spite of the later emphasis on the transference or analytical situation, the technique of free association has never been abandoned.

E. Glover points out that free association in the early stages of analysis —before the actual phantasy content is dealt with—can furnish clues to various unconscious trends, such as pre-genital fixations, types of resistance, narcistic attitudes, and neurotic trends. For example, anal tendencies are apparent in a reluctance to part with associations, resentment of interruption, etc.; urethral trends may underlie great loquacity; narcism is suggested in biographical recitals or tendencies to make one's own interpretations. The degree of affective discharge is also of significance—obsessional types are detached, unemotional; hysterical types are very emotional; narcistic types give stereotyped associations but display considerable feeling.

Rickman, in maintaining the superiority of the analytic technique to the psychiatric interview (of which he says, "Its pointed interrogations stimulate the patient to defense") points out how a statement can be checked up as to its significance, factual or delusional, by its setting in the stream of associations.

(2) Dream analysis. Freud has always stressed the analysis of dreams as an invaluable instrument for penetrating to the Ucs. The interest seems to lie less in interpreting the dream as a whole than in separating it into its various elements and using these as a starting point for free association. The dreamer is instructed to talk about the details of his dream, and specific trends and themes will emerge about which the associations will center; these lead finally to the discovery of the latent meaning in the unconscious content.

(3) Interpretation. A certain amount of interpretation or explanation of the material furnished by the patient is supposed to be offered at strategic points by the physician. In the beginning, Glover says these interpretations should take the form of encouraging explanations, and should always be "timed to take effect when the defensive systems have been really weakened." A "sense of touch" should be cultivated by the analyst. Interpretation may often become an effective weapon when a deadlock in the analysis occurs by making use of it to stimulate fancy. Freud points out the necessity for the analyst to communicate to the patient the connections he expects him to discover, but he says it must be done at the right place, that there is no use in trying to communicate the analyst's knowledge of the Ucs to the patient.

J. Glover, in describing a classical analysis, is at pains to emphasize the impersonal attitude of the physician. He writes as follows:

"Here the physician reduces to a minimum all personal contacts with his patient." He sits out of his patient's sight and only offers impersonal explanations of points which the patient can appreciate. "He does not argue or persuade, he does not praise or condemn. He does not advise." He merely enforces the fundamental rule of free association which may be difficult but is the only way to bring about the admission into consciousness of trains of thought that otherwise would be automatically censored. The overcoming by means of explanation of resistance to these unwelcome intruders is facilitated

Jung agrees with Freud that the dream "is an invaluable instrument' for penetrating to the unconscious, but he by no means believes that its chief function is wish-fulfilment. According to him, the dream is a natural psychic function which restores to life the ancient primordial images of the collective unconscious, which, becoming thus conscious, enlarge or widen the individual's horizon, bringing valuable self-knowledge. From his experience, Jung says, he has found that "by far the greater number of dreams have a compensatory character," that is, "they emphasize another side in each particular case in order to maintain the psychic equilibrium." Not only is mood corrected but dreams also have an educative value for the individual, they "create a picture that works far more effectively upon the feeling and understanding of the dreamer than would a learned discourse." Both for the patient and the analyst, dreams give valuable indications as to the fundamental tendencies of the psychic process, not only from the causal but also from the purposive point of view.

Discussing interpretation as a part of psychoanalytic technique, E. Glover admits that one of the greatest difficulties in analysis is when to speak and when to be silent, how much and how little to say.

Ferenczi acknowledges that interpretation deflects the course of free association, both by rousing the ideas expected by the analyst and imposing association-prohibitions. However, he points out that the interpretations offered are not irrefutable; their validity depends on whether they can be verified by memory material, or through repetition of earlier situations. Also, he says, the analyst always remains somewhat skeptical about his own interpretations and "must ever be ready to modify them or withdraw them completely."

by the fact that the analyst never appraises but only explains. Each successful explanation facilitates the production of more repressed mental content, and the path is opened to memories which give this repressed mental content a historical setting."

Freud says the analyst should "play the mentor as little as possible." It is desirable that the patient should make independent decisions. Only in the case of very young or helpless persons the function of physician and educator may be combined. He denies emphatically that an analyst ever advises giving sexuality full rein, but on the other hand, neither does he "take the part of conventional sex morality." Analysts are not "reformers."

E. Glover agrees that the pedagogic aim is not the goal of analysis. "The essential remodelling must be done by the patient." The analyst must only provide the setting—security, detached interest, and tolerance remove obstacles by analytic interpretation.

J. Glover points out that the authority of the analyst can be used in two directions, namely, either directly to influence the patient in a moral sense, or as the technical means of bringing into consciousness his forgotten infantile past, but he says most emphatically it cannot be carried along both of these divergent directions.

Ferenczi says that the analyst must "give full indulgence to his own unconscious." He quotes Freud as stating that this is the only way to grasp intuitively the expressions of the patient's unconscious "that are concealed in the manifest material of the manner of speech and behavior." The analyst does not listen with strained attention when the patient talks but by "suspended attention" allows scope to his own unconscious. There must be "a constant oscillation between the free play of phantasy and critical scrutiny on the part of the physician." The analyst must "yield himself passively to the play of his phantasy with the patient's ideas." The one exception to this is when a dream is being narrated, when every detail, every shade of expression, the exact wording, should be noted accurately by the analyst, and used for interpretation.

Reluctantly accepted as this phenomenon originally was by Freud and his followers, psychoanalysts seem agreed now not only on the desirability of utilizing this patient-physician relationship, but also, since its therapeutic value is so great, on the value of encouraging it. (Logically transference should be considered the fourth aspect of technique.)

The development of the transference, Freud postulated, is due to a "readiness for emotion," to be traced to an unsatisfactorily solved Oedipus complex. That is, the patient finds in the psychoanalytic treatment and in the person of the physician an opportunity for the re-enactment of an infantile child-father relationship. (See Dynamisms—Transference.) Experience showed that the patient's affectional feelings for the physician might take a sublimated form. (This occurs more frequently in men than in women.) A certain phase, known as negative transference, also frequently develops—that is, a hostile attitude to the physician. This may occur either simultaneously with the affectional relation or may appear later. These hostile feelings, however, connote an emotional attachment and also have their value therapeutically.

There are three stages or phases in an analysis, all connected with some aspect of the transference, each of which merges into the other to some extent. E. Glover describes these as follows:

(a) Opening phase. This is distinguished by the development of the transference, positive or negative, or an alternation of these. The patient finds himself in the old parental situation but with a parent who does not reprove or correct. This permits of a more or less unhampered development of the emotional relation on the patient's part. At this stage the analyst should be watching for clues that show the direction in which the patient's pleasure-principle tends to operate, stimulate free association, allay anxiety, and thus build up the transference as much as possible. Resistances should be dealt with in this phase only to the extent of "clearing the ground" for

The whole concept of transference, psychoanalysts agree, involves many subtleties, and its use requires expert skill and infinite caution. Freud says that once the transference has been established, everything depends on its being handled with the greatest dexterity, that the demands of the analytical technique at this point are very exacting; it is here that the most serious mistakes may be committed, or the most splendid results achieved. Any attempt to evade the difficulties by suppressing or neglecting the transference would, however, be senseless.

The critics of psychoanalysis have much to say about the part played by suggestion in the patient-physician relationship. Freud himself speaks of having "rediscovered suggestion in the shape of transference," and of the physician "with the aid of suggestion" making it possible for the patient to overcome resistances. It is contended, however, that the influence of the physician is confined to inducing the patient to perform a piece of mental work (the overcoming of his transference resistance) and to accept the physician's conviction of the inexpediency of conducting life on the pleasure-principle. Also, Freud claims that it is really impossible to get the patient to accept anything that does not agree with actuality—that incorrect interpretations on the part of the physician will inevitably fall away during the analysis.

Negative transference, E. Glover points out, may be due to projection of the patient's sense of guilt or self-criticism. It may show itself as hostility, depreciation, or reserve. Its origin lies in the reliving of the Oedipus situation, and it may be either a repetition of the phase when the child apprehends punishment on account of positive Oedipus wishes, or it may be a repetition of the inverted Oedipus—that is, the endeavor to realize libidinal tendencies through hostility or depreciation. Glover says it is very necessary to distinguish between negative transference and narcism in analysis. The reading of the physician's interpretations as a criticism or attack points to negative transference.

Alexander says that the period of negative transference is essential to every analysis, that successful analysis is assured only if the hate aspect is present—that is, if there is a "coaxing out" of the death instinct, a deflecting of the inward-turning aggression, back outward toward the environment (the analyst). He distinguishes three early phases, (a) primary transference—infantile intimidation, giving place to trust in more primitive representations of unconscious ideas, to allow primary processes to play their specific parts in guiding free associations. Evidences of more deep-lying resistances should be noted but not dealt with till later.

(b) Transference-neurosis. This is the term applied to that stage in the treatment when the earlier transference (positive or negative) becomes merged into a complete re-enacting of the infantile Oedipus experience, that is, not only does the analyst represent the parent as love-object, but all the old Ego attitudes and incest taboos are revived with a re-staging of the old conflict. This repetition of the complete Oedipus situation is stressed as an essential part of all analysis.

Glover points out that the analyst's effort from the beginning to keep the situation charged with affect, tends to make it take on an increasingly infantile coloring. Pre-genital thwartings and sadism are stirred up, and the patient essays to bind all this affect in the analyst, thus the transference-neurosis arises.

(c) Dissolution of the transference. Freud says that the transference-neurosis, "this new artificial neurosis," must be controlled or broken up. This, he says, is done "by proving to the patient that his feelings do not originate in the present situation . . . but merely repeat what happened to him at some other time." In other words, the repetition must be transformed into a recollection. In this way, the patient becomes free from the influences of his repressed impulses—"becomes and stays free . . . when the influence of the physician is removed." The libido, previously satisfied, at least partially, through symptoms, has become concentrated on the analyst, and the patient, in becoming free from the transference, is freed from his neurosis. Freud also says with regard to this dissolution phase, "The inner change brought about in the patient will accomplish this."

the analyst, with diminishment of neurotic fear, (b) negative transference—hate dares make its appearance, the analyst becoming the target, (c) secondary positive transference—the negative transference neutralized or erotized.

Writing of the transference-neurosis or analytical situation, Rickman claims that the analysis of the relationship between analyst and analysand "affords the clearest insight into the types of and motives for affective relationships between individuals that clinical psychology has yet evolved."

E. Glover describes the transference-neuroses phase as "a stage where the history of the patient's development, leading up to the infantile neurosis, is reënacted in the analytic room—the patient plays the part of actor-manager, pressing into service (like the child in the nursery) all the stage property that the analytical room contains, first and foremost, the analyst himself." There is, he says, a revival and reëxperience of "incest wishes and incest barriers," and he adds, "the conscious conviction through mental experience of the reality of the infantile Oedipus in all its strength and horror—this can occur nowhere else in human experience."

Though Jung also stresses the therapeutic value of the transference (or the psychological rapport, as he calls it), he has a very different conception of the dynamics of the phenomenon. He defines it as "the intensified tie to the physician which is a compensation symptom for the defective relationship to the present reality." He says, "The phenomenon of transference is inevitable in every fundamental analysis . . . the patient must find a relationship to an object in the living present, for without it he can never adequately fulfill the demands that adaptation makes upon him." Jung, however, emphasizes that he does not mean an object of sexual desire, but rather "an object of human relationship in which each individuality is guaranteed his proper place." "The individual relationship is for the patient an indispensable bridge; it must serve as a proof to him that his unique personality not only is acceptable but is indeed accepted, and that he himself is now in a position to build up a fully adapted relationship."

Freud himself writes of the transference as follows: "The decisive part of the cure is accomplished by means of the transference through which new editions of the old conflict are created. Under this situation the patient would like to behave as he had behaved originally, but by summoning all of his available psychic power, we compel him to reach a different decision. Transference then becomes the battlefield on which all the contending forces are to meet. The full strength of the libido, as well as the entire resistance against it, is concentrated in this relationship to the physician; so it is inevitable that the symptoms of the libido should be laid bare."

"In place of his original disturbance the patient manifests the artificially constructed disturbance of transference; in place of heterogenous unreal objects for the libido, you now have only the person of the physician, a single object, which, however, is also phantastic. The new struggle over this object is, however, raised to the highest psychic level, with the aid of the physician's suggestions, and proceeds as a normal psychic conflict. By avoiding a new suppression the estrangement between the Ego and the libido comes to an end, the psychic unity of the personality is restored. When the libido again becomes detached from the temporary object of the physician, it cannot return to its former objects but is now at the disposal of the Ego." (*General Introduction to Psychoanalysis.*)

Jung takes sharp issue with Freud as to the predominance of the sexual element in transference. He claims that when this occurs, it is brought about by the physician's own attitude, his exclusive concentration on the sexual motive. He also stresses the part played by the collective unconscious in the transference phantasies. He claims that after the first phantasies which are a projection of the personal unconscious and have personal memories for a foundation, that he has found repeatedly in his experience other phantasies appear in which the physician takes on the form of a god or demon, sometimes an animal. He asks, "Could the longing for a god be a passion, welling up from a more unsophisticated, darker source of instinct, a source perhaps even deeper and stronger than that from which the love for a human being springs?"

Rickman points out that there is a great contrast in the Freudian and Jungian methods of handling the transference. Freudians assume that every action of the patient during transference represents a repetition of a former psychic experience. It is the analyst's task to bring this to the patient's attention and get him to recollect the earlier psychic experience. In other words, something in the past has to be found to match the present experience. The less the analyst shows his personality, the more he is a blank screen on which the patient may project his phantasies, the more exact will be the reproduction of the whole early experience. The analyst has to do no more than detect and match the two things produced—the new mental experience centered on himself and the old one centered on some other person in the patient's past. His self-effacement should be as complete as possible, and he should deliberately refrain from playing the rôle of protector, guide, or father-imago. The Jungian analyst, Rickman says, plays a different rôle. He goes on the assumption that the neurotic lacks a goal or value in life, and that the analyst has a goal or value which he can communicate. He offers the possibility of attunement with the collective unconscious. Freudians offer a straightening out of the patient's past entanglements with the promise of limited improvement.

J. Glover writes very clarifyingly of transference. He says: "The relief which follows this process of integration enhances the affective bond between analyst and patient. The energies released by the cessation of conflict attach themselves to the concealed figure of the analyst and presently a new situation arises in which the patient no longer remembers his infantile past but *repeats it* in fantasies concerning this impersonal figure about whose actual personality and views of life he knows nothing save a readiness to face and explain unpleasant facts. In producing these transference phantasies, the patient has an opportunity of reliving and revising his infantile past. The analyst then becomes a blank screen upon which are projected pictures of the patient's infantile life, and his passivity, his refusal to blur these pictures by entering into reality relationships with his patient enables the latter to arrive at convincing emotional realization of the persisting infantile tendencies responsible for his neurosis. Again, the phantasied repetition of his early conflicts enables him to revise in the light of adult knowledge his crushing internal verdict on the crimes of infantile imagination."

The transference-neurosis as a psychoanalytic tool has various uses: (a) Every detail of the patient's behavior can be used to illustrate unconscious phantasies and Ego resistances, thus helping to convince him of the existence of these reconstructed infantile attitudes. (b) It makes possible the tracking down of early identifications and of recognizing specific Super-ego components. (c) The element of dramatization in the transference-neurosis makes the interpretation of the analyst more convincing—the patient has come as near as possible to the actual experience. Conviction is all the greater if the discrepancy between the emotion and the actual triviality of its occasion can be shown. (d) Many tendencies and experiences which have never been conscious find expression. This is the primary importance of the transference reproduction or reenactment—it is a way of discharge. (e) It becomes a "lever" or aid to recollection. (f) Transference phantasies may not only be proved as existing but may be brought into direct association with infantile impulses.

Rank says that Freud's interpretation or justification of the transference as the repetition of an earlier Oedipus situation is really a "flight" from the elements which are new in the situation. It should be approached as a new fact, as presenting "an *actual* relation of sentiments and not merely as the transference of the child's attitude toward the parents." In the analytic situation there has been an artificial production of a certain type of human relationships and "its origin, development, and passing should be analyzed as giving an insight into Ego psychology."

Schilder also thinks that analysis is concerned not only with the past but also with the present situation. In fact, the analysis of the present is the more important. Conflict can never be completely understood on the basis of the past, he says, because of "the persistence of a few irreducible elements."

According to Schilder, the general trend of the transference, that is, whether predominantly positive or negative, develops in the first few hours of analysis.

In the beginning of the analysis, Schilder says, the physician plays the rôle of the father and it is important to remember that he "never plays only one facet" of the father-imago in a complete analysis; pre-Oedipus attitudes to the father are likely to be present and must be reckoned with.

There is often a shifting of the physician's rôle from that of the father to that of the mother, and these cycles may frequently repeat themselves in the course of an analysis. Schilder thinks that Rank is right in pointing out that toward the end of the analysis the analyst becomes more and more the mother, that is, "he increasingly becomes the symbol of the general principle of protection where one is at home and safe." The psychoanalyzed person is faced with the sense of losing this protection, "and if the psychoanalysis is successful re-birth phantasies set in." Re-birth phantasies at this stage, Rank says, "may be taken for more than a metaphor."

What is spoken of as "counter-transference" must also be reckoned with in connection with the analytic situation. By this is meant impulses on the part of the analyst to respond to the patient's affectional trends. Schilder thinks that there is operative here an important psychological law regulating human relations and the patient's feelings will of necessity call for complementary ones on the part of the analyst. The latter must be aware of these complementary impulses, but, as Ferenczi says, he must not even yield inwardly to his own emotions, or as Schilder puts it, "He must never answer his patient in a human way." He points out that if the patient were given complete satisfaction it would be all the easier for him to "establish peace with his neurosis." Thus, the analyst has a double task of reform during analysis, first to observe the patient, scrutinize what he relates, and construct the patient's Ucs from his information and behavior; second, consistently to control or correct his own attitude toward the patient.

Rank and Ferenczi define the transference dissolution stage as the period when the Ego is "weaned" from the new libidinal situation and turned to reality. They both think that it is the most important stage in analysis. Theoretically, bringing the transference to life should make it difficult for an adult to cling to infantile reactions; the inner conflicts set up should promote detachment from the analyst. Actually, however, it is found that there are many cases in which dissolution is delayed, in spite of the removal of Ego resistances. Freud thinks the explanation of this is to be found in the repetition-compulsion principle, and this has led to the acceptance by psychoanalysts of the need for what is called "working through," or the process of assimilation of the physician's interpretation. In this connection, Ferenczi points out that dissolution delay may have something to do with the fact that the analytic treat-ment offers the patient "a new edition of his happy childhood." In fact the new edition is more attractive than the old one, due to the under-standing and lack of criticism on the part of the analyst. Freud thinks there are cases in which it is impossible to master and unshackle the transference and says that the analysis must then be terminated.

Jung says that on the problem of the dissolution of the transference "psychoanalytical theory sheds little or no light." Forcing a patient out of the transference, he thinks, creates danger of a relapse.

Resistance has been defined by Freud as "anything that interferes with the course of analysis." It is the work of the unconscious Ego. Though recollection or the recovery of lost memories is still regarded as a goal of psychotherapy, it is believed that these will be recovered with less difficulty if attempt is made by the analyst at the same time to uncover and surmount the resistances. Freud has outlined recently five kinds of resistances: (a) Ego unwillingness to give up repressive counter-charge. (b) Ego reluctance to renounce symptom gain or relief. (c) Transference resistance (an Ego resistance)—an attempt to evade recollection through re-enactment or repetition of infantile experience. (d) The Id repetition-compulsion urge. (In connection with this the term "working through" has arisen. Though the analysis seems to be completed, that is, the Ego resistances are broken down, the repetition-compulsion often causes a continuance of the transference neurosis.) (e) The need for punishment arising out of the demands of the Super-ego.

Ferenczi points out how free association may be made use of for the purpose of resistance. A superficial series of word associations, though it betrays unconscious material, does not give opportunity to achieve a thorough analysis of any particular ideas. The patient, he thinks, should be told of the intention which lies behind his meaningless associations. A sudden silence or a prolonged silence is to be interpreted as resistance.

E. Glover cites many examples of the various concrete forms resistance may take. These are general negativistic behavior (coming late, breaking free association rules, repudiation of analysts' interpretations, falling asleep, inaudible speech, etc.); pauses in free association, dearth of associations, screen memories; new symptoms or exacerbation of old ones; transference-neurosis. Both extreme fluency and extreme hesitation in giving free associations may be evidences of resistance, the former being only a seeming compliance with the analyst's desires and the material produced actually nothing but an exhibitionistic display, or a screen for deeper layers of unconscious phantasy, or a sort of dramatization instead of recollection.

Rickman says that when silences come in analysis, the patient is vaguely conscious of something troubling him—he feels restless and nervously apprehensive. This is due to the work of the unconscious Ego which is inhibiting the passage of a thought to the pre-conscious.

Alexander points out that resistances are more powerfully directed against a recognition of the repressing forces (the unconscious part of the Ego) than against the repressed tendencies. The Ego is more willing to face the latter than the former, since recognition of the former would mean the exposing of the Id-Super-ego, and the real significance of the neurotic symptoms.

J. Riviere warns against taking the wish for cure at its face value, since it may be a disguised expression of an unconscious phantasy and serve the purpose of a resistance. It should be analyzed just like everything else, since fundamentally no one wants to be analyzed.

Freud states the therapeutic aim as the replacing of the Ucs by the Cs. He says, "The neurotic struggle is a strife of forces, one of which has attained the level of the foreconscious and the Cs, while the other has been held back in the unconscious stage. That is why the conflict could have no outcome." A real decision can only be reached if the struggling parties can meet on the same ground, that is, on the conscious level. He also says, "The work of overcoming resistance is a fundamental task of the analytic cure." And again, he says the aim is to free the libido "from its present bonds which have estranged it from the Ego, and furthermore, to bring it once more to the service of the Ego."

According to Jones, the aim is "to strengthen the Ego at the expense of the Super-ego, to give it greater control over the repressed Ucs, and thus to bring about a more complete unity of the whole personality."

E. Glover says, "An essential part of the treatment relates to uncovering the archaic unconscious attitude of the Super-ego, tracing the factors in the child-parent relationship which has led to this particular set of attitudes, and so freeing the Ego from the necessity of carrying out various defense manoeuvers."

Alexander states the goal in terms of the Ego. The therapeutic aim, he says, is to strengthen the Ego, to remove the corrupt Super-ego and its punishment mechanism from the control of instinctual life and to bring the reënforced Ego into direct relations with the Id, to raise the level of the entire personality in the direction of the conscious Ego, to bring about a rapport between the Ego and the Id, to make the strengthened Ego take over the anachronistic functions of the over-severe Super-ego.

Recollection versus experience or abreaction as the goal of analytic treatment seems to be a current issue among psychoanalysts. Does the therapeutic value of the transference lie in the abreaction or discharge, potentialities of the experience, or in the possibilities it offers for historical reconstruction and emotional conviction; or as Freud insists, should it be used to stimulate actual memories with the resulting intellectual insight?

Alexander thinks that though complete recollection is impossible, "the more penetrating and the more thorough the treatment, the greater is the mass of recollection which emerges from repression." Feelings of conviction, he thinks, depend on the recollection of original pathological situations. The emergence of recollections, he also postulates, as the criterion of having "worked through" the transference-neurosis, and of being ready to renounce further repetitions. Sometimes, he says, it is impossible to get further than clear and easily interpretable repetitions. Again, he says, the analytic task is to permit "only such reliving as can be cleared up by insight, memories, feeling of conviction."

Schilder claims that the goal of an analysis should be the destruction in whole or in part, and the rebuilding of the Ego-ideal. In other words, analysis really undertakes the task of changing the character. First, however, there must be an analysis of the Id in order that material may be produced for an understanding of why the patient has built up his particular moral trends. The patient must be made to see that his desires relate to his Oedipus conflict, but it is even more important that he should recognize that he has built up his Ego-ideal according to what his father told him. He must be shown that his attitude to his father is a wrong one and that he has built up a faulty system of repression.

Ferenczi states the aim of analysis to be "to bring the unconscious components of the Id which operate automatically once more under the disposal of the Ego," and he quotes Freud as defining analysis to be "an instrument wherewith the Ego can continually possess itself of more of the Id."

The technical goal Freud stresses as "recollection and recognition." He believes that the unconscious strives for reproduction or repetition versus recollection and recognition by which he means "fitting the emotions into their place, both in the treatment and life history, subjecting them to rational consideration, and appraising them at their true psychical value." He believes that it is possible and desirable to get definite (not merely reconstructed by the analyst) memories aroused in the patient which he will recognize as fundamental. According to Freud an analysis is not complete "until all the obscurities of the case are cleared up, all amnestic gaps filled out, and the occasions which originally called out the suppressions discovered." He says that an analysis is successful only if it succeeds in removing the amnesia regarding the second to fifth year of childhood, when congenital libidinal factors are first awakened by actual experiences and become attached to certain complexes.

E. Glover stresses the making use of the transference-neurosis to help "memory work" but speaks of experience "when memory work fails" as an aid to "reconstruct before the patient irrecoverable parts of his development."

Ferenczi himself, however, speaks of the aim of psychoanalytic therapy as the bringing about of a mobilization of the repressed in the preconscious system by means of a reawakening of memories and "of reconstructions arrived at by necessity." Though he stresses experience (advocates intensifying the emotional reactions by "active therapy"), Ferenczi says that for him it is only a means for arriving at the roots of symptoms, and is thought of as something intellectual, the only guarantee against relapse." He emphasizes the necessity of interpretation "on parallel lines in respect to its infantile bearing," that is, for reconstruction purposes.

Ferenczi says, "The aim and end of psychoanalytic therapy now as always is to bring about a mobilization of the repressed in the pre-conscious system by means of re-awakened memories and of reconstructions arrived at by necessity."

E. Glover points out that the disappearance of symptoms is not to be trusted as a criterion of cure. He speaks of a change in dream content as being a sign that the treatment may be terminated. Dissolution of the transference seems to be commonly accepted as denoting cure.

Psychoanalysts state in various ways just what they believe to be the dynamic processes occurring in the course of an analytic treatment. Ferenczi speaks of "a process whereby using associative channels, or by means of increased tensions, repressed Id excitations are brought to consciousness in the face of Ego resistances. At other times it is a process whereby overstrong Id impulses are prevented from obtaining discharge by the mobilization of more powerful Ego forces." Elsewhere he says that analysis is a repetition "under favorable conditions of the reactions of the patient to frustration as it happened in childhood" and affords an opportunity to the analyst "to correct the disturbance in development which can be reconstructed historically."

Rickman describes analysis as "the work of attaching word presentations to ideas which were formerly incapable of making the union, owing to resistances—that is, there is a gain in strength for the Ego and an ultimate extension of the field of consciousness." Again he says, "Treatment consists in consolidating the Ego's capacity to tolerate the danger ahead. This is done by the arousing of past situations with appropriate affect and so affording the Ego a chance to re-experience consciously and to master consciously reactions that had before been dealt with reflexly and unconsciously. The fixations are undone by the Ego gaining more courage to face the primitive modes of instinct gratification (modification of Super-ego–Ego relationship) and acquiring more capacity to tolerate instinct impulse (Ego-Id relationship)."

E. Glover views what is taking place during analysis as a modification of the Super-ego. This he explains as due to the fact that the analytic situation being really a reproduction of the infantile Oedipus, it is dealt with as in childhood, i. e. deprivations and disappointments associated with parent attachments are compensated for by identifications. This time the identification is made with the analyst, so more adult attitudes should be introjected, not the "Thou shalts and shalt nots" of the parents.

According to Schilder the construction of a new Super-ego is brought about by effecting a substitutive identification with the analyst. He points out, however, that this does not mean identification with a particular personality, "but with someone who is looked upon as a useful member of human society, who is able to be happy," in other words, with a "purified analyst," that is, with a father and mother adapted to reality.

Alexander believes that through the transference the analyst comes to play the part of the Super-ego, and the patient being thus relieved from self-criticism begins to express openly his repressed tendencies. These are brought into genetic relationship with infantile memories or reconstructions of infantile experiences. Alexander also contends that recollection restores to the Ego its command over past repressions so the instinctual forces are at its disposal for fresh adaptations to reality—i. e. they become freely mobile instead of tonically bound forces.

Freud describes the analytical process as the reviving of an old conflict, the reopening of a case which has already been decided. At that time the Ego was weak and infantile and so denounced libidinal demands as dangerous. Now, however, it is stronger and more experienced, and so, with the aid of the physician, there should be a better issue to the conflict. He again describes the work of analysis as a separation of mental processes into constituent parts, into isolated instinctual elements. A new synthesis follows inevitably and automatically. Freud claims that the individual undergoes a significant inner change, that his psychic life is permanently

Jung says that the digging up of early childish complexes has no value except "in so far as they hamper present adaptation." "The therapeutic value of the minute and scrupulous pursuit of all the infantile phantasy roots depends not so much upon these relatively inessential demonstrations as upon the labor the physician gives himself to enter into the patient's psyche, whereby establishing a psychologically adapted relationship. For the patient is suffering precisely from the absence of such a relationship."

"lifted upon a higher plane of development," through the overcoming of resistances.

J. Glover, in discussing the place of what he calls "medical moralization" or deliberate attempts to synthesize, points out that any such efforts ignore "the most fundamental implication of the doctrine of mental conflict according to which forces, which in favorable circumstances should be harmoniously integrated, are disintegrated and kept asunder by the dynamic demarcation of Repression. By dissolving this sundering barrier and thus promoting the assimilation of the repressed into the main personality what is called analysis automatically achieves synthesis."

Ferenczi speaks of the aim of analysis as being a "kind of re-education," and again, as a.fight against habits by which he means a "substitution of real adaptations in place of those unsatisfactory habit-like methods of resolving conflict which we call symptoms."

Schilder says that in the case of a neurotic person psychoanalysis is undertaken on the assumption that he has the forces within himself for re-organizing his own Super-ego. Advice and education are generally unnecessary, and free association can be relied upon as adequate. In cases, however, where there is a very weak Super-ego, or a passive analysis does not lead to a spontaneous re-moulding of a Super-ego adapted to reality, the analyst should come to the rescue by pointing out errors in the early Super-ego formation and encouraging new attitudes.

Rank is not interested in the historical standpoint. "The essential agent is not intellectual insight into the historical origin, but emotional displacement of the instinctual impulses which are inhibited in the current conflict and its representation in the analytic situation." The historical factor, he thinks, is of no importance to the patient.

On the basis of his theory of "denial," Rank demands that there be an emotional reproduction rather than intellectual recollection. The latter, he says, may be only a resistance against "insight into the denial." The fact that denial has occurred is, he says, often more important than the content of the corresponding memory, "which one can about as easily elicit by questioning as reconstruct analytically."

The field of psychoanalytic therapy has been limited mainly to what are known as the Transference Neuroses (Hysteria, Anxiety neurosis, Obsessional neurosis), that is, the symptoms are all substitutive libidinous gratifications, and transference is the center of the cure. In contradistinction to these are the Narcistic Neuroses in which the capacity for transference is little or none, and the physician is rejected with indifference; such individuals have been considered practically inaccessible to psychoanalytic efforts. Freud's recent conception of three mental systems (the Id, Ego, Super-ego) has opened up new possibilities for exploring both the narcistic neuroses and the psychoses. Much stress is now being laid on the Super-ego, and Freud says that its attitude should be taken into account in all forms of mental disease. On the basis of these new dynamic conceptions, he defines the transference neurosis as a conflict between the Ego and the Id; the narcistic neurosis as a conflict between the Ego and the Super-ego; and the psychosis as a conflict between the Ego and reality. The pathogenic result of frustration, either through the Super-ego or the outer world, is dependent on whether the Ego remains true to its allegiance to the outer world and tries to subjugate the Id, or whether it allows itself to be overcome by the Id and torn from reality.

Psychoanalysts recognize certain limitations to their therapy. Freud, in discussing heredity, admits it is a barrier to psychoanalytic efforts; he says, "Do not think we underestimate it." Rickman, in his description of the various neuroses and psychoses, refers consistently to the constitutional factor in etiology. He speaks of constitutional "weak Ego tolerance of increase of erotic tension," "weakness of genital organization," "strengthening of oral libido," "weakness in Ego defense mechanism," etc. (A Survey—The Development of the Psychoanalytical Theory of the Psychoses.)

Of the influence of early childhood experiences in establishing a neurotic predisposition Freud writes, they "belong to the past and we cannot undo them." He also points out the potential obstacle to therapeutic efforts involved in a current unfavorable situation.

Reich emphasizes Freud's warning that psychoanalysts are dealing with "explosive material." He points out that there are certain cases in which "the Ego does not present that solid structure which is vital for a satisfactory termination of the analysis," that the Ego must be "strong enough to support the consciousness of material that has hitherto been repressed." Reich suggests that in such cases there should be a preliminary strengthening of the Ego by Ego analysis, "whatever that may prove to be"; also, it is necessary to retard the process of analysis "when the patient's associations and recollections, and in especial his incestuous conflicts, become conscious too rapidly," and there is what he calls "a flooding of consciousness with repressed material." Defects of the Ego, he says, are indicated by "such mighty eruptions of repressed material," and when these are not present the repressed material becomes conscious at a very slow rate.

On the whole, psychoanalysis has not been disposed to experiment therapeutically with the psychoses. Jones emphasizes the risk of analytic interference in psychotic conditions, adding "in any event, our knowledge in this field is as yet by no means extensive." Rickman says that he does not yet think it is possible to say what is a pre-psychotic condition. However, considerable theorizing with regard to the applicability of psychoanalytic concepts to the psychoses has been done. Two important contributions, attempting to bring psychiatric classifications into line with psychoanalytic concepts, are those of Schilder and Rickman. The latter has worked out a chart in which he compares the various neuroses and psychoses, as well as the normal individual, in respect to such psychoanalytic concepts as stage of libido fixation in regard to aim, relation to the object, Ego fixation, libido regression, Ego in relation to Id excitation, mode of repression, mode of dealing with the return of the repressed, Ego resiliency to external shocks or frustrations, Super-ego in relation to Ego, etc.

In addition to the analysis of neurotic individuals, character analyses and training analyses are also frequently undertaken. The former have reference to the so-called "neurotic characters" (see Repression). The latter refers to the fact that the chief requisite for practicing analysis is a personal analysis of the would-be analyst. Several Institutes have been established for this purpose.

To the objection so frequently raised that the majority of persons treated analytically are not worth the time expended upon them, Freud answers that he is not very much concerned whether this is true or not. His chief interest consists, and herein lies his main defense of his work, in the fact that through what he calls a moulding from within process versus a propping up from without, it is possible to "deepen that knowledge of the mental life which is just dawning upon us," and scientific gain should not be sacrificed to any practical considerations.

Child-analysis had its beginnings in Freud's *"Analysis of a Phobia in a Five-Year-Old Boy"* and has been in the process of development for the last twenty years. One of the pioneers in the movement, Melanie Klein, asserts that Freud's analysis of this child became the foundation stone of subsequent child analysis, since it showed "the presence of evolution of the Oedipus complex in children and demonstrated the form in which it operates in them; it also showed that these unconscious tendencies could most safely and profitably be brought into consciousness." The experiment was also justified in the fact that the boy recovered from his neurosis; it had the further significance of confirming discoveries already made through adult-analysis.

Freud has given his sanction to child-analysis. He writes of it, "Analyses of children yield various interesting results. Possibly, in future, they will grow in importance. As far as theoretical findings are concerned, there can be no doubt as to the value of these analyses. As children give unequivocal information on questions which only yield hazy results in the analyses of adults, the analyst is protected against mistakes which might have proved to be serious. Analyses of children have the added advantage, in that those moments are seized upon unaware, when a neurosis is in the process of development. There can be no mistake about such observations in children." (*The Problem of Lay-Analyses.*)

Ferenczi and Jones also are much interested in the possibilities of child-analysis. Jones says, "Although we have had as yet only a few years' experience in this work, the results, so far, have been most promising and instructive." He is, "convinced that in the future an important part of therapeutic analysis, perhaps the most important part, will lie in this sphere."

There are two main schools of child-analysis. In England, Melanie Klein, a pupil of Ferenczi, is at the head of the more radical group, while Anna Freud in Vienna represents a relatively conservative method of treatment and investigation.

Considerable difference in theory and method exists between the English and the Viennese schools. Klein believes in analyzing very young children, while Anna Freud takes children who are past the Infancy Period. Anna Freud does not believe that a child should be analyzed unless a neurosis is actually present, while Klein holds that analysis is helpful and should be undertaken in the case of children who show only behavior problems.

There is difference of opinion, too, between Anna Freud and Klein as to the degree to which the child's unconscious should be probed. Klein feels justified in suggesting interpretations to the child as to the symbolical nature of his acts during the analytic hour. She is convinced that in children there is a special relation to reality, and that "they endeavor to exclude and repudiate everything which is not in accordance with their unconscious impulses." Anna Freud does not think that the very young child's unconscious life reveals sufficiently the dynamic processes which will later underlie his personality development.

A good many differences of opinion appear to have arise between the English and Viennese schools, the controversies centering about the following:

(a) When analysis shall be undertaken. According to Anna Freud, Klein maintains that "every disturbance of the psychic or intellectual development of the child can be removed or, at least, be favorably influenced by analysis." A. Freud says, "The majority of Vienna analysts hold a different view and maintain that an analysis of the child is opportune only when real infantile neurosis is actually present." She herself also is inclined to insist on certain other precautions being taken as well, and suggests that analysis be limited to "children of analysts, of analyzed patients, or parents who contribute to analysis a certain trust and respect." Otherwise, she fears that new conflicts will be created for the child. A. Freud bases her conclusions on a "protracted analysis of some ten children." (*Technic of Child Analysis.*)

(b) Age of child. Klein analyzes very young children, from three to six years of age, as well as children in the latency and pubertal period. A. Freud speaks of the age of her patients as from six to eleven years.

(c) Unconscious content. Klein thinks that penetration into the Ucs can be carried far deeper in the child than in the adult. A. Freud says, "in the output of material from the Ucs, child analysis stands far behind adult-analysis." It "does not lead us beyond the boundary where the child becomes capable of speech."

(d) Transference. This appears to be one of the most important controversial issues. Klein strongly condemns A. Freud for her unanalytic methods of bringing about the transference, which she thinks can come about with the child just as with the adult. A. Freud thinks the initial situation of child and adult is very different, and that it is necessary to make deliberate efforts to win and hold the child at the beginning. Also, the child should be brought to a realization of its illness or naughtiness and to a definite wish for cure. Klein believes this quite superfluous.

Negative transference. A. Freud works definitely for a strong positive attachment, as she thinks actual constructive work can only be done in this way. Should a negative transference arise, she seeks to destroy it as quickly as possible. Klein is quite willing to work with the negative transference in the child, as in the adult, since she believes that the resolution of the negative transference is always followed by an increased posi-

The matter of transference is a very vital issue between the two schools. Klein proceeds with children just as in adult-analysis, that is she waits for positive transference to initiate itself and is quite willing to work with the negative transference if and when it arises. Anna Freud, on the other hand, thinks that the positive transference should be brought about and maintained by deliberate efforts on the part of the analyst, and if the negative transference arises, she endeavors to destroy it. Anna Freud does not believe that the child ever forms a transference in the sense that the adult does, since the actual parents are still in existence. Klein, true to her theory of the child's special relationship to reality believes that the whole Oedipus is worked out with parent imagos, so the existence of the actual parents will not hinder transference to the analyst.

Klein's theory that the Oedipus is entirely in the child's Ucs and is quite uninfluenced by his family situations, makes her feel quite at liberty to undertake a thorough-going analysis without any fear that the child's relationship to his parents will be in any way disturbed. Anna Freud is more fearful that analysis may disturb this relationship and is thus inclined to do less probing.

Another point at issue is to what degree it is wise to remove the child's repressions and inhibitions. Anna Freud takes the stand that the child's Super-ego is too immature to be trusted and thus his morale and character formation may be seriously damaged by disturbing the parent-child relation. Klein contends that the child's abreactions take place chiefly in the analytic hour and that they will not be carried over to his everyday environment.

tive transference, that is, that the release of hate feelings towards parents and siblings in part resolves them, so making it possible to strengthen the love attitude.

Transference-neurosis. Klein believes that the "true analytic situation" can be established with the child, since the Oedipus complex is quite unconscious, and the child's relations with the parent-imagos are quite independent of reality. Transference can, therefore, be made to the analyst without any disturbance of the actual child-parent relation. A. Freud is quite sure that the child does not form a transference-neurosis, explaining this on the basis that the parents "are actually in existence as love objects, not in fancy as with the adult neurotic." So the analyst must share with the parents the child's love or hate.

(e) The Oedipus. Much difference of opinion exists as to how deeply the Oedipus should be probed—or to what extent the child's instinctual life should be freed from repressions, and the child-parent relationship disturbed. Klein believes in a thorough-going analysis of the Oedipus, involving, as it does, the child's feeling of hate towards his parents. She maintains that the Super-ego is formed very early in the child's development. Also, she proceeds on the assumption that analysis liberates the child's capacity for love, and this craving will be strong enough as a motive for complying with social and cultural demands. J. Riviere suggests that when the child learns to tolerate frustration of his Oedipus desires and pre-genital strivings, the desires themselves diminish—that morality follows toleration as a matter of course.

Anna Freud thinks that though the Super-ego is present at a very early period, we must not overlook "the constant reciprocal relations between this Super-ego and the objects to which it owes its origin." The child's Super-ego, she thinks, is very immature, and the demands of conscience are "only of value to the child if the person responsible for its establishment remains intact as an object in the external world. Where it loses the relation to the object, it also loses the pleasure it had in fulfilling the requirement." She thinks it is "dangerous for the morale and character formation" to disturb the child-parent relation.

Klein claims that the child's abreactions occur chiefly in the analytic hour, while A. Freud maintains that the child acts out most of his abnormal reactions in the domestic environment. She also points out that parents and educators, for the most part, continue to make the same excessive demands on the child, so the prospects are that it will have to

There is very sharp disagreement regarding educative efforts on the part of the analyst. Klein is strongly opposed to any hint of pedagogy becoming associated with the analysis. She is convinced that education is no more necessary or desirable in the case of the child than in that of the adult. Anna Freud, distrusting as she does the strength of the child's own Super-ego, is quite convinced that the approval and disapproval of the analyst must be made very plain to the child.

The actual technique employed by the two schools naturally varies both because of their sharp theoretical differences and also because of the age of the children analyzed. Klein uses largely a play technique. She introduces play with tiny dolls, men, women, animals, cars, trains, through which the child is able to represent his mother, father, brothers, sisters, etc., and to enact all his most repressed unconscious phantasies. In addition, Klein supplies paper, pencils, scissors, string, balls, bricks, and above all, water. She proceeds on the principle that children have a very deep comprehension of symbolism, the language of the Ucs, and that they express themselves more easily and naturally through symbolic play than they do verbally. Klein claims that her play method is used only in connection with other methods of obtaining psychic material, and that she gets the same material in so many different performances and in such variety that an error about its meaning is impossible; this is also proved by the resolving and liberating effect of the interpretation. She says, however, that she does not consider an analysis satisfactorily concluded till the child can give free verbal expression to his representations, since speech is more closely linked with reality than play.

return to the ways of repression and neurosis, or to the alternative of actual gratification. For all of the above reasons, she feels that analysis should not be pressed too far.

(f) Rôle of education. Klein very definitely feels that the analyst should refrain from direct education, that, as with the adult, the unconscious attitude should be taken and no attempt made to mould the patient, but simply await developments. Any attempt at education, she thinks, is quite incompatible with analysis. She writes, "It is impressive to see in analysis how these destructive tendencies can be used for sublimation when we resolve the fixations—how the phantasies can be liberated for most artistic and constructive work. This is done in analysis only through purely analytical measures, not at all by advising or encouraging the child. From my experience, the latter way, which is the pedagogical one, cannot be combined with analytical work in the person of the analyst, but analysis prepares the ground for very productive pedagogical work."

Jones writes in this connection, "It is indispensable, however, that such an analysis be a real one, quite independent of any educative measure."

A. Freud says of the analyst, that he is not a "shadow" as in adult analysis. He must let the child see of what he approves and disapproves (which makes the transference-neurosis impossible). She says, "He must analyze and he must educate, must in one breath permit and forbid, loosen and hold in check again. If he does not succeed in this, the analysis will be a charter for all of the bad habits banned by society."

Freud himself says, "To be sure, in the interest of the child, it is necessary to combine analytical influence with educational measures. This is a technique still to be perfected."

(g) Technique. One of the best known experiments in analytical methods with children is Klein's play technique. She uses play with tiny dolls, animals, cars, trains, through which the child is able to represent his mother, father, brothers, sisters, etc., and to enact all his most repressed unconscious phantasies. In addition she supplies paper, pencils, scissors, string, balls, bricks, and above all, water. She proceeds on the principle that children have a very deep comprehension of symbolism, the language of the Ucs, and that they express themselves more easily and naturally through symbolic play than they do verbally. Klein claims that her play method is used only in connection with other methods of obtaining psychic material, and that she gets the same material in so

Child analysts seem to agree that children do not give free associations readily, and various methods, both of stimulating their phantasies and inducing them to give expression to these, are resorted to.

Dreams and day dreams are constantly employed in analyzing the child. Anna Freud (who represents a more conservative school of child analysis) points out that it is very easy for a child to comprehend the interpretation of a dream, and also that children are much more willing to relate their day dreams than are adults.

Klein emphasizes the need for continuous interpretation in order to allay the anxiety which the analytic treatment inevitably brings into the child's consciousness.

---

many different performances and in such variety that an error about its meaning is impossible; this is also proved by the resolving and liberating effect of the interpretation. She says, however, that she does not consider an analysis satisfactorily concluded till the child can give free verbal expression to his representations, since speech is more closely linked with reality than play.

A. Freud says of Klein's method that it is "of greatest value for the observation of the child." The child is transplanted from his domestic environment, his entire known world, to the non-interference of the analyst's room, and thus the opportunity is given to become familiar with its "aggressive inclinations, its capacity for sympathy, as well as its attitude toward the different objects and persons which are represented by the dolls." She also points out that the toy environment is manageable and subject to the child's will, so he may carry out all the actions which in the actual world would have to be largely expressed in phantasy. For this reason, she thinks the Klein technique "almost indispensable for intimate knowledge of the small child who is not yet sufficiently capable of expressing itself in words."

However, A. Freud does not think that Klein is justified in considering the child's play activity as equivalent to adult free associations. The state of transference in the adult, she says, "gives to even otherwise unimportant performances a symbolic significance," but according to her viewpoint the child is not concentrated in the analytic situation as is the adult, therefore, his play associations should not always be given a symbolic interpretation. All depends, she says, upon whether the child is "at all times and in every game wholly in the grip of the unconscious."

Aichhorn, who has done more work with adolescent delinquents than any other psychoanalyst, believes that the psychoanalytic technique is not utilizable for all such cases. It is valuable for those delinquents who are plainly neurotic; for the non-neurotic delinquent, it is valuable only as offering a means for a better understanding of the causes that lie back of the delinquency. He believes that some offenders must be led through education and training to conform with the social group. Many of these are not even ready for analysis, he thinks, and need a preliminary period of reëducation.

Several innovations have found their way into psychoanalytic therapeutic procedure. One of the most widely discussed of these experiments is Ferenczi's "active therapy." Ferenczi defends his method on the ground that Freud himself established the rule that analysis be carried on in a "state of abstinence," this being based on the theory that suffering (privation) is a motor power in therapy and it must, therefore, be maintained until the treatment is over; substitutive gratifications must be detected and forbidden. Freud also pointed the way, Ferenczi says, to his activity methods by directing anxiety-hysteria patients, whenever there came a stagnation in the analysis, "to seek just those critical situations which usually cause in them an attack of anxiety." By exposing himself to a phobic situation, the patient would overcome resistance to hitherto repressed material which would then become accessible to analysis.

Active therapy Ferenczi defines as the carrying out occasionally of tasks instead of a mere narration of ideas—the analyst remains inactive beyond the occasional encouraging of the patient to certain actions. Specifically, he says, it takes the form of prohibitions or injunctions directed toward the patient's relationships with family, friends, etc.; to the modification of personal habits (eating, sleeping, dressing, undressing); to methods of physical gratification (retention of excreta). Sometimes a ban is put on reading and artistic pursuits, when these seem to have a markedly substitutive value.

Ferenczi also thinks that the analyst is justified in interrupting the flow of associations and harking back to something brought forward earlier, if he feels that the patient is making use of the free association rule to "talk past the point," or for the purpose of resistance.

Rank disagrees with Ferenczi's active therapy on the principle that the analyst through his prohibitions plays the part of the "strict mother" instead of freeing the patient from his desire for her. He emphasizes the danger of allowing analysis to become an opportunity for the securing gratification of the "masochistic guilt feeling." The analyst must assume a passive attitude and compel the patient to build up a correctly functioning Super-ego instead of gratifying libidinally the primitive one.

The subject of active procedure and its practical application along the line of expediting psychoanalytic treatment has aroused keen interest among psychoanalysts. E. Glover says that the unsettled state of Ferenczi's own formulations on the subject has led to a great deal of uncertainty and misunderstanding. There has been a general tendency to await further investigation. According to Glover, the only pronouncement which has come from Freud in the matter is the statement that "all efforts to accelerate materially analytic treatment have come to nothing"; and again "the best way to shorten treatment is to carry it out correctly."

Glover claims that Ferenczi "has toned down his method considerably," and he himself thinks that "it is still open to theoretical discussion, whether a systematized policy of intervention, such as he (Ferenczi) recommends, does not carry with it some disadvantages. At the least before doing so one must be fairly certain that the possibilities of psychic remembering have been exhausted and that masochistic aspects of the transference have been fully ventilated." Ferenczi's system of "forced phantasy," Glover says, has been received with very general favor. "It differs, of course, from other active methods in that the patient is not stimulated to action."

According to Sachs, one important technical departure is the revealing of the primal trauma to the patient at the beginning of the transference, that is, before it is firmly established and consciously realized by the patient. Also, there is a reversal of the usual psychoanalytic course of analysis. The story is reconstructed from the base upward versus Freud's "spiral path."

473

"Forced phantasies" is another tool in Ferenczi's active therapy. There is a type of person, he says, "who both in analysis and life is particularly poor in phantasies if not actually without them, on whom the most impressive experiences leave no apparent trace." Such persons are able to reproduce, in memory, situations which should be accompanied by strong feeling- and phantasy-reactions, without showing any traces of either. Ferenczi does not hesitate to demand of these patients that they "fabricate" phantasies about their experience, that is, tell "all that comes into their mind without regard for objective reality." At times he even goes further, and if the patient, "in spite of the utmost pressure," produces nothing, he will tell him what he ought to have felt or phantasied in a given situation. When the patient finally accepts this, Ferenczi says he lays less weight on his own plot and more on the added details supplied by the patient.

There are three classes of forced phantasies, (1) positive and negative phantasies of the transference, (2) phantasies recollecting infancy, (3) onanistic phantasies. Ferenczi feels that his phantasy method is only justified at the end of the treatment and the analytic material as a whole must decide just what phantasies shall be put to the patient. He admits that there is always some risk about the experiment, that it may prolong rather than shorten the treatment. Also, though rarely, Ferenczi prohibits a patient's phantasy activities in certain cases. When habitual day dreaming is a symptom, he demands that these day dreams be forcibly interrupted and all the force exerted "in seeking out those psychical impressions which have been avoided through fear and which have switched the patients over onto the tracks of pathological phantasy."

Schilder thinks that there must often be some activity on the part of the physician, and advocates a certain amount of discussion as well as interpretation in cases where the patient is not convinced by his own free associations. It is often necessary to convince the patient that he has formed the wrong sort of Ego-ideal (Super-ego); also he must be shown that he is using his neurosis for a special purpose in his daily life. Discussion, however, should not be entered into until about the third or fourth month, and the analyst should be quite sure that the transference is well-established. Discussion should be based on the material produced in free association.

474

Rank's dream technique is strongly condemned by Ferenczi. He claims that "as a rule it is altogether unnecessary to give a translation of the separate elements of the dreams, but, especially in typical situations, perspicuous symbols or familiar complexes enable us to anticipate the interpretation, so that we may concern ourselves with the meaning of the dream in relation to the analysis as a whole." Again, Ferenczi quotes him as saying "there is no need whatever always to ask the patient for his associations in order to discover which part of the dream thoughts is the most important or the most intensely repressed."

Ferenczi has expressed himself very recently as being in agreement with Rank that "from the viewpoint of the analytic situation, the more courageous interpretation of dreams and symptoms is more successful." He criticizes Rank, however, as being unable to "resist the temptation to view the analytic situation too one-sidedly at the expense of the historical material." Freud, he concludes, is right in insisting that "analysis is effected through insight." He adds, however, "An exaggerated intellectualization of the analysis is no less wrong than the one-sided emotionalization of it. The former leads absolutely to the degrading of the analysis into a mere pedagogic measure, also to depriving oneself of all the advantages of the exploration of the unconscious."

Another interesting innovation is Clark's "Phantasy Method." Freud's admission of the inapplicability of the regularly employed psychoanalytic methods to narcistic neuroses, and the corroborative experience of his followers, Clark says, led him to devise a means of penetrating narcistic inaccessibility.

The patient lies on a couch, out of view of the analyst, with his eyes closed and is told to "imagine the subjective sensations of an infant, preferably from the first day of birth." Clark describes this as "comparable to inducing mild self-hypnosis," not unlike a form of day dreaming or "certain phases of psychogenic hallucinosis in which a mild degree of clouding of consciousness obtains." The analyst, he says, gets the best result by "literally dropping out of sight and becoming the quietest of listeners." The patient will then "drift out upon the tide of his phantasial production, communing with himself, as it were, and reliving his past experience."

The aim of active therapy, Ferenczi states to be as "nothing more and nothing less than to lay bare latent tendencies to repetition." It plays the part of *"agent provocateur"* and the repetitions must then be interpreted or reconstructed into memories. Through active interference with bowel functions, Ferenczi believes he can increase the patient's capacity for tolerating pain beyond the anxiety barrier, and so stimulate the courage necessary to reëstablish genital erotism. He points out that in this case the analyst's orders differ from the parental commands, in that in childhood these tend in the directions of weaning from pleasure gain—analysis affords suitable latitude to erotic play. The patients are convinced that they can stand more pain through efforts at retention of excreta; also, that they can exploit pain to extract further pleasure. "From this there arises a certain feeling of freedom, self-assurance . . . only with the assistance of this self-confidence will sexual tendencies of the advanced genital type be mobilized or courage gained to reactivate the Oedipus complex, and overcome the castration anxiety." Ferenczi cites clinical evidence in support of this. Renunciation of eating, or compulsory eating of certain foods which have been avoided, "can uncover the instinctual background of oral character traits."

His "forced phantasies," Ferenczi claims, have an unquestionable analytical value, both because they bring about the production or reproduction of scenes quite unexpected by both patient and physician "which leave an indelible impression on the mind of the patient" and which advance the analytical work perceptibly; also, because "they furnish a proof that the patient is, generally speaking, capable of such psychical productions of which he thought himself free, so that they give us a grasp of deeper research into unconscious repression." His active therapy, Ferenczi thinks, is especially valuable in "character analyses" in making possible the reduction to anal, urethral, and oral erotic interests.

Through the knowledge of transference and of active therapy, Ferenczi claims that psychoanalysis has been put in command not only of observation and interpretation but also of experiment. Psychoanalysts, he says, have now "become accustomed to deal with psychic quantities, just as with other energy masses."

Clark says that patients are often unable for several sessions to produce even a vague phantasy, but the analyst must not show any concern, and he must discourage requests for any other type of analysis. Soon, he says, vague thoughts and phantasies will begin to creep into the patient's mind which will often be met by many resistances and rationalizations. Little by little, the patient's data will assume "more definite shape and emotional content." He points out that the narcist can be encouraged to phantasy as a creative production. Actual memories are to be more or less disregarded. The patients are required to bring a written summary of the previous visit which is compared with the analyst's record. Sometimes, he says, a successful beginning of the phantasy method may be brought about by encouraging some form of creative art, in order to set free the Ego libido from its narcistic fixation; he warns, however, that this may do more harm than good.

For Clark the transference is "essentially narcistic or of the mother type, rather than the lover which so universally obtains in the ordinary transference-neurosis." He says, "the narcistic ideal is made up of desires and needs, fashioned out of the maternal identifications, and which are left unrequited at the weaning." The analyst becomes the parental surrogate upon which the narcist can place his infantile conflicts (unsatisfied longings of the weaning period), "and thus gain an insight into the process."

Clark does not claim that the phantasies he obtains are actual memories; he says it is not to be assumed that the "infantile period is anywhere near as clearly to be recalled as the patient's verbal statements show." He maintains, however, that these phantasies are proven to be psychologically true, that is, they "throw important light upon the emotional attitudes of the analysand in his earliest relationships with the mother and form the nucleus of his character and personality."

Instead of demanding, as does Freud, that the patient reënact his past, this process finally leading to recollections of past events coming into consciousness, Clark says his phantasy method renders this "superfluous to a certain extent." It is important only that the patient "reproduce his past in phantasies." The difference in the two techniques is marked, but Clark says that his method seems to be the only one which has been able to reach narcistic patients. He claims a three or four months recovery for several cases which for years had been resistant to ordinary analysis.

Regarding the dynamics of his procedure Ferenczi believes that the prohibitions which he issues to the patient disturb the habitual (pathological) pathways of discharge of excitations, and that the "new distribution of psychical tension, resulting from this transference, makes possible the activation of material till then lying hidden in the unconscious and allows it to become manifest in the associations." His theory is that since the awakening of a memory brings an emotional reaction or motor action, so the motor action can equally well expose the repressed memory. The activity aroused is only a means to an end, while catharsis, or abreaction of affect, was originally regarded as an end in itself. Ferenczi says "in requiring what is inhibited and inhibiting what is uninhibited, we hope for a fresh distribution of the patient's psychic, primarily of his libidinal, energy that will further the laying bare of repressed material." Again, he writes, "when the patient gives up pleasurable activities or masters painful ones, there arise in him new states of psychic tension, most often increases of tension, that disturb the peace of remote or deeply repressed psychic domains, hitherto spared by the analysis, so that the derivatives from this—in the form of ideas that can be interpreted—find their ways into consciousness."

Ferenczi, writing of the aim of analysis, agrees with Freud that, "The real triumph of our technique is when we are successful in changing the repetition tendency which shows itself in the analytic situation into memories." In defense of his active therapy, he says that he has found it to be necessary, however, for the analyst "to first of all not only permit but to encourage the repetition tendency. The advice I gave really helped the will to fight against certain neurotic habits, that is, to give up the subjective advantage of the primary and secondary gains in the neurosis." Ferenczi is at great pains, however, to make clear that active therapy should be used only occasionally and in exceptional cases. "Our purpose remains as before to bring the unconscious material into consciousness and to substitute an uncontrollable symptom-formation through insight and methods of release that are compatible with reality."

A very controversial problem in psychoanalytic circles at the present moment is that of the status which should be granted to lay analysis. Freud has come out quite unequivocally in favor of non-medical practitioners, though he does insist that no lay analyst should ever undertake an analysis unless the patient has been examined and the diagnosis established by a medical practitioner. Summed up briefly, his main arguments seem to be: (1) The medical curriculum being preoccupied with the physical aspect is unfavorable to the psychological way of thinking. (2) The fact that invaluable contributions have been made to psychoanalysis by non-medical men, so the exclusion of lay analysts might easily have the effect of hampering the natural development of psychoanalysis as a science. (3) That the applications of psychoanalysis to other scientific fields, e. g. sociology, pedagogy, etc. may well outweigh its application to the medical science. (4) The danger of psychoanalysis being "absorbed" by medicine. On the whole, it would seem as if the majority of Freud's adherents agree with Jones who feels that Freud is very one-sided in his viewpoint and is not taking sufficiently into account the risks involved in allowing non-medical persons to treat mental diseases. The consensus seems to be that all would-be analysts should be encouraged to take medical training. Alternative suggestions are that the lay analyst should work in close association with the properly qualified medical practitioner, or in lieu of medical training, there should be constructed a systematic psychoanalytic curriculum, including other allied sciences, as well as the medical. (Various opinions on this subject of well-known analysts, both medical and lay, are to be found in the *International Journal of Psycho-Analysis,* April, 1927.)

Very widely discussed and much disputed is Rank's birth trauma theory and the innovations which, based on this, he has introduced into psychoanalytic technique. According to Sachs, Rank looks upon the transference (or "analytic situation" as he prefers to call it) as a reproduction of the intra-uterine state. Rank himself says that in transference "object hunger" is manifested, but this is due "not merely to a reëstablishment of the Oedipus situation as such, or even a reëstablishment of the original libido relation to the mother." It serves also, he says, the purpose of "Ego unburdening," that is, it is "an attempt to solve one's Ego problems on an object," and it must be "made intelligible to the patient as an expression of Ego tendencies." Ferenczi says that according to Rank's view, "at the deepest instinctual level the biological attachment to the mother regularly dominates the analytical situation, whereas what Freud assigns to the analyst is in essentials a part of the father." Ferenczi says he has tried to test Rank's theory in this respect, but he discovered that when he shifted the stress on to the attachment to the mother, there was an absence of resistance, so he came to the conclusion that birth anxiety explanations are willingly accepted "precisely an account of their lack of current significance and are in fact taken over by the patient as a means of protection against the much more terrible castration anxiety."

Of Rank's technique, Ferenczi says, "it is not the technique of psychoanalysis but a modification of it which departs so widely from what has hitherto been practiced, that it would have been more straightforward to have described the book (*Technik der Psychoanalyse*) as the Rank technique. . . ." Sachs also asserts that Rank's technique is diametrically opposed in important particulars to psychoanalytic procedure.

The fundamental point of departure in Rank's technique is his setting a time limit at the very beginning of the analysis with the aim of definitely creating the original birth situation—that is, the patient must free himself from the analyst (the mother). He then interprets every utterance of the patient as a flight from the birth experience, and in this way he is given insight into his emotional life. Treatment is reëducation and consists in showing the patient the universality of his problem and suffering; others are no better than he. He thus loses the guilt feeling resulting from a false ideal. Rank asserts he has clinical evidence to justify his theory that analysis turns out to be finally a mastery of the incompleted birth trauma. Sachs, however, points out that Rank has given very few facts to support his theory, and Ferenczi says that both he and Freud reject it and think Rank unjustified in building up a technique on it.

APPENDIX

BIBLIOGRAPHIC SOURCES OF MATERIAL UTILIZED IN THIS BOOK

(For special articles to 1926 see Rickman's Index Psychoanalyticus)

Abraham, Karl, Trans., *Selected Papers on Psycho-Analysis*
Adler, Alfred, Trans., *The Neurotic Constitution*
        Trans., *The Practice and Theory of Individual Psychology*
Aichhorn, August, *Verwahrloste Jugend*
Alexander, Franz, *Psychoanalyse der Gesamtpersönlichkeit*—trans. by Glueck in press
Alexander, Franz, and Staub, Hugo, *Der Verbrecher und seine Richter*
Brill, A. A., *Psychoanalysis, Its Theory and Practical Application*
Deutsch, Helene, *Psychoanalyse der Weiblichen Sexualfunktionen*
Ellis, Havelock, *Studies in the Psychology of Sex,* Volume VII
Federn and Meng, Editors, *Das Psychoanalytische Volksbuch*
Ferenczi, Sandor, Trans., *Contributions to Psycho-Analysis*
        Trans., *Theory and Technique of Psycho-Analysis*
Flügel, J. C., *The Psycho-Analytic Study of the Family*
Freud, Anna, Trans., *Technic of Child Analysis*
Freud, Sigmund, Trans., *Collected Papers,* Vols. I, II, III, IV
        Trans., *Three Contributions to the Sexual Theory*
        Trans., *A General Introduction to Psychoanalysis*
        Trans., *Psychopathology of Everyday Life*
        Trans., *Group Psychology and the Analysis of the Ego*
        Trans., *Beyond the Pleasure Principle*
        Trans., *The Ego and the Id*
        Trans., *Inhibition, Symptom, and Anxiety* (in Archives of Psychoanalysis)
        Trans., *The Problem of Lay-Analyses*
        Trans., *The Future of an Illusion*
Graber, Gustav Hans, *Die Ambivalenz des Kindes*

Hinkle, Beatrice M., *The Re-Creating of the Individual*
Hitschmann, Eduard, Trans., *Freud's Theories of the Neuroses*
Holt, E. B., *The Freudian Wish*
Jones, Ernest, *Papers on Psychoanalysis*
          Psychoanalysis
Jung, C. G., Trans., *Two Essays on Analytical Psychology*
Low, Barbara, *Psycho-Analysis and Education*
MacCurdy, John T., *The Psychology of Emotion*
          Problems in Dynamic Psychology
Mitchell, T. W., *Problems in Psycho-Pathology*
Northridge, W. L., *Modern Theories of the Unconscious*
Rank, Otto, *The Trauma of Birth*
          Sexualität und Schuldgefühl
          Manuscript of Series of Lectures delivered in New York
          Manuscript of Series of Lectures delivered in Philadelphia
Reich, Wilhelm, *Der Triebhafte Charakter*
Reik, Theodor, *Geständniszwang und Strafbedürfnis*
Schilder, Paul, Trans., *Introduction to a Psychoanalytic Psychiatry*
Varendonck, J., *The Psychology of Day-Dreams*

PERIODICALS

American Journal of Psychiatry
Archives of Psychoanalysis
British Journal of Medical Psychology
Imago
International Journal of Psycho-Analysis
Internationale Zeitschrift für Psychoanalyse
Psychoanalytical Review

(Several manuscripts have been available as source material through the courtesy of the writers and translators thereof.)

INDEX

iii

viii

X

INDEX OF AUTHORS

* Indicates authors quoted too frequently to make listing of references practically valuable.

A
NOTE
ON THE
TYPE IN
WHICH THIS
BOOK IS SET

*This book is set
on the Linotype in
Granjon, a type which is
neither a copy of a classic
face nor an original creation.
George W. Jones drew the
basic design for this type from
classic sources, but deviated from
his model wherever four centuries of
type-cutting experience indicated an improvement or where modern methods of
punch-cutting made possible a refinement
that was beyond the skill of the sixteenth-
century originator. This new creation is based
primarily upon the type used by Claude Garamond
(1510–1561) in his beautiful French books and
more closely resembles the work of the founder
of the Old Style letter than do any of the various modern-day types that bear his name.*

THE STRUCTURE AND MEANING OF PSYCHOANALYSIS, which has gone through eight printings since it was first published in 1930, is the only book of its kind to survey the literature of psychoanalysis. It has been called "a Baedeker of the whole psychoanalytical movement," because it gives the definitions and points of view of every significant contributor to the movement from Freud through Adler, Jung, and Rank to many contemporary psychoanalysts.

The organization of these sources, frequently quoted or paraphrased, is unique. On the left-hand pages are given the orthodox theories of psychoanalysis, consisting for the most part of Freud's own statements. On the right-hand pages, in smaller type, are presented valuable exegetical paragraphs and various ideas set forth by psychoanalysts who hold to the major concepts of Freud but differ from him in minor matters of theory or practice. In the endeavor to keep the exposition unbiased, the authors refrain from offering any criticisms of their own. A detailed index enhances the value of their survey.

The practicing psychoanalyst or psychiatrist, the student, and the interested lay reader will find here the sources of psychoanalytic theory and a clear exposition of their bearing upon problems of personality and human conduct.